BIOTECHNOLOGY
AND
ENVIRONMENTAL MANAGEMENT

ENV BOOKS SERIES

BIOTECHNOLOGY AND ENVIRONMENTAL MANAGEMENT

Editors

Prof. Arun Arya
Offg. Head, Department of Environmental Studies
The Maharaja Sayajirao University of Baroda
Vadodara (GJ)
(India)

Dr. Raaz K Maheswari
Associate Professor,
Department of Chemistry
SBRM Govt PG College, Nagaur (Rajasthan)
(India)

&

Dr. Pawan Kumar 'Bharti'
Society for Environment, Health, Awareness of
Nutrition & Toxicology (SEHAT)
1775, Sohan Ganj, Near Clock Tower, Delhi - 110 007 (India)
E-mail: *gurupawanbharti@rediffmail.com*

DPH

DISCOVERY PUBLISHING HOUSE PVT. LTD.
INDIA

Published by:

Namit Wasan

DISCOVERY PUBLISHING HOUSE PVT. LTD.

4383/4B, Ansari Road, Darya Ganj
New Delhi-110 002 (India)
Phone : +91-11-23279245, 43596064-65
Fax : +91-11-23253475
E-mail : discoverypublishinghouse@gmail.com
namitwasan9@gmail.com
sales@discoverypublishinggroup.com

web : www.discoverypublishinggroup.com

***First Edition:* 2017**

ISBN: 978-93-5056-862-0

Biotechnology and Environmental Management

Printed at:
Infinity Imaging Systems
Delhi

ENV Books Series, India

Calls descriptive and error free chapters for upcoming volumes of books on various environmental issues. Send your manuscripts to envbooks@gmail.com

Founding Editor (Editor-in-Chief)

Dr. Pawan Kumar 'Bharti'

Society for Environment, Health, Awareness of Nutrition & Toxicology (SEHAT-India)
1775, Sohanganj, Near Clock Tower, Delhi-7, (India)
E-mail:*gurupawanbharti@rediffmail.com*

Other Important Titles by Editor-in-Chief:

1. **Advances in Biotechnology and Ecological Sciences**
   Bharti, P.K., Chauhan, A. and Ray, J. (eds.)
   (ISBN: 978-93-5056-358-8).
2. **Advances in Agriculture and Ecology**
   Bharti, P.K.; Chauhan, A. and Ezeaku Peter Ikemefuna (eds.)
   (ISBN: 978-93-5056-362-5).
3. **Agriculture and Environmental Biotechnology**
   Bharti, P.K. and Chauhan, A. (eds.)
   (ISBN: 978-93-5056-479-0).
4. **Agriculture Development and Sustainable Environment**
   Ray, J. and Bharti, P.K. (eds.)
   (ISBN: 978-93-5056-759-3).
5. **Agriculture Ecology and Environment**
   Bharti, P.K. and Olubukola O. Babalola (eds.)
   (ISBN: 978-93-5056-480-6).
6. **Agriculture Ecology, Sustainable Development and Agribusiness Management**
   Mehta Piyush; Sharma Pankaj; and 'Bharti' P.K. (eds.)
   (ISBN: 978-93-5056-851-4).
7. **Agriculture, Environment and Nano-science**
   Bharti, Pawan K. (ed.)
   (ISBN: 978-93-5056-760-5).
8. **Agricultural Practices and Crop Disease Control**
   Chauhan Alka and Sharma Anubhuti (eds.)
   (ISBN: 978-93-5056-859-0).

9. **Agro-biodiversity:** ***Conservation and Sustainable Development***
Sharma, Pankaj; Singh, Narayan; and Bharti, P.K. (eds.)
(ISBN: 978-93-505-782-1).

10. **Agro-forestry and Climate Change**
Bharti, Pawan K. and Singh, Narayan (eds.)
(ISBN: 978-93-5056-514-8).

11. **Agro-forestry and Sustainable Agriculture**
Sharma, Pankaj; Bharti, P.K. (eds.)
(ISBN: 978-93-5056-786-9).

12. **Aquaculture and Fisheries Environment**
Gupta, S.K. and Pawan K. Bharti (eds.)
(ISBN: 978-93-5056-408-0).

13. **Aquatic Biodiversity and Pollution**
Bharti, P.K.; Chauhan, A. and Kaoud, H.A.H. (eds.)
(ISBN: 978-93-5056-359-5).

14. **Aquatic Ecology and Biotechnology**
Bharti, P.K. and Zaki, M.S.A. (eds.)
(ISBN: 978-93-5056-451-6).

15. **Aquatic Environment and Toxicology**
Bharti, Pawan K. (ed.)
(ISBN: 978-93-5056-236-9).

16. **Biodiversity, Biotechnology and Environmental Conservation**
Bharti, P.K. and Bhandari, G. (eds.)
(ISBN: 978-93-5056-750-0).

17. **Biodiversity of Aquatic Ecosystem:** ***Significance, Threat and Conservation*** **(2013)**
Bharti, P.K. and Kaoud, H.A.H. (eds.)
(ISBN: 978-93-5056-297-0).

18. **Biological Diversity and Ecology**
Arya, M.K.; Bharti, P.K. and Ritesh Joshi (eds.)
(ISBN: 978-93-5056-785-2).

19. **Bioremediation and Microbial Biotechnology**
Gupta, Sandeep; and Bharti, P.K. (eds.)
(ISBN: 978-93-5056-783-8).

20. **Biotechnological Approaches and Water Ecosystem**
Zaki, M.S.A.; and Bharti, P.K. (eds.)
(ISBN: 978-93-5056-779-1).

21. **Biotechnology, Agro-ecology and Environment**
Chauhan, Avnish and Bharti, P.K. (eds.)
(ISBN: 978-93-5056-757-9).

22. **Clean Technologies and Environmental Protection**
Chauhan, A.; Sharma, S. and Bharti, P.K. (eds.)
(ISBN: 978-93-5056-731-9).

23. **Climate Change and Agriculture**
Bharti, P.K. and Chauhan, Avnish (eds.)
(ISBN: 978-93-5056-148-5).

24. **Climate Change and Biodiversity**
Bharti, P.K. and Chauhan, Avnish (eds.)
(ISBN: 978-93-5056-360-1).

25. **Climate Change, Disaster Management and Environment**
Chauhan, Alka; Bharti, P.K. (eds.)
(ISBN: 978-93-5056-784-5).

26. **Conservation and Cultivation of Medicinal Plants**
Bharti, P.K. and Singh Narayan (eds.)
(ISBN: 978-93-5056-740-1).

27. **Crop Productivity and Plant Disease Management**
Chauhan, Alka; Bharti, P.K. and Sadana, Deepti (eds.)
(ISBN: 978-93-5056-791-3).

28. **Eco-toxicology and Eco-technology**
Bharti, P.K. and Zaki, M. (eds.)
(ISBN: 978-93-5056-313-7).

29. **Environmental Biotechnology and Application**
Bharti, P.K. and Chauhan, Avnish (eds.)
(ISBN: 978-93-5056-262-8).

30. **Environmental Conservation and Biotechnology**
Chauhan, A. and P.K. Bharti (eds.)
(ISBN: 978-93-5056-512-4).

31. **Environmental Health and Problems**
Bharti, P.K. and Gajananda, Kh. (eds.)
(ISBN: 978-93-5056-263-5).

32. **Environmental Pollution and Biodiversity**
Bharti, P.K.; Chauhan, Avnish and Kumar, P. (eds.)
(ISBN: 978-93-5056-149-2).

33. **Farming Techniques and Crop Production**
Chauhan Alka; Sharma Anubhuti; Ray Jaswant and 'Bharti' P.K. (eds.)
(ISBN: 978-93-5056-855-2).

34. **Fisheries and Toxicology**
Zaki, M.S.A.; Bharti, P.K. and Chauhan, A. (eds.)
(ISBN: 978-93-5056-452-3).

35. **Fish Habitat and Aquaculture**
Bharti, P.K.; Gupta Kr. Sanjay (eds.)
(ISBN: 978-93-5056-744-9).

36. **Food Processing, Management and Nanotechnology**
Chauhan, Avnish; Bharti, P.K. (eds.)
(ISBN: 978-93-5056-796-8).

37. **Freshwater Ecosystem and Xenobiotics**
Bharti, P.K.; Zaki, M. and Chauhan, A. (eds.)
(ISBN: 978-93-5056-299-4).

38. **Heavy Metals and Metalloids in Biosphere:** ***Impacts & Assessment***
Chauhan, Avnish, Gupta, Sandeep; and Bharti, P.K. (eds.)
(ISBN: 978-93-5056-860-6).

39. **Limnology and Aquatic Science**
Sharma, S. and Bharti, P.K. (eds.)
(ISBN: 978-93-5056-735-7).

40. **Medicinal Plants:** ***Distribution, Utilization and Significance***
Sharma, P.; Bharti, P.K. and Narayan Singh (eds.)
(ISBN: 978-93-5056-734-0).

41. **Microbial Applications and Environment**
Bharti, Pawan K. (ed.)
(ISBN: 978-93-5056-515-5).

42. **Microbial Ecology and Habitat**
Bharti, Pawan K. (ed.)
(ISBN: 978-93-5056-514-8).

43. **Microbial Environment and Bioremediation**
Chauhan Alka; K. Rathoure Ashok; and K Maheshwari Raaz (eds.)
(ISBN: 978-93-5056-856-9).

44. **Natural Ecosystem and Climate Change**
Bharti, P.K., and Kh. Gajananda (ed.)
(ISBN: 978-93-5056-745-6).

45. **Pest Management and Agro-Techniques**
Biswas, Asim; Bharti, P.K., Chauhan, Avnish (eds.)
(ISBN: 978-93-5056-794-4).

46. **Prakriti me Aushadhi (*in Hindi*)**
Singh, J.R.; Bharti, P.K. and Bharti, B.
(ISBN: 978-93-5056-200-0).

47. **Seed Technology, Plant Growth and Cropping System**
Tyagi, P.K. and Bharti, P.K. (eds.)
(ISBN: 978-93-5056-738-8).

48. **Seed Treatment, Plant Heath and Agro-technology**
Chauhan, A. and Bharti, P.K. (eds.)
(ISBN: 978-93-5056-810-1).

49. **Soil Characteristics and Agro-ecology**
Avnish Chauhan and Bharti, P.K. (eds.)
(ISBN: 978-93-5056-758-6).

50. **Soil Contamination and Conservation**
Ezeaku, P.I. and Bharti, P.K. (eds.)
(ISBN: 978-93-5056-737-1).
51. **Soil Quality and Contamination**
Bharti, P.K. and Chauhan, Avnish (eds.)
(ISBN: 978-93-5056-361-8).
52. **Sustainable Aquaculture Management**
Gupta, S.K.; Bharti, P.K (eds.)
(ISBN: 978-93-5056-797-5).
53. **Waste Disposal and Management**
Bharti, P.K.; Tabassum, B. and Bajaj, P. (eds.)
(ISBN: 978-93-5056-729-6).
54. **Waste Generation and Utilization**
Bajaj Priya; Tabassum, B., and Bharti, P.K. (eds.)
(ISBN: 978-93-5056-792-0).
55. **Waste Management and Environmental Health**
Tabassum, B., Bajaj Priya, and Bharti, P.K. (eds.)
(ISBN: 978-93-5056-777-7).
56. **Water Resources** *Mapping Monitoring and Management*
Tyagi, P.K., Chauhan, Avnish and Bharti, P.K. (eds.)
(ISBN: 978-93-5056-861-3).
57. **Water Resources and Agriculture**
Bharti, P.K. and Ezeaku Peter Ikemefuna (eds.)
(ISBN: 978-93-5056-481-3).
58. **Waste Resources Management:** *Monitoring and Assessment*
Gupta, Sandeep and Bharti, P.K. (eds.)
(ISBN: 978-93-5056-799-9).

Preface

Biotechnology is the use of living systems and organisms to develop or make products, or any technological application that uses biological systems, living organisms or derivatives thereof, to make or modify products or processes for specific use. Biotechnology has shown a great promise in solving a plethora of environmental problems. Various categories of secondary agriculture and forestry wastes represent valuable resource materials for developing alternate energy as biofuels and other value added products such as sugars, phenols, organic acids, enzymes and animal feed, etc. However, waste material and environmental contaminants generated by various industries such as food and feed, pulp and paper and textile may lead to severe environmental pollution, if not managed properly. The energy, food and feed demand necessitate developing simple and economically viable technologies for environmental management and resource recovery. Microorganisms and their enzymes contribute significantly in utilization of plant residues, resource recovery and eventually in environmental pollution mitigation.

Controlling pollution at its source itself is an extremely effective approach towards a cleaner environment. Heavy metals like mercury, cadmium and lead are often present as pollutants in the wastewater of modem industry. The effects of mercury as pollutant have been known for quite some time now. These metals can be accumulated by some algae and bacteria, and thus removed from the environment. For instance, 'Pseudomonas aeruginosa' can accumulate uranium and 'Thiobacillus' can accumulate silver. Several companies in the US sell a mixture of microbes and enzymes to clean up chemical wastes including oil, detergents, paper mill wastes and pesticides.

Environmental biotechnology is is applied to and used to study the natural environment. Environmental biotechnology could also imply that one try to harness biological process for commercial uses and exploitation. The International Society for Environmental Biotechnology defines environmental biotechnology as "the development, use and regulation of biological systems for remediation of contaminated environments, and for environment-friendly processes (green manufacturing technologies and sustainable development)".

Environmental biotechnology can simply be described as "the optimal use of nature, in the form of plants, animals, bacteria, fungi and algae, to produce renewable energy, food and nutrients in a synergistic integrated cycle of profit making processes where the waste of each process becomes the feedstock for another process".

Consider an environment in which pollution of a particular type is maximum. Let us consider the effluents of a starch industry which has mixed up with a local water body like a lake or pond. We find huge deposits of starch which are not so easily taken up for degradation by micro-organisms except for a few exemptions. we isolate a few micro-organisms from the polluted site and scan for any significant changes in their genome like mutations or evolutions. The modified genes are then identified. This is done because, the isolate would have adapted itself to degrade/utilize the starch better than other microbes of the same genus. Thus, the resultant genes are cloned onto industrially significant micro-organisms and are used for more economically significant processes like in pharmaceutical industry, fermentations...etc.

Similar situations can be elucitated like in the case of oil spills in the oceans which require cleanup, microbes isolated from oil rich environments like oil wells, oil transfer pipelines...etc. have been found having the potential to degrade oil or use it as an energy source. Thus they serve as a remedy to oil spills.

Still another elucidation would be in the case of microbes isolated from pesticide rich soils These would be capable of utilizing the pesticides as energy source and hence when mixed along with bio-fertilizers, would serve as excellent insurance against increased pesticide-toxicity levels in agricultural platform.

But the counter argument would be that whether these newly introduced microorganisms would create an imbalance in the environment concerned. The mutual harmony in which the organisms in that particular environment existed may have to face alteration and we should be extremely careful so as to not disturb the mutual relationships already existing in the environment of both the benefits and the disadvantages would pave way for an improvised version of environmental biotechnology. After all it is the environment that we strive to protect.

The present book updates the subject content of biotechnology and biological tools and their applications in the conservation and management of environment, use of green technology and clean technology is the demand of the era, environmental management through the utilization implementation of biological agents, microbial use to make various useful products for human welfare, Reclaim the ecosystem and remediation of environmental pollutants, research on various fungus and bacteria for environment and agriculture.

Thanks are due to contributors from various organizations and publisher also. The book will be helpful for the researchers, academia working in the field of environmental biotechnology and use of green technology for the conservation and management of environment.

–Editors
(envbooks@gmail.com)

Contents

Pages: 1-35

BIOTECHNOLOGY AND ENVIRONMENTAL MANAGEMENT

Edited by: Prof. Arun Arya; Dr. Raaz K Maheswari & Dr. Pawan Kumar 'Bharti'

ISBN: 978-93-5056-862-0

Edition: 2017

Published by: Discovery Publishing House Pvt. Ltd., New Delhi (India)

1

Environmental Applications of Anaeroic Microorganisms

V.Davamani; E.Parameswari
T.Anitha and R.Poorniammal

INTRODUCTION

Many archaea colonize extreme environments. They include hyper thermophiles, sulfur-metabolizing thermophiles, extreme halophiles and methanogens. Because extremophilic microorganisms have unusual properties, they are a potentially valuable resource in the development of novel biotechnological processes. Despite extensive research, however, there are few existing industrial applications of either archaeal biomass or archaeal enzymes.

The Prokarya comprise two distinct domains, namely the Bacteria and the Archaea. The original classification based on 16S rRNA has been confirmed by extensive phylogenetic studies on a variety of macromolecules found in the patrimony of these microbes. Systematic classification of the Archaea, which are generally believed to originate from a single ancestor, has identified several major clusters based on physiological characteristics: hyperthermophiles (optimal growth temperatures higher than 70° C); methanogens (anaerobes with growth temperatures ranging from 0 to 100° C); extreme halophiles or Euryarchaeota (requiring high saline solutions, up to 20% sodium chloride, for growth); and sulfur-metabolizing thermophilic bacteria or Crenarchaeota.

Many archaea are extremophiles, microbes that not only tolerate, but grow optimally in habitats normally considered too severe for life. Although several extremophilic microorganisms have been known for 40 years, the search for extremophiles has intensified in the last decade for two main reasons. First, the range of conditions under which life can exist is now

Horticultural College and Research Institute, Tamil Nadu Agricultural University, Periyakulam, Tamilnadu, (India).

known to be much broader than previously thought, and this has led to the exploration of many hitherto uninvestigated habitats. Second, it is now recognized that attributes of organisms adapted to extreme environments have the potential to serve a wide array of industrial purposes.

In addition to unique amino acid sequences, extrinsic factors (e.g., protein folding systems) may be involved in extremophilic adaptation. Increasing the size of the genomic data set will indicate whether some adaptations are dependent on specific amino acid sequences or structural contexts (Haney *et al.* 1999). To this end, comparative studies of protein sequences from mesophilic and extremely thermophilic homologous microorganisms are needed. Haney *et al.* (1999) conducted such a study on *Methanococcus* species. Comparative studies at the molecular level (e.g., G + C content) or of amino acid alignment are also needed to identify highly conserved residues.

Many interesting enzymes have been isolated from extremophilic microbes (sometimes called extremozymes). Specific archaeal metabolites have also been purified and characterized and some of them have potential industrial uses. However, several technical difficulties have prevented the large-scale industrial application of enzymes and special metabolites from extremophilic sources, the most important being the availability of these compounds. Large-scale archaeal cultures are difficult to set up: medium evaporation has to be taken into account for hyperthermophilic cultures, and fermenters must be built of materials resistant to corrosion by the media required for growth of alkaliphiles, acidophiles and, particularly, halophiles. In addition, it is well established that the basal expression level of archaeal enzymes, although sufficient for their purification and characterization on a laboratory scale, is low with respect to that required for industrial purposes. As a consequence, scientific interest has focused both on the design of innovative bioreactors to achieve higher biomasses and metabolite production rates, and on the development of techniques for cloning and expressing archaeal enzymes in mesophilic cell factories. The successful coupling of these strategies has been demonstrated in several applications (Schiraldi *et al.* 2000, 2001).

In addition to the development of industrial production processes, basic research is also needed to determine how enzymes have adapted to extreme conditions at the molecular level. It has been shown that the modifications used by enzymes of psychrophiles to permit conformational flexibility at low temperatures are opposite to those that confer thermostability to proteins of thermophiles. Correlating the genetic code with specific chemico-physical characteristics provides a promising new approach to the development of customized industrial biocatalysts.

ANAEROBIC BACTERIA

An organism that does not use O_2 to obtain energy cannot grow under an air temperature, and for which O_2 is toxic. Mainly anaeorobs can be divided into two types, they are:

1. Facultative anaerobes
2. Strict (obligate) anaerobes

Facultative Anaerobes

An organism which does not require O_2 for growth (but may use it if available), which grows well under both aerobic and anaerobic conditions, and which oxygen is not toxic. Examples – *Streptococci*, Enterobacteriaceae – *E.coli* and yeast etc.

Obligate Anaerobes

An organism cannot grow in the presence of oxygen carry out fermentation where the final hydrogen acceptor is an organic molecule.

Examples – Methanogens and Clostridia etc.

OXYGEN TOXICITY TO ANAEROBES

Oxygen is potentially toxic to all living cells and oxygen intolerance is relative. Oxygen toxicity might be regarded as the ultimate consequence of exergonic reactions with, reduced compounds of biological materials, but even with hydrogen highly exergonic reactions do not normally occur without initiation by high temperature or catalysts. The normal triplet electronic state of oxygen is stable and high activation energy is required for the reactions to occur. Only singlet oxygen activated to a higher energy state, possibly by absorption of a photon, combines rapidly with a wide range of organic materials. This may be of relevance in photo-oxidation.

Possible Causes of Oxygen Toxicity

Oxygen is toxic to anaerobes because of the following reasons:

- Presence of free oxygen in the culture medium is incompatible with the attainment and maintenance of low Eh of the culture medium, required for growth. Preferential reduction of exogenous oxygen drains the organism of reducing power which it requires for biosynthetic purposes.
- The anaerobes are particularly vulnerable to oxygen because their metabolism and growth depend on key components (-SH compounds, iron, sulphur, proteins, tetrahydropteridines and flavo-proteins) liable to auto-oxidation.

It is therefore, likely that the toxic effects of oxygen do not result from a general oxidation of structural and functional components. Oxygen will however, react with some highly reduced compounds and many of these occur as a result of metabolism, accompanied by other substances such as cations of copper and iron which may act as catalysts. In the case of thiol containing enzymes direct oxygen inactivation and consequent interference with metabolism and growth may occur, but toxic effects of oxygen are found to include major changes to cell functions and rapid loss of viability. Such damage is presumably mediated by less direct means.

Attention was concentrated on this means by the discovery of Fredovich of superoxide dismutase (SOD) and the awareness that the primary reduction product of oxygen is usually the superoxide anion (O_2^-), a radical form by the addition of an electron. This radical is the anion of the hydro-peroxide radical (HO_2.), and in aqueous solution at biological pH values both will be present pKa = 4.69). The radicals are normally disposed rapidly' by dismutation to hydrogen peroxide and oxygen, the most reaction at pH 7.0 involving them both.

$HO_2. + 0_2^- + H^+ \quad > 0_2 + H_2O_2$ ($k = 10^8$ M^{-1} s^{-1})

In much of the normal aerobic metabolism this single electron reduction does not occur. For many oxygenases and cytochrome chains where oxidation is used productively, system has evolved to reduce the oxygen to water or incorporate it directly into larger molecular structures. It will be seen however that in other circumstances, both $0_2^{-\cdot}$ and hydrogen peroxide will inevitably be formed and, these oxygen reduction products appear to be the origin of toxic effects: The products are removed in most aerobic organism by catalase and peroxidases for hydrogen peroxide and SOD for the last enzyme increasing the spontaneous mutation rate of 0_2^- over a thousand fold.

There is much evidence that either hydrogen peroxide or 0_2^- alone is of limited reactivity and toxicity, but that their simultaneous presence is most undesirable. The derivative likely to be responsible is the hydroxyl radical (OH^-) which is so highly reactive with other radicals and organic molecules that the normal concentration of reactant molecules in both growth media and cytoplasm will ensure that the reaction is diffusion controlled, with OH^- -disappearing in a fraction of 1 um from the site of its origin.

The hydroxyl radical is therefore an oxygen reduction product readily capable of disrupting macromolecules such as DNA or membrane components which are crucial for cell viability. Hydrogen abstruction reactions of type (i) often have reaction rate constants of 10^{10} M^{-1} s^{-1} and are rather more likely than type (ii) on the basis of disruption of susceptible hydrogen atoms and also in terms of reaction rates. Compounds such as mannitol are therefore often used to 'quench' OH^- reactions. It should be noted that in complex biological systems with high concentratjons of susceptible molecules, added even when OH^- is present. In laboratory studies, formate and thiourea are also used to quench OH^- catalase to remove hydrogen peroxide and superoxide dismutase (SOD) to remove 0_2^-. Experiments using these and other approaches have shown that OH', hydrogen peroxide and 0_2^- are all involved in toxic effects when 0_2^- is generated.

The complete details unfortunately remain topics for speculation. This is partly because, although there is good evidence for reactions of the type described in experimental systems in which 02- is exogenously produced, by using xanthine oxidase, Jor example, direct oxygen toxicity is more difficult to examine. There are also other possibilities. These include for example, additional incestuous relationships of r-educed oxygen products, e.g.

$2OH. > H_2O_2OH + H_2O_2 > H_2O + HO_2$

And all the possibilities that different actions may occur in non-aqueous environment such as membranes and that cations may react as complexes and also that concept that superoxide is not essential for the formation of intra-cellular OU. There are reducing agents in the cytoplasm other than 02" which could maintain the concentration of Fe2+ and so maintain the Fentontype production of.on One aspect of this possibility is that the key enzymes with 0_2 labile sites could be directly inactivated thus initiating a series of ultimately lethal disturbances in metabolism.

There is some correlation between protective enzyme activity and oxygen tolerance. More of the oxygen-tolerant strains are found to have SOD and catalase than the oxygen-sensitive strains but it is not possible for SOD activity to be correlated with oxygen tolerance in any quantitative way. There are also other factors to be considered:

Rate of oxygen reduction: Anaerobic cultures are likely to have considerable powers of oxygen reduction, If O_2- is the reduction product, and toxic processes are initiated. On the other hand, low oxygen consumption reduces this risk. Extreme examples of this are spores of clostridia, whose dormancy makes them oxygen stable, even without the overall mechanisms of spore resistance.

Mode of oxygen reduction: In aerobes the main productive pathways of oxygen reduction yield water. Some anaerobes have been shown to reduce molecular oxygen to water by NADH oxidases, but this may be regarded as detoxifying mechanism rather than productive, because the NADH thus consumed is no longer available for reduction of metabolites.

Protective enzymes: In addition to SOD and catalase, bacteria may have peroxidases to maintain low levels of 0_2^- and hydrogen peroxide.

Cell composition: The macromolecules involved in bacterial oxygen damage are not known but DNA, cell membranes or proteins such as ferredoxins are most probable. With any of these, differences in composition or concentration of reactive sites explain degrees of sensitivity which appear to be in contradiction to the indications given by other properties such as protective enzymes.

Repair mechanism: Results from the study on *Escherichia coli* suggested that decreased resistance to hydrogen peroxide correlates well with loss of DNA-repair systems than loss of SOD or catalase and this might be extended to oxygenated anaerobes, where DNA damage has been demonstrated. It is possible that other macromolecular sites could be repaired.

Of all these factors, the most important is the primary reduction of oxygen. Modulations of other effects leading to provide a general explanation of variations in oxygen tolerance, but as yet cannot provide quantitative predictions.

METHANOGENS

The Archaea remain the most poorly understood domain of life despite their importance to the biosphere. Methanogenesis, which plays a pivotal role in the global carbon cycle, is Unique to the Archaea. Each year, an estimated 900 million metric tons of methane are biologically produced, representing the major global source for this greenhouse gas and contributing significantly to global warming. Methanogenesis is critical to the waste-treatment industry and biologically produced methane also represents an important alternative fuel source.

The methanogenic archae occupy a unique metabolic niche. These organisms are found in diverse anaerobic habitats ranging from aquatic and marine sediments to sewage digesters and the rumens and large intestines of herbivores and other mammals. In these habitats, the degradation of organic matter results in the production of H_2 and other intermediates by fermentative organisms. By maintaining an extremely low partial pressure of H_2, the methanogens keep fermentative pathways energetically favorable. Some methanogens may occupy niches where hydrogen is produced predominantly by geothermal reactions. Scientific curiosity and national economic imperatives have motivated to choose methanogens as the object of research nowadays. Biology of these organisms is only dimly understood at the molecular level.

What are Methanogens?

Methanogens are the unsung heroes of the global carbon cycle at the bottom of the food chain who break down the waste products of other organisms and release methane gas into the atmosphere. "Methanogens are critical players in the global carbon cycle and have potential uses for addressing human problems", says William W. Metcalf, a microbiologist at he University of Illinois at Urbana-Champaign. They are the unique group of microorganisms having CH4 as a stoichiometric product of their metabolism. Methanogens belong to the domain of life *Archaea*, kingdom *Euryarchaeotaea* (Boone *et al.*, 1993).

Why Methanogens?

Methane (CH4) and the other important green house gases (carbon dioxide (CO2), nitrous oxide oxide (N2O), and hydrofluorocarbons (HFCs) are changing the composition of the atmosphere. They absorb infrared radiations originating from the Earth's surface, the atmosphere, and clouds. Thus, heat is trapped within the surface-troposphere system, and the temperature at Earth's surface, and in the troposphere increases. Responsibility of green house gases in global climate change is now accepted. Since the Industrial Revolution in 1750, the concentration of green house gases in the atmosphere has increased dramatically. Although CH4 concentration in the atmosphere is low, when compared to the main green house gas CO2 (1,75 ppm versus 367 ppm), its capacity to absorb infrared radiations, and radiate energy back to earth gives it a 23 times higher global warming potential (GWP) than CO2 on a 100 years time horizon (IPCC, 2001). After the importance of CH4 as a green house gas was acknowledged (IPCC, 1990), much attention has been directed toward understanding its biogeochemical cycle.

Sources and Amount of Methane Production

Most of the CH4 produced annually is of anthropogenic origin (from 55 to 70%). The highest source of emissions is agriculture, with rice field, and domesticated ruminants responsible for 19 to 36% of total emissions. Natural CH4 sources are responsible for 30 to 45% of total emissions. Some of the natural sources of CH4 emissions are wetland soils (bogs, swamps, tundra, etc.), oceans, wild ruminants, and some insect species like termites with their methanogenic microbial symbionts. The biggest sources of natural CH4 emissions are wetlands, which emit 23 to 40% of the total annual CH4 emissions. Peat-forming wetlands (peatlands) are characterised by slow decomposition rates leading to an accumulation of peat; their organic soil below the water table is anoxic, and often acidic.

They represent the majority of the world's wetlands, and are therefore globally an important CH4 source. Between 10 and 20% of total CH4 emissions originate from peatlands situated in the northern latitudes (>45oN), although they cover only 3 % of the earth surface. Methane is almost exclusively produced by microbial activity.

History of Methanogens

In 1776, Alessandro Volta ran some experiments on combustible air that was reported to him by a friend, Father Carlo Campi. On a little boat in Lake Maggiore he started to poke and stir the bottom of an area covered with reeds. Upon doing this, Volta noticed a lot of air emerging and decided to collect some in a large glass container. Upon analysis of the air he noted that it burned a beautiful blue flame. It wasn't for nearly a century that firm evidence was collected that showed that the methane formation in these habitats was a microbial process.

The discovery of methanogens helped produce the idea for the kingdom *Archaeobacteria* that would include methanogens, some extreme halophiles, and some extreme thermophilic sulfur-dependant organisms. Methanogens can be used to produce methane (aka natural gas, biogas) from biomass and degrade and detoxify agricultural, municipal, and industrial wastes. Methane is also a big contributor to global warming, which is why a better understanding of how methanogenesis works is needed so that we can use methane as a renewable source of energy and limit its greenhouse gas effect

Metabolism

Most methanogens can grow on CO_2 and H_2 as their sole energy source. There are a few exceptions that only metabolize acetate, or reduce methanol with H_2, or use methylamine and methanol. For the majority that reduces CO_2 to CH_4, there are a few key coenzymes they need; coenzyme bound C_1-intermediates Methanofuran (MFR), tetra hydromethanopterin (H_4MPT), and coenzyme M (H-S-CoM). Other key coenzymes worth noting are F_{420} and *N*-7-mercaptoheptanoyl-*O*-phospho-L-threonine (H-S-HTP). Coenzyme F_{420} acts analogously to a quinone in electron transfer sequences by accepting the H^+ ions from the electron donor and supplying them to the electron acceptor. The other coenzyme, H-S-HTP, does the same task as F_{420} only in the last step of methanogenesis from CO_2 and H_2.

Metabolic and Physiological Diversity of Methanogens

Methanogens exhibit a widespread genetic diversity at the level of cellular systems. For example, *M. acetivorans* is distinct among all prokaryotes in possessing all of the four major molecular chaperoning systems, including the GroES/L system, which has not been described in any other archaeon. Additional examples of the genetic diversity of *Methanogens* are described below.

Methanogenesis

The only known energy-yielding process available to methanogenic organisms is methanogenesis and the importance of this metabolic process is reflected in the genome of *M. acetivorans*. Nearly 200 genes related to methanogenesis were identified. These include genes required for known steps in methanogenesis from methylated compounds such as methanol and methylated amines (the methylotrophic pathway; and those required for methanogenesis from acetate (the acetoclastic pathway. Many of these genes are present in multiple copies in the *M. acetivorans* genome. These include two or three copies each of genes encoding components of the methyl transferase systems for methanol, trimethylamine, dimethylamine and monomethylamine, and two copies of a six-gene operon encoding the acetyl-CoA decarbonylase/synthase (ACDS) complex essential for the acetoclastic pathway. The duplication of the ACDS complex in *M. acetivorans* is particularly striking; the two operons are 95% identical over a 6.6-kbp stretch, including a subsection of nearly 4 kbp with only 6 nucleotide changes.

Methanogenic Specialization

The biochemical functions of the multiple methanogenic genes provides strong evidence that *M. acetivorans* specializes in the utilization of acetate and a variety of one-carbon compounds as growth substrates. It is possible that these multiple gene copies provide added flexibility in the utilization of these substrates. The individual copies of the duplicated genes could display differential regulation or encode enzymes with altered kinetic properties, allowing the organism to rapidly change between substrates and to cope with variable substrateconcentrations. The emphasis on the utilization of multiple substrates is consistent with the hypothesis that *Methanosarcina* species succeed in nature by following a generalist strategy.

Hydrogen Utilization

M. acetivorans differs from many other *Methanosarcina* species in being incapable of growing methanogenically using H2 to reduce CO2 (the hydrogenotrophic pathway). The hydrogenotrophic pathway shares many steps in common with the oxidative branch of the methylotrophic pathway and utilizes the same enzymes for these steps, although the reactions are run in the reductive rather than the oxidative direction Electrons required only for the reduction reactions are provided by the oxidation of molecular hydrogen by enzymes known as hydrogenases. These hydrogenases are characteristic enzymes of the hydrogenotrophic pathway and would not be expected to play a role in the oxidative reactions. Therefore, it was surprising that most of the hydrogenases identified in hydrogenotrophic *Methanosarcina* species were also present in the *M. acetivorans* genome. The genes include a homolog of the *Methanosarcina barkeri frh* operon encoding an F420-reducing hydrogenase and homologs of two *Methanosarcina mazei* operons encoding F420-nonreducing hydrogenases (in which F420 is a redox coenzyme unique to methanogenesis). The identification of these hydrogenases in *M. acetivorans* strongly implies that it is capable of metabolizing hydrogen for purposes other than CO_2 reduction.

Carbon Monoxide Metabolism

Certain *Methanosarcina* species have been shown to grow using carbon monoxide (CO) as a methanogenic substrate. It has been hypothesized that oxidation of CO is mediated by the CO dehydrogenase (CODH), now known to be part of the multisubunit ACDS complex, during methanogenic growth on this substrate. Therefore, it was unexpected that *M. acetivorans* was found to contain two homologs of the single-subunit enzyme utilized by *Rhodospirillum rubrum* for growth on CO. The presence of this single-subunit enzyme indicates a possible alternative mechanism for methanogenic growth on CO. Furthermore, the fact that this enzyme is used by *R. rubrum* for nonmethanogenic growth on CO raises the surprising possibility that *M. acetivorans* may grow nonmethanogenically, using CO as a substrate.

Undiscovered Growth Substrates

A number of genes were identified indicating the possibility that other, as yet unidentified, growth substrates may be utilized by *M. acetivorans.* Methylotrophic methanogenesis begins with the transfer of the methyl group from a variety of substrates to coenzyme M, via two methyl-transferases, designated MT1 and MT2, and a substrate- specific methylotrophic corrinoid protein (containing a modified B12 derivative). Fourteen MT2 and 15 corrinoid protein- encoding genes were identified in the *M. acetivorans* genome. These include three proteins with both MT2 and corrinoid binding domains. Two of the MT2 homologs and 10 of the corrinoid proteins are known to be involved in the utilization of either methanol or methylated amines.

MICROBIOLOGY OF ANAEROBIC DIGESTION

Microbes as biocatalyst for methane generation are known for long time. But their actual identity as separate specialized group was established in sixties with ingenious techniques developed by Smith and Hungate and latter perfected by Bryant. Methanogenesis has traditionally been viewed as a two stage process, the acid forming and methane forming stages. In the first stage, the acid forming bacteria were thought ferment organic materials like carbohydrates, lipids and proteins to formate, acetate, propionate, butyrate, ethanol, hydrogen and carbon dioxide. In the second stage, the methanogenic bacteria convert fatty acids to methane.

Now at least four different trophic types of bacteria have been isolated from anaerobic digesters and recognized on the basis of substrate fermented and metabolic end products formed. The four metabolic groups included were (i) hydrolytic bacteria involved in the fermentation of variety of complex organic molecules (i.e. polysaccharides, lipids and proteins) into a broad spectrum of end products *viz.*, acetic acid, H_2/CO_2 and carbon compounds larger than methanol, (ii) the hydrogen producing acetogenic bacteria which included both obligate and facultative species that could ferment organic acids larger than acetic acid' (eg., butyrate, propionate) and neutral compounds larger than methanol (eg., ethanol, propanol) to hydrogen and acetate, (iii) the homoacetogenic bacteria which could ferment a very wide spectrum of multi; or one carbon compounds to acetic acid and (iv) methanogenic bacteria that could ferment CO_2 one carbon compounds, i.e., methanol, carbon monoxide, methylamine and acetate to methane.

Microorganisms Involved in Anaerobic Digestion

Fermentative Bacteria

Fermentative bacteria comprise consortium of many bacterial species. Many of these species are obligate anaerobes. but few facultative anaerobes such as enteric bacteria, *Streptococci* are also present. Anaerobic bacteria belonging to genera such as *Bacteroides, Bifioobactenum, Butyrivibrio, Clostridium, Eubacterium, Ruminococcus* etc., are predominant fermentative bacteria in anaerobic digester and rumen. In fact, the end products of fermentation of organic matter by fermentative bacteria in anaerobic digestion in biogas plant and animal rumen are closely comparable. Difference in the two however, lies in further utilization of end products. In the rumen the end products are absorbed by the rumen while in biogas plant they are further converted to biogas.

Cellulolytic Bacteria

Cellulose, the most abundant biopolymer in the biomass, has been studied with great interest for its degradation under anaerobic conditions. Anaerobic bacteria belong to genera *Acetivibrio, Clostridium,* and *Ruminococcus* are active anaerobic cellulose degrading organisms.through a step-wise hydrolysis glucose is produced which is further converted to pyruvate by

Embden-Meyerhoef-Parnas pathway. Depending upon the partial pressure of hydrogen, pyruvate is further fermented. When the partial pressure of hydrogen is low, acetate, H_2 and $C0_2$ are the major end products. On the other hand, when its high, ethanol, lactate, propionate, butyrate, H_2 and CO_2 are the major end products.

Proteolytic Organism

Many anaerobic bacteria, e.g., *Bacteroides, Butyrivibrio, Clostridium, Selenomonas* show proteolytic activity. Proteins are hydrolyzed first to peptides and then to amino acids. Different aminoacids are then decarboxylated and deaminated to organic acids, volatile fatty acids, H_2, CO_2 and NH_3. The branched chain amino acids such as valine, leucine and isoleucine are fermented to iso-butyrate, iso-valerate and D-2-methyl butyrate respectively. Aromatic amino acids such as phenylalanine, tyrosine and tryptophan are metabolized to Phenyl acetic acid, Phenyl propionic acid, indole etc.

Methanogens

The methanogens are the key organisms in the production of methane from waste materials; they are the only organisms able to break down acetate and hydrogen to gaseous end products. They require strict anaerobic condition for growth and a redox potential of about -300 m V. They have simple nutritional requirements and most species require only mineral salts With CO_2, ammonia and sulfide as extraneous mineral requirements. Some species can use cysteine instead of sulfide as their sulphur source. Some rumen species require addition of acetate, 2-methyl butyrate, coenzyme M, B-vitamins and a rumen fluid factor.

The methanogens are of two types based on their source of carbon for methane generation.

Aceticlastic Methanogens: Organisms which generate methane by using acetate as their carbon source.

Non-Acetlclastic Methanogens: These methanogens use hydrogen to reduce the carbon dioxide to form methane.

Aceticlastic Methanogens

Acetic acid has been shown to be the precursor of most (up to 75 %) of the methane produced in many anaerobic digesters. It has been established that methane is mainly formed directly from the methyl group of acetic acid rather than from reduction of Carbon dioxide as is the case with most other substrates.

Inspite of the known significance of acetate as an important intermediate in non-gastro intestinal methanogenesis, especially in the anaerobic sludge digestion system or in lake sediments, there has been little advancement in knowledge about this key reaction or the organisms involved. Radioactive tracer experiments from almost 30 years ago established the origin of methane from the methyl group of acetate and this route of methanogenesis.

Hydrogen Oxidizing Methanogens

In anaerobic environment the ultimate fate of the complete dissimilation of complex organic compounds such as protein and lipids is the formation of methane and carbon dioxide. The fermentation of carbohydrates, amino acids and long chain fatty acids initially leads to the formation of lower volatile fatty acids, alcohols and other neutral compounds, hydrogen and carbon dioxide. Hydrogen is rarely detectable since it is rapidly and preferentially oxidized by all known methane bacteria with the reduction of CO_2 to CH_4. In the absence of hydrogen removal, a mixture of products will accumulate and substrate utilization will be inhibited. The oxidation of hydrogen not only yields energy for methanogenic bacteria, it also provides an overall mechanism for terminal electron removal, thus permitting the continued breakdown of intermediate to the level of acetic acid.

Pathway of Anaerobic Digestion

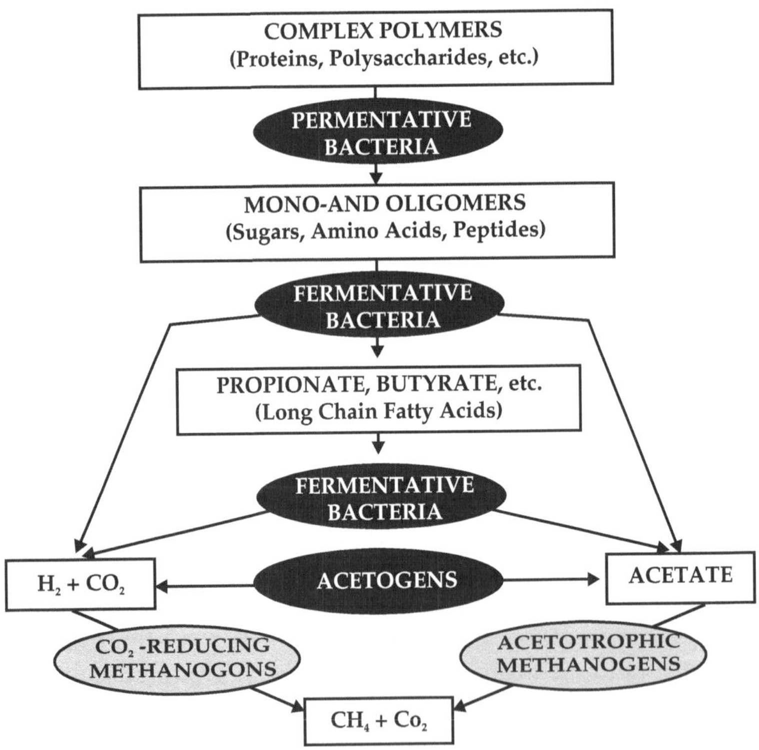

Biochemical Reactions Involved in the Conversion of Organic Matter

Acetogenic Reactions			ΔG° 25 °C (KJ mol-1)	ΔG° 55 °C (kJ mol-1)
Glucose + 12 H_2O	→	6 HCO_3^- + 12 H_2 + $6H^+$	+3.2	-51.8
Glucose + 4 H_2O	→	2 Acetate⁻ + 2 HCO_3^- + 4 H_2 + $4H^+$	-206.3	-232.2
Ethanol + H_2O	→	Acetate⁻ + 2 H_2 + H^+	+9.6	+1.7
Lactate⁻ + 2 H_2O	→	Acetate⁻ + HCO_3^- + 2 H_2 + H^+	-4.2	-12.6
Acetate⁻ + 4 H_2O	→	2 HCO_3^- + 4 H_2+ H^+	+ 104.2	+89.8
Propionate⁻ + 3 H_2O	→	Acetate⁻ + HCO_3^- + 3 H_2 + H^+	+ 76.5	+ 64.7
Propionate⁻ + 2 HCO_3^-	→	Acetate⁻ + 3 Formate⁻ + H^+	+ 72.4	+ 61.6
Butyrate⁻ + 2 H_2O	→	2 Acetate⁻ + 2 H_2+ H^+	+ 48.3	+ 39.5
Butyrate⁻ + 2 HCO_3^-	→	2 Acetate⁻ + 2 Formate⁻ + H^+	+ 30.6	+ 20.9
Homoacetagenic reactions				
Acetate⁻ + 4 H_2O	→	2 HCO_3^- + 4 H_2 + H^+	+ 104.6	+ 90.2
2 CO_2 + 4 H_2	→	Acetate⁻ + 2 H_2O	- 55.0	- 33.5
Methanogenic reactions				
4 H_2 + HCO_3^- + H^+	→	CH_4 + 3 H_2O	- 135.6	- 124.9
4 Formate⁻ + H_2O + H^+	→	CH_4 + $3HCO_3^-$	- 130.4	- 118.9
Acetate⁻ + H_2O	→	HCO3⁻ + CH_4	- 31.0	- 34.7

HIGH RATE ANAEROBIC BIO-REACTORS FOR ENERGY PRODUCTION

Bioenergy systems for alternate fuel production have attracted more attention in recent years in countries like India, where energy continues to be precious and high oil prices burden the economy. Anaerobic digestion of agro-industrial wastes is of positive environmental value since it combines waste stabilization with net fuel production. Energy conversion of organic matter by the biomethanation route (anaerobic digestion) is often advantageous than thermo-chemical routes since it is applicable to most types of high-moisture content organic feeds and is operated at low temperature and pressure with relatively high overall thermal efficiencies.

Need for High Rate Digesters

The popularity of biogas technology for large scale application has been limited essentially due to the slow rate and process instability of anaerobic digestion; the slow rate means large digester volumes (consequently greater costs and space requirements) and process instability means lack of assurance for steady energy supply. Once these two conventional disadvantages of anaerobic digestion are overcome the two major advantages - ability to generate energy and stable sludge's can favors anaerobic processes in the bio-waste management scenario.

Introduction of the Up-flow anaerobic filter, Up-flow anaerobic sludge blanket reactor, Anaerobic fluidized bed reactor and Up-flow anaerobic hybrid reactors have brought down the hydraulic retention time (HRT) of anaerobic digesters from 35-40 days of typical unstirred reactors (like conventional biogas digesters) to a few hours. Such drastic reduction in HRT had a radical impact on digester design considerations which favored size reduction and consequent reduction in digester costs. Further it has opened the possibility of treating high-volume low-strength wastes such as industrial effluents by anaerobic process.

Immobilized Cell Bio-reactors

Conventional digester designs consisting essentially of completely mixed, one-step continuous reactors without active biomass recycle were limited by the low specific growth rates of the methanogenic bacteria. The concept of biological solids recycle, which led to the introduction of the anaerobic contact or anaerobic activated sludge process, permitted a longer residence time for the active flora within the digester and resulted in more efficient waste stabilization and significantly higher gas volume efficiencies. Retention of the active biomass, independently of waste flow, considerably reduced the HRT resulting in a smaller digester volume. Efficient biological solids recycle means an effective separation of the bacterial cells from the effluent stream and this can be both troublesome and costly. In many instances a very high solids recycle rate is often warranted in order to maintain the required treatment efficiency.

Maintenance of the active flora within the reactor, independent of waste flow, is achieved in the second generation of high rate methane reactors by a mechanism which avoids the costly operational problems associated with the long retention time of conventional mixed reactors and the solids recycle system of the anaerobic contact process. The concept of retention and maintenance of biological growth on an inert support material forms the theoretical basis of almost all second generation *immobilized cell bio-reactor* designs. By maintaining a high concentration of active biomass within the reactor for long periods, these new designs allow efficient digestion of soluble wastes at hydraulic retention times of few days to several hours. They also ensure the treatment of both high and low strength soluble wastes to more satisfactory levels at more economically viable conditions.

Up-flow Anaerobic Filter (UAF)

In fixed film anaerobic systems like UAFs, the biomass is retained by attachment to an inert support medium and hence remains in the reactors for longer than the hydraulic residence time. It consists essentially of a column packed with an inert support material such as gravel, plastic, ceramic, fired clay, mussel shell etc. A range of support media have been used, by several workers depending on the type of reactor and the process geometry. The anaerobic filter initially developed by James C. Young in 1968 had random packed quartzite stones as matrix for cell immobilization. The distribution header for the filter is at the bottom of the unit, thereby creating an upward flow through the submerged matrix bed. Effluent re-circulation is sometimes practiced giving rise to higher up-flow liquid velocities. The first examples generally used rock media of 25-65 mm diameter, giving approximately 50% void volume. There were several studies in which the filters were tested on different types of waste-waters ranging from pretreated domestic wastewater to industrial waste-waters. Subsequently, different types of synthetic support media have been developed with void volumes up to 96%. A high proportion of the biomass (50%) is not strictly attached to the support media, but is rather held in the interstitial spaces of the filters. The hydraulic flow through the filters is low, so this interstitial biomass is retained. Waste-waters which contain a high concentration of suspended solids or a high degradable organic concentration tend to cause blockage or channeling within the filter.

Anaerobic filters have been used mainly for waste-waters which contain moderate organic concentrations (BOD 5000 mg/l) and low concentrations of suspended solids and are preferably warm. The overall loadings possible rarely exceed 10 kg COD $m^{-3}d^{-1}$ and for conventional 'stone' type media rarely exceed 5 kg COD $m^{-3}d^{-1}$. The treatment of carbohydrate based wastes reported that at low loadings (2 kg COD $m^{-3}d^{-1}$) approximately 90% COD removal is possible, while at higher loading rates (8-16 kg COD m-3d), the removal efficiency is reduced to approximately 40%. Provided that the filters are not overloaded, they produce biogas at the standard rate of 0.5 m^3kg^{-1} COD.

Up-flow Anaerobic Sludge Blanket (UASB) Reactors

The biomass in the anaerobic up-flow sludge blanket reactor is retained within the unit by development of highly settle able bacterial flocs, in the form of granules of 1-5 mm diameter. The anaerobic sludge in UASBs inherently attains good settling properties, provided the sludge is not exposed to heavy mechanical agitation. Well settle able sludge aggregates, dispersed under the influence of the biogas production (which is particularly quite heavy at higher organic space loads and in tall reactors), can be satisfactorily retained in the reactor by separating (collecting) the biogas in a gas collector system commonly referred as GSS (gas-solid separator) device. It is important to separate biogas from the biomass to prevent carry-over of granules into the treated effluent. The GSS device or three phase separator is crucial for UASB reactors and it acts as an in-built settler at the upper most part of the reactor which creates a zone in which gas is disengaged and biomass resettles into the sludge blanket. Sludge aggregates coalesce and settle out in the settler compartment, and then are allowed to slide back into the digester compartment beneath the GSS device.

Lettinga and co-workers found that high loadings could be applied once the granular sludge was formed. However, the granulation process did not occur with all wastes, for example slaughterhouse wastes and raw sewage did not cause granulation and rendering wastes only caused granulation at a slow rate. The slow start-up of UASB reactors is considered as one of the main drawbacks. Even though a considerable period of time is involved in cultivating a sufficient amount of well settle able (flocculent or granular) viable anaerobic sludge, once succeeded, the problem is solved. This is because anaerobic sludge can be preserved for long periods of time under unfed conditions, while excess anaerobic sludge cultivated in a full scale installation can be used for starting up new installations, even in the case that the new waste water is significantly different in composition, strength etc.

Development of granulated sludge is related to microbiological & biochemical factors, feedstock characteristics, and reactor conditions. The hydraulic retention time has to be such that filamentous and other non-settling bacteria are washed out of the reactor, particularly during startup. A two-stage process can be better, in which an acidification stage of short hydraulic retention time precedes the UASB. The feedstock is generally required to have a pH greater than 5.5 and sufficient alkalinity to ensure a stable operating pH. For soluble wastes, mixing from the biogas generation is sufficient to ensure adequate contact between sludge and the substrate to be treated. Hydraulic stresses in the reactor may result in occasional loss of granulation and subsequent washout of granules from the system. An important hydraulic parameter in UASB reactors is the superficial liquid up-flow velocity within the reactor. The up-flow velocity employed in most of the UASB reactors is about 1 mh-1 although values up to 6 mh-1 in laboratory scale reactors have also been reported. At high up-flow velocities granules may be disintegrated resulting in wash out of the fragments from the reactor. On the other hand at small up-flow velocities, a hollow core (filled with biogas) may appear within the granules, which makes them float and lead eventually to washout.

Up-flow Anaerobic Hybrid Reactors (UAHR)

Hybrid anaerobic digester was a new design instigated by Guiot and Van den Berg. The up-flow anaerobic hybrid reactor or the Up-flow Sludge Bed - Filter reactor hybridizes the UASB concept and random packing of a matrix in the top third of the reactor column. Many researchers evaluated the performance of this hybrid design. They reported that this configuration combined the advantages of both UASB and UAF while minimizing their limitations. The reactor was efficient in the treatment of dilute to high strength wastewater at high OLR and short HRT. The use of packing media only in the top portion of the reactor minimises channeling problem associated with UAF and loss of biomass due to floatation associated with poorly performing UASB reactors. Additionally, the packing material enhanced the development of granular sludge.

Anaerobic wastewater treatment without doubt can be regarded as a grown-up technology, although this is still not completely accepted everywhere. The UASB system so far is the most widely applied reactor concept. It has found successful application for a vast number of very different waste-waters including industrial effluents. Undoubtedly, various hybrid reactors have been developed which are becoming popular. The anaerobic treatment process very likely will find increasing application for treatment of industrial effluents, especially food processing waste waters. Even though at a limited scale in developing countries, there are also experiences with applying the process for the treatment of domestic sewage and its prospects look very promising in tropical and subtropical regions. Implementation of anaerobic treatment for this purpose can lead to tremendous savings in the investment of sewerage. It should also be emphasized here, that for the successful application of the anaerobic process it is a prerequisite, that the implementation is pursued with the necessary care bearing in mind that we are dealing with living organisms. This is true for the design, construction as well as the operation and maintenance of the system.

Ethanol Production

Ethanol production is another ancient industrial microbial process originally used for the manufacture of intoxicating liquor and latterly industrial alcohol. Ethanol is commonly produced as a fermentation product, but homoethanolic fermentation is a comparative rarity. With most organisms ethanol is only one of a mixture of fermentation products which may commenly include lactate, succinate, acetate, formate, hydrogen and carbon dioxide. The main organisms associated with homoethanolic fermentation are yeasts of the genus Saccharomyces and bacteria in the genus Zymomonas.

The current interest in the production of fuels and chemicals from biomass and waste materials has led to search for other potentially useful ethanologenic microbes particularly considered.

BIO HYDROGEN PRODUCTION

Benemann estimated that hydrogen production from wastewater has the greatest potential for economical near-term production of hydrogen from renewable resources—but only if hydrogen conversion efficiency could be increased to 60-80%. However, substantial technical barriers must be overcome to achieve such efficiency. Let us first further consider the case for hydrogen production from biomass, because some argue that it has the most immediate potential for hydrogen production. If biomass could be categorized as a carbohydrate such as glucose ($C_6H_{12}O_6$), the complete conversion of each mole (mol) of glucose would produce 12 mol of hydrogen.

$$C_6C_{12}O_6 + 6\ H_2O \rightarrow 12\ H_2 + 6\ CO_2$$

Fermentation of glucose by all known microbiological routes (primarily by *Clostridia*) produces up to 4 mol hydrogen/mol glucose. Woodward *et al.* achieved 96.7% conversion efficiency (11.6 mol hydrogen/mol glucose-6-phosphates) only by using enzymes, not bacteria. They coupled enzymes from the oxidative pentose phosphate cycle with hydrogenases purified from

Pyrococcus furiosus. Thus, there are no known naturally occurring biochemical routes for achieving anywhere near the required 60–80% conversion efficiency. A thermophilic organism has recently been isolated that may be able to achieve higher conversion efficiencies. However, its biochemical route of hydrogen production is unknown, and claims of high hydrogen production conversion have not been independently verified or shown to be economical.

The main challenge to fermentative production of hydrogen is that only 15% of the energy from the organic source can typically be obtained in the form of hydrogen. While a conversion efficiency of 33% is theoretically possible for hydrogen production from glucose, only half of this is usually obtained under batch and continuous fermentation conditions. Four mol of hydrogen are made from glucose if 2 mol of acetate are produced, but only 2 mol of hydrogen are produced when butyrate is the main fermentation product. Typically, 60–70% of the aqueous product during sugar fermentation is butyrate.

$$C_6H_{12}O_6 + 2\,H_2O \rightarrow 4\,H_2 + 2\,CO_2 + 2\,C_2H_4O_2$$

$$C_6H_{12}O_6 \rightarrow 2\,H_2 + 2\,CO_2 + C_4H_6O_2$$

Anaerobic-systems Producing Hydrogen as Fuel for Conventional Fuel Cells

Various bacteria and algae, e.g. *Escherichia coli, Enterobacter* aero-genes, *C. butyricum, Clostridium acetobutylicum* and *Clostridium perfringens*, are known to be active for hydrogen production under anaerobic condition. The most effective hydrogen-producing microorganism is *C. butyricum. E. coli* and *Enterobacter* aero-genes are facultative anaerobes and ferment both glucose and lactose as a carbon source to produce hydrogen.

The conversion of carbohydrate to hydrogen is achieved by a multienzyme system. In bacteria, it involves the conversion of glucose to 2 mol of NADH, a reduced form of coenzyme 1, namely *b*-nicotinamide adenine dinucleotide of the vitamin niacin, and 2 mol of pyruvate formed by Embden–Meyerhof pathway. Pyruvate is then oxidized through a pyruvate–ferredoxin oxidoreductase producing acetyl-CoA, CO_2 and reduced ferredoxin. NADH–ferredoxin oxidoreductase oxidizes NADH and reduces ferredoxin. The reduced ferredoxin is reoxidized to form hydrogen by hydrogenase. As a result, 4 mol of H_2 are produced from 1 mol of glucose under ideal conditions as shown below. In practice, however, H_2 yield is only about 25% of the theoretical value. Improvement in H_2 production is possible by genetic engineering techniques and screening of new hydrogen-producing bacteria.

A H_2/O_2 fuel cell comprising a platinum-black–nickel mesh anode and a palladium-black–nickel mesh cathode, and separated by a nylon filter operating at room temperature was connected to a bioreactor producing hydrogen. The current and voltage output were dependent on the rate of hydrogen production in the fermenter. For example, an open-circuit voltage

(*V*oc) of 0.95 V and a short-circuit current density (*I*sc) of 40 mA/cm_2 were obtained at a H_2 flow of 40 ml/min. The biological fuel cell operating under steady-state conditions for a week produced a continuous current between 500 and 550 mA.

$$\text{Glucose} + 2\text{NAD}^+ \xrightarrow[\text{Embden–Meyerhof pathway}]{\text{Multienzyme}} 2\text{ Pyruvate} + 2\text{NADH} \quad (1)$$

$$\text{Pyruvate} + \text{Ferredoxin}_{ox} \xrightarrow[\text{Oxidoreductase}]{\text{Pyruvate–ferredoxin}} \text{Acetyl-CoA} + CO_2 + \text{Ferredoxin}_{red} \quad (2)$$

$$\text{NADH} + \text{Ferredoxin}_{ox} \xrightarrow[\text{Oxidoreductase}]{\text{NADH–Ferredoxin}} \text{NAD}^+ + \text{Ferredoxin}_{red} \quad (3)$$

$$\text{Ferredoxin}_{red} + 2H^+ + 2e^- \xrightarrow{\text{Hydrogenase}} \text{Ferredoxin}_{ox} + H_{2-} \quad (4)$$

$$H_2 \rightarrow 2H^+ + 2e^- \text{ (at aonde)} \quad (5)$$

NEWLY FOUND REDOX ENZYMES FROM ANAEROBES SUITABLE FOR BIOCONVERSIONS

Purified redox enzymes or microbial cells have been used as stereo selective redox biocatalysts for many years. The reducing enzymes applied were usually pyridine nucleotide dependent. New enzymes for this purpose were found and introduced for preparative work. The application of isolated pyridine nucleotide dependent enzymes on a preparative scale requires coenzyme regeneration. As far as cells are concerned, mostly various types of yeasts have been applied. Methods have been studied for controlling the enantioselectivity of reductions with baker's yeast.

Some time ago we became interested in redox enzymes occurring in anaerobes. We assumed that during evolution, in the absence of noticeable concentrations of dioxygen in the earth atmosphere redox enzymes may have been evolved creating carbon-hydrogen bonds, which are not stab-le in the presence of oxygen. It was known, that strict anaerobes contain redox enzymes such as hydrogenases, reversible carbon monoxide dehydrogenases, nitrogenases and others, which are hardly found in aerobes. The presence of carbon-hydrogen forming enzymes was screened by using resting anaerobes such as *clostridia* or anaerobically grown facultative anaerobes as catalysts for the reduction of various unsaturated compounds such as ketones, 0x0 acids, 2-enoates, 2-enones and non-activated carboxylic acids, at the expense of dihydrogen, formate or carbon monoxide. We found that the C-C double bonds of non-activated 2-enoates, the C-0 double bonds of 0x0 acids and aldehydes or even non-activated carboxylic acids can be reduced by non-pyridine nucleotide dependent enzymes with dihydrogen, formate or carbon monoxide. It turned out that interesting unknown redox enzymes exist in strict and facultative anaerobes, if the latter are grown under strict anaerobic conditions. Some of the newly detected enzymes together with suitable methodologies are of interest for preparative work.

BIOPOLYMER DEGRADATION

Thermoanaerobes possess amylolytic, xylonytic and cellulolytic enzyme activities. A great deal of our understanding of cellulose degradation has come from studying the cellulose system in anaerobes.

The Cellulosomes

Multienzyme Machines for Degradation of Plant Cell Wall Polysaccharides.

During the years, the cellulosome has become a major paradigm for microbial degradation of cellulose and as a model for the formation of multi-component hetero-complexes. Cellulosomes are composed of a conglomerate of subunits, each of which comprises a set of interacting functional modules. A multi-functional integrating subunit (called scaffoldin) is responsible for organizing the cellulolytic subunits into the multi-enzyme complex. This is accomplished by the interaction of two complementary classes of domain, located on the two separate types of interacting subunits, i.e., a cohesin domain on scaffoldin and a dockerin domain on each enzymatic subunit. The high-affinity cohesin-dockerin interaction defines cellulosome structure. The scaffoldin subunit also bears a cellulose-binding domain (CBD) that mediates attachment of the cellulosome to its substrate.

A number of studies have been devoted to furthering the understanding of the enzymic degradation of cellulose. In order to solubilize crystalline cellulose substrates, bacteria and fungi produce either a collection of free cellulases and or multicellulase complexes known as cellulosomes. Despite these studies, the exact mechanism by which either isolated enzymes or multi-component enzymic systems are able to attack and digest crystalline biopolymers, such as cellulose, remains a mystery.

Cellulose-based materials are usually complex substrates consisting of a hierarchy of structures. In Nature, the polymer chains of native cellulose (or cellulose I) are organized into slender crystalline microfibrils. The micro fibrils themselves are further assembled into plant cell walls, the tunica of some sea animals, pellicles of bacterial origin, etc. The microstructure of the crystalline micro fibrils also adds a degree of complexity to the picture; in addition to variable amounts of amorphous components, the cellulose micro fibrils also consists of crystalline nanodomains of two distinct allomorphs: cellulose Ia and Ib. Within a given cellulose sample, the fraction of the Ia and Ib phase depends on its source. It has been established that these two phases exhibit different susceptibilities towards chemical as well as enzymic reagents. Thus, with a complex solid such as cellulose, the kinetics of enzymic digestion depends on both the macro- as well as the micro-structure of the substrate.

Establishing the relative influence of parameters such as accessibility, crystallinity and nanostructure of the substrate is one of the major hurdles that have to be cleared for the full understanding of the enzymic degradation of cellulose.

The availability of models of cellulose micro fibrils and different crystalline forms has advanced our understanding of cellulose biodegradation. In this context, the model substrates have been subjected to the action of either individual enzymes or controlled mixtures of enzymic components. Using this approach, each micro fibrils or crystal has an equivalent accessibility, and thus only the contributions of crystallinity and the perfection of the desired substrate have to be taken into account. To date, structural and morphological studies on the digestion of model cellulose crystals have been achieved, essentially with fungal enzymes from *Trichoderma reesei* and *Humicola insolens.* In these studies, ultrastructural observations revealed the processivity and or synergism of these enzyme systems. In some cases, spectroscopic evidence has also shown that the Ia phase of cellulose was more susceptible toward enzyme degradation than the Ib counterpart.

Clostridium thermocellum produces a highly active cellulase system that consists of a high-M(r) multienzyme complex termed cellulosome. Hydrolytic components of the cellulosome are organized around a large, noncatalytic glycoprotein termed CipA that acts both as a scaffolding component and a cellulose-binding factor. Catalytic subunits of the cellulosome bear conserved, noncatalytic subdomains, termed dockerin domains, which bind to receptor domains of CipA, termed cohesin domains. CipA includes nine cohesin domains, a cellulose-binding domain, and a specialized dockerin domain. Proteins of the cell envelope carrying cohesin domains that specifically bind the dockerin domain of CipA have been identified. These proteins may mediate anchoring of the cellulosomes to the cell surface. Cellulase complexes similar to the cellulosome of C. thermocellum are produced by several cellulolytic clostridia. High-M(r) multienzyme complexes have also been identified in anaerobic rumen fungi. The architecture of the fungal complexes also seems to rely on the interaction of conserved, noncatalytic docking domains with a scaffolding component. However, the sequence of the fungal docking domains bears no resemblance to the clostridial dockerin domains, suggesting that the fungal and clostridial complexes arose independently.

The thermophilic cellulolytic anaerobic strain, Bacteroides sp. P-1 was isolated from a thermophilic anaerobic digester. The growth and adherance of cells to insoluble microcrystalline cellulose (avicel) and the production of avicelase, carboxymethymethylcellulase (CMCase) of xylanase when grown on avicel, carboxymethylcellulose (CMC) or xylan as sole source of carbon, indicated that this Bacteroides sp. P-1 was found to be a cellulosome producing strain. When grown on avicel, the Bacteroides strain produced cellulase, xylanase, ethanol and organic acids, especially acetic acid. The crude extracellular cellulosome type enzyme from the Bacteroides strain could adsorp on microcrystalline cellulose and hydrolyzes raw agricultural residues such as rice straw, bagasse and corn hull and corn cob effectively.

Occurance of Cellulosome in Cellulolytic Microorganisms

Anaerobic bacteria	*Clostridium thermocellum* C.Cellulovorans C.Cellulolyticum C.Josui Acetivibrio cellulolyticus Bacteroides cellulosolvens Ruminococcus albus R.flavefaciens
Aerobic bacteria Anaerobic fungi	*Vibrio* sp Neocallimastix sp Piromyces sp *Orpinomyces sp*

General Strategies of Cellulose Hydrolysis and Utilization by Anaerobic Bacteria

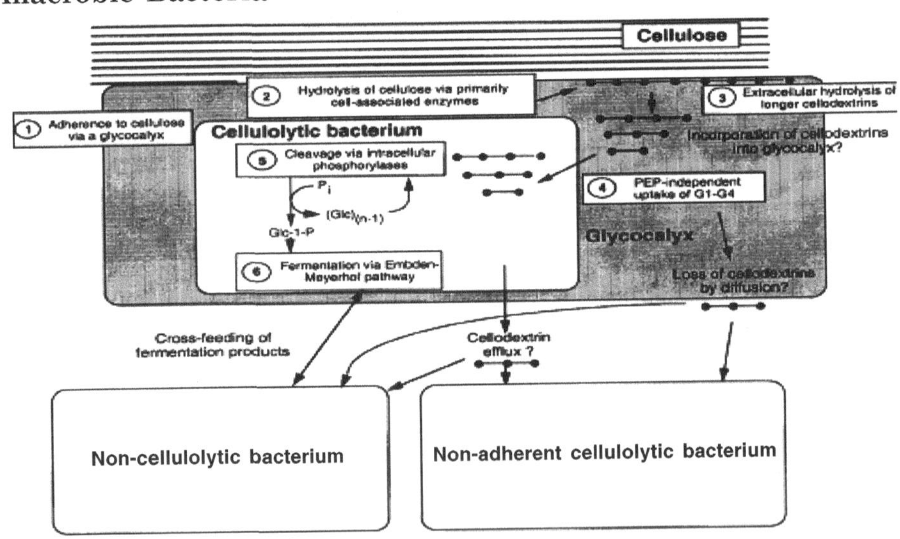

INNOVATIVE FERMENTATION PROCESSES FOR THE PRODUCTION OF ARCHAEAL BIOMASS, ENZYMES AND METABOLITES

A major limitation to the industrial application of archaeal enzymes and metabolites is the low productivity of the fermentation processes as a result of low growth rates and low biomass yields. To overcome these limitations, attention has been focused on studying the physiology of archaea of biotechnological interest and on designing bioreactors and bioprocesses that increase productivity. Because of the unconventional environmental conditions needed for the cultivation of extremophiles, contamination problems are minimal. Therefore, a continuous culture approach has been widely adopted. Continuous culture experiments have provided insights into the significance of specific enzymes, in addition to clarifying stress responses and unusual physiological characteristics of hyperthermophilic and extremely thermoacidophilic microorganisms.

To improve biomass yield of the hyperthermophilic archaeon *Pyrococcus furiosus*, Raven *et al.* (1992) used continuous cultures with defined and minimal media and achieved a maximal cell density of 108 cells ml–1 when *P. furiosus* was grown on starch (Raven and Sharp 1997). Rinker *et al.* (1999) cultivated the hyperthermophilic heterotrophs *Metallosphera sedula, P. furiosus* and *Thermococcus litoralis* in a chemostat and observed the production of exopolysaccharides. Continuous cultures of *Methanobacterium thermoautotrophicum* were performed at different gassing rates using continuous measurements of the growth-limiting factor H2, and a simple unstructured mathematical model was developed and verified. Another extremely thermophilic methanogen, *Methanococcus jannaschii*, was grown in continuous culture to evaluate the correlation between hydrogenase activity and parameters such as growth rate and pressure (Tsao *et al.* 1994).

Optimization of the growth medium is also of key importance in the production of extremophilic biomasses for subsequent exploitation in industry. Particular interest has focused on the cultivation of anaerobic archaea, because their sensitivity to oxygen is a major obstacle to cultivation and to the development of genetic exchange systems in archaea. Godfroy *et al.* (2000) exploited a gas-lift bioreactor for the continuous culture of *Pyrococcus abyssi* ST549 on carbohydrates, proteinaceous substrates or amino acids and found that the disaccharides maltose and cellobiose did not support growth, whereas proteinaceous materials, such as peptone or amino acids in the presence of sulfur, were good substrates. The use of waste products as substrates for extremophilic biomass production is an attractive option for producing enzymes and metabolites for commercial exploitation. *Sulfolobus solfataricus* MT4 grown at 87 °C in a 100-l fermenter on whey supplied directly from dairy farms yielded 80 g of dry biomass per mole of lactose.

Research attention has also focused on the development of culture techniques that result in high cell densities. To date, successful approaches for improving biomass yield and enzyme or metabolite production have involved either fed-batch cultures or the development of special bioreactors that allow easy removal of toxic metabolites and replacement of nutrients. Efficient production of *Sulfolobus solfataricus* DSM 1617 was achieved by a fed-batch technique (Park and Lee, 1997). In these studies, maximum cell yield (dry biomass) was 23 g l-1, when constant volume was maintained by continuous replacement of evaporated water. The kinetic parameters and a athematical model of the fermentation process were evaluated. The effects of yeast extract and other complex components on metabolite formation (e.g., ammonia) and cell yield were also reported. A novel corrosion-resistant bioreactor composed of polyetherether ketone, tech glass (borosilicate glass), silicium nitrate ceramics and silicon nitrite ceramics was used for the cultivation of two recently isolated extreme halophilic archaea that produce poly-_-glutamic acid and poly-_-hydroxybutyric acid, respectively (Hezayen *et al.* 2000). Batch fermentations on *n*-butyric acid as carbon source yielded a cell density (dry biomass) of 2.3 g l–1, with the accumulation of poly-_-hydroxybutyric acid comprising up to 53% of the dry biomass. Although the application of fed-batch techniques coupled with media optimization have facilitated in vitro culture of archaea in sufficient quantities to permit physiological studies and the isolation of numerous enzymes of industrial interest, it has not been possible to scale-up these techniques for largescale production.

Bioreactor Scale Cultivation of Archaea: Continuous and High Cell Density Fermentation. Abbreviation: *T*opt = Optimal Growth Temperature

Microorganism	T_{opt} (°C)	Cultivation mode	Reference
Metallosphera sedula	74	Continuous	Rinkar *et. al.* 1999
Methanobacterium thermoautotrophicum	65	Continuous growth-limiting factor H_2	Schills *et al.* 1996
Mehanococcus jannaschii	85	Medium optimization CSTR	Mukhopadhyay *et al.* 1999
Mehanococcus jannaschii	80-85	Continuous	Tsao *et al.* 1994
Pyrococcus abyssi ST549	95	Continuous	Godfroy *et al.* 2000
Pyrococcus furiosus	90	Dialysis	Krahe *et al.* 1996
Pyrococcus furiosus	90	Continuous	Raven *et al.* 1992
Pyrococcus furiosus	90	Batch on starth-based medium	Raven and sharp 1997
Pyrococcus furiosus	98	Continuous	Rinker *et al.* 1996
Sulfolobus shibatae	75	Dialysis	Krahe *et al.* 1996
Sulfolobus solfatarious Gθ	75	Microfiltration	Schiraldi *et al.* 1999
Sulfolobus solfataricus MT4	87	Batch on whey-based medium	Romano *et al.* 1992
Thermococcus barosli	82.5		Durraud *et al.* 1998
Thermococcus litoralli	85-88	Batch and continuous	Rinkar and Kelly 2000

Industrial Potential of Archaeal Enzymes and Metabolites

Most of the archaeal bio products and bioprocesses that have been developed in industry so far are based on the unconventional properties of archaeal biomasses or of their enzymes and metabolites. Here we describe several promising applications that have been developed in the past decade, and highlight the few applications that have already reached the market.

Biotechnological Applications of Archaeal Biomasses

Despite the potential of microorganisms from the domain Archaea, their industrial application has not been exploited, except in microbiological waste treatment processes. Biological methanogenesis is applied to the anaerobic treatment of sewage sludge, and agricultural, municipal and industrial wastes, where the maintenance of a desired methanogenic flora is achieved by innoculation. Methanogens are a taxonomically and phylogenetically diverse group of microorganisms that obtain energy for growth from the reaction leading to methane production. Methanogens use only a small number of compounds, H_2 or one-carbon atom compounds, and this specialization makes them dependent on other organisms for a supply of substrates in most anaerobic environments (Boone *et al.* 1993).

Many bioreactor configurations have been exploited to increase the efficiency of anaerobic digestion, such as the rotating biological contactor, the anaerobic baffle reactor and the upflow anaerobic sludge blanket reactor, and several largescale plants are in operation (Rehm and Reed, 1999). Recently, a methanogenic process has been established on a lab-scale for the anaerobic digestion of the organic fraction of municipal gray-waste based on a mixed archaeal population; the reactors have been fed daily and held in steady state for over 2 years. These examples illustrate the potential for coupling waste treatment processes to biogas production, thereby recovering energy from an unavoidable process. Halophilic archaea have also been evaluated for bioremediation in harsh environments, for the degradation of organic pollutants and in the treatment of concentrated textile waste waters, particularly the first dye bath liquor from the dying process, which contains a high salt load (Margesin and Schinner, 2001). Biosurfactant-producing halophilic bacteria can play a significant role in the accelerated remediation of oil-polluted saline environments. Lovley (2001) examined the degradation of hydrocarbons by archaeal microbes under anoxic conditions. Sulfate-reducing microorganisms belonging to the domain Archaea have been isolated for their capacity to degrade alkanes anaerobically. In aquatic sediments, the anaerobic oxidation of methane with sulfate as electron acceptor has been reported and is assumed to involve the reversal of methanogenesis catalyzed by archaea with the scavenging of an electron-carrying metabolite by sulfate-reducing bacteria.

Archaeal Enzymes of Biotechnological Interest

In addition to the potential uses of archaeal biomasses, natural and modified archaeal enzymes also present huge possibilities for industrial applications. The biotechnological value of these enzymes is related not only to their direct applications, but also to the knowledge acquired from molecular sequences and crystallographic studies. Such knowledge will permit the redesign of conventional enzymes for use as biocatalysts in harsh industrial conditions. Widespread use of DNA polymerases from hyperthermophilic archaea may portend future common use of extremophile enzymes in biotechnology, although none of the novel enzymes from these microorganisms has yet achieved significant industrial application because of difficulties encountered in their large-scale production. Efforts to resolve or ameliorate these difficulties are likely in the near future.

Many archaeal enzymes involved in carbohydrate metabolism, particularly those from the glycosyl hydrolase family, are of special interest to the industrial biotechnology sector. The starch processing industry, which converts starch into more valuable products such as dextrins, glucose, fructose and trehalose, can profit from the exploitation of thermostable enzymes. In all starch processing conversions, high temperatures are required to liquefy starch and make it accessible to enzymatic attack. Enzymes from mesophilic organisms are currently employed in these processes, but this is likely to change in the near future when the advantages of the integrated utilization of amylases, pullulanases and glucosidases recently isolated from hyperthermophilic sources are harnessed.

Archaeal Metabolites for Biotechnology

Some archaeal metabolites, such as proteins, osmotically active substances (so-called compatible solutes), exopolysaccharides and special lipids have potential industrial applications. Halophilic archaea offer a multitude of actual or potential biotechnological applications. Compatible solutes produced by halophilic archaea include mannosylglycerate (MG) and diglycerol phosphate, and they have also beeen identified in *P. furiosus*, *P. woesei* and *Archaeoglobus fulgidus*. The stabilizing effect ofMGon several enzymes subjected to heating or freeze-drying was superior to that of other stabilizers.

Strategies for Cloning and Expression of Archaeal Enzymes and their Industrial Use

Because archaeal enzymes are adapted to extreme environments, they are unusually stable. They are therefore suitable candidates for applications in industrial processes that are performed under harsh conditions, such as high temperatures or in the presence of organic solvents or high ionic strength. For the same reasons, they are also ideal model molecules for investigations aimed at elucidating the mechanisms of chemicophysical stability of proteins. Biologists already use the extremophilic enzyme Taq polymerase from *Thermus aquaticus*. In addition to the isolation of new enzymes, the spectrum of available enzyme capabilities could be expanded by random mutagenesis and directed evolution. Genes encoding several enzymes from extremophiles have been cloned in mesophilic hosts, with the objective of overproducing the enzyme and altering its properties to suit commercial applications. *Escherichia coli*, *Bacillus subtilis* and yeasts have been used successfully as mesophilic hosts for several archaeal genes.

The expression system has to be chosen based on the intended use of the expressed protein. To obtain a sufficient amount of a recombinant enzyme for basic characterization, *E. coli* expression is recommended, because this host is easily grown in the laboratory and the vectors are well characterized. Expression in yeasts has advantages for large-scale industrial production. Furthermore, because yeast is a "generally recognized as safe" organism, it represents an ideal pilot system for the production of enzymes for the food technology industry. Recombinant enzymes can be obtained by cloning and expressing synthetic gene. Fusi *et al.* (1995) reported the expression of P2 ribonuclease from *S. solfataricus* in which the codon of the gene was modified to include those triplets that are widely used in *E. coli* cells to enhance protein expression.

This modification was achieved by reverse translation of the amino acid sequence into a degenerate nucleotide sequence and synthesis by PCR amplification of overlapping primers. To overcome the limitations of different codon usage for heterologous expression of archaeal enzymes, successfully cloned and expressed in *E. coli* a carbamoyl phosphatase synthetase (CPSase) from *Pyrococcus abyssi*. Overexpression of the CPSase gene was achieved by cotransformation of the host cells with a plasmid encoding tRNA synthetases for low-frequency *E. coli* codons. Ishida *et al.* (1997) were able to obtain efficient production of a thermophilic 3-isopropylmalate dehydrogenase with a GC-rich coding gene in *E. coli*, by providing a leader open reading frame.

The method chosen to express an extremophilic enzyme needs to take into account the downstream processes used for enzyme purification. The major findings of studies on the cloning and expression of archaeal enzymes can be summarized as follows. (1) Archaea utilizes the universal genetic code and their genes are translated by Eukarya and Bacteria. (2) The expression product maintains its natural properties including its thermophilicity and thermostability. (3) The rigid structure of thermophilic proteins at low temperature appears to prevent their degradation by host proteases, leading to an accumulation of recombinant enzyme. Recombinant extremophile enzymes are generally inactive under optimal host growth conditions, and the difference in observed biomass between different recombinants may be explained by specific interference in the replication cycle of the host by the heterologous gene expressed. (4) Thermostable enzymes can easily be purified from mesophilic protein contaminants by sequential thermal precipitation steps. After thermal denaturation, the only remaining enzymatic activity is that of the thermophilic protein expressed, which generally has a purity sufficient for industrial applications (Schiraldi *et al.*, 2001).

HYPERTHERMOSTABLE CELLULOLYTIC AND HEMICELLULOLYTIC ENZYMES

Cellulose and hemicelluloses are the most abundant polysaccharides in nature. They build structural components of plant cell walls and are associated with lignin and other polysaccharides. Therefore, microbial degradation of cellulose and hemicelluloses has enormous economic potential for the conversion of plant biomass into fuels and chemicals. Cellulolytic microorganisms play an important role in the biosphere by recycling cellulose.

Cellulose is an unbranched linear homopolymer of glucose units linked by β-1, 4-D-glucosidic bonds, that forms insoluble, crystalline microfibrils which are highly resistant to enzymatic hydrolysis. The cellulolytic enzyme system is composed of at least three different enzymes: endoglucanase, cellobiohydrolase and β-glucosidase, which act together in synergism. Xylans, major components of the hemicelluloses and the second most abundant polysaccharides in nature, are branched heteroglycans with a backbone of β-1,4-linked D-xylose residues. Branches consist of α-1, 3-linked L-arabinofuranosyl and α-1, 2- linked 4-O-methyl-glucuronic acid residues. Complete hydrolysis of these complex molecules requires the interaction of a number of main chain-and side-chain- leaving enzyme activities (Leuschner and Antranikian, 1995). Both cellulolytic and hemicellulolytic enzymes have been found in fungal species, especially in *Trichoderma reesei* and various bacteria.

Several applications of these enzymes are being developed for textile, food and paper pulp processing. These applications are based on the modification of cellulose and hemicelluloses by partial hydrolysis. Total hydrolysis of cellulose into glucose, which could be fermented into ethanol, isopropanol or butanol, is not yet economically feasible. Developments of pretreatment process and fermentation efficiency including improvements of enzyme properties are necessary. One of major drawbacks in industrial terms is that most cellulases and hemicellulases apparently lack thermostability. Currently, considerable interest is focused on the use of hemicellulases in the processing of paper pulp. Use of xylanases in bleaching step has been shown to reduce the amount of chlorine required to achieve comparable levels of paper brightness. However, the mesophilic enzymes currently in use have limitations due to high temperature used in bleaching.

Cellulolytic and Hemicellulolytic Enzymes Produced by Hyperthermophiles

Thermophilic bacteria have received considerable attention as sources of highly active and thermostable cellulolytic and xylanolytic enzymes. There are thermostable cellulolytic enzymes characterized from thermophilic cellulolytic bacteria such as *Clostridium thermocellum, Caldocellum saccharolyticum* and *Acidothermus cellulolyticus*. The most stable of these, from *Acidothermus*, has a half-life of less than 20 min. at 85° C. Recently, hyperthermal cellulases and hemicellulases have been isolated and some of them have been purified and characterized. Most of the enzymes isolated from hyperthermophiles genus *Thermotoga* have temperature optima at 90° C or higher and some, such as cellobiohydrolase from *Thermotoga* sp. strain FjSS3-B.1, are even active at 108°C. The unusual properties of these enzymes have resulted in the development of the novel biotechnology processes that can be accomplished within a wide range of conditions, including the reactions that are beyond the capability of biologically based systems.

Summary of cellulolytic and hemicellulolytic enzymes produced by hyperthermophiles

Enzymes	Organisms	Enzyme Properties			References
		T optimum (°C)	pH (optimum)	MW (kDa)	
	Aerobes				
Endoglucanase	*Rhodothermus marinus*	95	7.0	49	Hreggvidsson *et al.* (1996)
	Acidothermus cellulolyticus	81	5.0	72	Sakon, *et al.* (1996)
	Anaerobes				
Cellobiohydrolase	*Thermotoga* sp. FJSS3-B.1	100-105	6.8-7.8	36	Ruttersmith and Daniel (1991, 1993)
Endoglucanase	*Thermotoga neapolitana*	95, 106	6.0, 6.0-6.6	29,30	Bok *et al.* (1998)
	Thermotoga maritima	95	6.0	27	Bronnenmeier *et al.* (1995)
	Caldocellum saccharolyticum				Te'o *et al.* (1995)
	Caldocellulosiruptor - saccharolyticus				Bergquist *et al.* (1999)
	Dictyoglomus twgidus				Bergquist *et al.* (1999)
Exoglucanase	*Thermotoga maritima*	95	7.5	29	Bronnenmeier *et al.* (1995)
	Caldocellulosiruptor - saccharolyticus				
Xylanase	*Thermotoga* sp. FJSS3-B.1	100	5.3	31	Leuschner and Antranikian (1995)
	Thermotoga maritima MSB8	92, 105	6.2, 5,4	120, 40	Wimerhalter and Liebl (1995)
	Thermotoga thermaruni	90	6.0	40	Leuschner and Antranikian (1995)
	Dictyoglomus thermophilum	85	6.5	39.8	Morris *et al.* (1998)
					Gibbsetal. (1995)
Arabinofurano-sidase/β-Xylo-sidase	*Thermotoga* sp. FJSS3-B.1			92	Ruttersmith and Daniel (1993)
	Pyrococcus furiosus	102-105			Kengen *et al.* (1993)
β-Glucosidase/ (β-Galactosidase	*Thermotoga* sp. FJSS3-B.1		7.0	75	Ruttersmith and Daniel (1993)
	Pyrococcus furiosus	102-105	5.0	230	Kengen *et al.* (1993)
	Thermotoga maritima		6.2	95	Leuschner and Antranikian (1995)
	Sulfolobus solfataricus MT4				Leuschner and Antranikian (1995)
β-Mannanase	*Caldocellum saccharolyticum*	80	6.0		Gibbs *et al.* (1993): Morris *et al.* (1995)
	Caldibacillus cellulovorans	85	6.0	30.7	Sunna *et al.* (2000)

Potential Applications

The driving force behind research on hyper thermal enzymes is the promise of being able to use enzymes effectively at extreme temperatures in industrial processing. The exquisite specificity of an enzyme-mediated reaction is difficult to mimic with conventional chemical catalysis. Moreover, enzyme catalysis can eliminate the need for multistep reactions and their often unwanted waste production from side reaction.

Paper pulp Bleaching

Considerable attention is currently focused on the use of hemicellulases in processing of paper pulp, particularly, in bleaching step. Bleaching, essentially the removal of lignin from pulp has traditionally been carried out using toxic chemicals such as chlorine and hypochlorite. This step is necessary for aesthetic reasons and for improvement of paper properties. Additionally, bleached kraft pulp is the most important pulp produced today. The production is approximately 65-70 millions ton a year, corresponding to a value of more than 50 billion US$. Presently, bleaching of kraft pulp uses large amounts of elemental chlorine and chlorine dioxide. By-products from using these chemicals are chlorinatedorganic, resulting from the substitution reaction of chlorine with lignin. It has been found that xylanases can facilitate the release of lignin so that much less chlorine needs to be used. This could have important environmental consequences since the chlorine combined with phenolics derived from lignin results in pollution of paper mill effluents. Hyperthermostable xylanases isolated from hyperthermopiles have a high potential for biotechnological application in kraft pulp prebleaching. The first part of the process in production of kraft pulp involves debarking and chipping of the wood logs followed by a strong alkaline cooking where the main part of the lignin is dissolved and then washed away.

The result is a strong colored pulp, which has to be bleached in order to get a white pulp for paper production. The traditional bleaching of pulps has been done in multistages, which can vary by the chemicals that are used. A typical bleaching sequence is (C+D)-(E+O)-D-(E+P)-D wherein C is elemental chlorine, D is chlorine dioxide, E is sodium hydroxide sometimes used in the presence of O, oxygen, and/or P, peroxide. On the other hand, the process with xylanases is very simple with a pH and temperature adjustment. After xylanases are mixed into the pulp, which is kept in a holding tank for 1-3 h, the pulp is bleached in the normal way after one wash. However, due to the removal of some of the residual lignin and an opening of the structure, the chlorine consumption is much lower. A study shows xylanase treatment of pulp enable chlorine use to be replaced completely and a higher brightness pulp to be achieved without alteration of strength properties.

Clarifying Agent

The use of xylanases has been proposed for clarifying juices, wine and beer; for extracting coffee, plant oil and starch; for improving the nutritional properties of agricultural silage; for macerating plant cell walls; for producing food thickener and for providing different textures to bakery products. Many of these applications do not strictly require pure xylanases, the presence of cellulases and/or pectinases is often desirable.

Some of them have been reported to be currently in use. These enzymatic reactions usually are not carried out at moderate temperatures with conventional enzymes due to the risk of bacterial contamination. Given the availability of enzymes that function at sufficiently high temperatures, aseptic conditions could be maintained. This makes enzyme use to modify and improve food characteristics attractive. For instance, lactose in dairy products could be hydrolyzed with minimal risk of contamination. Furthermore, economical heat pretreatment can be developed for hydrolysis of cellulose and hemicelluloses since improvement of enzymatic hydrolysis at high temperature are feasible.

Enhancing the Flow of Oil

In addition, hyperthermophilic enzymes might also be used to enhance the flow of oil or gas in drilling operations. Practically, product flow to the well bore has been stimulated by forcing out open crevices in the surrounding bedrock which is done by flooding the well with a natural polymer (e.g., guar gum) solution and sand particles, capping the well and then pressurizing the bedrock until it fractures. The viscous polymer solution carries the sand through the fractures, propping open cracks for oil or gas flow. To facilitate product flow, the polymer solution is thinned by chemically oxidizing the gum or hydrolyzing its sugar linkages with β-1,4-mannanase and α- 1,6-galactosidase. As temperature increases with depth (120° C or higher), using conventional enzymes, which have limited stability above 80° C, is unsuccessful. Moreover, these enzymes are active at low temperatures so they would hydrolyze the gum before the polymer solution is introduced into the well. Recently, a hyperthermophilic hemicellulase has been isolated. These enzymes are able to hydrolyze guar gum at elevated temperatures and have limited activity at lower temperatures so that implementation of oil production by these enzymes could be feasible.

TRANSFORMATION OF DIOXINS BY ANAEROBIC BACTERIA

Mixed cultures of anaerobic bacteria capable of reductively dechlorinating freshly spiked 1, 2, 3, 4-tetrachlorodibenzo-p-dioxin (1, 2, 3, 4-TeCDD) were obtained from freshwater sediments of streams near Bitterfeld, Germany. All of these sediments have been impacted by industrial wastewater for decades, but have comparably low levels of polychlorinated dibenzo-p-dioxins and -furans (PCDD and PCDF), not exceeding 500 ng toxicity equivalents (I-TEQ) per kg dry weight. Reductive dechlorination of 1,2,3,4-TeCDD in the primary enrichments as well as dechlorination of trichlorinated dioxin congeners in subsequent transfers showed that dioxin-dechlorinating bacteria could be enriched from these low-level contaminated sites. The amount of two transformation products, 1,3- and 2,3-dichlorodibenzo- p-dioxin was different in the studied cultures, demonstrating preferential substitution of chlorine in either peri- or lateral positions of the molecule. Ten different dioxin-dechlorinating cultures were analyzed with a 16S rDNA-based polymerase chain reaction (PCR) approach to detect phylotypes of bacteria known to be able to reductively dechlorinate several halogenated aliphatic and aryl compounds. Using this qualitative approach, we could not assign a specific dechlorination pathway to the presence or absence of specific dehalogenating organisms. However, it was shown that members of *Desulfitobacterium* and *Dehalococcoides* were present in all communities studied, including cultures from Spittelwasser sediments and might be involved in reductive dehalogenation of chlorinated dioxins.

Examples

Desulfuromonas chloroethenica, Dehalobacter restrictus, Desulfomonile tiedjei Dehalococcoides ethenogenes, Dehalospirillum multivorans

REMEDIATION OF ACID MINE DRAINAGE

Acid mine drainage (AMD) is one of the most widespread and serious forms of water pollution, affecting both developing nations and post-industrial countries including the UK. AMD is caused when sulphide ores (primarily pyrite, FeS2) are exposed to oxygen and moisture through mining activities, leading to the formation of sulphuric acid. However, several forms of anaerobic respiration including Fe (III) and sulphate reduction are alkali-generating anaerobic processes that can potentially reverse acidification caused by pyrite oxidation.

ANTICANCER EFFICACY ANAEROBIC BACTERIA AS GENE THERAPY VECTORS TARGETING TUMOR HYPOXIA/NECROSIS

A major obstacle in cancer gene therapy is selective tumor delivery. Studies have suggested that genetically engineered anaerobes of the genus *Clostridium* might be gene therapy vectors because of their ability to proliferate selectively in the hypoxic/necrotic regions common to solid tumors. However, the tumor colonization efficiency of the strain previously used was insufficient to produce any antitumor effect. For the first time the successful transformation of *C. sporogenes*, a clostridial strain with the highest reported tumor colonization efficiency, with the E. coli cytosine deaminase (CD) gene and show that systemically injected spores of these bacteria express CD only in the tumor. This enzyme can convert the nontoxic prodrug 5-fluorocytosine (5-FC) to the anticancer drug 5-fluorouracil (5-FU). Furthermore, systemic delivery of 5-FC into mice previously injected with CD-transformed spores of C. sporogenes produced greater antitumor effect than maximally tolerated doses of 5-FU. Since most human solid tumors have hypoxic and necrotic areas this vector system has considerable promise for tumor-selective gene therapy.

A major advantage of the clostridial delivery system is that not only is it tumor specific, it has also proved itself to be safe in humans. The lack of pathogenicity of these organisms was initially demonstrated by Mose *et al*, who injected themselves with spores of *C. sporogenes* (a strain later named *C. oncolyticum*), and experienced a mild fever as the only side-effect. The safety of *C. oncolyticum* was substantiated in clinical trials with cancer patients with a variety of solid tumors and also in more recent trials in non-cancer patients with a *C. beijerinckii* strain. Because anticancer drug delivery is typically given on multiple occasions to allow normal tissues to recover, it would be advantageous if the clostridial therapy could also be given on multiple occasions. In this respect it is helpful that the recombinant clostridia are injected as spores, which do not elicit an immune response.

BIOLOGICAL COLOUR REMOVAL BY STRICTLY ANAEROBES OR FACULTATIVE MICROORGANISMS INCUBATED UNDER ANAEROBIC CONDITIONS

Under anaerobic conditions a low redox potential (< -50 mV) can be achieved, which is necessary for the effective decolourisation of dyes. Colour removal under anaerobic conditions is also referred as dye reduction in which literature mostly covers the biochemistry of azo dye reduction. The azo bond cleavage „ŸN.N„Ÿ involves a transfer of four-electrons (reducing equivalents), which proceeds through two stages at the azo linkage. In each stage two electrons are transferred to the azo dye, which acts as a final electron acceptor:

$$(R_1\text{–N=N–}R_2) + 2e^- + 2H^+ \rightarrow R_1\text{–HN–NH–}R_2$$

(*Hydrazo intermediate*)

$$(R_1\text{–HN–NH–}R_2) + 2e^- + 2H^+ \rightarrow R_1\text{–}NH_2 + R_2\text{–}NH_2$$

(*Reductive cleavage of the azo bond*)

Examples of facultative and strictly anaerobic bacterial cultures, which were able to decolourise azo dyes under anaerobic conditions

Organism	Dyes	Avtivity	Decolour (%)	Comments
Clostridium perfringens ATCC 3626	Amaranth Methyl Orange Orange H Tartrazine	µ mol/ml/h 0.74 0.62 0.70 0.67	– – –	Dye concentration of 0.033 mM.
Bacteroides fragilis	Amaranth Orange H Tartrazine	µ mol/ml/h 0.30 0.20 0.08	66.0 37.0 9.0	After 6 h of incubation. Dye concentration of 0.1 nM.
Pseudomonas GM3	Acid Violet 7 Reactive Blue 2 Acid Green 27 Acid Red 183 Indigo Carmine	– – – – –	97.4 18.3 75.6 20.1 69.0	After 72 h of incubation. Dye Concentration of 100 mg/l.

(Contd...)

Organism	Dyes	Avtivity	Decolour (%)	Comments
		μ mol/min/g protein		
Sphingomonas xenophanga BN6	Acid Red 27	0.10	–	Dye concentration of 0.1 mM.
	Acid Orange 20	0.10	–	
	Acid Orange 7	0.30	–	
	Acid Red 14	0.20	–	
	Acid Yellow 23	0.10	–	
	Acid Black I	0.30		
		AU × 10^{-1}/mg protein		
Enterococcus faecalis	Methyl Red	1.81	99.4	After 20 h of incubation. Dye Concentration of 0.2 mM
	Orange H	1.39	95.1	
	Orange G	1.20	64.1	
	Amaranth	1.37	99.5	
Eubacterium biforme	Tartrazine	–	4.0	After 150 minutes of incubation. Dye concentration of 2 mM
	Sunset Yellow	–	22.0	
	Methyl Orange	–	79.0	
	Orange H	–	81.0	
	Amaranth	–	19.0	
	Allura Red 40	–	11.0	

Reductive Decolourisation of Dyes by Thermophilic Anaerobic Organisms

The colour removal achieved under anaerobic conditions is also called reductive decolourisation, which is composed of a biological part, i.e. the reducing equivalents are biologically generated, and a chemical part, i.e. the formed electrons reduces chemically the dyes.

Results indicated that acidogenic bacteria and methanogenic archaea play important roles in this reductive process. Experiments with the thermophilic methanogens *Methanothermobacter thermoautotrophicus*.H and a *Methanothermobacter*-related strain NJ1 revealed that these strains were unable to reduce the dye in the absence of the redox mediator, riboflavin. This suggested that anaerobic dye reduction is not a universal property among methanogenic archaea and that redox mediators may play an important role for allowing some microbial groups, commonly found in wastewater treatment systems, to participate more effectively in reductive decolourisation of dyes.

REFERENCES

Boone, D.R., W.B. Whitman and P. Rouviere. 1993. Diversity and Taxonomy of Methanogens. In: Methanogenesis: Ecology, Physiology, Biochemistry, and Genetics. Ed. J.G. Ferry. Chapman and Hall, London, pp. 35-80.

De Rosa, M., A. Morana, A. Riccio, A. Gambacorta, A. Trincone and O. Incani. 1994. Lipids of the Archaea: A New Tool for Bioelectronics. Biosens. Bioelectron. 9: 669-675.

Fusi, P., M. Grisa, E. Mombelli, R. Consonni, P. Tortora and M. Vanoni. 1995. Expression of a Synthetic Gene Encoding P2 Ribonuclease from the Extreme Thermoacidophilic Archaebacterium *Sulfolobus solfataricus* in Mesophylic Hosts. Gene 154: 99-103.

Godfroy, A., N.D. Raven and R.J. Sharp. 2000. Physiology and Continuous Culture of the Hyperthermophilic Deep-sea vent Archaeon *Pyrococcus abyssi* ST549. FEMS Microbiol. Lett. 186: 127-132.

Haney, P.J., J.H. Badger, G.L. Buldak, C.I. Reich, C.R. Woese and G.J. Olsen. 1999. Thermal Adaptation Analyzed by Comparison of Protein Sequences from Mesophilic and Extremely Thermophilic *Methanococcus* Species. Proc. Natl. Acad. Sci. 96: 3578-3583.

Hezayen, F.F., B.H. Rehm, R. Eberhardt and A. Steinbüchel. 2000. Polymer Production by Two Newly Isolated Extremely Halophilic Archaea: Application of a Novel Corrosion-resistant Bioreactor. Appl. Microbiol. Biotechnol. 54: 319-325.

Ishida, M., M. Yoshida and T. Oshima. 1997. Highly Efficient Production of Enzymes of an Extreme Thermophile, *Thermus thermophilus*: A Practical Method to Overexpress GC-Rich Renes in *Escherichia coli*. Extremophiles 1: 157-162.

Margesin, R. and F. Schinner. 2001. Potential of Halotolerant and Halophilic Microorganisms for Biotechnology. Extremophiles 5: 73-83.

Park, C.B. and S.B. Lee. 1997. Constant Volume Fed-batch Operation for High Density Cultivation of Hyperthermophilic Aerobes. Biotechnol. Tech. 11: 277-281.

Raven, N. and R.J. Sharp. 1997. Development of Defined and Minimal Media for the Growth of the Hyperthermophilic Archaeon *Pyrococcus furiosus*. FEMS Microbiol. Lett. 146: 135-141.

Raven, N., N. Ladwa, D. Cossar and R. Sharp. 1992. Continuous Culture of the Hyperthermophilic Archaeon *Pyrococcus furiosus*. Appl. Microbiol. Biotechnol. 38: 263-267.

Rehm, H.J., G. Reed, A. Pühler and P. Stadler. 1999. Biotechnology: Environmental Processes I. Vol. 11a. 2nd Edn. Wiley, New York, pp. 458-468.

Rinker, K.D. and R.M. Kelly. 2000. Effect of Carbon and Nitrogen Sources on Growth Dynamics and Exopolysaccharide Production of the Hyperthermophilic Archaeon *Thermococcus litoralis* and Bacterium *Thermotoga maritima*. Biotechnol. Bioeng. 69: 537-547.

Schiraldi, C., A. Martino, M. Acone, I. Di Lernia, A. Di Lazzaro, F. Marulli, M. Generoso, M. Carteni and M. De Rosa. 2000. Effective Production of a Thermostable _-Glucosidase from *Sulfolobus solfataricus* in *Escherichia coli* Exploiting a Microfiltration Bioreactor. Biotech. Bioeng. 70: 670-676.

Schiraldi, C., M. Acone, M. Giuliano, I. Di Lernia, C. Maresca, M. Cartenì and M. De Rosa. 2001. Innovative Fermentation Strategies for the Production of Extremophilic Enzymes. Extremophiles 5: 193-198.

Tsao, J.H., M.K. Kaneshiro, S. Yu and D.S. Clark. 1994. Continuous Culture of *Methanococcus jannaschii*, an Extremely Thermophilic Methanogen. Biotechnol. Bioeng. 43: 258-261.

Pages: 36-49

BIOTECHNOLOGY AND ENVIRONMENTAL MANAGEMENT

Edited by: Prof. Arun Arya; Dr. Raaz K Maheswari & Dr. Pawan Kumar 'Bharti'

ISBN: 978-93-5056-862-0

Edition: 2017

Published by: Discovery Publishing House Pvt. Ltd., New Delhi (India)

2

Signifying Plant Microbe Interaction

K.D. Kamble*

ABSTRACT

"United we stand" is also applicable to variety of life forms which are staying in association with each other irrespective of differentiation in species/genera/kingdom. Independent survival has many limitations particularly with regards to requirements of solubilized elements. Autotrophs can grow independently but their growth is considerably influenced by microbes surrounding them. Communication of this sort is popularly referred as plant and microbe dialogue. Sound dialogue between plant and rhizobacteria benefits each other and also suppress pathogenic bacteria in the vicinity. A thin line determines which will infect first either rhizobacteria or pathogens. This chapter focuses natural aspects of plant microbe relationship, the necessity of interaction and ways to make this plant microbe bond stronger.

INTRODUCTION

Role of prokaryotes in nature cannot be ignored as popularly exemplified by nitrogen fixation and recycling of organic matters. Considerable amount of nitrogen is fixed by these bacteria making available to plants. Bacteria are symbionts of plants as well as animals. In animals these act as probiotic which inhibit pathogenic bacteria by making conditions unfavorable, some also produce antibiotics of bacterial origin like colicin. Vitamins are also produced by probiotics which are absorbed by intestinal cells. In brief these bacteria are highly beneficial to animals by means of protection and provision of some vital nutrients. Similar kinds of benefits

* Department of Microbiology, Sant Gadge Baba Amravati University, Amravati, Maharashtra, (India).

are also provided to plants by bacteria in fact more than animals. At the same time negative associations should also be mentioned which are by means of disease causing microorganisms. Number and variation in microbial species around an organism can produce valuable information regarding association between living microbe interactions and dominance of microbes in this relationship. Culturing methods are developed with event of time still culture independent approaches particularly 16S rDNA sequencing exceeds in reporting broader bacterial communities (Little *et al*, 2008). Overall rhizospheric microbes consist of rhizobia, mycorrhizae, endophytes and plant-growth promoting rhizobacteria (PGPR) and parasitic interactions with other plants, pathogenic microbes and invertebrate herbivores.

Cell signaling is a phenomenon which exists between plants/ animals and microbial communities. In this chapter major focus is on plant-microbe dialogue.

Cell to cell communication within plant was studied way back in 1879 for the first time which was called as cytoplasmic bridges. Eduard Strasburger in 1901 coined the term "plasmodesmata" to these cytoplasmic bridges. Now it is evident that a complex regulatory network is a part of signaling between neighboring cells. Intercellular connections in fungi are by means of pores in septa; the cross walls on mycelia. Septa were described by De Bary in 1884, however it was Wahrlich (1893) who clearly showed the signaling is by means of cytoplasmic inclusions in septa i.e. pores in septa (Bloemendal and Kuck, 2013).

With cell to cell communication within eukaryotes the beginning of cell communication between plants and microbes must be noted. Arbuscualr mycorrhizae are thought to be described as early as 1842 by Nageli. Association between plants and fungi was given the name "mycorhiza" by Frank (1887) which was later deviated to "mycorrhiza" by Kelly (1931). Though presence of mycorrhizae was shown 150 years back but its existence dates before 450 million years as revealed by paleobotanical studies (Remy *et al*, 1994). It was major breakthrough when Remy *et al*, (1994) showed evidence for presence of mycorrhizae before 450 million years. *Bacillus radicicola* was the name designated by Beijerinck to rhozobia studied way back in 19th century. Later *Rhizobium* was the name coined by Frank. It was in 1904 when Hiltner noticed the region surrounding roots was quite high in bacterial population. The reason for such high bacterial number is that considerable amount of carbon fixed by plants is secreted theough root exudate which is utilized by bacteria that in turn help plants by acting as biofertilizers, rhizoremediators, photostimulators, stress controllers eventually designated as plant growth promoting rhizobacteria (Lugtenberg and Kamilova. 2009).

The organic compounds released through root exudates includes monosaccharides, polysaccharides, peptides, aromatic compounds, aliphatic compounds, fatty acids, sterols, phenolics, enzymes, polypeptides, plant growth regulators and secondary metabolites. Secondary metabolites like flavonoids of plants are released at the stage of seed germination. Flavonoids, ethylene, auxin and cytokinin are important metabolites that determine rhizobial nodule efficiency. When released from seed coats flavonoids acts as inducers for the nod genes (nodulation genes) of bacteria responsible for Nod factor synthesis (Subramanian *et al*, 2006). Mixture of flavonoids and other organic compounds can help outgrow rhizobacteria but the process is initiated by secretion of flavonoids used as source of carbon by rhizobia which in turn synthesize lipochitooligosaccharides, called Nod factors (NFs), triggering the nodule developmental process. Rhizobial selectivity for nodule formation is determined by membrane-localized LysM receptor kinase which differentiates among Nod factors synthesized by various bacteria. In Lotus and Medicago root hairs curl to form niche for rhizobial colony which later turns into root nodule (Madsen *et al.*, 2011; Radutoiu *et al.*, 2003, 2007).

Ethylene is a stress hormone affecting wound response and is involved in defense also. The amount of ethylene makes a fine demarcation between pathogenic and symbiotic microbial attack. A high degree of complexity exists between ethylene signaling pathway, auxin and cytokinin pathway (Desbrosses and Stougaard, 2011). The developmental stages of plants are influenced by interaction with microbes thereby making nodulation as inducible process. Accumulation of auxin occurs at the time of rhizobial infection or nodulation factor application. Auxin transport inhibitors leads to disruption of polar auxin transport resulting in reduced nodulation. Decreased number of nodules was also observed in transgenic soybean lines with reduced level of flavonoids. Evidences are enough to state the role of cytokinin in root nodulation. Tropical application of cytokinin to roots of *Sesbania rostrata* resulted in formation of root nodules (Dehio and de Bruijn, 1992). Mutant analysis of cytokinin receptor gene affects the nodulation process. The loss of gene resulted in large number of infectious threads but very few nodules. Conversely gain of gene spontaneously resulted in nodule formation (Murray *et al.*, 2007).

Since last decade of genome sequencing out of 358 genes of *Arabidopsis thaliana*; an extensively studied plant for genomics, 244 are confirmed (Meinke *et al*, 2008). Vast data available on *Arabidopsis thaliana* employing genetics and bioinformatics studies have revealed many facts about root biological networks. A high degree of complexity is found in eukaryotic gene regulation similar is found in expression of genes by various factors. Beside gene regulation by conventional transcription factors diffusible proteins, secreted peptides, hormones, mRNA or miRNAs affects. The site and time of gene expression is future area of research regarding plant microbe interactions. Species of *Rhizobium* and *Agrobaterium* are extensively studied at gene level focusing on extrachromosomal gene expressions whereas chromosomal gene expressions of other microbial communities are still to be detailed. Obviously functional prediction of all genes is not an easy task, further how many genes are involved in microbial communication and regulation of genes in these processes if predicted can make this interaction even stronger.

REASONS TO STUDY PLANT-MICROBIAL INTERACTION

Plant-microbe affection leads to several applications. Beside extensively studied nitrogen fixation by nodule rhizobial interaction other important areas include extraction of metals, detoxification of land, and emergence of drought resistant and salt resistant plants. Plant-microbe interaction to enhance plant productivity is preferred over genetically engineered plants because plant cloning procedures are tedious, expression of engineered plants many times is not uniform and the suspect of horizontal gene transfer in nature. At the same time transgenic plants with fungicidal proteins are ineffective against insect and bacterial pathogens i.e. one type of pathogen is controlled with emergence of another type. Following applications stress the necessity of plant microbe interactions.

In addition to making nitrogen easily assimilable to plants, rhizobacteria outgrow around the roots which in turn controls infection by pathogenic bacteria. Among the predominant species around plants are *Bacillus* and *Pseudomonas*. Species of *Bacillus* in rhizosphere also protect plants from pathogenic bacteria and fungi by producing antimicrobial compounds like bacteriocin. For field application on crops either bacterial formulation are directly used or antibiotics can be purified and applied afterwards. Ericin is found effective against *C. michiganensis*, which causes bacterial canker on tomato. Similarly Bac 14B is found effective in reducing excessive infections caused by *A. tumefaciens* (Abriouel *et al*, 2011). Among widely studied bioactive agent is thuricin (Lee *et al*, 2009). Antimicrobial compound thuricin is beneficial by three ways firstly it caused curling of root hairs thereby enhancing root nodulation. Secondly, direct application of thuricin to leaves and roots enhanced the plant growth. Finally it's similarity with bacteriocin makes it an effective antimicrobial agent.

Symbiotic relationship does exist between a plant and microbe before the seed germinates; in fact endophytes are transferred from mother plant to seeds and this relationship is made stronger when a seed encounters soil microbes. The number and variation of rhizobial flora affects the plant growth as exemplified with *S. littoralis*. Weight of *S. littoralis* was reduced by mycorrhizal treatments i.e. *R. irregularis*. Experiment was carried with single and double inoculations using *R. irregularis* and its variant which revealed dual inoculated plant performance was stronger than single inoculations (Pangesti *et al*, 2013).

Phosphate solubilization is one of the initial applications of rhizobacterial studies. With event of time phosphate solubilization remained one of the application; others included resistance to pesticides, antibiotics like phosphonomycin, salt tolerance and pH tolerance. Actually rhizobacteria which can fulfill all these criteria is recently extracted by Zhao *et al*, (2013). The bacterium is designated *Pseudomonas chlororaphis* which also had antifungal activity against *Fusarium oxysporum, Magnaporthe grisea, Botrytis cinere* etc.

It is hard to believe rhizobacteria helps plant grow in high salt conditions. This role is played indirectly through 1-aminocyclopropane-1-carboxylate (ACC) deaminase enzyme synthesized by few bacteria like *Achromobacter piechaudii*. High salt concentration as with other stressful conditions causes the plant root to secret ethylene which in turn has a regulatory activity to infection by rhizobacteria. ACC deaminase catalyzes the cleavage of ACC to ammonia and ketobutyrate. A direct relationship does exist between levels o f ACC and ethylene. Hence to control ethylene levels one way is to control ACC (Mayak *et al*, 2004).

Consequences of flood on plants can be controlled by plant growth promoting rhizobacteria. Flooding conditions often occurs in a season when plant growth also accelerates. This leads to anaerobic conditions in roots during which ACC is not converted to ethylene as the enzyme ACC oxidase requires oxygen for this step which further results in transport of ACC to shoot system where aerobic conditions are maintained that ultimately damages the plant by process of epinasty, leaf chlorosis, necrosis and reduced fruit yield. The remedy is to treat plants with PGPR or induce ACC producing gene to plants so that it is expressed as and when required (Grichko & Glick, 2001).

Similarly abilities of rhizobacteria for drought resistance have also been studied by Marasco *et al* (2012). Similar enzyme is also involved in this process. Careful selection of ACC deaminase producing rhizobacteria under water stress was initially carried followed by influence on plants in vivo under drought. The screened bacteria belonged majorly to genera *Citrobacter, Klebsiella, Achromobacter* and *Acinetobacter*. Pepper plants were irrigated with and without rhizobacterial suspensions and were suddenly exposed to water stress for twelve day period. It was observed that after eight days controlled plants were severely affected whereas those with rhizobacteria showed remarkable resistance. Re-watering of plants was done after twelve days and root growth was observed. Roots showed a robust growth with 40-60% than control. This clearly shows for specific period at least rhizobacteria helps water stress conditions.

A conjugative effect of plant and rhizobacteria in metal detoxification or restoration of degraded lands can certainly increase land under cultivation. It is important to stress the basis of plant- microbe metal extraction process. As is evident rhizosphere is rich in microbial population which enhances the bioavailability of metals by processes such as bioleaching and biotransformation in soil. Bacteria reduce metals either by assimilatory or dissimilatory processes, membrane bound or intracellular mechanisms for cellular metabolism. Another important mechanism is production of organic compounds i.e. siderophores, carboxylic acids or acidic exopolysaccharides etc that can bind or reduce metal cations thereby enhancing availability of metals to plants. Plant diseases markedly affect productivity enabling excessive use of chemical pesticides. Excessive use of chemical pesticides over the last few decades affected soil fertility as well as other side effects including biomagnifications that caused environmental as well as health hazards. A shift to plant growth promoting rhizobacteria is therefore a safer strategy to control plant pathogens as it is well established fact that rhizobacteria inhibits the plant pathogens. These secondary metabolites include siderophores, antibiotics, volatile metabolites and enzymes with different modes of action against plant pathogens (Saraf *et al*, 2014).

Physiology, growth and development of plants are affected by toxic metals. Indirect effects constitutes molecular signals, quorum sensing within bacterial communities, release and exchange of nutrients and off course a dialogue between plant and microbe. These metals can be converted to non-toxic compounds or can be extracted from a metal contaminated site in a process called bioremediation. A highly complex network does exist when phytoremediation combines with microbes referred quite correctly as "underground orchestra" by Alexander Kamnev (2008). Controlled use of metals that too in an easily assimilable form is required by plants as exemplified by iron uptake. Iron is one of the elements of high demand in living systems required as cofactors, metalloenzymes and in metabolism of chlorophyll. Excluding few chemolithotrohic bacteria no cell can obtain energy from elemental iron directly nor can utilize for cellular processes. Chelation of iron is therefore necessary for acquisition by plants. Siderophores are one of the molecules with low molecular weight which has high affinity for iron and are easy to assimilate (Katiyar and Goel, 2004).

Recently bacterial consortia was prepared to study the combined effect of plant and bacteria on survivability of plant in presence of toxic metals like Cu, Pb, Zn and Cd. Bacterial selection was based on resistance to heavy metals and also abilities for plant growth promotion. The consortia consisted of *Pseudomonas* sp. *Stenotrophomonas maltophilia*, *Rhizobium* sp., *Niabella* sp., *Curtobacterium flaccumfaciens*, *Streptomyces violarus*, *Streptomyces* sp., *Plantibacter*sp., *Niabella* sp. and *Bacillus cereus*. Mycorrhizae were obtained from roots of plant species like *Rosmarinus officinalis*, *Ranunculus bullatus* and *Carlina corymbosa* etc. The bacterial consortia and mycorrhizae were grown with plant species i.e. *Euphorbia pithyusa*. Finally the metal content was analyzed in in plant and soil samples after drying at 50 °C overnight. Results clearly indicated that a fine consortium was effective in bioaugmentation. The microbial activity was responsible to enhance own growth as well as plant growth in presence of heavy metals. The soil without microbial inoculation displayed less functional diversity indicating the microbial community is adapting with plant and changing the conditions around *E. pithyusa* (Sprocati *et al*, 2013).

Consortial studies have been carried by Langella *et al*, (2013) on grasses. Generally grasses are considered metal excluders but when combined with rhizobacteria in consortia significant extraction of metals was observed. Pot experiments were carried selecting *F. rubra* and *A. capillaries* for extraction of mixture of metals like Cd, Cu, Mn, Ni, Pb, Sr, Zn and U. Samples were collected from multi-metal polluted site in Germany and copper mine in Sweden for which separate microbial consortia of varied bacteria were studied. Results stress careful selection of bacteria in consortium development, plant and properties of soil. Generally the native flora from same soil which is already adapted to the soil can yield better results. Grasses have been used as metal extractor for the first time with significant extraction. These are economic, fast growing and easy to remove hence highly convenient for metal extraction when combined with rhizobia. Combination of grasses with other plants infected by rhizobacteria is also suggested for better metal extraction.

Conclusively there are limitations to individual capabilities of bacteria and plant as in case of detoxification combined effect can yield better results. Considerable area of land is uncultivable because of mines and salt content. Emergence of grasses and rhizobacteria must ultimate strategy for phytoremediation. Case might be of salt resistance, restoration of abandoned mines, flood/drought/insect/fungi resistant plant it is not individual role of plant or bacteria rather a conjugative effort. Another important thing is careful selection of plant as well as rhizobacteria. Whether to go for single rhizobacterium like *Pseudomonas chlororaphis* which is proved to be a model rhizobacterium that can fulfill or criterion mentioned above or consortia of rhizobacteria which can outgrow and resist pathogenic bacteria still remains a question. Behavior of experimental rhizobacteria on field is also hampered by environmental factors and content of soil more precisely nutritive value of soil and physical factors like salt, pH and temperature. Therefore it is suggestive to go for pre-adapted rhizobacteria be grown in abundance and used in similar fields.

ENHANCING PLANT MICROBE INTERACTION

Emergence of above mentioned applications stress to focus on newer strategies to enhance plant microbe interactions. The richness of microbial diversity is responsive to the changing environment of soil which is largely dependent on agricultural practices. Cultivating single crop year after year might hamper varied microbial flora around crops. A changing environment is rich in microbial diversity. Off course many microbial aspects are still unclear in this regard. The relationship between plant and microbe can be made stronger by genetic and non-genetic engineering approaches. While making this relationship stronger one must think of environment around these two partners. Major purpose of plant microbe interaction is to increase crop productivity by replacing or reducing chemical pesticides or fertilizers.

Modification of protocols employed for formulation of rhizobacteria with seeds, selection of metal, pesticide and salt resistant rhizobacteria, over expression of certain enzymes/molecules during this interaction are few important approaches that can positively affect plant microbe relationship. In addition to soil profiling, properties of rhizobacteria as well as plants can contribute to stronger plant microbe relationship.

Conventional approaches include addition of gum during rhizobia and seed formulation. While applying rhizobacteria to plant care must be taken to increase survivability of these bacteria in field trials. These methods are being modified by replacement of adhesives as in case of soybean and *Bradyrhizobium japonicum*. Use of xanthan and exopolyacrylamide during formulation increased viability of *Bradyrhizobium japonicum* 23.3 times during storage condition. Plant growth regulators like biosil and ivin were also found effective for survival of rhizobia (Titova *et al*, 2011). Change in nitrogen levels around seeds can affect nodulation both positively and negatively. Reducing nitrogen content around seeds has already been reported to enhance nodulation. On the contrary optimum levels of NH_4^+ showed enhancement in nodulation. Studies were carried on *Medicago truncatula* and *Sinorhizobium meliloti* with NH_4^+ and NO_3^- as source of nitrogen. A threefold increase in nodulation was observed compared to control when 0.5 mM NH_4^+ was used (Fei and Vessey, 2009).

Single rhizobial inoculation may not be advisable. Co-inoculation as used with soybean might be effective with other plants also. Rather a combination of rhizobacteria and mycorrhizae also is a productive process. Colonization and nodulation efficiency was markedly increased when soybean plant was infected with co-inoculation by *Bacillus amyloliquefaciens* strain LL2012 and *Bradyrhizobium japonicum*. *B. japonicum* is a proven plant growth promoting rhizobacteria hence *B. amyloliquefaciens* was confirmed for nitrogen fixing, phosphate solubilization, siderophores production and phytoharmone producing abilities (Masciarelli *et al*, 2014).

Organopesticides and copper containing compounds are heavily used for pest management. These are not selective against pest only and beneficial soil flora is considerably damaged. Selection of pesticide resistant rhizobia in such soil can be done prior to which a survey of pesticides and quantification of pesticides in soil is necessary. Zawoznik and Tomaro (2005) investigated the effect of acetolactate synthase (ALS)-inhibiting herbicide chlorimuron-ethyl on *B. japonicum*. Growth of *B. japonicum* was not affected by this herbicide however nodulation was decreased by 38%, total fresh biomass by 25% and leghemoglobin content by 40%. The results revealed application of chlorimuron-ethyl has to at the optimum level which should not affect growth of *B. japonicum* and also that rhizobia might help in tolerance to ALS inhibitors.

In a similar manner copper containing compounds are widely used as microbicidal agents in agricultural fields. Copper tend to accumulate in fields and can affect rhizobial populations. The resistance to copper stress was achieved by Laguerre *et al*, (2006) during eight year study. The rhizobia under study included *Rhizobium leguminosarum* infecting *Vicia sativa* and rhizobial species infecting *Phaseolus vulgaris*. The study was carried for eight years which mentioned a reduction in the *Rhizobium* population and also on plant growth. At the same time a new lineage was extracted which had resistance to copper levels compared to other species (Laguerre *et al*, 2006).

Rhizobial infection to plants is also based on signaling molecules which in case are synthesized by rhizobia also. A low molecular weight exopolysaccharide (EPS) i.e. succinoglycan is produced in case of *Sinorhizobium meliloti* which induces root hairs in alfalfa and *Medicago truncatula*. Succinoglycan is polysaccharide composed of octasaccharide repeating units of 1 galactose and 7 glucose residues, modified with succinyl, acetyl, and pyruvyl substituents. Mutants deficient in synthesizing succinoglycan cannot induce nodulation (Jones and Waker, 2008). Further, Jones (2012) clearly showed that overproduction of succinoglycan was not detrimental to plants; in fact enhancement in symbiotic relationship of *S. meliloti* was observed. In future genetically engineered rhizobial strains might be incorporated with succinoglycan producing gene so that symbiotic relationship enhances and crop production increases.

The genetic basis of legume-rhizobium relationship pertaining to nodulation is difficult to simplify. Particularly in concern to abortive nodulation where nodule formation takes place but nodules cannot perform nitrogen fixation. To develop an understanding of incompatibility between plant and rhizobia wide range of strains of *S. meliloti* and diverse species of *Medicago* as host were selected. Symbiotically incompatible host were screened which were further selected for their abilities to overcome incompatible condition. This phenotypic change was brought about by loss of accessory plasmid. The plasmid confers a limiting symbiotic host range which has to be excluded from cell in order to select unusual hosts (Crook *et al*, 2012). Wide range of host can be availed to rhizobia by this approach.

As mentioned previously microbe nodule interaction is a complex network regulated by range of biomolecules. Recently role of Micro-RNAs (miRNAs) in nodule development is depicted by Yan *et al*, (2013) which was poorly elucidated before. The role of miRNAs during developmental stages in eukaryotes is well studied phenomenon. In plants miRNAs controls the expression of genes involved in plant development, floral organs and flowering time. Ectopic expression of soybean miR172 resulted in enhancement of nodulation as well as increase in nitrogenase activity.

Complex interaction between prokaryotes and eukaryote exist which is being referred to as interkingdom signaling. Microbial coordinated activity was first time observed in *Vibrio fischerii* in the form of bioluminescence. This phenomenon of quorum sensing is found in various biological processes and is also a significant phenomenon in the interkingdom signaling which is one of the mechanism found in plant-microbe interaction (Badri *et al*, 2009).

Burkholderia phytofirmans is popular as plant growth promoting bacteria residing in rhizosphere and also colonization inside the plant roots. Quorum sensing techniques to establish cell to cell contact was adopted for efficient colonization of *Arabidopsis thaliana* plants. Quorum sensing was devised by using N-acyl homoserine lactone (AHL) (Zuniga *et al*, 2013). AHL influences the plant growth either by affecting the hormones or by development roots or root hairs. However the exact mechanism is still unknown. The involvement of bacterial AHL is not the entire mechanism of quorum sensing. In *Rhodopseudomonas palustris* it has been observed that a precursor of plant origin i.e. p-coumarate is required for synthesis of AHL (Schaefer *et al*, 2008).

The process is further complicated by involvement of proteins referred as solo or orphan proteins which respond to endogenously produced AHL (Smith and Ahmer, 2003). These proteins do exist in bacteria such as *Rhodospirillum*, *Citreicella*, *Rhizobium*, *Sinorhizobium*, *Agrobacterium*, *Xanthomonas* and *Pseudomonas*. The solo proteins bind to DNA upstream of the target site bringing conformational changes which recruits RNA polymerase. In absence of signaling molecule the similar proteins acts as repressors (Zhu and Winans, 2001; Minogue *et al*, 2001).

A solo protein from *Sinorhizobium meliloti* called NesR was found to affect methyl cycle. NesR mutant were unable to grow in high salt concentration, detergent and in media with glycine betain as single carbon source and were also less competitive for nodulation. This revealed the importance of NesR to avoid stress condition by utilizing various carbon sources and to communicate with plant for nodulation.

Enzyme based strategies involves exploitation of some key enzymes of nodule rhizobial relationship/ controlled expression of enzymes. Although series of enzymes are involved during various stages of nodulation, apyrases and trehalase are among one. Apyrases are diverse nucleotide triphosphatases found in animals, yeast and plants involved in modulation of neuro-transmission, glycosylation of oligosaccharides in lumen and mobilization of phosphate respectively. In plants apyrases perform range of activities viz. membrane depolarization, hormonal activity, calcium oscillations and signal transductions which are significant phenomenon of nodulation. This is obvious to go for genetic engineering experiments to obtain enhance copies of apyrases leading to enhanced nodulation. Soybean apyrase was cloned to *Lotus japonicus* and was expressed constitutively. The selection of *L. japonicus* was based on the fact that it is easily expressed and transformed. Transgenic *L. japonicus* had larger infection zones leading to a total of 30-40% enhancement in the nodulation suggesting apyrase involvement in early nodulation (McAlvin and Stacey, 2005). Presence of trehalose during nodulation directly affects rate of nodulation which in turn is controlled by enzyme trehalase. Down regulation of this enzyme was achieved by Barraza *et al*, (2013). The gene was knocked down by RNA interference in common bean which ultimately leads to higher trehalose content, bacteroid number, nodule biomass and nitrogenase activity.

Genomics and proteomics studies are quite helpful since compatibility among host and rhizobia can be studied prior to field trials. Involvement of transcriptional and translational factors during nodulation can also be availed using omics approaches. Impact of a single or an array of proteins and a key step in plant-microbe interaction are few more areas where omics can significantly contribute. Knowing such proteins or steps can be further regulated for overexpression of metabolites so as to increase plant-microbe interaction. One more important information genomics can yield is selectivity of rhizobial infection to host plant, factors contributing and proteins contributing to enhancement in host range. Since genome sequences of plant available are very scary and rhizobial genome sequences are also very less because of the fact that more than 90% bacteria are not cultured and also it is not practically feasible to culture bacteria from all environment. Still genome sequences of these bacteria in immediate vicinity of the plant can be availed by metagenomics and their interaction can be studied. Though various mechanisms have been reported for enhancement of plant microbe interaction it is necessary to go for a comparative studies among all these methods so as to come up with an efficient practical approach that can enhance plant- microbe interaction leading to plant growth and productivity which today is largely based on chemical fertilizers.

REFERENCES

1. Abriouel, H., Franz, C.M., Omar, N.B., & Gálvez, A. (2011). Diversity and Applications of Bacillus bacteriocins. *FEMS microbiology reviews*, *35*(1), 201-232.
2. Badri, D.V., Weir, T.L., van der Lelie, D., & Vivanco, J. M. (2009). Rhizosphere Chemical Dialogues: Plant–microbe Interactions. *Current Opinion in Biotechnology*, *20*(6), 642-650.
3. Barraza, A., Estrada Navarrete, G., Rodriguez Alegria, M.E., Lopez Munguia, A., Merino, E., Quinto, C., & Sanchez, F. (2013). Down Regulation of PvTRE1 Enhances Nodule Biomass and Bacteroid Number in the Common Bean. *New Phytologist*, *197*(1), 194-206.
4. Beijerinck, M.W. (1888). Cultur des *Bacillus radicola* aus den Kno¨ llchen. *Bot. Ztg*. 46, 740-750.
5. Bloemendal, S., & Kück, U. (2013). Cell-to-cell Communication in Plants, Animals, and Fungi: A Comparative Review. *Naturwissenschaften*, 100(1), 3-19.
6. Crook, M.B., Lindsay, D.P., Biggs, M.B., Bentley, J.S., Price, J.C., Clement, S.C., & Griffitts, J.S. (2012). Rhizobial Plasmids that Cause Impaired Symbiotic Nitrogen Fixation and Enhanced Host Invasion. *Molecular Plant-Microbe Interactions*, 25(8), 1026-1033.

7. Dehio, C., & Bruijn, F.J. (1992). The Early Nodulin Gene SrEnod2 from Sesbania Rostrata is Inducible by Cytokinin. *The Plant Journal*, 2(1), 117-128.
8. Desbrosses, G.J., & Stougaard, J. (2011). Root Nodulation: A Paradigm for How Plant-microbe Symbiosis Influences Host Developmental Pathways. *Cell Host & Microbe*, *10*(4), 348-358.
9. Fei, H., & Vessey, J.K. (2009). Stimulation of Nodulation in Medicago Truncatula by Low Concentrations of Ammonium: Quantitative Reverse Transcription PCR Analysis of Selected Genes. *Physiologia plantarum*, 135(3), 317-330.
10. Frank, B. (1887). Ueber Neue Mycorhiza-Formen. *Ber Deut Bot Ges*, 5, 395-409.
11. Frank, B. (1890). *Over the Pilzymbiose of legumes*. P. Parey.
12. Grichko, V.P., & Glick, B.R. (2001). Amelioration of Flooding Stress by ACC Deaminase-containingplant Growth-promoting Bacteria. *Plant Physiology and Biochemistry*, 39(1), 11-17.
13. Hiltner, L. (1904). Over Recent Experiences and Problems in the Field of Bodenbakteriologie Paying Particular Attention to Green Manure and Fallow.*Works from the German Agricultural Society*, 98, 59-78.
14. Jones, K.M. (2012). Increased Production of the Exopolysaccharide Succinoglycan Enhances Sinorhizobium Meliloti 1021 Symbiosis with the Host Plant Medicago Truncatula. *Journal of bacteriology*, *194*(16), 4322-4331.
15. Jones, K.M., & Walker, G.C. (2008). Responses of the Model Legume Medicago Truncatula to the Rhizobial Exopolysaccharide Succinoglycan. *Plant signaling & behavior*, 3(10), 888-890.
16. Kamnev, A.A. (2008). 13 Metals in Soil versus Plant-microbe Interactions: Biotic and Chemical Interferences.
17. Katiyar, V., & Goel, R. (2004). Siderophore Mediated Plant Growth Promotion at Low Temperature by Mutant of Fluorescent Pseudomonad*". *Plant Growth Regulation*, 42(3), 239-244.
18. Laguerre, G., Courde, L., Nouaim, R., Lamy, I., Revellin, C., Breuil, M.C., & Chaussod, R. (2006). Response of Rhizobial Populations to Moderate Copper Stress Applied to an Agricultural Soil. *Microbial Ecology*, 52(3), 426-435.
19. Langella, F., Grawunder, A., Stark, R., Weist, A., Merten, D., Haferburg, G., & Kothe, E. (2014). Microbially Assisted Phytoremediation Approaches for Two Multi-element Contaminated Sites. *Environmental Science and Pollution Research*, 21(11), 6845-6858.
20. Lee, K.D., Gray, E.J., Mabood, F., Jung, W.J., Charles, T., Clark, S. R., ... & Smith, D.L. (2009). The Class IId bacteriocin thuricin-17 Increases Plant Growth. *Planta*, 229(4), 747-755.
21. Lugtenberg, B., & Kamilova, F. (2009). Plant-growth-promoting Rhizobacteria. *Annual Review of Microbiology*, 63, 541-556.
22. Madsen, E.B., Antolín Llovera, M., Grossmann, C., Ye, J., Vieweg, S., Broghammer, A., ... & Parniske, M. (2011). Autophosphorylation is Essential for the in vivo Function of the Lotus Japonicus Nod Factor Receptor 1 and Receptor Mediated Signalling in Cooperation with Nod Factor Receptor 5. *The Plant Journal*, 65(3), 404-417.
23. Marasco, R., Rolli, E., Ettoumi, B., Vigani, G., Mapelli, F., Borin, S., ... & Zocchi, G. (2012). A Drought Resistance-promoting Microbiome is Selected by Root System Under Desert Farming. *PLoS One*, 7(10), e48479.
24. Masciarelli, O., Llanes, A., & Luna, V. (2014). A New PGPR Co-inoculated with Bradyrhizobium Japonicum Enhances Soybean Nodulation. *Microbiological Research*, 169(7), 609-615.

25. Mayak, S., Tirosh, T., & Glick, B.R. (2004). Plant Growth-promoting Bacteria Confer Resistance in Tomato Plants to Salt Stress. *Plant Physiology and Biochemistry*, 42(6), 565-572.
26. McAlvin, C.B., & Stacey, G. (2005). Transgenic Expression of the Soybean Apyrase in *Lotus japonicus* Enhances Nodulation. *Plant physiology*, 137(4), 1456-1462.
27. Meinke, D., Muralla, R., Sweeney, C., & Dickerman, A. (2008). Identifying Essential Genes in Arabidopsis thaliana. *Trends in Plant Science*, 13(9), 483-491.
28. Minogue, T.D., Trebra, M.W.V., Bernhard, F., & Bodman, S.B.V. (2002). The Autoregulatory Role of EsaR, a Quorum Sensing Regulator in Pantoea Stewartii ssp. Stewartii: Evidence for a Repressor Function. *Molecular Microbiology*, 44(6), 1625-1635.
29. Murray, J.D., Karas, B.J., Sato, S., Tabata, S., Amyot, L., & Szczyglowski, K. (2007). A Cytokinin Perception Mutant Colonized by Rhizobium in the Absence of Nodule Organogenesis. *Science*, 315(5808), 101-104.
30. Nageli, C. (1842). Pilze im Innern von Zellen. *Linnaea*, 16, 278-285.
31. Pangesti, N., Pineda, A., Pieterse, C.M., Dicke, M., & Van Loon, J.J. (2013). Two-way Plant Mediated Interactions Between Root-associated Microbes and Insects: from Ecology to Mechanisms. *Frontiers in Plant Science*, 4, 414.
32. Radutoiu, S., Madsen, L.H., Madsen, E.B., Felle, H.H., Umehara, Y., Grønlund, M., ... & Stougaard, J. (2003). Plant Recognition of Symbiotic Bacteria Requires Two LysM Receptor-like Kinases. *Nature*, 425(6958), 585-592.
33. Radutoiu, S., Madsen, L.H., Madsen, E.B., Jurkiewicz, A., Fukai, E., Quistgaard, E. M., ... & Stougaard, J. (2007). LysM domains Mediate Lipochitin–oligosaccharide Recognition and Nfr Genes Extend the Symbiotic Host Range. *The EMBO journal*, 26(17), 3923-3935.
34. Remy, W., Taylor, T.N., Hass, H., & Kerp, H. (1994). Four Hundred-million-year-old Vesicular Arbuscular Mycorrhizae. *Proceedings of the National Academy of Sciences*, 91(25), 11841-11843.
35. Saraf, M., Pandya, U., & Thakkar, A. (2014). Role of Allelochemicals in Plant Growth Promoting Rhizobacteria for Biocontrol of Phytopathogens. *Microbiological Research*, *169*(1), 18-29.
36. Schaefer, A.L., Greenberg, E.P., Oliver, C.M., Oda, Y., Huang, J.J., Bittan-Banin, G., ... & Harwood, C.S. (2008). A New Class of Homoserine Lactone Quorum-sensing Signals. *Nature*, 454(7204), 595-599.
37. Smith, J.N., & Ahmer, B.M. (2003). Detection of Other Microbial Species by Salmonella: Expression of the SdiA regulon. *Journal of bacteriology*, 185(4), 1357-1366.
38. Sprocati, A.R., Alisi, C., Pinto, V., Montereali, M.R., Marconi, P., Tasso, F., ... & Marini, F. (2014). Assessment of the Applicability of a "Toolbox" Designed for Microbially Assisted Phytoremediation: The Case Study at Ingurtosu Mining Site (Italy). *Environmental Science and Pollution Research*, *21*(11), 6939-6951.
39. Subramanian, S., Stacey, G., & Yu, O. (2006). Endogenous Isoflavones are Essential for the Establishment of Symbiosis Between Soybean and Bradyrhizobium Japonicum. *The Plant Journal*, 48(2), 261-273.
40. Titova, L.V., Brovko, I.S., Leonova, N.O., Votselko, S.K., Iutinskaia, G.A., & Patyka, V.F. (2011). Role of Biocompatible Adhesives in the Increase of Rhizobia Physiological Activity and Productivity of Soybean-rhizobia Symbiosis. *Mikrobiolohichnyi zhurnal (Kiev, Ukraine:* 1993), 74(6), 9-16.
41. Yan, Z., Hossain, M.S., Wang, J., Valdés-López, O., Liang, Y., Libault, M., ... & Stacey, G. (2013). miR172 Regulates Soybean Nodulation. *Molecular Plant-Microbe Interactions*, 26(12), 1371-1377.

42. Zawoznik, M.S., & Tomaro, M.L. (2005). Effect of Chlorimuron Ethyl on Bradyrhizobium Japonicum and its Symbiosis with Soybean. *Pest Management Science*, 61(10), 1003-1008.

43. Zhao, L.F., Xu, Y.J., Ma, Z.Q., Deng, Z.S., Shan, C. J., & Wei, G. H. (2013). Colonization and Plant Growth Promoting Characterization of Endophytic Pseudomonas Chlororaphis Strain Zong1 Isolated from Sophora alopecuroides Root Nodules. *Brazilian Journal of Microbiology*, 44(2), 629-637.

44. Zhu, J., & Winans, S.C. (2001). The quorum-sensing transcriptional regulator TraR requires its cognate signaling ligand for protein folding, protease resistance, and dimerization. *Proceedings of the National Academy of Sciences, 98*(4), 1507-1512.

45. Zuniga, A., Poupin, M.J., Donoso, R., Ledger, T., Guiliani, N., Gutiérrez, R.A., & González, B. (2013). Quorum Sensing and indole-3-acetic Acid Degradation Play a Role in Colonization and Plant Growth Promotion of Arabidopsis thaliana by Burkholderia Phytofirmans PsJN. *Molecular Plant-Microbe Interactions*, 26(5), 546-553.

Pages: 50-69

BIOTECHNOLOGY AND ENVIRONMENTAL MANAGEMENT

Edited by: **Prof. Arun Arya; Dr. Raaz K Maheswari & Dr. Pawan Kumar 'Bharti'**

ISBN: 978-93-5056-862-0

Edition: **2017**

Published by: **Discovery Publishing House Pvt. Ltd., New Delhi (India)**

3 Nano Remediation of Environmental Pollutants

E. Parameswari
V.Davamani
T. Anitha

Due to the rapidly increasing population and to increasing demands for the devices that many associate with a high standard of living, such as cars, televisions, washing machines, etc., we are increasingly being faced with the challenge of pollution control, decontamination and maintenance of soil, water and air quality. There are two main approaches to these problems: the first is to control pollution at source to minimize or eliminate waste production or harmful emissions; the second is to remedy the pollutants that accumulate in the environment. Considering the enormous scale of soil and groundwater contamination, the complexity of the task seems intractable. Nanotechnology offers a number of promising solutions to these environmental issues and represents a new approach to the clean up of contaminated sites and waste streams, particularly for those substances that are highly toxic, persistent, or difficult to treat using conventional means. Nanotechnology also includes green manufacturing and green energy production to reduce pollution at source. Nanotechnology promises the creation of improved, more specific, faster and more cost effective solutions for pollution treatment. The early impact of nanotechnology research has been seen mostly in remediation and treatment technologies (Masciangioli and Zhang, 2003).

The use of nanotechnology in the improvement of a contaminated site to prevent, minimize or mitigate damage to human health or the environment is known as Nanoremediation. In general, remediation technologies can be grouped into categories using thermal, physico-chemical or biological methods. The various techniques usually work well when applied to a specific

Horticultural College and Research Institute, Tamil Nadu Agricultural University, Periyakulam, Tamilnadu, (India)

type of water pollution, though no readily available treatments were discovered that could clean all types of pollutants. Due to the complex nature of many polluted waters, it is frequently necessary to apply several techniques to soil from a particular location to reduce the concentrations of pollutants to acceptable levels. Numerous reports have examined how nanoparticles can be used for pollution treatment and contaminant remediation.

POTENTIAL APPLICATIONS OF NANO SCALE MATERIALS

Zero-valence state metals (such as Fe^{o}, Zn^{o}, Sn^{o} and Al^{o}) are surprisingly effective agents for the remediation of environmental pollutants. Zero-valent iron in particular has been the subject of numerous studies over the last 10 years and Nanosized Zero-Valent Iron (NZVI) technology is becoming an increasingly popular choice for treatment of hazardous and toxic wastes, and forremediation of contaminated sites.

The high surface area and surface reactivity compared with granular forms enable the nanoparticles to remediate more pollutants at a higher rate and with a lower generation of hazardous byproducts (Zhang, 2003). Many different nano scale materials have been explored for remediation, such as nano scale zeolites, metal oxides, carbon nano tubes and fibers, enzymes and various noble metals. These particles include self assembled monolayers on mesoporous supports (SAMMS), ferritin, dendrimers, and metalloporphyrinogens. Recently, a variety of nanomaterials for potential use to adsorb or destroy contaminants as part of either *in situ* or *ex situ* processes.

(i) Nanoscale zero-valent iron particle

Nanoscale zero-valent iron particles, with primary particle size less than 100nm, are made by avariety of vendors and shipped as highly concentrated slurries, for use as a reagent to destroyorganic contaminants and immobilize inorganic contaminants in groundwater. Several studieshave shown that NZVI is very effective for the degradation of halogenated solvents such aschlorinated methanes, brominated methanes, trihalomethanes, chlorinated ethenes, chlorinatedbenzenes and other polychlorinated hydrocarbons in groundwater. NZVI wasalso shown to be effective against some pesticides, heavy metals, and dyes. NZVI can bedistributed into the subsurface using a variety of carrying fluids. Among the most common are water, nitrogen gas, and vegetable oil. Slurries of water and NZVI powder can be injected intothe contaminated zone using nitrogen gas as a carrier. This helps the iron powder disperse in thesubsurface and create contact between the contaminants and the iron. Alternatively, NZVI canbe mixed with vegetable oil and water to create an emulsion, which is then injected into thecontaminant zone (ESTCP, 2006). Researchers hypothesized that chlorinated solventspreferentially diffuse through the vegetable oil and react with the iron inside the emulsiondroplet. NZVI will typically be received as stabilized aqueous slurry.

Bare NZVI (Figure 3.1) is composed of a core which consists primarily of zero-valent or metalliciron while the mixed valent [*i.e.*, Fe (II) and Fe (III)] oxide shell is formed as a result ofoxidation of the metallic iron (Figures 1 and 1a.). Iron typically exists in the environment as iron(II)-and iron (III)-oxides, and as such, ZVI is a manufactured material. Thus far, applications ofZVI have focused primarily on the electron-donating properties of NZVI. Under ambientconditions, NZVI is fairly reactive in water and can serve as an excellent electron donor, whichmakes it a versatile remediation material (Stumm and Morgan, 1996).

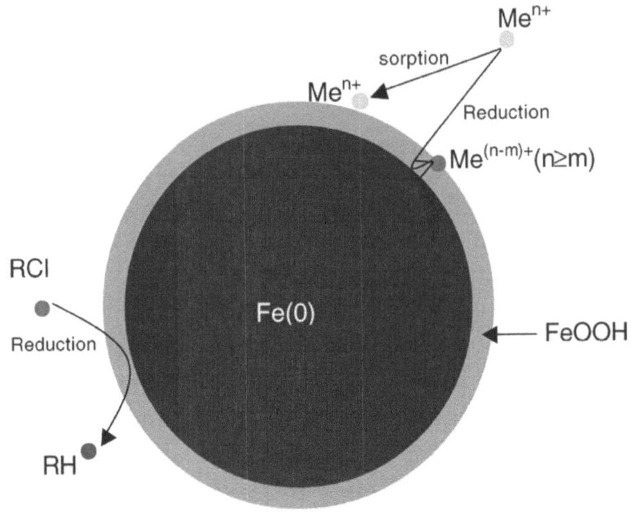

Fig. 3.1: The Core-shell Model of Zero-valent Iron Nanoparticles

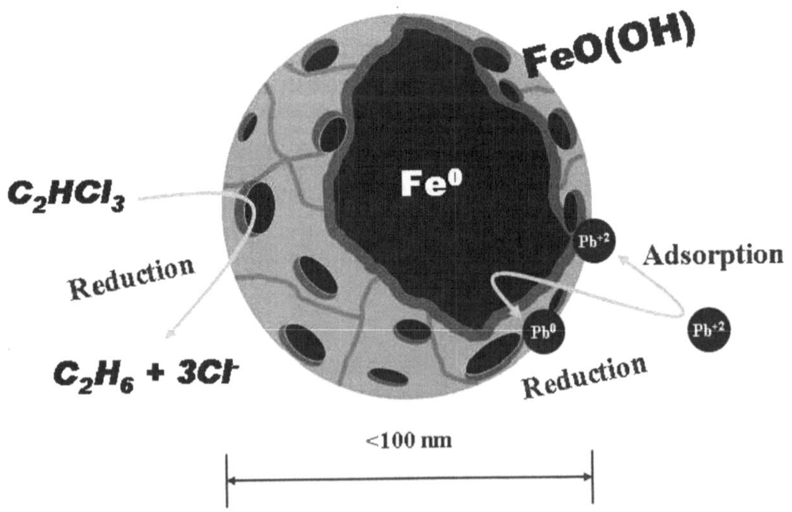

Fig. 3.1a: A more Three-dimensional View of a Zero-valent Iron Nanoparticle

The core consists of mainly zero-valent ironoxides/hydroxides formed from the oxidation of zero-valent iron. The shell provides sites for chemical complexformation (*e.g.*, chemosorption) (Li Elliot and Zhang, 2006).

This figure also shows the porosity of the nanoparticle, which is also an important factor in physicochemical reactivity. Zero-valentnanoironcan also be coupled with trace metals (*ex.* Pt, Pd, Ag), showing significantly enhanced reaction. Nanoiron ispotentially benign to the environment and, ultimately, is mainly transformed into Fe_3O_4 and Fe_2O_3, which areabundant on earth (Copyright © 2007 GeoNano Environ. Tech., Inc.).

According to the core-shell model, the mixed valence iron oxide shell is largely insoluble underneutral pH conditions and may protect the ZVI core from rapid oxidation.

NZVI works best under anaerobic conditions, especially in the case of beta-elimination reactions.Decreased dissolved oxygen (DO) levels and increased Oxidation Reduction Potential (ORP) ($\leq$ -400mV) are ideal conditions to facilitate targetcontaminant degradation (USEPA, 2005). ORP depends on the transfer of electrons betweenchemical species and determines the reduction potential of an aqueous solution. Like pH, thereduction potential represents an intensity factor. It does not characterize the capacity of thesystem for oxidation or reduction in much the same way that pH does not necessarilycharacterize the buffering capacity. Reduction potential measurement is useful as an analyticaltool in monitoring changes in an aqueous system rather than determining their absolute value.

Besides toxic chlorinated compounds such as TriChloroEthane (TCE), NZVI has been shown to able to degradeother compounds found at contaminated sites such as the organic contaminant trinitrotoluene(TNT), pesticides (DDT), heavy metals (Hg, Ni, Cd, etc.), organic dyes (chrysoidin), andinorganic anions (Table 3.1) (Li Elliot, and Zhang, 2006).

Table 3.1: Common contaminants that can be remediated by iron nanoparticles (Li Ellio and Zhang, 2006)

(i) Chlorinated MethanesTrihalomethanes
Carbon tetrachloride (CCl_4) Bromoform ($CHBr_3$)
Chloroform ($CHCl_3$) Dibromochloromethane ($CHBr_2Cl$)
Dichloromethane (CH_2Cl_2) Dichlorobromomethane ($CHBrCl_2$)
Chloromethane (CH_3Cl)

(ii) Chlorinated Benzenes Chlorinated Ethenes
Hexachlorobenzene (C_6Cl_6) Tetrachloroethene (C_2Cl_4)
Pentachlorobenzene (C_6HCl_5) Trichloroethene (C_2HCl_3)
Tetrachlorobenzenes ($C_6H_2Cl_4$) *cis*-Dichloroethene ($C_2H_2Cl_2$)
Trichlorobenzenes ($C_6H_3Cl_3$) *trans*-Dichloroethene ($C_2H_2Cl_2$)

(iii) Pesticides Other Polychlorinated Hydrocarbons
DDT ($C_{14}H_9Cl_5$) PCBs
Lindane ($C_6H_6Cl_6$) Pentachlorophenol
1,1,1-trichloroethane

(Table Contd...)

(iv) Organic Dyes Other Organic Contaminants
Orange II (C16H11N2NaO4S) N-nitrosodiumethylamine (NDMA) (C4H10N2O)
Chrysoidin (C12H13ClN4) TNT (C7H5N3O6)
Tropaeolin O (C12H9N2NaO5S)
(v) Heavy Metals Inorganic Anions
Mercury (Hg2+) Perchlorate (ClO4-)
Nickel (Ni2+) Nitrate (NO3-)
Cadium (Cd2+)
Lead (Pb2+)
Chromium (Cr(VI))

(ii) Semiconductor Photocatalysts

Semiconductor photocatalysts such as titanium dioxide (TiO_2), zinc oxide (ZnO), iron oxide (Fe_2O_3) and tungsten oxide (WO_3) act as photocatalysts (Nagaveni, 2004). Due to their light absorbing capabilities, they are employed in a variety of applications. Both titanium dioxide and zinc oxide can be used as pigments to provide whiteness for substances, such as paint and paper. The ability of photocatalysts to absorb ultraviolet light makes them useful in sunscreen as well as cosmetics to provide opaqueness to the creams or lotions. These properties also can be exploited for antimicrobial coatings; the photocatalytic properties allow thin coatings to be self cleaning and to have disinfecting properties after exposure to UV radiation. Photocatalysts have the ability to oxidize organic pollutants into nontoxic materials. Traditionally, TiO_2 has been used in advanced photochemical oxidation (APO) processes for environmental remediation because of its low toxicity, high photoconductivity, high photostability, availability, and low cost (Nagaveni, 2004). Field and pilot scale applications have demonstrated the ability of TiO_2 to remediate fuel contaminated groundwater containing benzene, toluene, ethylbenzene, and xylene (BTEX) compounds. In addition, TCE, Methyl-*tert*-butyl ether (MTBE), chloroform, ethylbenzene, and nitrobenzene can be destroyed by semiconductor photocatalysis.

(iii) ZnO nanoparticles

Recently, ZnO has been proposed as a dual function photocatalytic material. Kamat *et al.* (2002) reported that ZnO possessed both sensing and remediating capabilities for organic contaminants in water. The study concluded that the ZnO films showed a high degree of sensitivity on the order of 1 ppm to aromatic compounds such as chlorinated phenols. Under UV lighting, the films degraded the aromatic compounds.

(iv) Nanotubes

Nanotubes are engineered molecules most frequently made from carbon. They are electrically insulating, highly electronegative and easily polymerized. Nanotubes have also been made from titanium dioxide and have demonstrated potential for use as a photocatalytic degrader of chlorinated compounds. Bench scale research has shown titanium dioxide nanotubes to be particularly effective at high temperature, capable of reducing contaminant chemicals by greater than 50 percent in three hours (Xu, 2005). Bench scale tests using ferritin, an iron storage protein, have indicated that it can reduce the toxicity of contaminants such as chromium and technetium in surface water and groundwater to facilitate remediation. Like titanium dioxide, ferritin is photocatalytic; in one bench scale project, the addition of visible light caused ferritin to reduce toxic, water soluble hexavalent chromium to the less toxic trivalent chromium, which is not water soluble and precipitates out of solution. Dendrimers are hyper branched, well organized polymer molecules made up of three components: core, branches, and end groups. Dendrimer surfaces terminate in several functional groups that can be modified to enhance specific chemical activity. Fe^0/FeSnanocomposites, synthesized using dendrimers as templates, could be used to construct permeable reactive barriers for the remediation of contaminated groundwater. Bench scale research has indicated that dendrimers have flexible delivery options (Diallo, 2006).

Metalloporphyrinogens are complexes of metals with naturally occurring, organic porphyrin molecules. Batch reactor experiments have shown that metalloporphyrins are capable of reducing chlorinated hydrocarbons such as trichloroethylene, trichloroethene (TCE), perchloroethylene (PCE) and carbon tetrachloride under anoxic conditions to remediate contaminated soil and groundwater, with some structures showing a reduction of TCE and PCE by greater than 90 percent from the original concentration (Dror, 2005). Researchers are also using nanotechnology to develop membranes for water treatment, desalination, and water reclamation. These membranes incorporate a wide variety of nanomaterials, including nanoparticles made of alumina, zero valent iron, and gold (Theron, 2008). Carbon nanotubes can be aligned to form membranes with nanoscale pores to filter organic contaminants from groundwater (Mauter, 2008). Some materials can be made with surface functional groups to serve as adsorbents to scavenge specific contaminants from waste streams. SAMMS particles consist of a nanoporous ceramic substrate coated with a monolayer of functional groups tailored to preferentially bind to the target contaminant. The functional molecules covalently bond to the silica surface, leaving the other end group available to bind to a variety of contaminants. Contaminants successfully sorbed to SAMMS particles include radionuclides, mercury, chromate, arsenate, pertechnetate, and selenite.

BIOGENICALLY ENHANCED nZVI CONTAMINANT DEGRADATION

(i) Metal Catalyst: Bimetal Nanoparticles

Bimetallic nanoscale particles (BNPs) increase the kinetics of the redox reactions involved in contaminant remediation, and thus perform as a catalyst to this reaction. Palladium and iron BNPs are commercially available and currently the most commonly used in site remediation. The reactivity of the nanoscale iron particles can be significantly enhanced by depositing a small amount (less than 0.1 percent) of a noble metal (palladium, platinum, nickel, silver, etc.) on the surface of the iron, which creates bimetallic nanoscale particles (USEPA, 2008). Tee (2006),using Fe^{o}/Ni and Fe^{o}/Pd BNPs, observed a TCE degradation rate constant that was two orders of magnitude higher than bulk iron and NZVI, indicating that the bimetallic nanoparticles are more efficient at degrading TCE when compared to the monometallic iron nanoparticles. It has been postulated that atomic hydrogen adsorbed on the reductant surface (Hads) is responsible for bimetal reactivity. In bimetallic systems, Hads could be generated through the dissociative chemisorption of H_2, itself generated *in situ* via water reduction. Alternatively, Hads could be produced as an intermediate to H_2. It was also suggested that *ab*sorbed atomic hydrogen (Habs) within the metal additive lattice, rather than surface-*ad*sorbed atomic hydrogen (Hads), represents the reactive entity in iron-based bimetallic systems. Differences in the reactivity of Pd and Pt electrodes toward 4-chlorophenol have been attributed to the substantially greater solubility of atomic hydrogen in Pd relative to Pt (Zhang, 2003).

Laboratory research on TCE degradation at Oak Ridge National Laboratory (ORNL) led to the first reported observation of degradation byproducts, including vinyl chloride (VC), when using monoiron nanoparticles. In order to enhance dechlorination reaction rates and minimize byproduct formation, (BNP) systems of palladized iron were developed (and patented). It has been observed that the surface area normalized rate constant (Ksa) of Fe/Pd nanoparticles for the degradation of tetrachloromethane is over twoorders of magnitude higher than that of microscale iron nanoparticles (Li, Elliot, and Zhang, 2006). Zhang (2003) has given an overview of the synthesis, characterization and use of NZVIparticle and BNPs such as Fe0/Pd0, Fe0/Pt0, Fe0/Ag0, Fe0 /Ni0, Fe0/Co0, and Fe0/Au0 in environmental remediation. These nanoparticles can reduce a variety of organic pollutants (*e.g.*,chlorinated alkanes and alkenes, chlorinated benzenes, pesticides, organic dyes, nitro aromatics,PCBs) and inorganic anions (*e.g.*, nitrates) in aqueous solutions to less toxic and less recalcitrant by-products. NZVI and bimetallic NZVI nanoparticles have also been successfully used to reduce redox-active metal ions such as Cr(VI) to less toxic and less mobile Cr(III) species.

Work done by Xu and Zhao (2007) indicated the potential of using stabilized NZVI and phosphate-based nanoparticles as soil amendments, to reductivelyimmobilize Cr(VI) and also reduce the bioaccessibility of Cu in soils (Cundy Hopkinson, and Whitby, 2008). The Naval Air Engineering Station (NAES) in Lakehurst, NJ, conducted a series of bimetallic nanoscale particle (BNP) applications from 2001 to 2003 to treat groundwater containing chlorinated solvents. Based on successful results, a full-scale application was completed in 2003 to treat two contaminant source areas at the facility. The plumes consist primarily of tetrachloroethene (PCE), TCE, and 1,1,1-trichloroethane (TCA), and degradation products such as *cis*-dichloroethene (*cis*-DCE) and vinyl chloride. The selected BNP slurry contained iron particles averaging 50 nm in diameter and coated with trace (0.1 percent by weight) palladium that served as a catalyst for redox reactions. The slurry was injected directly into the aquifer across the treatment area over a period of 13 days using direct-push technology at 15 injection points. Overall, TCE and DCE concentrations decreased an average of 79 and 83 percent, respectively, and the average total volatile organic compound (VOC) concentration decreased 74 percent. Presence of the hydrogenation catalyst (Pd, Pt, Sn, Ni, Ag, etc.) is likely to be the object of regulatory scrutiny (USEPA, 2005). Many of these metals were used historically in ways that foster human oral exposure such as dentistry and food preservation.

The use of palladium is the most extensively researched metal as a catalyst for BNP with zerovalentiron. Tratnyek and Sarathy in 2008 found that, in general, 1,2,3-trichloropropane (TCP)exhibits little or no reaction with mild reductants (including construction-grade ZVI) but is dechlorinated by strong reductants (like palladized NZVI). Figure 3.2 shows a summary of degradation pathways that are most promising for TCP degradation in soil and groundwater.

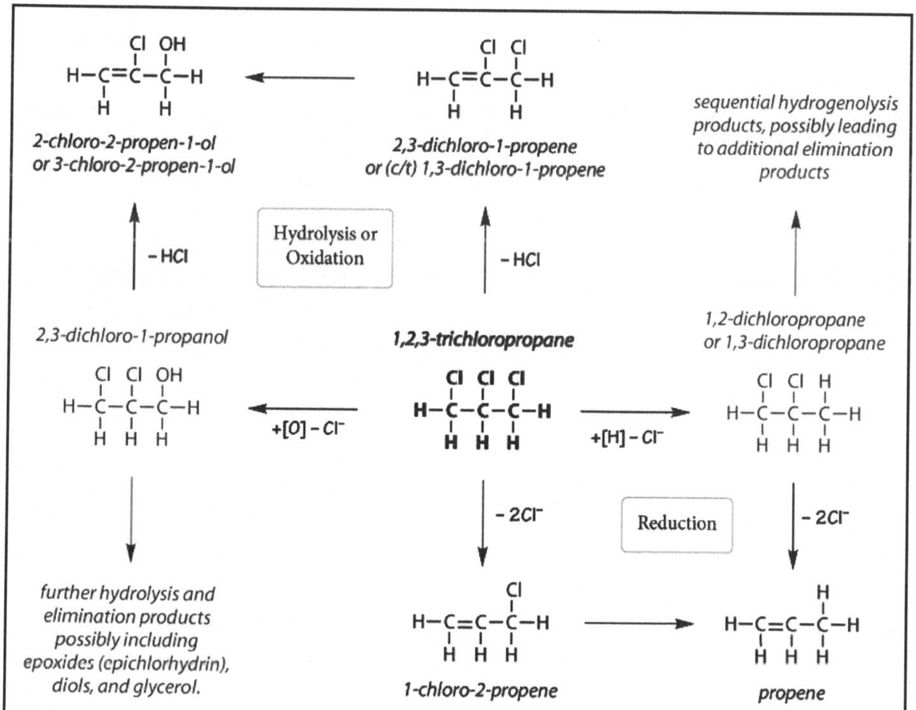

Fig. 3.2: Anticipated Primary Reaction Pathways for Degradation of TCP

Oxidation, hydrolysis, and hydrogenolysis are represented by the horizontal arrows. Elimination (dehydrochlorination) and reductive elimination (reductive ®-elimination) are shown with vertical arrows. [O] represents oxygenation(by oxidation or hydrolysis), [H] represents reduction. Gray indicates products that are likely to be of lessersignificance (Tratnyek and Sarathy, 2008).

Doping palladium on the surface sets up a galvanic couple, which increases the rate of corrosionof the iron, thus increasing the rate of dechlorination. Palladium andnickel have also been found to significantly enhance the dechlorination of perchloroethylene(PCE) in a zero-valent silicon/water system (Doong, Chen, and Tsai, 2003).

(ii) Emulsified Zero-Valent Iron

Dense non-aqueous phase liquid (DNAPL) at the source zone of contaminated areas has been amajor problem that inhibits the remediation process at contaminated sites and prevents siteclosure. DNAPLs are a common cause of environmental contamination at thousands of Department of Energy, Department of Defense, National Aeronautics and Space Administration (NASA), and private industry facilities around the country (AFCEE, 2008). To deal with thisongoing problem, researchers have developed emulsified zero-valent iron, or EZVI (Figure 3.3). EZVI is a surfactant stabilized emulsion with NZVI that is also biodegradable. The surfactantsurrounds the nanoparticle to form very small colloid droplets consisting of an oily membranearound the zero-valent iron nanoparticle while suspended in water. The surfactant emulsion iscommonly made of some type of vegetable oil. Edible oils have been used in a variety of locations throughout the United States to stimulate anaerobic biodegradation of chlorinatedsolvents and other contaminants (ESTCP, 2006). Not only would these particular emulsifiersstimulate microbial activity, but they would also allow for better mobility while forming ahydrophobic membrane around the NZVI, making them miscible to the DNAPL, such astrichloroethene (TCE), which is also hydrophobic. By using surfactants that attract the organicspecies to the surface of the NZVI, the contact time can be increased, thus allowing a morecomplete reaction. This is particularly important when using NZVI in a permeable barrier wherethe contaminated water usually flows through (McDowall, 2005).

Encapsulating NZVI in a hydrophobic membrane protects the nanoscale iron from othergroundwater constituents such as inorganics that might otherwise use some of the iron's reducingcapacity, thereby reducing the mass of NZVI available to treat target contaminants, and affectoverall project costs. According to researchers, when using EZVI, TCE diffuses through the oilmembrane into the interior aqueous phase of the emulsion particle. There it will undergoreductive dechlorination facilitated by the zero-valent iron particles (USEPA, 2006). This willmaintain a concentration gradient across the oil membrane and provide a driving force for TCEmolecules to continue entering the micelle. The final by-products of non-chlorinatedhydrocarbons from the reaction can then diffuse out of the emulsion into the surroundinggroundwater. It is expected that increased destruction of chlorinated solvents can be achievedusing EZVI through increased contact between the DNAPL and the nano-sized iron and through providing vegetable oil and surfactant components, which enable the material to serve as a longtermelectron donor and to augment biological degradation.

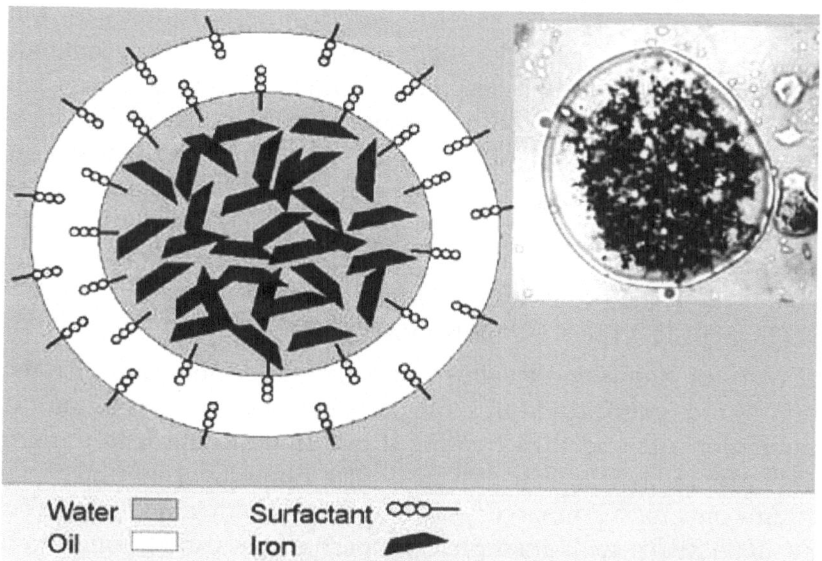

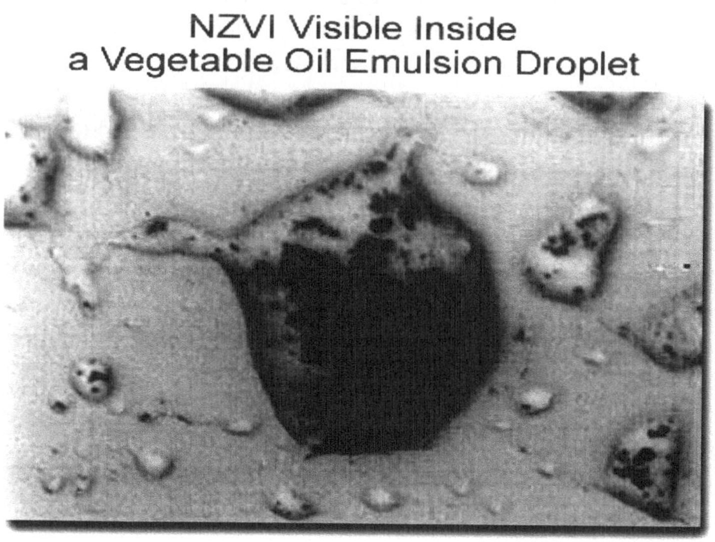

Figs. 3.3 and **3.3a:** EZVI Emulsion Droplets Containing Nanoscale Iron Particles in Water Surrounded by anOil-Liquid Membrane

EZVI is usually composed of surfactant, biodegradable vegetable oil, water, and nanoscaleiron. The emulsion particles (or micelles) that formed from this mixture contain a nucleus of iron suspended inwater, surrounded by an oil membrane. The surfactant keeps the micelles intact and well-distributed (dense nonaqueousphase liquids [DNAPLs])

Based on the documented case studies showed the majority of field applications have utilized nano iron. In conjunction with nano iron's diverse group of target contaminants, the field scale deployment of the particles can be achieved in a variety of ways. Nanoparticles can be mixed with water to form slurry that can be injected using pressure or gravity into a contaminated plume (Zhang, 2003). Once injected, the particles remain in suspension, forming a treatment zone. Particles of iron can be used in *ex situ* and *in situ* slurry reactors to treat soil, sediment, and solid waste. In cases of water and/or wastewater treatment, anchoring nanoparticles onto a solid matrix, such as activated carbon, can prove extremely effective. The injection of nano iron into the ground represents the most common deployment of this technology thus far. Overall the process provides a number of remedial benefits.

EX SITU APPLICATION OF NANOPARTICLES

Ex situ or pump and treat systems operate on the basis of removing contaminated groundwater from the ground, downstream of the contamination site and then treating it before returning it to the ground. SAMMS are created by self assembly of a monolayer of functionalized surfactants onto mesoporous ceramic supports, resulting in very high surface areas (~1000 m^2/g) with adsorptive properties that can be tuned to target contaminants such as mercury, chromate, arsenate, pertechnetate, and selenite. Dendritic polymers are another type of nanostructured material that has the potential for use in remediation. Both of these types of nanostructured adsorbants are most likely to be applied *ex situ*, where they can be recovered with the concentrated hazardous material that they adsorb. Nanotechnologies that affect remediation by contaminant degradation rather than adsorption are particularly attractive for organic contaminants. A well established approach for remediation of organic contaminants is photooxidation and the potential benefits of quantum sized photocatalysts have long been recognized for contaminant degradation applications. However, as with the absorptive technologies described above, photooxidation with nanostructured semiconductors is primarily an *ex situ* strategy, in this case because effective illumination usually requires that treatment be done in a reactor that is designed for this purpose. With this technology "it takes a long time to achieve cleanup goals, it has been demonstrated to spread contamination in some cases, and it is expensive to operate and maintain," requiring continual energy input (USEPA, 2004).

IN SITU APPLICATION OF NANOPARTICLES

Nanomaterials have highly desired properties for *in situ* applications. Because of their minute size and innovative surface coatings, nanoparticles may be able to pervade very small spaces in the subsurface and remain suspended in ground water, allowing the particles to travel farther than larger, macrosized particles and achieve wider distribution. For *in situ*nano remediation, no ground water is pumped out for aboveground treatment, and no soil is transported to other places for treatment and disposal (Otto *et al.*, 2008).

Most of the field application of nanoparticles for remediation at full scale have focused on nZVI and related products. Full scale commercial applications of nZVI in remediation are quickly becoming common, and there already are competitive markets among purveyors of nZVI materials and geotechnical service providers with various methods for deploying nZVI. The rapid emergence of remediation technologies based on nZVI has obscured and perhaps even exacerbated some pervasive misconceptions regarding the fundamental principles underlying this technology and the practical implications of its use in the environment. A common type of *in situ* remediation method, currently used to clean up contaminated groundwater is the permeable reactive barrier (PRB). PRBs are treatment zones composed of materials that degrade or immobilize contaminants as the groundwater passes through the barrier. They can be installed as permanent, semi permanent or replaceable barriers within the flow path of a contaminant plume.

Site Characteristics and Evaluation

Nanoremediation, has site specific requirements that must be met in order for it to be effective. Adequate site characterization is essential, including information about site location, geologic conditions, and the concentration and types of contaminants. Geologic, hydro geologic, and sub surface conditions include composition of the soil matrix, porosity, hydraulic conductivity, ground water gradient and flow velocity, depth to water table, and geochemical properties (pH, ionic strength, dissolved oxygen and concentrations of nitrate, nitrite, and sulfate). All of these variables need to be evaluated before nano particles are injected to determine whether the particles can infiltrate the remediation source zone, and whether the conditions are favourable for reductive transformation of contaminants.

The sorption or attachment of nanoparticles to soil and aquifer materials depends on the surface chemistry of soil and nano particles, ground water chemistry, and hydro dynamic conditions. The reactions between the contaminants and the nZVI depend on contact or probability of contact between the pollutant and nano particles (USEPA, 2008).

Injection Process and Technology

Nano scale ZVI particles used for remediation are usually about 50-300 nm in diameter (USEPA, 2005). Due to the fast aggregation process, it is difficult to get aggregates smaller than 1 μm in the field despite mixing. Aquatest identified an injected concentration of 1-2 g/L to be sufficient for plume treatment and to ensure particle mobility. They found that the particle mobility decreases with increasing concentration. Other experts found higher concentrations (10-30g/L) to be more mobile. It was agreed though that there is a trade off between injection velocity and injected concentration.

A slurry of nZVI can be introduced into the subsurface using a variety of carrying fluids such as water, nitrogen gas or vegetable oil. This helps dispersing the nZVI particles in the target area. Nano scale ZVI has a relatively short lifetime which typically requires more than one treatment to remediate a site. The required total mass of nZVI and the injection interval (number of reinjections) depends on: volume of contaminated soil and groundwater, contaminant concentration, phase (separate or dissolved) and total mass, aquifer characteristics including permeability and anisotropy, groundwater chemistry and incidental biodegradation rates.

Studies at the University of Stuttgart have shown that within 20 min the particles moved between 100-900 mm at an injection velocity of 0.6 m/h to 3.2 m/h respectively (at a constant concentration of 30 g/L). In a radial flow from the injection point, the velocity decreases exponentially with an increasing distance from the injection point. Typically, nZVI injection is accomplished with the following four methods:

1. Direct push techniques
2. Pneumatic fracturing techniques
3. Pressure pulse techniques
4. Liquid atomization injection techniques

The direct push method involves driving direct push rods, similar to small drilling augers, progressively deeper into the ground. This method allows materials to be injected without having to install permanent monitoring wells. Pneumatic fracturing uses air to create a fracture network of preferential flow paths in rock around the injection point to allow liquids and vapors to be transported quickly through fractured rock. This method of injection improves access to contaminants and allows liquids to flow freely (Zhang, 2003). Pressure pulse technology utilizes large amplitude pulses of pressure to insert the nZVI slurry into porous media at the water table; the pressure then excites the media and increases fluid level and flow. Liquid atomization injection is a technology that introduces an nZVI fluid mixture into the subsurface using a carrier gas. The nZVI liquid gas combination aerosolizes, allowing for more effective distribution; this method can be used in geologic formations with lower permeability (NAVFAC, 2008).

Research is ongoing into Methods of injection that will allow nanoparticles to better maintain their reactivity and increase their access to recalcitrant contaminants by achieving wider distribution in the subsurface.

Creating nZVI on site reduces the amount of oxidation the iron undergoes, thereby reducing loss in reactivity. Researchers in green chemistry have successfully created nZVI in soil columns' using a wide range of plant phenols then allows greater access to the contaminant and creates less hazardous waste in the manufacturing process (Varma, 2008). Figure1illustrates the basic principles of the methods of remediating contaminated groundwater using nanoscale iron. In (Fig 3.4.a) a conventional 'permeable reactive barrier' made with millimetre sized construction grade granular Fe; (Fig 3.4.b) a 'reactive treatment zone' formed by sequential injection of nanosized Fe to form overlapping zones of particles adsorbed to the grains of native aquifer material; and Fig. 3.4.c treatment of densenonaqueous phase liquid (DNAPL) contamination by injection of mobile nanoparticles. In (b) and (c), nanoparticles are represented by black dots and zones that are affected by nanoparticles are represented as pink plumes. In (b), the nanoparticles are assumed to have little mobility in the porous medium; whereas in (c), nanoparticles modified to impart significant mobility are necessary. Note that reaction will only occur when contaminant either dissolved in the groundwater or as DNAPL comes into contact with the Fe surfaces.

Post injection observations of the subsurface indicate an increase in pH (due to the formation of hydroxyl ions) and a decrease in the oxidation reduction potential (ORP) (due to the reducing conditions that are created). A lower ORP would most likely favour anaerobic bacteria growth, which in turn may promote increased degradation. Other chemicals formed when using particles such as nZVI may include hydrogen gas and Fe^{2+} ions, which would further promote microbial growth. After an nZVI injection, the ORP tends to decrease sharply before becoming stable (Zhang, 2003).

Monitoring

Continuous site monitoring is crucial to assure long term effects. If rebound effects are observed, reinjection may be necessary. Generally, the Oxidation Reduction Potential (ORP) levels are a good long term monitoring performance parameter.

Poursaberi *et al.* (2012)revealed that the Nanoscale zero-valent iron (nZVI) particles were synthesized by theaqueous phase borohydride reduction method, and the synthesizedNZVI particles were used for the degradation of Basic Yellow 28(BY28) dye in aqueous solution. The influence of experimental variables such asreaction time, nZVI particle dosage and pH were studied on the decolorizationof BY28. Mixing an aqueous solution of 100 mg L^{-1} BY28 with 2 g L^{-1} Fe^{o} resulted in 98.2% loss of BY28 within 15 min. The color removal efficiency wasfound to be increased with decrease in initial pH of dye solution and nZVIexhibited good color removal efficiency at acidic pH. Solvent extraction of theFe0 revealed that BY28 removal was not through adsorption, but throughdegradation, as Fe0 treatment of BY28 lead to new chromatographic peaks(degradation products) in HPLC analysis.

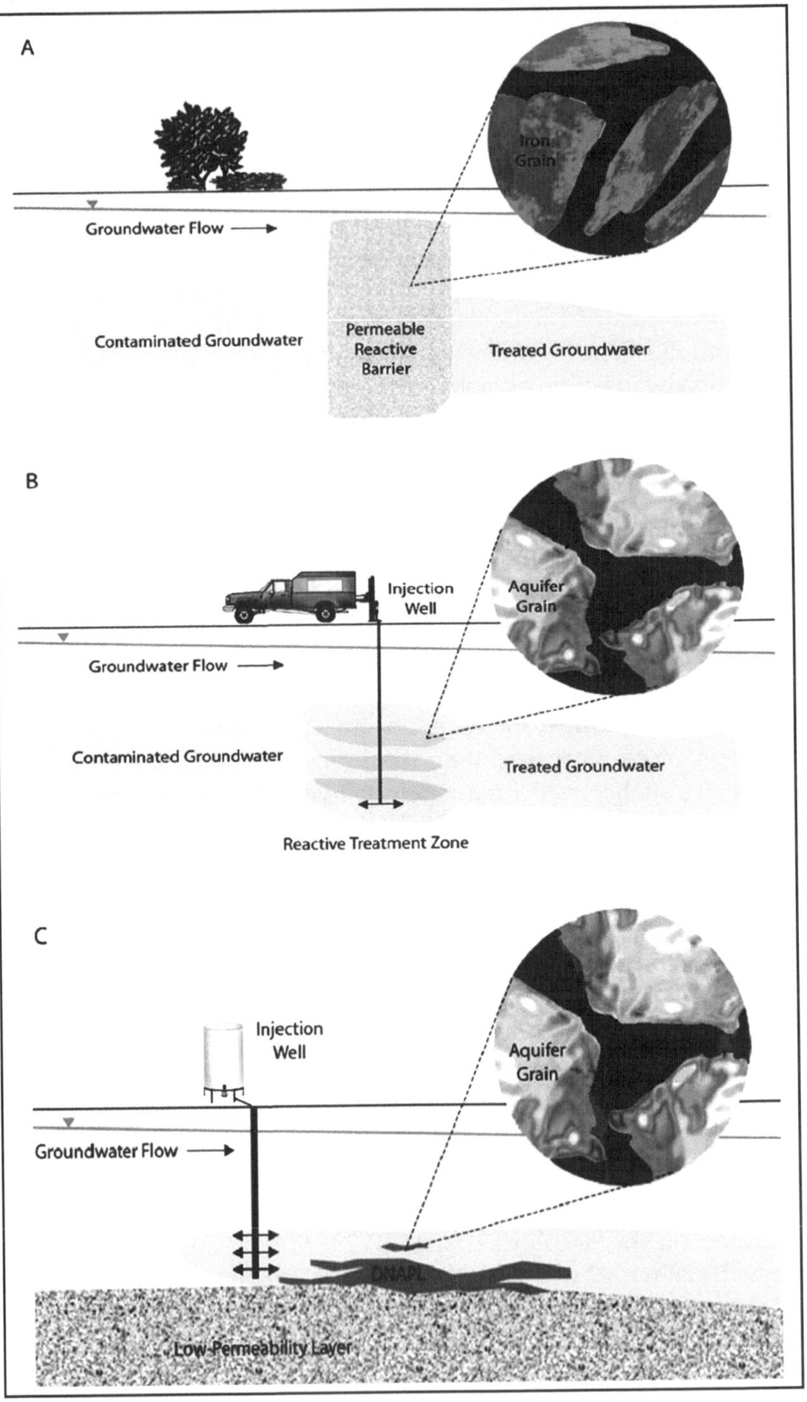

Fig. 3.4: Three Approaches to Application of nZVI Particles for Groundwater Temediation

Impact on Human and Environmental Health

Some nanomaterials that enter animal tissues may be able to pass through cell membranes orcross the blood-brain barrier. This may be a beneficial characteristic for such uses as targeteddrug delivery and other disease treatments, but could result in unintended impacts in other usesor applications. Inhaled nanoparticles may become lodged in the lung or be translocated, and thehigh durability and reactivity of some nanomaterials raise issues of their fate in the environment.It may be that in most cases, nanomaterials will not be of human health or ecological concern.However, at this point, not enough information exists to assess environmental exposure for mostengineered nanomaterials. This information is important because Environmental Protection Agency (EPA) will need a soundscientific basis for assessing and managing any unforeseen future impacts resulting from theintroduction of nanoparticles and nanomaterials into the environment. A nanomaterials riskassessment work sheet by the DuPont Chemical company in 2007 stated that toxicity, humanhazard, and environmental fate and effects data available from potential suppliers of NZVI arehighly variable in both quality and completeness. It also stated that in many cases, it is not clearfrom the information provided whether the Environmental Health and Safety (EHS) data arebased on the NZVI or on larger sized iron powder. Typical warnings include:

- Skin irritation
- Eye irritation
- Harmful if inhaled – irritating to mucous membranes and upper respiratory tract.
- May be harmful if swallowed. Large doses will produce a laxative effect.
- Toxicological properties have not been thoroughly investigated.
- Dissolved iron and manganese concentrations in groundwater may increase.

nZVI that is released into the air in the form of particulate matter could cause the first three aforementioned effects. Particulate matter triggers an acute inflammatory response in the lung,thus stimulating the secretion of cytokines, chemokines, ROS (reactive oxidation species), andtranscription factors (Gwinn and Vallyathan, 2006). Naturally occurring and engineered nanoparticles can remain airborne over a long period because of the small size and light weight(Biswas and Wu, 2005). Therefore, an increased likelihood that they will travel long distances, and interact with gases and other airborne particles is possible. When considering the fact thatmost nanoparticles are suspended in some type of liquid, surfactant medium, or pumped directly into the soil and water for contaminated groundwater remediation purposes, this may not be an important factor. There has been some toxicological research done on nanomaterials but not NZVI directly. It has been proposed that the induction of intracellular oxidative stress seems to be a key event of thebiological effects of many nanomaterials. Once inside the cell, nanomaterials may induce intracellular oxidative stress by disturbing the balance between oxidant and antioxidant processes. A study by Hu *et al.* (2009) found that certain nano-sized metal oxides exhibited toxicity according to their ionic charge. Lethal dose at 50 percent mortality rate (LD50) was calculated after certain metal oxide nanoparticles were exposure to *E. coli* bacteria. This particular bacteria strain was used as the test organism because it commonly exists in the environment and in the human body. *E. coli* also is simple to culture and easy to use inoperation. Table 3.2 gives a brief summary of those results.

Table 3.2: LD50 of *E. coli* after exposure to nano-sized metal oxides

Sl. No.	Nanoparticles	Cation Charge	FW	LD50 mg/L
1	ZnO	2+	81.39	21.1
2	CuO	2+	79.54	64.5
3	Al2O3	3+	101.96	326.1
4	La2O3	3+	325.82	456.9
5	Fe2O3	3+	159.69	638.3
6	SnO2	4+	150.69	1045.6
7	TiO2	4+	79.9	1104.8

There is a correlation with the cationcharge of the metal oxide nanoparticles and their toxicity. ZnO is the most toxic to *E. coli* at 21 mg/L and TiO2 isthe least toxic at 1104.8 mg/L (Hu *et al.*, 2009).

The induction of intracellular oxidative stress seems to be a key event of the biological effects ofmany nanomaterials. Hydrophobic nanomaterials (*i.e.*, nano-sized EZVI) can penetrate throughtissue and pass into the lymphatics (Gwinn and Vallyathan, 2006). Once inside the cell,nanomaterials may induce intracellular oxidative stress by disturbing the balance betweenoxidant and antioxidant processes. Microorganisms typically have an overall negative chargeassociated with their surface particles at neutral pH in solution.The negatively charged cell membrane surface can associate with the positively charged metaloxide particles, resulting in electrostatic condensation. Assumably, *E. coli* will attract lowercharged cations on per cell basis; therefore, greater cytotoxicity is exerted via the lower valentcations (Hu *et al.*, 2009). A trend that can be observed in table 3.2 is that there is a correlationwith the ionic charge and the toxicity of the metal oxides, with ZnO being the most toxic with acation charge of 2+ and TiO2 being the least toxic with a charge of 4+. Fe2O3, which is one ofthe precipitates of zero-valent iron during exposure to certain contaminants and in the presenceof oxygen, was also found to be one of the less toxic metal oxides with a cation charge of 3+.

Table 3.2 indicates that as the cationic charge increases, the toxicity of the metal oxide nanoparticles decreases. Thus it can be surmised that there is a decrease in toxicity (reactivity)as the cationic charge begins to increase. In the case of NZVI, cationic charge increases as itgoes from Fe0 to Fe2+ and finally to Fe3+ (ferric oxide) during chemical transformation onceentering a groundwater aquifer.

Treatment of cell cultures with nano-sized uncoated iron oxide (Fe2O3) revealed a cell-typespecific response when exposed to human mesothelioma cells and a rodent fibroblast cells. Slower proliferating 3T3 (rodent fibroblast) cells were only slightlyaffected by addition of up to 30 ppm iron oxide, while the cell parameters MTT-conversion andDNA content of faster growing MSTO (human mesothelioma) cells were drastically reducedupon exposure to as little as 3.75 ppm iron oxide(Brunner *et al.,* 2006). This information has significance in the treatment of particular types of cancer, as well understanding theenvironmental fate of nano-sized iron particles.

Nanoremediation has the potential to reduce the overall costs of cleaning up large scale contaminated sites, reduce cleanup time, eliminate the need for treatment and disposal of contaminated dredged soil, and reduce some contaminant concentrations to near zero, and it can be done *in situ*. In order to prevent any potential adverse environmental impacts, proper evaluation, including full scale ecosystem wide studies, of these nano particles needs to be addressed before this technique is used on a mass scale. Nanotechnology based products and processes promise to be ecologically beneficial in terms of energy consumption, materials saving, replacements of toxic materials and resource preservation. However, several questions such as the toxicity of nanoparticles, the capacity to recycle products generated by nanotechnologies and the degree of environmental compatibility of nanotechnology production processes need to be answered.

REFERENCES

AFCEE (Air Force Center for Engineering and Environment). 2008. Workshop on *In Situ* Biogeochemical Transformation of Chlorinated Solvents; Prepared for: AFCEE, Brooks City-Base, Texas; Environmental Security Technology Certification Program, Arlington,VA; and Naval Facilities Engineering Service Center, Port Hueneme, CA.

Biswas, P. and Wu, C.Y. (2005). Critical Review: Nanoparticles and the Environment. Journal of the Air and Waste Management Association, 55: 708-745.

Brunner, T.J., Wick, P., Manser, P., Spohn, P., Grass, R.N., Limbach, L.K., Brunink, A., and Stark, W.J. (2006). In Vitro Cytotoxicity of Oxide Nanoparticles: Comparison to Asbestos, Silica, and the Effect of Particle Solubility. *Environ. Sci. Technol.*, 40, 4374-4381.

Cundy, A.B., Hopkinson, L., and Whitby, R.L.D. (2008). Use of Iron-based Technologies in Contaminated Land and Groundwater Remediation: A Review. Elsevier; *Science of the Total Environment* 400: 42-51.

Diallo, M., P. Hudrlik and A. Hudrlik. 2006. Fe°/FeSD Endrimer Nano Composites for Reductive Dehalogenation of Chlorinated Haliphatic Compounds: Synthesis, Characterization and Bench Scale Laboratory Evaluation of Materials Performance. *Power Point Presentation*. 2006. Available at: http://www.howard.edu/CEACS/news/HBCU_MI/Howard%20-Diallo.ppt.

Doong, R.A., Chen, K.T., Tsai, H.C. (2003). "Reductive Dechlorination of Carbon Tetrachloride and Tetrachloroethylene by Zerovalent Silicon-Iron Reductants." *Environmental Science and Technology*, 37 (11) pp. 2575-2581.

Dror, I., D. Baram and B. Berkowitz. 2005. Use of Nanosized Catalysts for Transformation of Chloroorganic Pollutants. *Environmental Science and Technology,* 39(5): 1283-1290.

ESTCP (Environmental Security Technology Certification Program). 2006. "Protocol for Enhanced *In Situ* Bioremediation Using Emulsified Edible Oil." Prepared by: Industrial Environmental Services. May 2006, Cleared for Publication by: Department of Energy (DOD) June 8, 2006.

Gwinn MR., Vallyathan V. (2006) Nanoparticles: Health Effects—Pros and Cons. Environ Health Perspec. 114(12): 1818-1825.

Hu, X., Cook, S., Wang, P., Hwang, H., Liu, X., and Williams, Q.L. (2009). "*In vitro* Evaluation of Cytotoxicity of Engineered Metal Oxide Nanoparticles", *Science of Total Environment,* 407(8:) 3070-3072.

Kamat, P., H. Rebecca and N. Roxana. 2002. A "Sense and Shoot" Approach for Photocatalytic Degradation of Organic Contaminants in Water. *Journal of Physical Chemistry B,* 106(4): 788-794.

Lien, H.L., Elliott, D.S., Sun, Y.P. and Zhang, W.X. (2006). Recent Progress in Zero Valent Iron Nanoparticles for Groundwater Remediation; *Journal of Environmental Engineering and Management*, 16 (6), pp. 371-380.

Masciangioli, T and W. Zhang. 2003. Environmental Nanotechnology: Potential and Pitfalls. *Environmental Science and Technology,* 37, 102-108.

Mauter, M.S and M. Elimelech. 2008. Environmental Applications of Carbon-based Nanomaterials. *Environmental Science and Technology,* 2008; 42(16): 5843-5859.

Nagaveni, K., G. Sivalingam, M.S. Hegde and M. Giridhar. 2004. Photocatalytic Degradation of Organic Compounds Over Combustion-synthesized Nano-TiO_2. *Environmental Science and Technology,* 38(5): 1600-1604.

NAVFAC (Naval Facilities Engineering Command).2005. Cost and Performance Report: Nanoscalezerovalent Iron Technologies for Source Remediation. Available at: http://www.clu.org/download/remed/cr-05-007-env.pdf.

OCETA (Ontario Centre for Environmental Technology Advancement). 2003. Pressure Pulse Technology (PPT) for Recovery of Nonaqueous Phase Liquids. *OCETA Environmental Technology Profiles,* pp. 452-569.

Otto, M., M. Floyd and S. Bajpai. 2008. Nano Technology for Site Remediation. *Remediation,* 19(1): 99-108.

Poursaberi, T.M. Hassanisadi, F. Nourmohammadian. 2012. Application of Synthesized Nanoscale Zero-Valent Iron in the Treatment of Dye Solution Containing Basic Yellow 28. Prog. Color Colorants Coat. 5: 35-40.

Stumm, W.; Morgan, J.J. (1996). Aquatic Chemistry: Chemical Equilibria and Rates in Natural Waters; Wiley Interscience: New York.

Tratnyek, P.G., and Sarathy, V., (2008). Fate and Remediation of 1,2,3- Trichloropropane: Proceedings of the Sixth International Conference on Remediation of Chlorinated and Recalcitrant Compounds (Monterey, CA; May 2008). ISBN 1-57477-163-9, published by Battelle, Columbus, OH.

USEPA. 2004. Cleaning up the Nations Waste Sites: Markets and Technology Trends. EPA 542-R-04-015. http://www.epa.gov/tio/download/market/2004market.pdf.

USEPA. (U.S.EPA Workshop on Nanotechnology for site Remediation). 2005. http://epa.gov/ncer/publications/workshop/pdf/10_20_05_nanosummary.pdf.

USEPA. 2008. Nano Technology for site Remediation: Fact Sheet. EPA 542-F-08-009. Washington, DC. 236-328.

Varma, R. 2008. Greener Synthesis of Noble Metal Nanostructures and Nanocomposites. Presented at the *U.S. EPA Science Forum: Innovative Technologies – Key to Environmental and Economic Progress*. May 20-22.

Xu, Y.H. 2005. Removal of Copper from Contaminated Soil by Use of Poly (Amidoamine) Dendrimers. *Environmental Science and Technology,* 39(7): 2369-2375.

Xu, Y.H., and Zhao, D.Y. (2007). Reductive Immobilization of Chromate in Water and Soil Using Stabilized Iron Nanoparticles. *Water Res.* 41: 43-50.

Zhang, W. 2003. Nanoscale Iron Particles for Environmental Remediation: An Overview. *Journal of Nanoparticle Research,* 5: 323-332.

Pages: 70-112

BIOTECHNOLOGY AND ENVIRONMENTAL MANAGEMENT

Edited by: **Prof. Arun Arya; Dr. Raaz K Maheswari & Dr. Pawan Kumar 'Bharti'**

ISBN: 978-93-5056-862-0

Edition: **2017**

Published by: **Discovery Publishing House Pvt. Ltd., New Delhi (India)**

4

Genetic Manipulation of *Nicotiana tobaccum* L. and *Solanum lycopersicum* L. Plants with Annexin Gene using *Agrobacterium* Mediated Transformation Method

S. Chethan; C.V. Soumya Moudgalya
M. Shanthala; B. Dinesh and S. Rajashekara*

ABSTRACT

The ligated pGPTV vector carrying *Annexin* gene was transferred to the competent cells of *E.coli* (DH5αstrain) without any antibiotic resistance plasmid.Tri Parental Mating (TPM) was carried out by using *Agrobacterium* LBA4404 strain, *E.coli* strain pRK 2013 (having helper plasmid) and DH5αstrain of *E.coli* containing pGPTV with Annexin gene plasmid.Genomic DNA was isolated from the transgenic plantlets grown on ST media by using CTAB extraction method. *Neomycin phosphotransferase II*(nptII gene) with 800 bp was used as selectable marker system to show the presence of gene of interest. Forward and Reverse primer for nptII gene was used to carry out the PCR analysis and its amplification confirmed the presence of Annexin gene in the recombinant plantlets.Application of PCR analysis for Tobacco (*Nicotiana tabacum*) plant showed Lanes 1-4 and 6-8 loaded with the genomic DNA obtained from the transgenic tobacco plantlets. Similarly, PCR analysis for Tomato (*Solanium lycopersicum)* plant showed Lanes 2-8 loaded with the genomic DNA obtained from the transgenic tomato plantlets. Presence of Annexin gene was confirmed by the amplified bands that were clearly visible. The results obtained at the end of PCR analysis was the amplification the bands of nptII gene confirming the successful transformation of both

* Centre for Applied Genetics, Department of Studies in Zoology, Bangalore University, Jnana Bharathi Campus, Bengaluru - 560 056 (India)

Tobaccoand Tomato with annexin gene. Genetic manipulation of tomato plant through *A. tumefaciens* to form a transgenic plant by incorporating the annexin gene into plant's genomic DNA.*Agrobacterium tumefaciens* mediated transfer of DNA is a natural method of transformation of plants and this technology has been used for the production of transgenic tomatoes expressing a variety of heterologous proteins. Transgenic plants obtained in this study will further have to be subjected to field trails to prove their effectiveness.

INTRODUCTION

Transgenic Plants

Transgenic plants are the one who's DNA has been modified using genetic engineering techniques. The aim is to introduce a new trait to the plant which does not occur naturally in the species. A transgenic plant contains a gene or genes that have been artificially inserted. The inserted gene sequence is known as the "Transgene". It may come from an unrelated plant or from completely a different species. The purpose of inserting a combination of genes into a plant is to make it as useful and as productive as possible. This process provides advantages like improved shelf life, higher yield, improved quality, pest resistance, heat tolerance, cold and drought resistance and resistance against a variety of biotic and abiotic stresses. Transgenic plants can also be produced in such a way that they express foreign proteins with industrial and pharmaceutical values. Plants made up of vaccines or antibodies are especially striking as plants are free of human diseases, thus reducing the screening costs for viruses and bacterial toxins (Herbers and Sonnewald, 1999).

The first transgenic plants were reported in 1983, since then many recombinant proteins have been expressed in several important agro-economic species of plants including tobacco, tomato, corn, potato, banana etc. (Hammond and McGarvey1999).

In present research *Nicotiana tabacum* (tobacco), *Solanium lycopersicum* (tomato) and *Arabidopsis thaliana* are the most genetically modified plants due to well-developed transformation methods, easy propagation and well-studied genomes (Koornef *et al.*, 2010). *Arabidopsis thaliana* serves as model organism for other plant species. Transgenic plants are alsobeing used for bioremediation of contaminated soils having, mercury, cadmium, selenium and organic pollutants like polychlorinated biphenyls. These pollutants can be removed from soils by using transgenic plants containing genes for bacterial enzymes (Meagher, 2000).

Among the most important tools in the genetic engineer's tool kit are enzymes that perform specific functions on DNA. Restriction enzymes recognize and cuts the DNA at a specific region and the Ligase enzyme join the ends of two DNA fragments. These two along with other enzymes enable the manipulation and amplification of DNA. These are the essential components for joining the DNA of two unrelated organisms (Ray 1995).

Locating Genes for Plant Traits

Identifying and locating genes for agriculturally important traits is currently the most limiting step in the transgenic process. We still know relatively little about the specific genes required for enhancing yield potential, improving stress tolerance, modifying chemical properties of the harvested product or otherwise affecting plant characters. Usually, identifying a single gene involved with a trait is not sufficient; scientists must also understand how the gene is regulated, what other effects it might have on the plant and how it interacts with other genes active in the same biochemical pathway. Public and private research programs are investing heavily into new technologies to rapidly sequence and determine the functions of genes of most important crop species. These efforts should result in identification of a large number of genes potentially useful for producing transgenic varieties (Ausubel *et al.*, 1992).

Designing Genes for Insertion

The first step is to choose and isolate the gene that will be inserted into a plant of our interest (James and Clive, 2012). The gene which is to be inserted can be isolated using restriction enzymes which cuts the DNA into fragments and gel electrophoresis is run to separate them out according to their respective lengths (Alberts *et al.*, 2002). Polymerase chain reaction can also be used to amplify a gene segment which can then be isolated through gel electrophoresis. If the chosen gene on the donor organism's genome has been well studied, it may be present in a genetic library (Kaufmanand Nixon, 1996).

The designed genes must consist of the following genes in their stretch of sequence: Marker gene, Promoter gene, Transgene and Terminator sequence.

The gene to be inserted into the plant of interest must be combined with other genetic elements in order for it to work properly. The gene fragment that is to be inserted must contain a promoter and a terminator gene as well as a selectable marker gene. The promoter region initiates transcription of the gene and can be used to control the location and level of gene expression, while the terminator region ends transcription. The selectable marker which in most cases confers antibiotic resistance to the organism is needed in order to determine the cells that are transformed with the new gene. The constructs are made using recombinant DNA techniques such as restriction digestions, ligations and molecular cloning (Berg and Metz, 2010).

Transforming Plants

Transformation is the heritable change in a cell or an organism brought about by the uptake and establishment of introduced DNA. Transformation via *Agrobacterium* has been successfully practiced in dicots (broadleaf plants like soybeans, tobacco and tomatoes) for many years, but only recently it is being effectively practiced in monocots (grasses and their relatives). In general, the *Agrobacterium* mediated transformation method is preferred to the gene gun method because of the greater frequency of single-site insertions of the foreign DNA, making it easier to monitor (Hamza, 1993).

Agrobacterium Mediated Method of Plant Transformation

Agrobacterium tumefaciens is a remarkable species of soil-dwelling bacteria that has theability to infect plant cells with a piece of its DNA. When the bacterial DNA is integrated into a plant chromosome, it effectively hijacks the plant's cellular machinery and uses it to ensure the proliferation of the bacterial population. Many gardeners and orchard owners are unfortunately familiar with *A. tumefaciens* because it causes crown gall diseases in many ornamental and fruit plants (Ko and Korban, 2004).

The DNA of an *A. tumefaciens* cell is contained in the bacterial chromosome as well as in another structure known as the Ti (tumour-inducing) plasmid. The Ti plasmid contains a stretch of DNA termed T-DNA (~20 kb long) that is transferred to the plant cell during the infection process. A series of virulence (*vir*) genes directs the infection process (Lopez *et al.*, 2004). *Agrobacterium tumefaciens* can infect a plant only through wounds. When a plant root orstem is wounded, it gives off certain chemical signals. In response to those signals, the *vir* genes of *A. tumefaciens* become activated and direct a series of events necessary for the transfer of the T-DNA from the Ti plasmid to the plant's chromosome (Gelvin, 2003).

Types and Functions of *vir* Genes

Types of *vir* genes are *vir*A, *vir*C, *vir*G, *vir*E, *vir*E1, *vir*D, *vir*D1, *vir*D2, *vir*H. Functions of *vir* genes are (a) they help in copying the T-DNA sequence (b) attach a product to the copied T-DNA strand to act as a leader (c) add proteins along the length of the T-DNA possibly as a protective mechanism (d) open a channel in the bacterial cell membrane through which the T-DNA passes.

The T-DNA then enters the plant cell through the wound. It is not clear how the bacterial DNA moves from the cytoplasm to the nucleus of the plant cell or how the T-DNA becomes integrated into the plant chromosome. Most of the time, plant DNA does not exist as an exposed strand but it is wrapped with histone proteins in a super coiled state. One speculation is that the T-DNA waits until the plant DNA is being replicated or transcribed and then inserts itself into the exposed plant DNA (Howard *et al.*, 1992).

To use *A.tumefaciens* as a transgene vector, scientists have removed the tumour-inducing section of T-DNA, while retaining the T-DNA border regions and the *vir* genes. The transgene is inserted between the T-DNA border regions, where it is transferred to the plant cell and becomes integrated into the plant's chromosomes (Gelvin, 2003).

Selection of Successfully Transformed Tissues

Following the gene insertion process, plant tissues are transferred to a selective medium containing an antibiotic or herbicide depending on which the selectable marker was used. Only plants expressing the selectable marker gene will survive and it is assumed that these plants will also possess the transgene of interest (When grown on selective media, only plant tissues that have successfully integrated the transgene construct will survive).Thus subsequent steps in the process will only use these surviving plants (Raj *et al.*, 2005).

Regeneration of whole Plants

To obtain whole plants from transgenic tissues such as immature embryos, they are grown under controlled environmental conditions in a series of media containing nutrients and hormones by a process known as tissue culture. Once whole plants are generated and produce seeds, evaluation of the progeny begins. This regeneration step has been a stumbling stage in producing transgenic plants in many species but specific varieties of most crops can now be transformed and regenerated (Sharma *et al.*, 2009).

Plant Breeding and Testing

Intrinsic to the production of transgenic plants is an extensive evaluation process to verify whether the inserted gene has been stably incorporated without detrimental effects to other functions of the plant, its product quality or the intended agro ecosystem. Initial evaluation includes attention to: Activity of the introduced gene, Stable inheritance of the gene and unintended effects on plant growth, yield and quality.

If a plant passes these tests, most likely it will not be used directly for crop production, but it will be crossed with improved varieties of the crop. This is because only a few varieties of a given crop can be efficiently transformed and these generally do not possess all the producer and consumer qualities required by modern cultivars. The initial cross to the improved variety must be followed by several cycles of repeated crosses to the improved parent and this process is known as backcrossing. The goal is to recover as much of the improved parent's genome as possible with the addition of the transgene from the transformed parent (Newell, 2000).

The next step in the process is multi-location and a multi-year evaluation trial in greenhouse and field environments to test the effects of the transgene and overall performance. This phase also includes evaluation of environmental effects and food safety (Richard *et al.*, 2007).

Gene Cloning

The term gene cloning" refers to a wide variety of techniques that makes it possible to manipulate DNA in order to return it to living organisms where it can function normally. Essentially it involves isolating a piece of DNA from an organism and introducing it into a cloning host. It is therefore possible to study the cloned DNA or production of the protein encoded by the gene. The cDNA may be inserted into vectors and then cloned. The choice of vector represents the most important consideration in molecular cloning experiments (Krebs *et al.*, 2010).

Many bacteria contain an extra chromosomal element of DNA known as a plasmid DNA. This is relatively small, covalently closed circular molecule, which carries genes for antibiotic resistance, conjugation or the metabolism of unusual substrates. One of the most notable plasmids, termed pUC19 was widely adopted for cloning of small DNA fragments in *E.coli*. Ithas an antibiotic resistance gene for ampicillin and contains an origin of replication enabling the vector to replicate in *E.coli* (Lodge *et al.*, 2007).

Plasmid vectors permit the identification of recombinant clones by looking for insertion inactivation of either antibiotic resistance genes or *lacZ*. However, potential recombinant clones still needs to be analyzed. This involves purifying the plasmid DNA from individual clones and cutting it with restriction enzymes in order to analyze the size of the fragments produced (Krebs *et al.*, 2010).

Restriction endonucleases recognize certain DNA sequences and cleave them in a defined pattern. Covalent joining of ends on each of the two strands may be brought about by the enzyme DNA ligase, which enables the construction of recombinant DNA fragments. However, it is often convenient to cut a vector with two restriction endonucleases which do not produce complementary overhanging ends (described as sticky ends and are generated by cleavage).

EcoRI is one of the most commonly used restriction enzyme and it is produced by the bacterium *E.coli* strain RY13 (Walker and Rapley, 2000).

The next step in cloning a gene is to find a way of joining the DNA molecules together in a new combination (termed as recombinant). The most commonly used DNA ligase is a protein produced by a bacteriophage known as T4. In the energy consuming process of ligation, DNA ligase catalyzes the formation of a covalent phosphodiester bond between the 5 phosphate on one DNA strand and a 3 hydroxyl on another (Krebs *et al.*, 2010).

The final step is described as the transformation which involves the introduction of the new recombinant plasmid into host bacterial cell. For the DNA to get into the bacterial cell, selection of the cells containing the plasmid is necessary. Considering that the host bacterial cell is not naturally capable of transformation, these host cells needs to be treated chemically and must be electrophoresed in order to enable them to take up the foreign DNA (Lodge *et al.*, 2007).

Gene Carrying Vector (pUC 19)

pUC 19 is the donor of the desired Annexin gene. It carries Annexin gene in its multiple cloning sites. The size of pUC 19 is 2.7 Kbp, it has an origin of replication in *E.coli*. It has a gene for ampicillin resistance and a multiple cloning site for restriction enzymes (Yanisch-Perron, 1985).

Plasmid Guss Plant Transformation Vector (pGPTV)

pGPTV is a binary vector. Its size is 13Kbp long, consists of origin of replication for both *E.coli* and *Agrobacterium tumefaciens*. It has gene for Neomycin phosphotransferase (nptII) that confers resistance to Kanamycin. It has poly cloning site for unique restriction enzymes, lacks *vir* genes and requires a helper strain with only *vir* region in order to transfer the desired gene into the host plant cell. It also contains T-DNA border sequences (Charles, 1995).

Introduction to Annexin Gene

Annexins are an evolutionarily conserved, homologous, and structurally related to super family of Ca^{2+} dependent phospholipid-binding proteins. They exist in some prokaryotes and all eukaryotes with varying number across various organisms (Gerke *et al.*, 2002; Laohavisit *et al.*,2011; Clark *et al.*, 2012; Jami *et al.*, 2012). Plant annexin was first identified in tomato (Boustead *et al.*, 1989) and the first plant annexin multigene family was detected from the model plant *Arabidopsis thaliana* (Clark *et al.*, 2001).

In the past decade, studies on plant annexin multigene families were mostly focused on identification and characterization in rice, mustard and tomato (Jami *et al.*,2008, 2009, 2010; Laohavisit *et al.*, 2011; Lu *et al.*, 2012). Structurally, plant annexins consist of four annexin repeats of approximately 70 amino acids, and only the first and fourth repeats contain the observed motif of GxGT-(38 residues)-D/E for calcium binding (Geisow *et al.*, 1986). For plant annexins, there are five main invitro protein activities. These functions include nucleotide phosphodiesterase (ATPase and GTPase) activity (McClung *et al.*, 1994), peroxidase activity (Gorecka *et al.*, 2005), cytoskeletal binding (Hayes *et al.*, 2004), regulation of glucan synthesis (Andrawis *et al.*, 1993) and transport (Hofmann *et al.*, 2000; Laohavisit *et al.*, 2009, 2010, 2012).

These functions suggested that plant annexins are involved in a wide range of processes including reproductive and vegetative development and responses to environmental stimuli. Differential expression had been observed during the cell cycle (Proust *et al.*,1999), primary and lateral root development (Clark *et al.*, 2001; Bassani *et al.*, 2004), tuber enlargement (Sheffield *etal.*, 2006), vasculature development (Clark *et al.*, 2001), fiber elongation of cotton (Yang *et al.*, 2008), cork formation (Soler *et al.*,2007), embryogenesis (Gallardo *et al.*,2003), pollen andseed germination (Buitink *et al.*,2006; Dai *et al.*, 2006; Yang *et al.*,2007) and petal senescence and fruit ripening (Bianco *et al.*, 2009; Bai *et al.*, 2010).

Genetic and transgenic evidence indicated that annexins play a vital role both in abiotic and biotic stress responses (Lee *et al.*, 2004; Jami *et al.*, 2008; Konopka-Postupolska *et al.*, 2009; Divya *et al.*, 2010). For instance, the over-expression of mustard *AnnBj1* gene enhanced salt and drought tolerance in transgenic cotton and tobacco (Jami *et al.*, 2008; Divya *et al.*, 2010). A recent study indicated that *AnnAt1* gene and *AnnAt4* gene function cooperatively in response to drought and salt stresses (Huh *et al.*, 2010). These studies indicated that some plant annexins could be vital candidates for genetic engineering to enhance stress resistance of crops. A recent study performed a genome-wide survey of annexin multigene families in 16 plant species and identified 149 genes.

TOBACCO

Tobacco belongs to the nightshade family (*Solanaceae*) and it is indigenous to North and South America, Australia, Southwest Africa and the South Pacific. The English word "tobacco" originates from the Spanish and Portuguese. However, it is indigenous to some parts of the globe. It is now grown all over the globe as a commercial crop because of its economic value, but in some parts of the globe growing tobacco plant is considered as a crime because of its effect on human health.

The classification of tobacco is given below:

Classification:

Kingdom : Plantae
Phylum : Magnoliophyta
Class : Magnoliopsida
Order : Solanales
Family : Solanaceae
Genus : *Nicotiana*
Species : *Nicotiana tabacum*L.

Tobacco is a tall leafy annual plant that belongs to the Solanaceae family. It is an annual herb, shrub or small tree from 0.9 to 1.5m tall according to the variety. Tobacco includes numerous species, which are grown throughout the world. One species (*Nicotiana tabacum*), common tobacco is the main source of commercial tobacco used today.

Nicotiana tabacum is a native of Tropical and Sub Tropical America but it is nowcommercially cultivated worldwide. It is referred to as a cash crop because it is grown for sale and not for use on the farm. Other varieties are cultivated as ornamental plants or grow as a weed (Goodman and Jordan 2005).

Every part of the plant except the seed contains nicotine, but the concentration is related to different factors such as species, type of land, culture or weather conditions. The concentration of nicotine increases with the age of the plant. Tobacco leaves contain 2 to 8% of nicotine combined as malate or citrate. The distribution of the nicotine in the mature plant is widely variable: 64% of the total nicotine exists in the leaves; 18% in the stem, 13% in the root and 5% in the flowers (Durkin *et al.*, 2012).

TOMATO

Tomato is an edible, often red berry-type fruit of the nightshade *Solanum lycopersicum*, commonly known as a tomato plant. Tomatoes are consumed in diverse ways, including raw, as an ingredient in many dishes, sauces, salads, and drinks. The English word tomato comes from the Spanish word, tomate, derived from the Nahuatl (Aztec language) word tomatl. It first appeared in print in 1595.

The classification of tomato is given below:

Classification:

Kingdom : Plantae
Division : Magnoliophyta
Class : Magnoliopsida
Order : Solanales
Family : Solanaceae
Genus : *Solanum*
Species : *Solanum lycopersicum*L.

The species originated in Central and South America and its use as a food originated in Mexico, and spread throughout the world following the Spanish colonization of the Americas. Its many varieties are now widely grown, sometimes in greenhouses in cooler climates. The plants typically grow to 1-3 meters (3-10 ft.) in height and have a weak stem that often sprawls over the ground and vines over other plants. It is a perennial in its native habitat, although often grown outdoors in temperate climates as an annual. An average common tomato weighs approximately 100 grams.

While tomatoes are botanically and scientifically the berry-type fruits of the tomato plant, they can also be considered a culinary vegetable, causing some confusion.

There are around 7,500 tomato varieties grown for various purposes. Tomato varieties are roughly divided into several categories, based mostly on shape and size (Valero *et al.,* 2011).

No comprehensive study has been carried out with respect to annexin gene incorporation into the plant of our choice (tobacco and tomato). Hence, the present study was carried out with the objectives given below:

- Clone Annexingene into plant transformation vector pGPTV to generate a recombinant plasmid and its introduction into tobacco and tomato plants through *Agrobacterium* mediated transformation technique in order to generate a transgenic tobacco and tomato plants.
- Transfer of Annexin gene construct into plant's genomic DNA by using leaf disc preparation, co-cultivation and selection media transfer.
- Leaf disc containing gene construct survives on selection media containing antibiotics like Kanamycin, Augmentin and Cefatoxin and those were allowed to grow into calli, which indicate the presence of gene of interest.
- The presence or absence of the gene of interest was further confirmed by extraction and isolation of genomic DNA from transgenic plants, which were then subjected to the PCR analysis.

MATERIALS AND METHODS

Biological Cultures (Sambrook *et al.*, 1989)

- Glycerol stocks of DH5α cells (Basic strain of *E.coli*) containing pUC19/ANNEXIN and pGPTV vector.
- Plain DH5α cells (Basic strain of *E.coli*) for competent cell preparation
- *Agrobacterium tumefaciens* receptor strain LBA4404
- *E.coli* cells with pRK2013 Helper strain.

Microbial Media (Sambrook *et al.*, 1989)

Table 4.1: Components of Lauria - Bertini (LB) broth media

Sl. No.	Components	Concentration
1.	Tryptone	10g
2.	Yeast extract	10g
3.	NaCl	5g
4.	pH	7
5	Distilled water	1000 ml

Table 4.2: Components of Lauria - Bertini Agar (LB-agar) media

Sl.No.	Components	Concentration
1.	Tryptone	10 g
2.	Yeast extract	10 g
3.	NaCl	5 g
4.	pH	7
5.	Agar	15 g
6.	Distilled water	1000 ml

Antibiotic (AB) medium

Medium used for Tri Parental Mating is called AB medium and is divided into 3 parts:

Table 4.3: Components for AB salt(5x)

Sl.No.	Components	Concentration
1.	NH_4CL	0.5 g
2.	$CaCL_2$	0.075 g
3.	$MgSO_4.7H_20$	0.15 g
4.	$FeSO_4.7H_20$	1.25 g
5	KCl	0.075 g

Table 4.4: Components for AB buffer (pH – 7.0) (X)

Sl. No.	Components	Concentration
1.	K_2HPO_4	1.5 g
2.	NaH_2PO_4	0.5 g

Table 4.5: Components for AB agar media

Sl. No.	Components	Concentration
1.	AB 5X salts	20 ml
2.	AB 5X buffer	20 ml
3.	D - Glucose	0.5%
4.	Agar	1.5%

When AB medium is supplemented with antibiotics (Kanamycin 50 µg/ml, Rifampicilin 10 µg/ml and Streptomycin 100 µg/ml) it is referred to as AB-KRS plates.

Murshiage and Skoog (MS) Medium (Murshiage and Skoog 1962)

MS medium is a basal medium used for laboratory cultivation of plant cell cultures. The preparation is divided into 6 parts:

(i) Major salts (Macronutrients)
(ii) Minor salts (Micronutrients)
(iii) Iron source
(iv) Amino acids and Vitamins
(v) Carbon source and Agar
(vi) Hormones

Regeneration (RT) Medium

It is the modification of MS medium with growth hormones added.

Selection (ST) Medium

It is the modification of RT medium with antibiotics added.

Antibiotics

Table 4.6: Components for ST media

Sl. No.	Components	Concentration
1.	Kanamycin	250 µg/ml
2.	Rifampicilin	200 µg/ml
3.	Streptomycin	50 µg/ml

Stock of Antibiotics

1. Ampicillin (100 µg/ml)
2. Kanamycin (50 µg/ml)
3. Streptomycin (100 µg/ml)

4. Augmentin (250 µg/ml)
5. Cephatoxin (200 µg/ml)

Plasmid Isolation (Sambrook *et al.*, 1989)

Table 4.7: Components for saline Tris-EDTA (STE) buffer

Sl. No.	Components	Concentration
1.	NaCl	0.1 M
2.	Tris–HCl (pH 8.0)	10 mM
3.	EDTA (pH 8.0)	1 Mm

Table 4.8: Components for solution I

Sl. No.	Components	Concentration
1.	Glucose	50 mM
2.	EDTA (pH 8.0)	10 mM
3.	Tris–HCl (pH 8.0)	25 mM

Table 4.9: Components for solution II (Prepared fresh)

Sl. No	Components	Concentration
1.	NaOH	0.2 N
2.	SDS	1%

Take 3ml of AFDDW (Autoclaved Filtered Double Distilled Water) add 200 µl of NaOH and make the volume up to 6 ml with AFDDW then add 1 ml of 10% SDS and make the final volume up to 10 ml with AFDDW.

Table 4.10: Components for solution III

Sl. No	Components	Concentration
1.	5M Potassium acetate	10 mM
2.	Glacial Acetic acid	11.5 ml
3.	Distilled water	28.5 ml

Table 4.11: Components of Tris-EDTA (TE) buffer

Sl. No	Components	Concentration
1.	EDTA (pH 8.0)	1 mM
2.	Tris–HCl (pH 8.0)	10 mM

Other Chemical Components

Chloroform : Isoamyl Alcohol (24:1)

24 ml of chloroform and 1 ml of isoamyl alcohol was added and mixed together and stored in dark away from sunlight.

Phenol : Chloroform : Isoamyl Alcohol (25:24:1)

25 ml of phenol, 24 ml of chloroform and 1 ml of isoamyl alcohol was added and mixed together and stored in dark at 40° C.

3M Sodium Acetate

346.09 g of Sodium Acetate was dissolved in 800 ml of distilled water and volume was made up to 1 L by volumetric flask, stored at 40° C.

70% Ethanol

70 ml of 100% ethanol was mixed with 30 ml of distilled water to make up 70% concentration.

2.5M Ammonium Acetate

192.7 g of sodium acetate was dissolved in 800 ml of distilled water and the volume was made up to 1 L by volumetric flask and stored at 4° C (Sambrook *et al.*, 1989).

Agarose Gel Electrophoresis (Dolnik, 1997)

Requirements – Agarose Gel powder, TAE buffer, EtBr solution and gel loading dye.

EtBr (10 mg/ml)

10 mg of EtBr was dissolved in 1 ml of Sterile Double Distilled Water to prepare a stock EtBr solution of 10 mg/ml concentration.

Table 4.12: Components for gel loading dye gel loading dye

Sl. No	Components	Concentration
1.	Bromophenol Blue	0.25%
2.	Xylene Cyanol	0.25%
3.	Glycerol or Sucrose	5 ml

Genomic DNA Extraction (Sambrook *et al.*, 1989)

Table 4.13: Components for extraction buffer

Sl. No	Components	Concentration
1.	Tris – HCl	100 mM
2.	NaCl	1.4 M
3.	EDTA	20 mM
4.	CTAB	2%
5.	β Mercaptoethanol	0.4%
6.	PVP (Poly Vinyl Pyrrolidone)	1%

5M NaCl

292.2 g of NaCl was dissolved in 800 ml distilled water and volume was made up to 1L by volumetric flask, dispensed in aliquots and sterilized by autoclaving.

Other Requirements (Sambrook *et al.*, 1989)

Biological Enzymes

RNase A (10 mg/ml)

EcoR1 and Xbal (1µl)
Bacteriophage T4 DNA Ligase enzyme(0.5µl)
Taq enzyme (1 Unit)

Buffers Required

OPAB buffer 10X – for restriction enzymes
10X Ligase buffer – for ligation reaction
10X Assay buffer – for PCR

STE buffer, Tris EDTA (TE) buffer, 1X TAE buffer, for Gel loading, Genomic DNA extraction buffer (CTAB) and PCR reaction mixture.

Chemicals

Mixture of 4 dNTP's, Primers (Forward and Reverse primers), 0.1 M $CaCl_2$, AFDDW, 70% Ethanol (ice cold), isopropanol (ice cold), Absolute Alcohol (ice cold), Equilibrated phenol, Double distilled water, Agarose, Standard solutions of known DA concentrations in the range of 0-60 ng/µl in TE, Tween – 20 solution, 0.1% Mercuric chloride solution, 70% Methanol.

Instruments and Apparatus

Autoclave, Incubator, Rotatory shaker, Electrophoresis unit, Centrifuge tubes, Eppendorf tubes, Ultra violet transilluminator, Orbital shaker, Laminar air flow, Water bath, Micro pipettes, Pestle and Mortar, Speed vacuum desiccator, Sterile tooth pick, Spirit lamp, Ice maker, Blade, Parafilm,Glass ware, Test tubes, Spreader, Petri plates, Conical flask, Beaker, Measuring cylinder, PCR.

Plasmid DNA Isolation

Plasmid DNA was isolated according to the procedure given below (Sambrook *et al.*, 1989).

PROTOCOL:

1. 100µl of bacterial glycerol stock was added into 50ml of LB broth containing the respective antibiotics (that is Kanamycin for pGPTV and Ampicillin for pUC19- Annexin). These conical flasks were incubated overnight at 37° C on the orbital shaker.
2. The cultures were transferred into sterile centrifuged tubes and Chilled on an ice bath for 5 min at 4 °C. The cells were harvested by centrifugation at 6000 rpm for 6 min at 4° C.
3. The supernatant was discarded and 3 ml of solution-I was added to the pellet. The vial was vortexed gently to get uniform suspension. The vial was kept in ice for 10 minutes and shifted to room temperature.
4. 6 ml of freshly prepared solution-II was added to the vial and mixed well. The tubes were incubated for 10 minutes at room temperature and shifted to ice for 1 minute.
5. 4.5 ml of solution-III was added and mixed well and then kept on an ice-bath for 10 minutes. Then centrifuged at 12,000 rpm for 12 minutes.

6. The supernatant was transferred to fresh tubes and 0.6V of isopropanol was added and mixed well. The tubes were left at room temperature for 30 minutes to allow the DNA to precipitate. This was then centrifuged at 10,000 rpm for 10 minutes. The DNA was observed as a white pellet sticking to the sides of the tubes.
7. The tubes were air-dried for few min and the pellet was dissolved in 0.8ml of 1X TE.
8. The contents were shifted into 2ml eppendorf tubes and 10-12µl of RNase-'A' was added into each tube. The tubes were then incubated at 37° C for 30 minutes. This step allows the denaturation of any RNA content in the preparation.
9. After 30 minutes,an equal volume of phenol: chloroform: isoamyl alcohol was added and centrifuged at 12,000 rpm for 12 minutes. The supernatant was transferred to fresh tubes. This process was repeated twice or thrice.
10. Than equal volume of chloroform: isoamyl alcohol mixture was added to the supernatant and centrifuged at 12,000 rpm for 12 minutes. The supernatant was transferred to fresh eppendorf tubes.
11. To the supernatant 0.1V of 3M sodium acetate was added and mixed gently. Two volumes of absolute alcohol was added and kept at- 20° C overnight. This step allows the re-precipitation of the plasmid DNA.
12. The vial was centrifuged at 12,000 rpm 12 minutes at 4° C. The pellet contained plasmid DNA.
13. Pellet was washed with ice cold 70% ethanol.
14. Pellet was dried in a speed vacuum desiccator for about 10 minutes.
15. Pellet was re-dissolved in 30µl-40µl of 1 x TE buffer (depending on the size of the pellet).

Agarose Gel Electrophoresis

This was conducted according to the protocol given below (Dolnik, 1997).

PROTOCOL

Preparation of the Gel:

1. The edges of a clean, dry glass plate were sealed with tape, so as to form a mold. The combs were positioned 0.5- 0.1 mm above the plate, so that the complete well is formed when the agarose is added. Two combs with six wells each were placed so as to get 12 wells in a single gel.
2. Sufficient electrophoresis buffer (1X TAE) was prepared - to fill the electrophoresis tank and to prepare the gel.
3. 0.8% agarose gel was prepared by dissolving 0.4g of agarose in 50 ml of 1 × TE buffer by heating at a temperature above 60° C. The solution was cooled to 60° C and Ethidium Bromide (From a stock solution of 10mg/ml in water) was added to get a final concentration of 0.5µg/ml.

4. The gel was poured in gel casting unit with combs.
5. After the gel was completely set, the combs and tapes were carefully removed and the gel was mounted in the electrophoresis tank.
6. Enough electrophoresis buffers, to cover the gel to a depth of about 1mm were poured in the electrophoresis tank.

Loading of Samples: 10µl of DNA samples were taken in a separate eppendorf tubes and 1.5µl of gel loading buffer was added to each tube and mixed well. The gel-loading buffer is available as a stock of 6X concentration. Thus based on the volume of DNA sample, loaded dye is added to give a final concentration of 1X (Van Holde *et al.,* 1998).

PROTOCOL:

1. With the help of micropipette, the samples were loaded into appropriate wells.
2. The lid of gel tank was closed and electric leads were attached, so that the DNA will migrate towards the anode. A voltage of 50-100V/cm was applied. The gel was run until bromophenol blue and xylene cyanol FF have migrated the appropriate distance through gel.
3. After electrophoresis for 1:30to2:00 hours, the electric current was turned off and leads were removed. The lid of tank was opened and the gel was observed under UV transilluminator (Skyrinou *et al.,* 2009).

Restriction Digestion

This was done according to the protocol given below (Krebs *et al.,* 2010).

Double Digestionprotocol

1. DNA samples of 20.00 ml of pUC19/Annexin and 30.00µl of pGPTV were taken in a sterile microfuge tubes and mixed with double distilled water to give the required volume
2. 2.5µl of the appropriate 10X-restriction digestion buffer was added and mixed by tapping the tubes. The tubes were spun for few seconds.
3. 1µl of restriction enzymes EcoRI and XbaI each were added and mixed by tapping the tubes.The tubes were spun for few seconds in a micro centrifuge
4. Both the tubes were incubated at 37° c overnight in a water bath.
5. The restriction is stopped by adding 0.5M EDTA (pH 8.0) to a final concentration of 10mM.
6. The DNA samples were analyzed directly on 0.8% agarose gel by adding 4.1µl of gel loading dye to each tube containing the reaction mixture were loaded into slot cast on 0.8% agarose gel containing ethidium bromide.
7. After the run was complete the gel was observed under UV transilluminator for the vector (pGPTV) and insert (Annexin) bands.

Gel Elutionprotocol

It was done according to the protocol given below (Ausubel *et al.*, 1992).

1. DNA was digested with desired restriction enzymes and fractionated electrophoretically through an agarose gel that contains ethidium bromide of 0.5mg/ml.
2. After electrophoresis, the bands were located under ultraviolet fluorescence. An incision was made in the gel ahead of the desired band (towards positive electrode. A rectangle piece of agarose was cut).
3. The agarose along with the band was taken out and transferred into fresh eppendorf tube and crushed well.
4. Then 2.5M Ammonium acetate - (350ml) was added and crushed well until the agarose completely dissolves in the tube.
5. Centrifuge at 12,000 rpm for 5min at 4° C.
6. Take supernatant in fresh eppendorf tubes and add 2.5 volumes of absolute ethanol and store at –20° C for overnight.
7. Centrifuge at 12,000 rpm for 20 min 4°C to get DNA pellet.
8. The pellet was washed with 70% ice cold ethanol.
9. This was centrifuged at 12,000 rpm for 10 min at 4° C.
10. The pellet was dried in speed vacuum desiccator for 5 to 7 min and dissolved in 50ml of 1X TE.
11. The insert (Annexin) band was eluted. The pGPTV vector band was eluted.
12. Their concentration of plasmid DNA was estimated by the spot method

Protocol for Estimating the Concentration of Dna in Small Volume Using Spot Test

This test is done by following the procedure given below (Ausubel *et al.*, 1992).

1. Standard solutions of known DNA concentrations were prepared in the range of 0-50 ng/µl in TE or distilled water.
2. On a piece of parafilm, 2.5µl of 5ng/µl solution of Ethidium bromide was arranged and a standard curve was prepared by mixing 2µl of standard DNA solution each. 0, 1, 5, 15, 30 and 50 ng/µl standards were used.
3. The samples of DNA fragment preparation (2µl) were mixed each with 2.5µl of Ethidium Bromide on a parafilm.
4. The parafilm was then placed on a UV transilluminator and visualized under UV light.
5. The fluorescence of the DNA fragment preparation was compared with the standard curve in order to estimate its concentration.

Ligationprotocol

It was done according to the protocol given by Krebs *et al.*, (2010).

1. A clean sterile 1.5 ml eppendorf tubes were taken.
2. In the eppendorf tube 2.8 µl (14 ng) of insert DNA (Annexin) was taken and to it 7.5 µl (75ng) of vector DNA (pGPTV) was added. This gave a molar concentration of 1:2.
3. 2µl of 10X ligase buffer and 1µl of ligase enzyme were added to each tube.
4. Double distilled water was added to the tube to make up the reaction volume to 20µl.
5. The tube containing the reaction mixture was incubated at 12° C to 14° C overnight.
6. The ligation mixture was used to transform competent *E.coli* cell to check for successful ligation reaction.

Ligation Calculations: The standard statement goes that:

1µg OF DNA having 1000 bp = 1.52 PICOMOLES

- pGPTV (DNA) has 13,000 bp =>
  ∴ 1 µg of pGPTV = 0.116 Pico moles.
- Annexin (insert DNA) has 1200 bp =>
  ∴ 1 µg of Annexin = 1.25 Pico moles
- Concentration of pGPTV vector DNA = 10ng/µl.
- Concentration of Annexin insert DNA =5ng/µl.
- If we have 1µg (=1000 ng) of pGPTV DNA → concentration is 0.116 picomoles.
- If we use 75ng of pGPTV DNA (by taking 7.5µl of vector of the above concentration) → we get a molarity of 0.00870 picomoles.
- Since we need a molar ratio of 1:2: vector: insert, if we take 0.00870 picomoles of vector then 0.01740 picomoles of insert will be required.
- We know that 1µg (=1000 ng) of Annexin DNA will have 1.25 picomoles. But we need 0.01740picomoles. Hence we need to take (0.01740*1000)/1.25= 14 ng of Annexin insert DNA.
- We know that concentration of Annexin insert DNA = 5 ng/µl. So to get 14 ng of Annexin we need to take 2.8µl of Annexin of this concentration.
- Thus 7.5µl of vector + 2.8µl of insert give a molar concentration of 1:2 (Lodge *et al.*, 2007).

This ligated mixture is used for preparation of transforming cells.

Protocol for Competent Cell Preparation

The competent cells were prepared according to the procedure given below by Sambrook *et al.*, (1989).

1. 20μl of bacterial glycerol stock was added to 8ml of LB media.
2. The test tube was incubated overnight at 37° C on the orbital shaker.
3. The culture was scaled up by adding 0.6ml of the grown culture into 25ml LB broth. The culture was incubated for 3 hours at 37° C on a shaker.
4. The cells were aseptically transferred to sterile centrifuged tubes. The culture was cooled to 0° C by storing the tubes on ice for 5 minutes.
5. The cells were recovered by centrifugation at 6,000 rpm for 6 minutes at 4° C. (Higher rpm causes formation of a hard pellet and hence 6,000 rpm is ideal for pelleting the cells).
6. The media was decanted from the cell pellet. The tubes were kept in inverted position for 1 minute on a tissue paper to allow the last traces of media to drain away.
7. The pellet was resuspended in 5ml of ice cold 100mM $CaCl_2$, and stored on ice for 20 minutes. The tubes were swirled intermittently for the pellet to completely dissolve in $CaCl_2$.
8. The cells were recovered by centrifugation at 6,000 rpm for 6 minutes at 4° C.
9. The supernatant was decanted from the cell pellet, and tubes were kept in inverted position for 1 minute to allow the last traces of supernatant to drain away.
10. The pellet was resuspended in 1.5ml of 100mM $CaCl_2$. The cells are now competent and can either be used for transformation or can be stored frozen.

Transformation of Competent Cells

The competent cells were transformed by following the protocol given below (Sambrook *et al.*, 1989).

1. Three sterile eppendorf tubes were taken and labeled appropriately. The following were added to each of the tubes.
   (a) 150μl of competent cells alone. (To be plated on LB plain).
   (b) 150μl of competent cells alone. (To be plated on LB Kan plate).
   (c) 150μl of competent cells + ligated samples were added.
2. The tubes were stored on ice for 20 minutes.
3. The tubes were transferred to water bath for 100 seconds at 42° C to give it the heat shock. This period is sufficient for transformation to get effected. The tubes were rapidly transferred to an ice bath. They were allowed to chill for 2 minutes.
4. 900μl of LB broth was added to each tube and the tubes were incubated on a shaker at 37° C for 1 hour to allow the bacteria to recover and express the antibiotic resistance marker encoded by the plasmid.
5. The tubes were centrifuged at 6,000 rpm for 3 minutes to pellet the cells. The cells were then dissolved in 150μl of fresh LB broth and plated.

6. The tube containing only competent cells was plated on LB plain, LB (Amp) and LB (Kan) plates.
7. Tubes containing competent cells with ligated samples were plated on LB (Kan) plates.

Protocol for Triparental Mating

It was carried out according to the protocol given below (Sambrook *et al.*, 1989).

1. *Agrobacterium tumefaciens* LBA 4404 was streaked to get isolated colonies on AB minimal medium with 10µg Rifampicin and incubate at 28° C.
2. Both *E.coli* having pRK-2013 and *E.coli* having pGPTV with gene of interest were separately streaked to get isolated colonies on LB agar medium containing 50µg/ml Kanamycin and incubated at 37° C overnight.
3. One loopful each of pRK 2013, pGPTV–Annexin and *Agrobacterium* strain LBA 4404 were mixed on yeast extract peptone plate without any antibiotics and incubated at 28° C for 12-18 hours.
4. A loopful of mixed culture from YEP plate was taken and diluted with 1ml of 0.9% NaCl, made serial dilutions till 10^{-6}.
5. 200µl of 10^{-1} & 10^{-3} dilutions were taken and spread on AB minimal medium containing 50µg/ml Kanamycin, 10µg/ml Rifampicin and 100µg/ml Streptomycin and incubated at 28° C for 2 days and then observed for the growth.
6. Isolated colonies were observed in plates containing 10^{-1}-and 10^{-4} dilutions.

Agrobacterium Plasmid DNA Isolation

The agrobacterium plasmid DNA was isolated according to the protocol given below (Sambrook *et al.*, 1989).

1. One colony from 10^{-1} AB-KRS plate was taken in a sterile toothpick and inoculated in 10ml of LB broth, having appropriate antibiotics and incubated at 28° C overnight.
2. The culture was centrifuged at 6,000 rpm for 6 minutes at 4° C.
3. The supernatant was discarded and the pellet was dissolved by adding 1ml of solution–I and incubated at room temperature for 10 minutes.
4. 2 ml of freshly prepared solution – II was added and mixed by inverting the tubes and incubated at room temperature for 10 minutes.
5. 300µl of Alkaline Phenol was added and mixed by vortexing.
6. Immediately 150µl of 3M sodium acetate was added and mixed by inversion and incubated at -20° C for 20 minutes.
7. It was then centrifuged at 10,000 rpm for 3 minutes and the supernatant was collected quickly.
8. To the supernatant 12µl of RNase 'A' was added (10mg/ml) and incubated at 37° C for 30 minutes.

9. Equal volume of phenol: chloroform was added and mixed by inversion and centrifuged at 12,000 rpm for 12 minutes at 28° C.
10. The aqueous phase was collected and equal volume of phenol: chloroform was added again centrifuged at 12,000 rpm for 12 minutes at 28° C.
11. Aqueous phase was collected and equal volume of chloroform: isoamyl alcohol (24:1) was added and mixed by inversion and centrifuged at 12,000 rpm for 10 minutes at 28° C.
12. The aqueous phase was collected and 2 volumes of ice-cold 96% ethanol was added and mixed by inversion.
13. It was then kept at – 20° C for 1-2 hours and then centrifuged at 12000 rpm for 12 minutes at 4° C.
14. The supernatant was discarded and the pellet was dried in speed vacuum desiccator.
15. The pellet was suspended in 25µl of TE.
16. 10 µl of DNA was used for running on an agarose gel, 1-2µl for back transformation of *Agrobacterium* into *E.coli.*

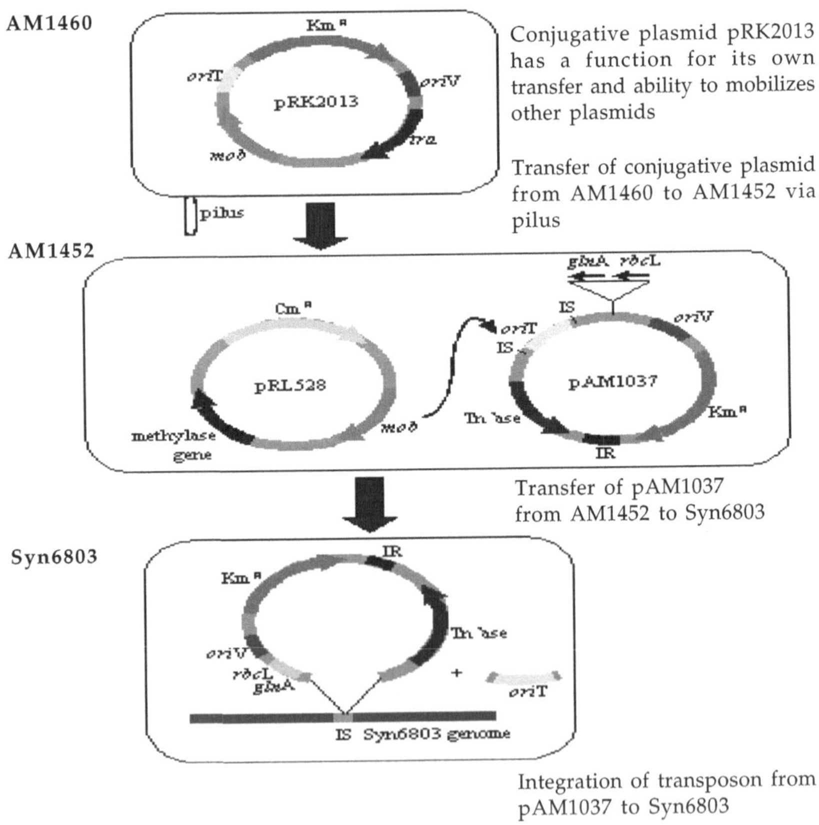

Fig. 4.1: Schematic Representation of Tri parental Mating. (*Courtesy:* Mo Bi Tec Molecular Biotechnology)

Confirming the Presence of the Gene of Interest

Isolation of Genomic DNA

The genomic DNA was isolated according to the procedure given below (Sambrook *et al.*, 1989).

Day 1 procedure:

1. 150mg of tobacco callus growing on selection media was crushed in 500µl of extraction buffer in eppendorf tubes.
2. The samples were incubated at 50° C for 10 minutes and then 500µl of sevag (chloroform: isoamyl alcohol 24:1) was added
3. The tubes were kept on shaker for 15 minutes.
4. They were then centrifuged at 12,000 rpm for 12 minutes at room temperature.
5. Following the centrifugation, the supernatant was transferred to a fresh eppendorf tube and DNA was precipitated by adding equal volume of isopropanol (500µl) and 0.5 volume of 5M NaCl and tubes were incubated at 20° C for overnight.

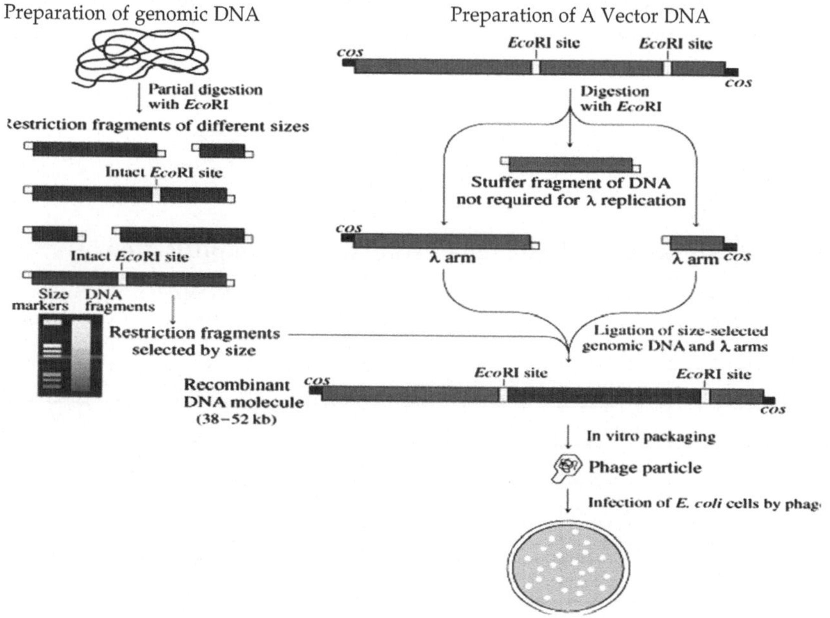

Fig. 4.2: Schematic Representation of Gene Cloning.
(*Courtesy:* Mo Bi Tec Molecular Biotechnology)

Day 2 procedure:

1. The DNA was recovered by centrifugation at 12,000 rpm for 12 minutes at 4° C. The pellet was washed with 1ml of absolute ethanol and the pellet was resuspended in 500µl of TE.

2. 10μl of RNase 'A' was added and incubated at 37° C for 30 minutes.
3. Following the 30 minutes incubation, equal volumes of phenol: chloroform (1:1) was added and centrifuged at 12,000-rpm for12 minutes at room temperature. This step was repeated twice.
4. Equal volume of chloroform: isoamyl alcohol (24:1) was added and centrifuged at 12,000 rpm for 12 minutes at room temperature.
5. Then the DNA was reprecipitated by adding 0.1 volume of 3M sodium acetate and 2 volumes of absolute alcohol to the aqueous layer and incubated at -20° C overnight.
6. DNA was recovered by centrifugation at 12,000 rpm for 12 minutes at 4° C and the pellet was air-dried.
7. The pellet was washed with 1ml of 70% ethanol.
8. Using speed vacuum desiccator the pellet was dried for 5 minutes and resuspended in 50μl of TE buffer.
9. 10μl of samples was used for loading and bands were observed.

Polymerase Chain Reaction

Polymerase chain reaction (PCR) is a technique which is used to amplify the number of copies of a specific region of DNA, in order to produce enough DNA to be adequately tested. This was first produced by Kerry Mullis in 1985 and received the Nobel Prize for developing PCR in 1993. This technique can be used to identify with a very high-probability, disease-causing viruses and/ or bacteria, a deceased person, or a criminal suspect (Bartlett *et al.*, 2003).

PROTOCOL:

Table 4.14: Showing total reaction mixture for PCR amplification

Sl. No.	Plasmid DNA	Genomic DNA	10x buffer (μl)	4dNTPs mixture (μl)	Forward Primer (μl)	Reverse Primer (μl)	Taq Polymerase (μl)	DD water (μl)
1.	–	7.50	2.5	2.25	0.75	0.75	0.75	10.50
2.	1.50	6.00	2.5	2.25	0.75	0.75	0.75	10.50
3.	–	6.00	2.5	2.25	0.75	0.75	0.75	12.00
4.	1.50	6.50	2.5	2.25	0.75	0.75	0.75	10.00
5.	–	9.50	2.5	2.25	0.75	0.75	0.75	8.50
6.	–	10.00	2.5	2.25	0.75	0.75	0.75	8.00
7.	–	10.00	2.5	2.25	0.75	0.75	0.75	6.50
8.	1.00	15.00	2.5	2.25	0.75	0.75	0.75	3.00

The genomic DNA, which was extracted from the transformed tobacco plants, was subjected to PCR amplification in order to confirm the presence of gene of interest. All the above mentioned ingredients were mixed and prepared for the total number of reactions including negative control with a primer, DNA template and Taq polymerase. The content of the tubes are mixed with brief spin and then tubes were placed in the PCR amplification machine with the program set.

Forward primer – 5′ CTG AAT GAT CTG CAG GAC GAGG 3′

Reverse primer - 3′ GCC AAC GCT ATG TCC CGA TGA 5′

These are the primers for neomycin phosphotransferase II which is present in pGPTV.

The PCR works on the following principle steps of:

Denaturation: At 94° C for 5 minutes

Annealing of primers: At 55°C a melting temperature of primers dictates 1 minute because, higher the annealing temperature more specific the reaction would be

Td = 4(G+C) + 2(A+T)

Td = Temperature at which one half of the primers are annealed to their target sequence.

Enzymatic extension: At 72° C for 1 minute. This temperature is determined by optimum temperature for polymerase activity (McPherson *et al.*, 1995).

The steps were programmed, so as to be repeated for 35 cycles to get the amplified DNA.

Plant Tissue Culture

Introduction to Plant Tissue Culture

Plant tissue culture is the science of growing plant cells, tissues or organs isolated from the mother plant on an artificial media. Tissue culture is commonly used as a collective term to describe all kinds of in-vitro plant cultures. Tissue cultures are started from pieces of whole plants, which are called as explants. Plant tissue culture is also widely termed as Micro propagation and in-vitro clonal selection (Bottino, 1981).

Plant material will only grow in-vitro when provided with specialized media. A medium usually consists of a solution of salts supplying the major and minor elements necessary for the growth of whole plants together with various vitamins, amino acids, carbohydrate source (e.g., sucrose).

To replace the carbon, which the plant normally fixes from the atmosphere by photosynthesis. To improve growth many media also include plant growth regulators, one of the most commonly used media is the MS media (Murashige and Skoog) developed in 1962.

Protocol for Media Preparation

1. The constituents given in the table 4.15 were weighed and dissolved in 500ml of double distilled water. The contents are mixed thoroughly on a magnetic stirrer.
2. The volume was made to 1 litre with double distilled water
3. The ph was adjusted to 5.6-5.8 with 1N NaOH.

4. The agar was weighed and added to the solution and melted.
5. Then the media was poured into the culture bottles and it was sealed and autoclaved (Murashige and Skoog 1962).

Table 4.15: Composition of MS media

	Elements	Mg/lit.
1.	**Major Elements**	
	NH_4NO_3	1650
	KNO_3	1900
	$MgSO_4.7H_2O$	370
	$CaCl_2.2H_2O$	440
	KH_2PO_4	170
2.	**Minor Elements**	
	$MnSO_4.4H_2O$	22.3
	KI	0.83
	H_3BO_3	6.2
	$ZnSO_4.7H_2O$	8.6
	$CuSO_4.5H_2O$	0.025
	$Na_2Mo_4.2H_2O$	0.25
	$CoCl_2.6H_2O$	0.025
	$FeSO_4.7H_2O$	27.8
	Sodium EDTA	37.8
3.	**Vitamins**	
	Pyridine HCl	0.5
	Nicotinic Acid	0.5
	Thiamine HCl	0.1
	Myoinositol	100
4.	**Amino Acid**	
	Glycine	2.0
5.	**Sucrose**	30,000
6.	**Gelrite**	8,000

Surface Sterilization of Explants

Explants are of different kinds and the correct choice of explants material is important:

1. Leaves from 4-week-old healthy tobacco and tomato plants were taken and cut on the margins using a sterile scalpel to get leaf discs of about .2 cm × .2 cm.
2. All these leaf discs were placed in regeneration medium with adaxial portions downwards (as it is the most responsive portion to nutrients, and the leaf tissue of the leaf to cease growing and dividing) and incubated under conditions of light and temperature in the growth room for 2 days.

Leaves are surface sterilized. Tween-20 (detergent) acts as a surfactant and removes the dirt from the surface of leaves. Mercuric chloride acts as a sterilant and kills any microorganism present in the leaves. Providing aseptic techniques are strictly adhered to during excision and transfer to culture medium.

1. Wash the tobacco and tomato leaves in water containing few drops of tween-20 solution for 8 minutes with intermittent shaking under sterile conditions and decant the water.
2. Continue washing the leaves with sterile double distilled water until lather is completely removed.
3. Swab the laminar airflow cabinet with 70% methanol within the cabinet, rinse the leaves with autoclaved double distilled water three times.
4. Treat leaves with 70% ethanol for 30-40 seconds.
5. The leaves are treated with 0.1% mercuric chloride solution for 2-2.5 minutes.
6. Wash with autoclaved double distilled water five times for 1.5-2 minutes each (George 1993).

Co-Cultivation of Tobacco Leaf Discs with *Agrobacterium tumefaciens*

The isolated colonies of *Agrobacterium* (from 10^{-1} AB-KRS plate of TPM) having recombinant plasmid were inoculated in LB broth containing kanamycin (50 mg/ml) and were incubated overnight at 28° C.

1. The pre-incubated tobacco leaf discs were put in a sterile bottle containing*Agrobacterium tumifaceins* culture. The culture had to be diluted with LB broth such that the broth contains 5×10^8 cell/ ml (usually 1:20 dilutions for an overnight culture). It was swirled gently for 10 minutes.
2. The leaf discs were taken out; the excess of culture was blotted on a filter paper.
3. The infected leaf discs were transferred to a regenerating (RT) medium and incubated for 2 days in dark.
4. During this time, the virulence genes in the bacteria would have been induced, the bacteria would be bound to the plant cells around the wounded edge of the explants and the gene transfer process would have occurred (Newell 2000).

Selection Media Transfer

After the transformation had occurred, the leaf discs were given final wash with double distilled water for 3 to 4 times with Augmentin. Then the leaf discs were transferred to the selection media.

The Selection medium contains Augmentin (250 mg/ ml), Cefatoxin (200 mg/ml) and Kanamycin (50 mg/ml). Augmentin is added to prevent the excessive multiplication of *Agrobacterium,* Cefatoxin is added to prevent the growth of any other bacteria on the medium and *Kanamycin* is added to inhibit the growth of non-transformed plant cells. The leaf discs were blotted on sterile filter paper and placed on the selection media and incubated for obtaining regenerates.

After two weeks of incubation the transformed cells grew into callus and showed initiation of shoots. During the fourth week the direct regenerates were transferred to fresh regeneration media containing 250 mg/ ml Augmentin and 50 mg/ ml Kanamycin for proper establishment of the regenerate (George 1993).

RESULTS AND DISCUSSIONS

Plasmid Isolation and Purification

The plasmid DNA of pUC 19 vector having the desired Annexin gene (3Kbp) and the plasmid DNA of the binary vector pGPTV (13 Kbp) were isolated from *E.coli* (DH5á strain) by alkaline lysis method and their isolation was confirmed by plasmid DNA bands obtained in agarose gel electrophoresis as shown in the figure 4.3.

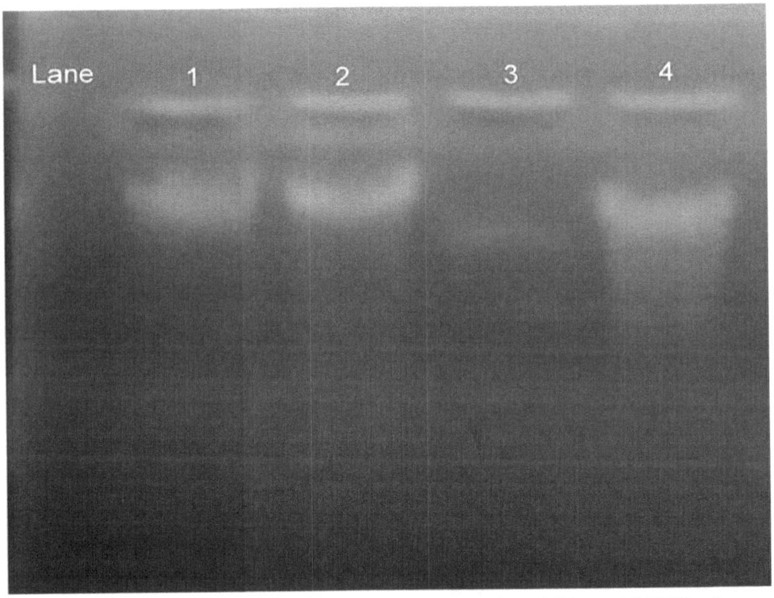

Fig. 4.3: Gel Documentation Showing the Isolated Plasmid DNA of pUC 19 Vector with Annexin Gene and Plasmid DNA of pGPTV Vector

Lane 1 and 2- plasmid DNA of pUC 19,Lane 3 and 4- plasmid DNA of pGPTV vector.

Restriction Digestion

The purified pUC 19/Annexin and pGPTV plasmid were restriction digested using the restriction enzymes EcoRI and XbaI. Both these enzymes cut the plasmid at the multiple cloning sites and produce blunt ends. After restriction digestion 40µl of the digested product was run on 0.8% agarose gel. On visualization of the gel, two band patterns were observed as in figure 4.4. Lane 1-showing the digested product of pUC19 with Annexin gene. The first band is the plasmid DNA of pUC19 vectors and the second band is the gene of our interest, Annexin. During restriction digestion the enzymes EcoRI and XbaI cut at the multiple cloning sites between which the Annexin gene lies. This separates the Annexin gene from the plasmid vector carrying it and gives us a separated band of Annexin which is as observed in lane 1. Lane 2 shows the undigested form of pUC19 plasmid. Lane 3 shows digested band of pGPTV vector. The restriction enzymes have cut open the circular pGPTV DNA by removing a small part in the plasmid making it a linear one. Hence two bands are observed first band being pGPTV plasmid vector of our interest and second band part is the eluted part. Lane 4 shows the undigested circular pGPTV plasmid vector. The bands obtained on the gel show good quality of insert Annexin and vector pGPTV which confirms the successful restriction digestion with EcoRI and XbaI. The vector and insert thus obtained can be further used for ligation reaction. The digested plasmid shown in the band pattern in the gel were cut by gel elution technique and purified from other reaction mixture. Then the dot spot test was done to calculate the concentration of pGPTV and Annexin gene.

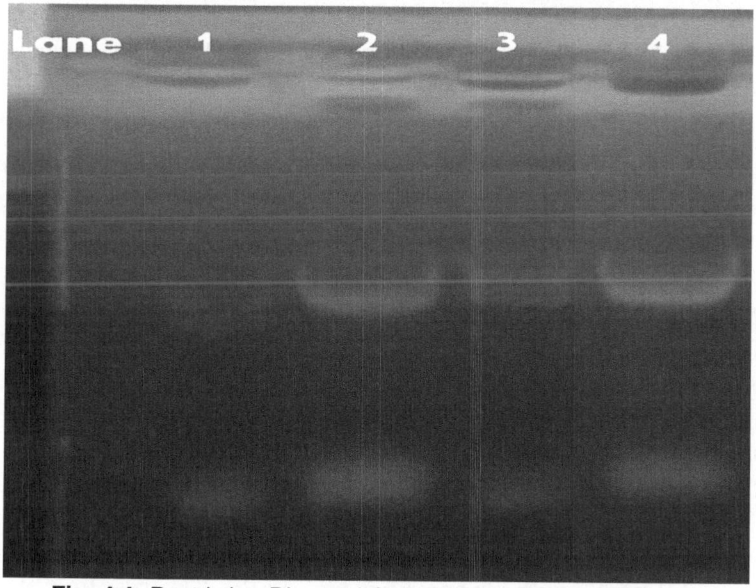

Fig. 4.4: Restriction Digested Samples Showing Separated Bands of pUC 19 Vector/Annexin Gene and pGPTV Vector

Lane 1- digested pUC 19 with Annexin gene, Lane 2- undigested pUC 19, Lane 3- digested pGPTV and Lane 4- undigested pGPTV vector.

Dot spot test to calculate the concentration of pGPTV plasmid and Annexin gene

The concentration of pGPTV and Annexin gene obtained from gel elution was determined by Dot spot test method by comparing it with the spots of known concentration of standard DNA under UV transillumination. The concentration of the pGPTV (denoted as V in the Fig. 4.5) and Annexin gene (denoted as I in the Fig. 4.5) was found to be 10ng/µl and 5ng/µl respectively.

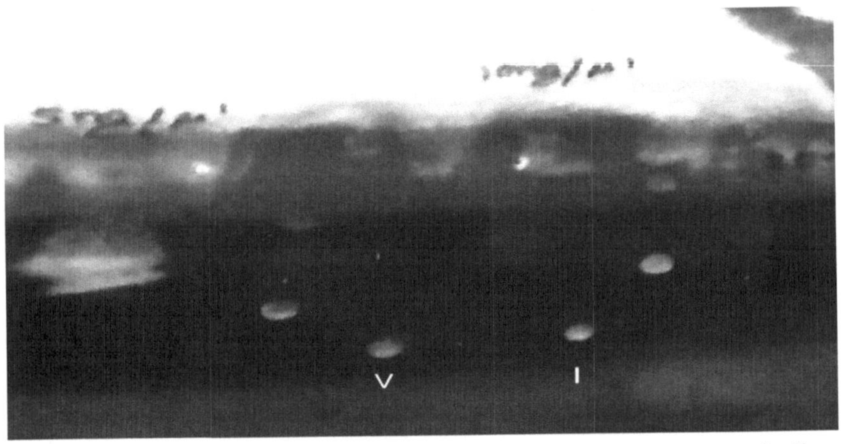

Fig. 4.5: Dot Spot Test showing the Concentration of Insert Gene Annexin (I) and Vector pGPTV (V) with Different known Concentration of Standard DNA

Ligation of the insert annexin gene with the vector pGPTV

The ligation reaction mixtures of pGPTV and Annexin gene were mixed in the ratios 1:2 The concentration of plasmid was lesser than the concentration of Annexin gene. Later the ligated mixture was used for the preparation of transforming cells.

Transfer of the ligated pGPTV vector carrying Annexin gene

The ligated pGPTV vector carrying Annexin gene was transferred to the competent cells of *E.coli* (DH5αstrain) without any antibiotic resistance plasmid. The competent cells were prepared by using the calcium chloride heat shock method which was later used for transformation.

The competent cells without being treated with ligation mixture were plated on LB agar plate with Kanamycin Fig. 4.6(a) and the competent cells that were prepared by using the calcium chloride heat shock method were grown on LB broth with Kanamycin Fig. 4.6(b). The results obtained are depicted in the Fig. 4.6(a) and Fig. 4.6(b). Competent cells alone that were plated on LB agar plate with Kanamycin was a negative control since it showed no growth on the plate, Fig. 4.6(a) and Competent cells transformed with pGPTV/ Annexin vector showed growth on the LB plate with Kanamycin Fig. 4.6(b).

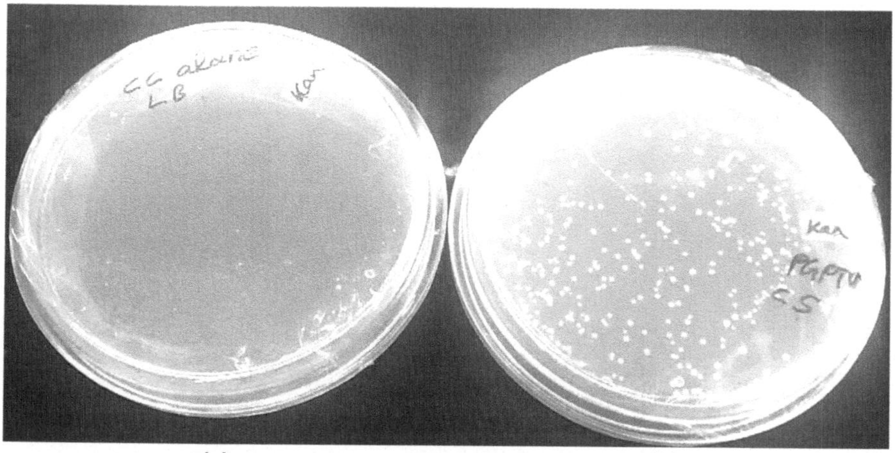

(a) (b)

Fig 4.6: Culture Plates of LB Broth with Kanamycin

Plate(a) showing the absence of growth of CC, Plate(b) showing the growth of CC confirming the successful transfer of pGPTV/Annexin gene ligation mixture to CC.

The growth in plate (b) confirms the successful ligation of Annexin gene with pGPTV vector. The presence of nptII gene (found in association with Annexin gene) gives resistance to kanamycin, begin the reason behind the growth of competent cells on plate (b).

Tri Parental Mating

The Tri Parental Mating (TPM) was carried out by using *Agrobacterium* LBA4404 strain, *E.coli* strain pRK 2013 (having helper plasmid) and DH5αstrain of *E.coli* containing pGPTV with Annexin gene plasmid. All these bacterial strains were first streaked separately on the plane LB media and Fig. 4.7(a) shows the three strains used for TPM. The three bacterial colonies grown on LB media were mixed, serially diluted and spread on the Antibiotic (AB) medium containing three antibiotics Kanamycin, Rifampicin and Streptomycin media to prove the successful transfer of Annexin gene into *Agrobacterium* by TPM and to check whether the transformants possess the Annexin gene Fig. 4.7(b). These isolated colonies of *Agrobacterium* were used for the co-cultivations with leaf disc.

Plant Tissue Culture; Agrobacterium Infection to Leaf Disc

The tobacco and tomato leaf discs were infected with *Agrobacterium* by Co-cultivation method. The infected leaf discs were inoculated on the regeneration media (RT) and incubated to allow the growth of *Agrobacterium*. After incubation, leaf discs were transferred to ST media. Only the transformed leaf discs survived on this media as the media contained kanamycin and *Agrobacterium* growth was reduced by the action of cephatoxin.

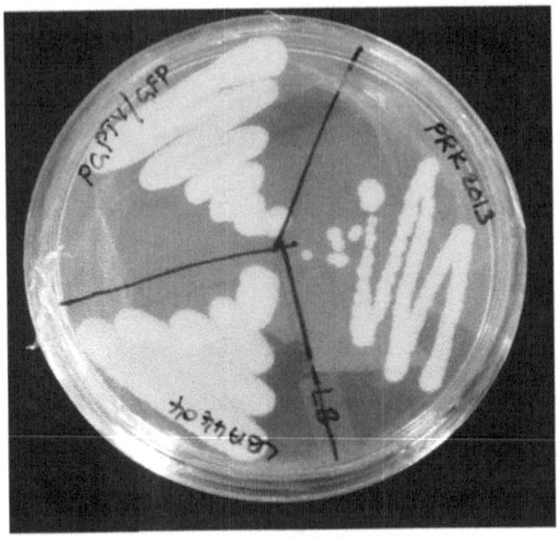

(a)

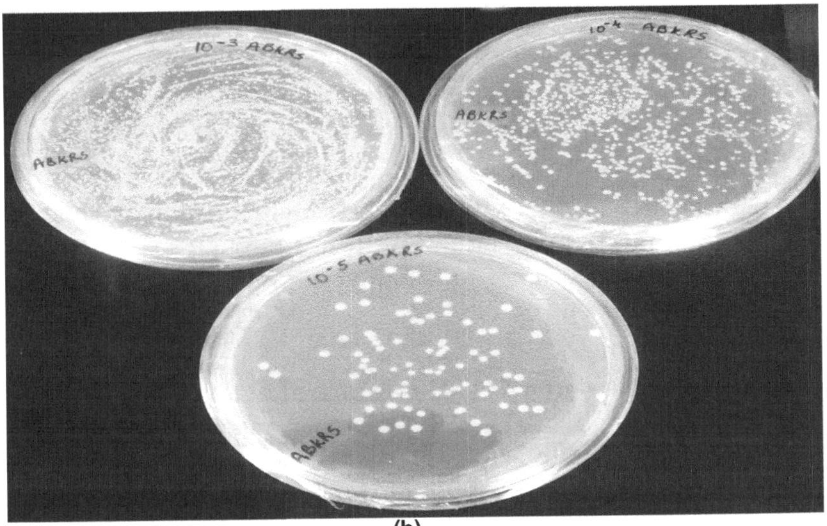

(b)

Fig. 4.7: Culture Plates showing Tri Parental Mating (TPM)
(a) The Three Cultures used for TPM. (b) Dilutions of
Transformed Colonies Obtained from TPM

Fig. 4.8(a) and Fig. 4.10(a) Shows the growth of *Agrobacterium* infected leaf disc in RT medium. The growth was observed as a slimy layer of *Agrobacterium* formed around the tobacco and tomato leaf discs respectively. Fig. 4.8(b) and Fig. 4.10 (b) showing the leaf discs transferred from RT to ST media. Fig. 4.8(c) and Fig. 4.10(c) shows the development of leaf disc into callus after 15-20 in ST media. After the degeneration of the old media, the callus was supplemented with fresh medium to grow. After 70-80 days growth of tobacco and tomato plantlets were observed (Fig. 4.9 and 4.11). This was used for genomic DNA isolation.

Fig. 4.8: Culture Bottles showing Methods Involved in Plant Tissue Culture carried out with *Agrobacterium* Infected Leaf Discs of Tobacco. (a) Leaf Discs of Tobacco Inoculated on Regeneration Media (RT) (b) Leaf Discs of Tobacco Transferred to Selection Media (ST) from RT Media, (c) Transgenic Callus Growth was Observed from the Infected Leaf Discs of Tobacco

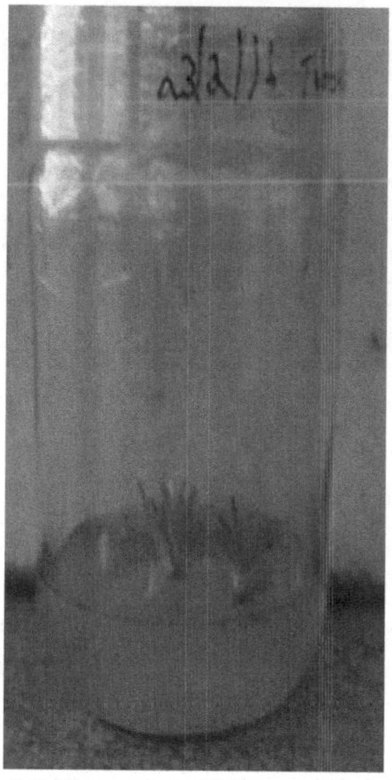

Fig. 4.9: Transgenic Tobacco Plantlets

Fig. 4.10: Pictures showing Methods Involved in Plant Tissue Culture carried out with *Agrobacterium* Infected Leaf Discs of Tomato. (a) Leaf Discs Inoculated on RT Media, (b) Leaf Discs Transferred to ST Media, (c) Transgenic Callus Growth was Observed from the Infected Leaf Discs of Tomato

Fig. 4.11: Transgenic Tomato Plantlets

Genomic DNA Isolation

The genomic DNA was isolated from the transgenic plantlets grown on ST media by using CTAB extraction method. The DNA isolated from the plantlets of transgenic tobacco and transgenic tomato along with gel loading dye were run on agarose gel in different lanes. A good concentration and pure quality of bands were obtained on the gel which was eluted to check for the presence of Annexin gene in the transformed plants. The presence of Annexin gene in the genomic DNA of tobacco and tomato plantlets were confirmed by comparison with non-transgenic plant's genomic DNA samples (Fig. 4.12).

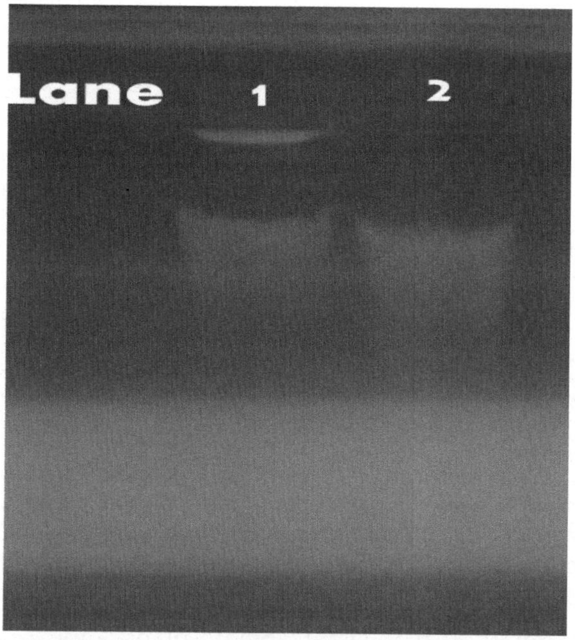

Fig. 4.12: Gel Documentation showing the Genomic DNA of Transgenic Plantlets. Lane 1: Band Obtained from Genomic DNA Isolated from the Plantlets of Transgenic Tobacco. Lane 2: Band Obtained from Genomic DNA Isolated from the Plantlets of Transgenic Tomato

Polymerase Chain Reaction (PCR) results to confirm successful transformation of Tobacco and Tomato plants into Transgenic plants

In order to confirm the presence or absence of Annexin gene in the transgenic plants, the Genomic DNA of the transgenic pantlets, genomic DNA of transformed plantlets + plasmid DNA, were subjected to PCR amplification and the results were interpreted based on the observation of the band thickness and its clarity after subjecting them to gel electrophoresis. The nptII (neomycin phosphotransferase) gene (800 bp) was used as selectable marker system to show the presence of gene of interest. Forward and Reverse primer for nptII gene was used to carry out the PCR analysis and its amplification confirmed the presence of Annexin gene in the recombinant plantlets.

For PCR analysis of Tobacco plant, Lane1, Lane 2, Lane 3, Lane 4, Lane 6, Lane 7 and Lane 8 were loaded with the genomic DNA obtained from the transgenic tobacco plantlets. The presence of Annexin gene was confirmed by the amplified bands that were clearly visible. For the purpose of comparison, the genomic DNA sample of non-transgenic tobacco plant (as negative control) was loaded in Lane 5, which showed no amplification in the band due to absence of nptII gene (Fig. 4.13).

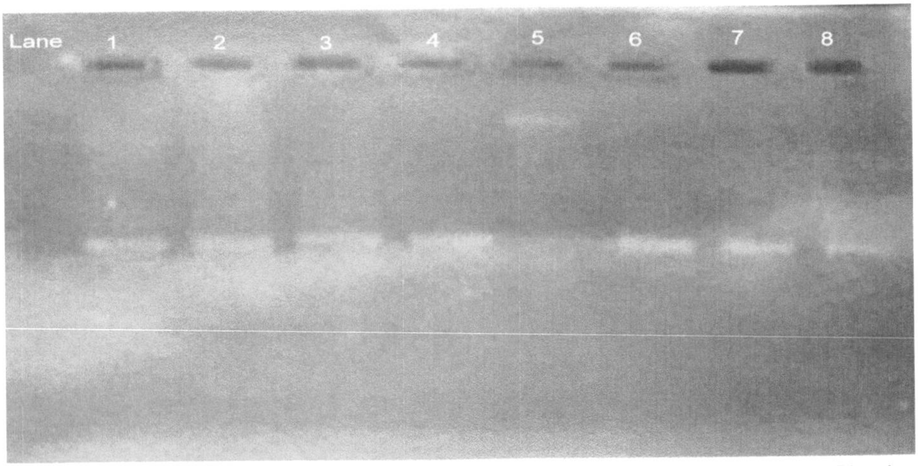

Fig. 4.13: Profile of PCR Amplified DNA (Genomic DNA of Transformed Tobacco Plantlets and Genomic DNA of Non-transformed Tobacco Plant). Lane 1, 3, 6 and 7: Genomic DNA Sample 1, 3, 5 and 6 of Transformed Tobacco Plantlets. Lane 2, 4 and 8: Genomic DNA Sample 2, 4 and 7 of Transformed Tobacco Plantlets + Plasmid DNA. Lane 5: Genomic DNA Sample of Non-transformed Tobacco Plantlets

Simalarly, for PCR analysis of Tomato plant, Lane 2, Lane 3, Lane 4, Lane 5, Lane 6, Lane 7 and Lane 8 were loaded with the genomic DNA obtained from the transgenic tomato plantlets. The presence of Annexin gene was confirmed by the amplified bands that were clearly visible. The genomic DNA sample of non-transgenic tomato plant was loaded in Lane 1 which did not shown amplification because of the absence of nptII gene (Fig. 4.14).

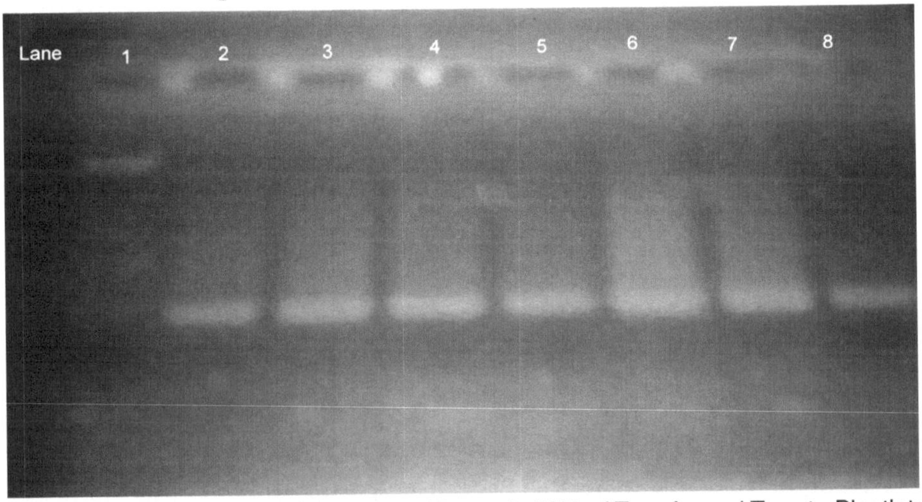

Fig. 4.14: Profile of PCR Amplified DNA (Genomic DNA of Transformed Tomato Plantlets and Genomic DNA of Non-transformed Tomato Plant). Lane 1: Genomic DNA Sample of Non-transformed Tomato Plantlets, Lane 2, 4, 5, 6 and 7: Genomic DNA Sample 1, 3, 4, 5, and 6 of Transformed Tomato Plantlets, Lane 3 and 8: Genomic DNA Sample 2 and 7 of Transformed Tomato Plantlets + Plasmid DNA

In the previous study, the annexin gene was isolated from the plasmid DNA of pUC19 which was incorporated into pGPTV vector. The pGPTV vector having Annexin gene was then transferred to competent cells which was then transferred into *Agrobacterium tumifaceins* by Tri Parental Mating method. The sterilized leaf discs of Tobacco and Tomato plants were infected with *Agrobacterium tumifaceins* having annexin gene by co-cultivation method and were allowed to develop into plantlets whose genomic DNA were isolated. The genomic DNA thus obtained were subjected to PCR analysis with plasmid DNA along with the genomic DNA of transformed plantlets which served as a positive control and the genomic DNA of non-transformed plant served as a negative control. The result observed at the end of PCR analysis was the amplification the bands of nptII gene confirming the successful transformation of both Tobacco and Tomato with annexin gene. Genetic manipulation of tomato plant (*Lycopersicum esculantum)* through *Agrobacterium tumefaciens* to form a transgenic plant by incorporating the annexin gene into plant's genomic DNA (Mishra *et al.*, 2010).

Broothaerts *et al.*, (2005) have shown that non *Agrobacterium* species-*Rhizobium* sp.NGR234, *Sinorhizobium meliloti* and *Mesorhizobium loti* are capable of genetically transforming different plant tissues and plant species but their advantage over *agrobacterium* is not yet confirmed and *Agrobacterium* remains the most favored tool for plant genetic engineering. Thus, we attempted the transfer of Annexin gene through *Agrobacterium* into tomato and tobacco.

Zhongbao *et al.*, (2015) had previously identified and characterized annexin gene in *Arabidopsis thaliana* and rice and they also isolated and characterize the annexin genes in maize across a whole genome using bioinformatics, microarray and real time PCR methods. Annexins act as targets of calcium signals in eukaryotic cells and recent results have revealed that they play an important role in plant stress responses by up regulation of mRNA to overexpress AnnAt1 protein found in Arabidopsis (Konopka-Postupolska *et al.*, 2009).

Mortimer *et al.*, (2008) observed that hydrogen peroxide accumulation in guard cells was reduced in overexpressing plants and increased in knockout plants both before and after treatment with abscisic acid. Oxidative protection resulting from AnnAt1 overexpression could be due to the low level of intrinsic peroxidase activity exhibited by this protein in vitro. The in vitro properties of annexins and their known dynamic distribution patterns suggests that they could be central regulators or effectors of plant growth and plant stress signaling. Potentially, they could operate in signaling pathways involving cytosolic free calcium and reactive oxygen species.

In the present study tobacco and tomato leaves were infected with *Agrobacterium tumefaciens* by co-cultivation at the range of 26 to 28° C. Many studies were conducted on Co-cultivation of host plants with *Agrobacterium tumefaciens* at different temperatures ranging from 24° C-28° C for transformation of plants like tobacco, soybean, rice, potato and cotton (Krugel *et al.*, 2002; Paz *et al.*, 2006; Terada *et al.*, 2004; Anderson *et al.*, 2003 and Leelavathi *et al.*, 2004). *Agrobacterium tumefaciens* mediated transformation is generally used for genetic transformation of higher plants. Several experimental factors important for the increase of β-Glucuronidase (GUS) reporter gene activity were evaluated by Sunjung (2006) in her study using leaf disks of tobacco and also found that co-cultivation at a temperature of 20° C to be the most critical factor to obtain the reproducible enhancement of GUS activity, but at 25° C the highest GUS activity and transformation efficiency were seen. The effect of temperature on Co-cultivation of Agrobacterium mediated plant transformation was tested by Dillen *et al.*, (1997)andKapila *et al.*, (1997). The pattern of plant annexin gene expression was studied by Margret *et al.*, (1992) from tomato, potato and barley.

We utilized *in vivo* grown tomato and tobacco plants for co-cultivation with *A.tumefaciens* and the transformed callus tissue was obtained by using cefatoxin, kanamycin and augmentin which prevented the excessive growth of *A.tumefaciens* and other bacterial cells by allowing only the kanamycin resistant ones to grow. Shantha *et al.*,(2012) have shown the genetic manipulation of tomato (*Lycopersicum esculentum*) plant with Wheat Germ Agglutinin (WGA) gene using *Agrobacterium* mediated transformation in order to get resistance against the insects through the use of insect control protein gene, a glycoprotein with molecular weight of 34000 Da. Toxic effect appears to be mediated through binding of the lectins (WGA) to glycoproteins in the insect leading to the disruption of gut epithelial cells and are believed to be nature's own insecticides.

Transgenic tomato plants that express an *anti-Salmonella enterica* single chain variable fragment (ScFv) have been produced. It is an antibody that binds to lipopolysaccharide of *S. enterica*, was used as a tool diagnosis and detection, as a therapeutic agent, and in applications such as water system purification (Richard *et al.*, 2007). Sharma *et al.*,(2009) reported that *Agrobacterium tumefaciens* mediated transfer of DNA is a natural method of transformation of plants and this technology has been used for the production of transgenic tomatoes expressing a variety of heterologous proteins like the beta amyloid protein, used as a vaccine against Alzheimer's disease and human factor IX. The transgenic plants obtained in this study will further have to be subjected to field trails to prove their efficiency.

CONCLUSION

Plants are constantly being subjected to both abiotic and biotic stresses which cause reduction in yield, quality and growth rate. So we have to deal with some aspects of Recombinant DNA Technology and Molecular Biology in combination with Plant Tissue Culture techniques in order to produce genetically engineered plants (here tobacco and tomato plants).

To get genetically engineered tobacco and tomato plants having the desired character, we followed a standard protocol to isolate the plasmid DNA of pUC19 vector which had Annexin Gene (the gene of our interest). The plasmid DNA was subjected to restriction digestion with the help of restriction enzymes like EcoRI and XbaI to get fragments of DNA which were then subjected to electrophoresis to release Annexin gene. Then the Annexin gene was gel eluted and ligated with the help of DNA ligase enzyme. The Annexin gene from pUC19 was then incorporated into pGPTV vector. The pGPTV vector having Annexin gene was then transferred into *Agrobacterium tumifaceins* by Tri Parental Mating method. Then the leaf discs of both tomato and tobacco were infected with *Agrobacterium tumifaceins* by co-cultivation method and were cultured on MS media for 2 days and these leaf discs were transferred to ST media. In about 2 weeks, only those leaf discs which got infected by *Agrobacterium* started developing into callus and showed initiation of root and shoot. By the end of 4th week these regenerates were transferred to RT media and were allowed to grow into plantlets for 90 days.

From these plantlets the Genomic DNA was isolated and was subjected to restriction digestion. The restricted fragments were then subjected to PCR cycles for amplification of genes which was done in order to check for the presence of Annexin gene in the genomic DNA of genetically modified tobacco and tomato plants. The concentration of bands obtained by PCR showed maximum amplification of nptII gene there by confirming the successful transformation of both tobacco and tomato plants.

The presence of Annexin gene in plants makes it resistant to draught like abiotic stresses and this Annexin gene was successfully transferred into both tobacco and tomato plants by Agrobacterium mediated transformation technique efficiently. The tobacco and tomato plantlets generated by this method may also have resistance for other abiotic stress conditions like increased salinity and acidity of the soil, change in soil pH etc.

This Agrobacterium mediated transformation technique is economically cheaper and can be efficiently used for genetic modification of other commercial crops like wheat, barley, rice etc. and make them resistant to various abiotic stresses. Problems arising due to excessive requirement of water by plants can be solved by genetically modifying them by inserting Annexin gene and making them draught resistant, there by catering the needs of areas having water problems. These varieties of plants will grow efficiently even with minimum water supply and are more adaptive to any abiotic stress factors thus enabling their better growth.

REFERENCES

Alberts, B., Johnson, A. and Lewis, J. (2002): Isolating, Cloning, and Sequencing DNA. (4th ed.). Garland Science, New York.

Anderson, M., Trifonova, A., Anderson, A.B., Johansson, M., Bulow, L. and Hofvander, P.(2003): A Novel Selection System for Potato Transformation Using a Mutated AHAS Gene. *Plant Cell Reproduction*,22: 261-267.

Andrawis, A., Solomon, M. and Delmer, D. P. (1993): Cotton Fiber Annexins: A Potential Role in the Regulation of Callose Synthase. *Plant Journal,* 3: 763-772.

Ausubel, B., Kingston, M., Seidman, S. and Struh (1992): Short Protocols in Molecular Biology, II Edition, *Green Publishing Associates & John Wiley and Sons*. 34: 459-474.

Bai, S., Willard, B., Chapin, L.J., Kinter, M.T., Francis, D.M., Stead, A.D., Jones, M.L. (2010): Proteomic Analysis of Pollination-induced Corolla senescence in Petunia. *Journal of Experimental Botany,* 61: 1089-1109.

Bartlett, J.M.S. and Stirling, D. (2003): A Short History of the Polymerase Chain Reaction. *Methods in Molecular Biology*, 226: 3-6.

Bassani, M., Neumann, P.M. and Gepstein, S. (2004): Differential Expression Profiles of Growth Related Genes in the Elongation Zone of Maize Primary Roots. *Plant Molecular Biology,* 56: 367-380.

Berg, P. and Mertz, J.E. (2010): Personal Reflections on the Origins and Emergence of Recombinant DNA Technology. *Genetics,* 4(1): 9-17.

Bianco, L., Lopez, L., Scalone, A.G., Di Carli, M., Desiderjo, A., Benvenuto, E. and Perrotta, G. (2009): Strawberry Proteome Characterization and its Regulation during Fruit Ripening and in Different Genotypes. *Journal of Proteomics,* 72: 586-607.

Bottino, P.J. (1981): Methods in Plant Tissue Culture. *Kemtec Educational Corp*. Kensington, Maryland. 1: 65-72.

Boustead, C., Smallwood, M., Small, H., Bowles, D. and Walker, J.H. (1989). Identification of Ca^{2+} Dependent Phospholipid-binding Proteins in Higher Plant Cells. *FEBS Letters,* 244: 456-460.

Broothaerts, W., Mitchell, H.J., Weir, B., Kaines, S., Smith, L.M.A., Yang, W., Mayer, J.M., Roa, R.C. and Jefferson, R.A. (2005): Gene Transfer to Plants by Diverse species of Bacteria. *Nature*,433: 629-633.

Buitink, J., Leger, J.J., Guisle, I., Vu, B.L., Wuillème, S., Lamirault, G., Le Bars, A., Le Meur, N., Becker, A. and Küster, H. (2006): Transcriptome Profiling Uncovers Metabolic and Regulatory Processes Occurring during the Transition from Desiccation-sensitive to Desiccation-tolerant Stages in Medicago Truncatula Seeds. *Plant Journal,* 47: 735-750.

Charles, H.S.(1995): Introduction of Cloning Plasmids into *Agrobacterium tumefaciens*. Plant Gene Transfer and Expression Protocols. *Methods in Molecular Biology*, 49: 33-37.

Clark, G.B., Morgan, R.O., Fernandez, M.P. and Roux, S.J. (2012): Evolutionary Adaptation of Plant Annexins has Diversified Their Molecular Structures, Interactions and Functional Roles. *New Phytology*,196: 695-712.

Clark, G.B., Sessions, A., Eastburn, D.J. and Roux, S.J. (2001): Differential Expression of Members of the Annexin Multigene Family in *Arabidopsis*. *Plant Physiology,* 126: 1072-1084.

Dai, S., Lei, L., Chen, T., Chong, K., Xue, Y. and Wang, T. (2006): Proteomic Analysis of *Oryza sativa* Mature Pollen Reveal Novel Proteins Associated with Pollen Germination and Tube Growth. *Proteomics*,6: 2504-2529.

Dillen, W., De Clercq, J., Kapila, J., Zambre, M., Van Montagu, M. and Angenon, G. (1997): The Effect of Temperature on *Agrobacterium tumefaciens*-mediated Gene Transfers to Plants. *Plant Journal*, 12: 1459-1463.

Divya, K., Jami, S.K. and Kirti, P.B. (2010). Constitutive Expression of Mustard Annexin, AnnBj1 Enhances Abiotic Stress Tolerance and Fiber Quality in Cotton Under Stress. *Plant Molecular Biology*, 73: 293-308.

Dolnik, V. (1997): Capillary Zone Electrophoresis of Proteins. *Electrophoresis*, 18: 2353-2361.

Durkin, S., Brennan, E. and Wakefield, M. (2012): "Mass Media Campaigns to Promote Smoking Cessation Among Adults: An Integrative Review." *Tobacco Control*,21: 127-138.

Gallardo, K, Le Signor, C., Vandekerckhove, J., Thompson, R. D. and Burstin, J. (2003): Proteomics of Medicago Truncatula Seed Development Establishes the Time Frame of Diverse Metabolic Processes Related to Reserve Accumulation. *Plant Physiology*, 133: 664-682.

Geisow, M., Fritsche, U., Hexham, J., Dash, B. and Johnson, T. (1986): A Consensus Amino Acid Sequence Repeats in Torpedo and Mammalian Calcium-dependent Membrane Binding Proteins. *Nature*, 320: 636-638.

Gelvin, S.B. (2003): *Agrobacterium*-mediated Plant Transformation: The Biology Behind the Gene Jockeying Tool. *Microbiology and Molecular biology*,67: 16-37.

George, E.F. (1993): Plant Propagation by Tissue Culture Part I and Part II: In Practice. Second Edition, Exegetics Limited, Edington.

Goodman and Jordan. (2005): *Tobacco in History and Culture: An Encyclopaedia* (Detroit: Thomson, Gale). 15: 137-141.

Gorecka, K.M., Konopka-Postupolska, D., Hennig, J., Buchet, R. and Pikula, S. (2005): Peroxidase Activity of Annexin 1 from *Arabidopsis thaliana*. *Biochemistry and Biophysics*, 336: 868-875.

Hammond, J. and McGarvey, P. (1999): (eds.) Plant Biotechnology: New Products and Applications. 240.

Hamza, S. (1993): Reevaluation for Conditions for Plant Regeneration and *Agrobacterium* Mediated Transformation from Tomato. *Journal of Experimental Botany*, 44(12): 1837-1845.

Hayes, M.J., Rescher, U., Gerke, V. and Moss, S.E. (2004): Annexin Actin Interactions. *Traffic*. 5: 571-576.

Herbers, K. and Sonnewald, U. (1999): Production of New/Modified Proteins in Transgenic Plants. *Current Opinion Biotechnology*,10: 163-168.

Hofmann, A., Proust, J., Dorowski, A., Schantz, R. and Huber, R. (2000): Annexin 24 from *Capsicum annuum* X-ray Structure and Biochemical Characterization. *Journal of Biological Chemistry*, 275: 8072-8082.

Howard, E.A., Zupan, J., Citovsky, V. and Zambryski, P. (1992): The VirD2 Protein of *A.tumefaciens* Contains a C-terminal Bipartitie Nuclear Localization Signal: Implications for Nuclear Uptake ofDNA in Plant Cells. *Cell*, 68: 109-118.

Huh, S.M., Noh, E.K., Kim, H.G., Jeon, B.W., Bae, K., Hu, H.C., Kwak, J.M. and Park, O. K. (2010): *Arabidopsis* Annexins AnnAt1 and AnnAt4 Interact with Each Other and Regulate Drought and Salt Stress Responses. *Plant Cell Physiology*, 51: 1499-1514.

James. and Clive. (2012): "Global Status of Commercialized Biotech/GM Crops". ISSA No-44.

Jami, S.K., Clark, G.B., Ayele, B.T., Ashe, P. and Kirti, P.B. (2012): Genome-wide Comparative Analysis of Annexin Superfamily in Plants. *PLoS ONE*,7(11): e47801.

Jami, S.K., Clark, G.B., Swathi, T.A., Handley, C. and Roux, S.J. (2008): Ectopic Expression of an Annexin from *Brassica juncea* Confers Tolerance to Abiotic and Biotic Stress Treatments in Transgenic Tobacco. *Plant Physiology and Biochemistry,* 46: 1019-1030.

Jami, S.K., Dalal, A., Divya, K. and Kirti, P.B. (2009): Molecular Cloning and Characterization of Five Annexin Genes from Indian Mustard (*Brassica juncea* L.Czern and Coss). *Plant Physiology and Biochemistry,* 47: 977-990.

Jami, S.K., Hill, R.D. and Kirti, P.B. (2010): Transcriptional Regulation of Annexins in Indian Mustard, *Brassica juncea* and Detoxification of ROS in Transgenic Tobacco Plants Constitutively Expressing AnnBj1. *Plant Signal Behaviour,* 5: 618-621.

Kapila, J., De Rycke, R., Van Montagu, M. and Angenon, G. (1997). *Agrobacterium*-mediated Transient Gene Expression System for Intact Leaves. *Plant Science,*122:101-108.

Kaufman, R.I. and Nixon, B.T. (1996): Use of PCR to Isolate Genes Encoding Sigma 54-dependent Activators from Diverse Bacteria. *Journal of Bacteriology,*178(13): 3967-3970.

Ko, T. and Korban, S. (2004): Enhancing the Frequency of Somatic Embryogenesis following *Agrobacterium*-mediated Transformation of Immature Cotyledons of Soybean (*Glycine max* (L.) Merrill). *In Vitro Cell Development Biology-Plant,*40: 552-558.

Konopka-Postupolska, D., Clark, G., Goch, G., Debski, J., Floras, K.,Cantero, A., Fijolek, B., Roux, S. and Hennig, J. (2009): The Role of Annexin 1 in Drought Stress in *Arabidopsis*. *Plant Physiology,* 150: 1394-1410.

Konopka-Postupolska, D., Greg, C., Grazyna, G., Janusz, D., Krzysztof, F., Araceli, C., Bartlomiej, F., Stanley, R. and Jacek, H.(2009). The Role of Annexin 1 in Drought Stress in Arabidopsis1. *Plant Physiology,*150: 1394-1410.

Koornef, M. and Meinke, D. (2010): The Development of Arabidopsis as a Model Plant. *Plant Journal of Cell Molecular Biology,* 61(6): 909-921.

Krebs, J.E., Goldstein, E.S. and Kilpatrick, S.T. (2010): Lewin's Essential Genes. 2nd Edition. *Jones and Bartlett Publishers, London,* 343: 459-473.

Krugel, T., Lim, M., Gase, K., Halitschke, R. and Baldwin, I. T. (2002): *Agrobacterium*-mediated Transformation of *Nicotiana attenuata,* a Model Ecological Expression System. *Chemoecology,* 12: 177-183.

Laohavisit, A., Brown, A.T., Cicuta, P. and Davies, J.M. (2010): Annexins: Components of the Calcium and Reactive Oxygen Signaling Network. *Plant Physiology,* 152: 1824-1829.

Laohavisit, A., Davies, J.M. (2011): Annexins. *New Phytology,* 189: 40-53.

Laohavisit, A., Mortimer, J.C. and Demidchik, V. (2009): *Zea mays* Annexins Modulate Cytosolic Free $Ca^{2+}$and Generate a Ca^{2+} Permeable Conductance. *Plant Cell,* 21: 479-493.

Laohavisit, A., Shang, Z., Rubio, L., Cuin, T.A., Véry, A., Wang, A., Mortimer, J.C., McPherson, N., Coxon, K.M. and Battey, N.H. (2012): *Arabidopsis* Annexin1 Mediates the Radical-activated Plasma Membrane Ca2^{+}-and K^{+}-permeable Conductance in Root Cells. *Plant Cell,* 24: 1522-1533.

Lee, S., Lee, E.J., Yang, E.J., Lee, J.E., Park, A.R., Song, W.H. and Park, O.K. (2004): Proteomic Identification of Annexins, Calcium Dependent Membrane Binding Proteins that Mediate Osmotic Stress and Abscisic Acid Signal Transduction in Arabidopsis. *Plant Cell,* 16: 1378-1391.

Leelavathi, S., Sunnichan, V.G., Kumria, R., Vijaykanth, G.P., Bhatnagar, R.K., Reddy, V. S.(2004): A Simple and Rapid Agrobacterium-mediated Transformation Protocol for Cotton (*Gossypiumhirsutum* L.): Embryogenic calli as a Source to Generate Large Numbers of Transgenic Plants. *Plant Cell Reproduction,* 22: 465-470.

Lodge, J., Lund, P. and Minchin, S. (2007): Gene Cloning Principles and Applications. 1st Edition. Taylor and Francis, Abingdon, 4: 23-27.

Lopez, S.J., Kumar, R., Pius, P.K. and Muraleedharan, N. (2004): *Agrobacterium tumefaciens* Mediated Genetic Transformation in Tea (*Camellia sinensis* (L.) O. Kuntze). *Plant Molecular Biology,* 22: 201a-201j.

Lu, Y., Ouyang, B., Zhang, J., Wang, T. and Lu, C. (2012): Genomic Organization, Phylogenetic Comparison and Expression Profiles of Annexin Gene Family in Tomato (*Solanum lycopersicum*). *Gene,* 499: 14-24.

Margaret, F.S., Gurr, S.J., McPherson, M.J., Roberts, K. and Bowles, D.J. (1992). The Pattern of Plant Annexin Gene Expression. *Biochemistry Journal,* 281: 501-505.

McClung, A.D., Carroll, A.D. and Battey, N.H. (1994): Identification and Characterization of ATPase Activity Associated with Maize (*Zea mays*) Annexins. *Biochemistry Journal,* 303: 709-712.

McPherson, M.J., Hamesh, B.D. and Taylor, G.R. (1995): PCR2, A Practical Approach, Kirl Press, 35: 205-218.

Meagher, R.B. (2000): Phytoremediation of Toxic Elemental and Organic Pollutants. *Current Opinion of Plant Biology,* 3(2): 153-162.

Mishra, S.P., Bhat, S., and Singh, S. (2010): Genetic Manipulation of Tomato Plant with Annexin Gene Through Agrobacterium Mediated Transformation. *The Bioscan,*5(2): 331-334.

Mortimer, J.C., Laohavisit, A., Macpherson, N., Webb, A., Brownlee, C., Battey, N.H. and Davies, J.M. (2008). Annexins: Multifunctional Components of Growth and Adaptation. *Journal of Experimental Botany,* 59: 533-544.

Murashige, T. and Skoog, F. (1962): A Revised Medium for Rapid Growth and Bioassays with Tobacco Tissue Culture. *Physiology of Plant,*15, 473-497.

Newell, C.A. (2000): Plant Transformation Technology. Developments and Applications. *Molecular Biotechnology,* 16: 53-65.

Paz, M.M., Martinez, J.C., Kalvig, A.B., Fonger, T.M. and Wang, K. (2006): Improved Cotyledonary Node Method Using an Alternative Explant Derived from Mature Seed for Efficient *Agrobacterium* Mediated Soybean Transformation. *Plant Cell Reproduction,* 25: 206-213.

Proust, J., Houlné, G., Schantz, M.L., Shen, W.H. and Schantz, R. (1999): Regulation of Biosynthesis and Cellular Localization of SP32 Annexins in Tobacco BY2 Cells. *Plant Molecular Biology,* 39, 361-372.

Raj, S.K., Singh, R., Pandey, S.K. and Singh, B.P. (2005): *Agrobacterium*-mediated Tomato Transformation and Regeneration of Transgenic Lines Expressing *Tomato Leaf Curl Virus* Coat Protein Gene for Resistance Against TLCV Infection. *Current Science,* 88(10): 1674-1679.

Ray, Wu. (1995): Recombinant DNA Methodology II. *Academic Press,* 8: 485-496.

Richard, M., Twyman, Schillberg, S. and Fischer, R. (2007): Molecular Farming of Antibodies in Plants. *Improvement of Crop Plants for Industrial Uses,* 435-469.

Sambrook, J., Fritsch, E.F. and Maniatis, T. (1989): Molecular Cloning: A Laboratory Manual. *Cold Spring Harbor Laboratory Press,* Cold Spring Harbor, New York, 1 and 2: 1-33.

Shantha, S.L., Padma, S.G., Bhat, S.K.C. and Rao, R.B. (2012): Genetic Manipulation of Tomato Using WGA Gene Through *Agrobacterium* Mediated Transformation. Kathmandu University. *Journal of Science, Engineering and Technology,* 8: 36-43.

Sharma, M.K., Solanke, A.U., Jani, D., Singh, Y. and Sharma, A.K. (2009): A Simple and Efficient Agrobacterium-mediated Procedure for Transformation of Tomato. *Journal of Biosciences,* 34(3): 423-433.

Sheffield, J., Taylor, N., Fauquet, C. and Chen, S. (2006): The Cassava (*Manihotesculenta Crantz*) Root Proteome: Protein Identification and Differential Expression. *Proteomics,* 6: 1588-1598.

Skyrinou, K.C., Raptopolou, C.P., Psycharis, V., Kessissoglou, D.P. and Psomas, G. (2009). Structure, Cyclic Voltammetry and DNA-binding Properties of the bis (pyridine) bis(sparfloxacinato) nickel(II) complex. *Polyhedron,* 28: 3265-3271.

Soler, M., Serra, O., Molinas, M., Huguet, G., Fluch, S. and Figueras, M. (2007): A Genomic Approach to Suberin Biosynthesis and Cork Differentiation. *Plant Physiology,* 144: 419-431.

Sunjung, P. (2006): *Agrobacterium tumefaciens*-mediated Transformation of Tobacco(*nicotiana tabacum*) eaf disks: Evaluation of the Co-cultivation Conditions to increaseβ-glucuronidase gene activity. M.S., Korea University, Korea.

Terada, R., Asao, H. and Iida, S. (2004): A Large-scale *Agrobacterium*-mediated Transformation Procedure with a Strong Positive-negative Selection for Gene Targeting in Rice (*Oryza sativa*) *Plant Cell Reproduction,* 22: 653-659.

Valero, M.A., Vidal, A. and Burgos, R. (2011): Meta-analysis on the Role of Lycopene in Type 2 Diabetes Mellitus. *Nutritional Hospital (Meta-analysis) (in Spanish),* 26(6): 1236-1241.

Van Holde, K.E., Johnson, W.C. and Shing Ho, P. (1998): Principles of Physical Biochemistry, *Prentice-Hall Inc.,* New Jersey, 213-233.

Walker, J.M. and Rapley, R. (2000): Molecular Biology and Biotechnology. 4th Edition. The Royal Society of Chemistry, Cambridge.

Yang, M., Xie, X., Zheng, C., Zhang, F., He, X. and Li, Z. (2008): *Agrobacterium tumefaciens* Mediated Genetic Transformation of *Acacia Crassicarpa* via Organogenesis. *Plant Cell, Tissue and Organ Culture,*95: 141-147.

Yang, P., Li, X., Wang, X., Chen, H., Chen, F. and Shen, S. (2007): Proteomic Analysis of Rice (*Oryza sativa*) Seeds during Germination. *Proteomics,* 7: 3358-3368.

Yanisch-Perron, C. (1985): Improved M13 Phage Cloning Vectors and Host Strains: Nucleotide Sequences of the M13mp18 and pUC19 Vectors. *Gene,* 33, 103-119.

Zhongbao Zhang, Xianglong Li, Meng Han, and Zhongyi Wu. (2015): Genome-wide Analysis and Functional Identification of the Annexin Gene Family in Maize (*Zea mays* L.).*Plant Omics Journal,*8(5): 420-428.

Pages: 113-126

BIOTECHNOLOGY AND ENVIRONMENTAL MANAGEMENT

Edited by: Prof. Arun Arya; Dr. Raaz K Maheswari & Dr. Pawan Kumar 'Bharti'

ISBN: 978-93-5056-862-0

Edition: 2017

Published by: Discovery Publishing House Pvt. Ltd., New Delhi (India)

5 Microbial Enzymes and its Role on Pollution Management

Anitha, T.; E.Parameswari
V. Davamani and R.Poorniammal

INTRODUCTION TO ENZYMES

Enzymes are biological catalysts that facilitate the conversion of substrates into products by providing favorable conditions that lower the activation energy of the reaction. An enzyme may be a protein or a glycoprotein and consists of at least one polypeptide moiety. The regions of the enzyme that are directly involved in the catalytic process are called the active sites. An enzyme may have one or more groups that are essential for catalytic activity associated with the active sites through either covalent or noncovalent bonds; the protein or glycoprotein moiety in such an enzyme is called the apoenzyme, while the nonprotein moiety is called the prosthetic group. The combination of the apoenzyme with the prosthetic group yields the holoenzyme.

ENZYME NOMENCLATURE

Enzyme names apply to a single catalytic entity, rather than to a series of individually catalyzed reactions. Names are related to the function of the enzyme, in particular, to the type of reaction catalyzed (Lehninger, 2004).

ENZYME CLASSIFICATION

The ultimate identification of a particular enzyme is possible through its enzyme commission (E.C.) number. The assignment of E.C. numbers is described in guidelines set out by the International Union of Biochemistry. All known enzymes fall into one of these six categories. The six main divisions are: (1) oxidoreductases, (2) transferases, (3) hydrolases, (4) lyases,

Horticultural College and Research Institute, Tamil Nadu Agricultural University, Periyakulam Tamil Nadu, (India)

(5) isomerases, and (6) igases (synthetases). Oxidoreductases catalyze the transfer electrons and protons from a donor to an acceptor. Transferases catalyze the transfer of a functional group from a donor to an acceptor. Hydrolases facilitate the cleavage of C–C, C–O, C–N, and other bonds by water. Lyases catalyze the cleavage of these same bonds by elimination, leaving double bonds (or, in the reverse mode, catalyze the addition of groups across double bonds). Isomerases facilitate geometric or structural rearrangements or isomerizations. Finally, ligases catalyze the joining of two molecules.

New technologies for waste disposal that use high-temperature incineration and chemical decomposition (e.g., base-catalyzed dechlorination, UV oxidation) have evolved. Although they can be very effective at reducing wide a range of contaminants but at the same time have several drawbacks. These methods are complex, uneconomical, and lack public acceptance. The associated deficiencies in these methods have focused efforts towards harnessing modern-day bioremediation process as a suitable alternative.

Bioremediation is a microorganism mediated transformation or degradation of contaminants into nonhazardous or less-hazardous substances. The employability of various organisms like bacteria, fungi, algae, and plants for efficient bioremediation of pollutants has been reported (Vidali, 2001). The involvement of plants in the bioremediation of pollutants is called as phytoremediation. The process of phytoremediation is an emerging green technology that facilitates the removal or degradation of the toxic chemicals in soils, sediments, groundwater, surface water, and air (RTDF). Genetically, engineered plants are also in use. For instance arsenic is phytoremediated by genetically modified plants such as *Arabidopsis thaliana* which expresses two bacterial genes. One of these genes allows the plant to modify arsenate into arsenite and the second one binds the modified arsenite and stores it in the vacuoles (Leung, 2004).

The process of bioremediation mainly depends on microorganisms which enzymatically attack the pollutants and convert them to innocuous products. As bioremediation can be effective only where environmental conditions permit microbial growth and activity, its application often involves the manipulation of environmental parameters to allow microbial growth and degradation to proceed at a faster rate.

The process of bioremediation is a very slow process. Only certain species of bacteria and fungi have proven their ability as potent pollutant degraders. Many strains are known to be effective as bioremediation agents but only under laboratory conditions. The limitation of bacterial growth is under the influence of pH, temperature, oxygen, soil structure, moisture and appropriate level of nutrients, poor bioavailability of contaminants, and presence of other toxic compounds. Although microorganisms can exist in extreme environment, most of them prefer optimal condition a situation that is difficult to achieve outside the laboratory. Most bioremediation systems operate under aerobic conditions, but anaerobic environments may also permit microbial degradation of recalcitrant molecules. Both bacteria and fungi rely on the participation of different intracellular and extracellular enzymes respectively for the remediation of recalcitrant and lignin and organ pollutants.

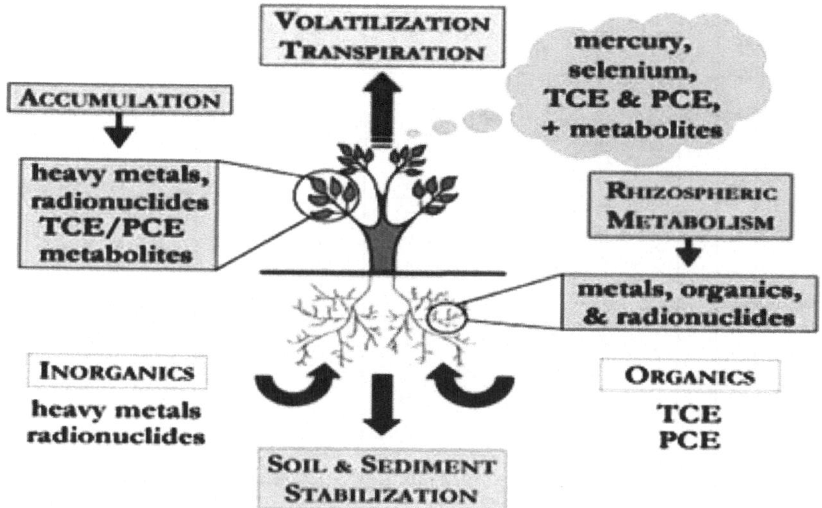

Fig. 5.1: Concept of Bioremediation

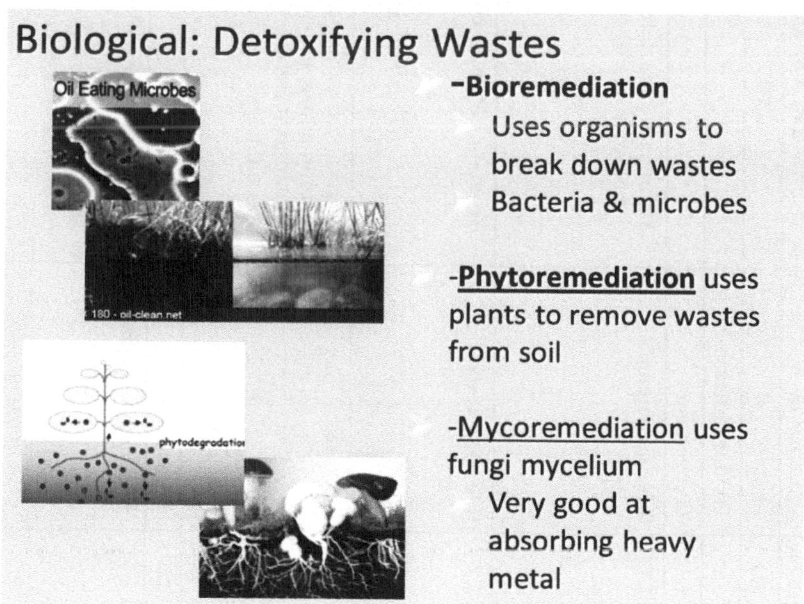

Fig. 5.2: Biological means of Detoxifying Wastes

Table 5.1: Microbial enzymes in bioremediation

Sl.No.	Enzyme	Substrate/Pollutant	Reaction	Applications
(1)	(2)	(3)	(4)	(5)
1.	**Oxidoreductase**			
1.1	**Oxygenase**			
1.1.1	**Monooxygenase**	Alkane, steroids, fatty acid, and aromatic compounds	Incorporation of oxygen atom to substrate and utilize substrate as reducing agent. Desulfurization, dehalogenation, denitrification, ammonification, and hydroxylation of substrate	Protein engineering, bioremediation, synthetic chemistry, and so forth.
1.1.2	**Dioxygenase**	Aromatic compounds	Introduction of two oxygen atom to the substrate results in intradiol cleaving and extradiol cleaving with the formation of aliphatic product.	Synthetic chemistry, pharmaceutical industry, bioremediation, and so forth.
1.2	**Laccase**	Ortho and paradiphenols, aminophenols, polyphenols, polyamines, lignins, and aryldiamines.	Oxidation, decarboxylation and demethylation of substrate.	Food industry, paper and pulp industry, textile industry, nanotechnology, synthetic chemistry, bioremediation, cosmetics, and so forth.
1.3	**Peroxidase**			
1.3.1	**Lignin peroxidase**	Halogenated phenolic compounds, polycyclic aromatic compounds and other aromatic compounds	Oxidation of substrate in the presence of cosubstrate H_2O_2 and mediator like veratryl alcohol.	Food industry, paper and industry, pharmaceutical pulp industry, textile industry, bioremediation, and so forth.

(Table Contd…)

(1)	(2)	(3)	(4)	(5)
1.3.2	**Manganese peroxidase**	Lignin and other phenolic compounds	In the presence of Mn^{2+} and H_2O_2 the co-substrate catalyses oxidation of Mn^{2+} to Mn^{3+}which results in an Mn^{3+} chelateoxalate, which in turn oxidizes the phenolic substrates.	Food industry, Paper and pulp industry, textile industry, pharmaceutical industry, bioremediation, and so forth.
1.3.3	**Versatile peroxidase**	Methoxybenzenes and phenolic aromatic	The enzyme catalyzes the electron transfer from an oxidizable substrate, with the formation and reduction of compound I and compound II intermediates.	Industrial biocatalyst, bioremediation, and so forth.
2.	**Hydrolase**			
2.1	**Lipase**	Organic pollutants such as oil spill	The hydrolysis of triacylglycerols to glycerols and free-fatty acids	Control of oil spills, detergent production, baking industry, paper and pulp industry, personal care products, and so forth.
2.2	**Cellulase**	Cellulosic substance	Hydrolyses the substrate to simple carbohydrates.	Textile manufacturing. detergent production, paper and pulp industry, bioremediation, and so forth.
2.3	**Protease**	Proteins	Enzymes that hydrolyze peptide bonds in aqueous environment.	Leather, laundry, biocatalyst, bioremediation, and so forth.

ROLE OF ENZYMES

(i) Microbial Dioxygenases

Dioxygenases are multicomponent enzyme systems that introduce molecular oxygen into their substrate. Aromatic hydrocarbon dioxygenases belong to a large family ofRieskenonheme iron oxygenases. These dioxygenases catalyze enantiospecifically the oxygenation of wide range of substrates. Dioxygenases primarily oxidize aromatic compounds and, therefore, have applications in environmental remediation. All members of this family have one or two electron transport proteins preceding their oxygenase components. The crystal structure of naphthalene dioxygenase has confirmed the presence of a Rieske (2Fe–2S) cluster and mononuclear iron in each alpha subunit (Arora, 2014).

The catechol dioxygenases serve as part of nature's strategy for degrading aromatic molecules in the environment. They are found in the soil bacteria and involved in the transformation of aromatic precursors into aliphatic products. The intradiol cleaving enzymes utilize Fe(III), while the extradiol cleaving enzymes utilize Fe(II) and Mn(II) in a few cases.

(ii) Microbial Oxidoreductases

The detoxification of toxic organic compounds by various bacteria and fungi and higher plants through oxidative coupling is mediated with oxidoreductases. Microbes extract energy via energy-yielding biochemical reactions mediated by these enzymes to cleave chemical bonds and to assist the transfer of electrons from a reduced organic substrate (donor) to another chemical compound (acceptor). During such oxidation-reduction reactions, the contaminants are finally oxidized to harmless compounds (Singh, 2003).

The oxidoreductases participate in the humification of various phenolic substances that are produced from the decomposition of lignin in a soil environment. In the same way, oxidoreductases can also detoxify toxic xenobiotics, such as phenolic or anilinic compounds, through polymerization, copolymerization with other substrates, or binding to humic substances. Microbial enzymes have been exploited in the decolorization and degradation of azo dyes.

Many bacteria reduce the radioactive metals from an oxidized soluble form to a reduced insoluble form. During the process of energy production, bacterium takes up electrons from organic compounds and use radioactive metal as the final electron acceptor. Some of bacterial species reduce the radioactive metals indirectly with the help of an intermediate electron donor. Finally precipitant can be seen as the result of redox reactions within the metal-reducing bacteria.

Chlorinated phenolic compounds are among the most abundant recalcitrant wastes found in the effluents generated by the paper and pulp industry. These compounds are produced upon the partial degradation of lignin during pulp bleaching process. Many fungal species are considered to be suitable for the removal of chlorinated phenolic compounds from the contaminated environments. The activity of fungi is mainly due to the action of extracellular oxidoreductase enzymes, like laccase, manganese peroxidase, and lignin peroxidase, which are released from fungal mycelium into their nearby environment. Being filamentous, fungi can reach the soil pollutants more effectively than bacteria.

Water polluted with phenolic compounds can be de-contaminated by plants with the help of enzymes exuded by their roots. The plant families of Fabaceae, Gramineae, and Solanaceae are found to release oxidoreductases which take part in the oxidative degradation of certain soil constituents. Phytoremediation of organic contaminants has been generally focused on three classes of compounds: chlorinated solvents, explosives, and petroleum hydrocarbons (Que, 1996).

(iii) Microbial Oxygenases

Oxygenases belong to the oxidoreductase group of enzymes. They participate in oxidation of reduced substrates by transferring oxygen from molecular oxygen (O_2) utilizing FAD/NADH/NADPH as a cosubstrate. Oxygenases are grouped into two categories; the monooxygenases and dioxygenases on the basis of number of oxygen atoms used for oxygenation. They play a key role in the metabolism of organic compounds by increasing their reactivity or water solubility or bringing about cleavage of the aromatic ring. Oxygenases have a broad substrate range and are active against a wide range of compounds, including the chlorinated aliphatics. Generally the introduction of O_2 atoms into the organic molecule by oxygenase results in cleavage of the aromatic rings. Historically, the most studied enzymes in bioremediation are bacterial mono- or dioxygenases. A detailed study of the role of oxygenases in biodegradation process is available.

Halogenated organic compounds comprise the largest groups of environmental pollutants as a result of their widespread use as herbicides, insecticides, fungicides, hydraulic and heat transfer fluids, plasticizers, and intermediates for chemical synthesis. The degradation of these pollutants is achieved by specific oxygenases. Oxygenases also mediate dehalogenation reactions of halogenated methanes, ethanes, and ethylenes in association with multifunctional enzymes (Fetzner, 2003).

(iv) Monooxygenases

Monooxygenases incorporate one atom of the oxygen molecule into the substrate. Monooxygenases are classified into two subclasses based on the presence of cofactor: flavin-dependent monooxygenases and P_{450}monooxygenases. Flavin-dependent monooxygenases contain flavin as prosthetic group and require NADP or NADPH as coenzyme. P_{450} monooxygenases are heme-containing oxygenases that exist in both eukaryotic and prokaryrotic organisms. The monooxygenases comprise a versatile superfamily of enzymes that catalyzes oxidative reactions of substrates ranging from alkanes to complex endogenous molecules such as steroids and fatty acids. Monooxygenases act as biocatalysts in bioremediation process and synthetic chemistry due to their highly region-selectivity and stereo selectivity on wide range of substrates. Majority of mono-oxygenase studied previously are having cofactor, but there are certain monooxygenases which function independent of a cofactor. These enzymes require only molecular oxygen for their activities and utilize the substrate as reducing agent.

The desulfurization, dehalogenation, denitrification, ammonification, hydroxylation, biotransformation, and biodegradation of various aromatic and aliphatic compounds are catalyzed by monooxygenases. These properties have been explored in recent years for important application in biodegradation and biotransformation of aromatic compounds. Methane mono-oxygenase enzyme is the best characterized one, among monooxygenases. This enzyme is involved in the degradation of hydrocarbon such as substituted methanes, alkanes, cycloalkanes, alkenes, haloalkenes, ethers, and aromatic and heterocyclic hydrocarbons. Under oxygen-rich conditions, mono-oxygenase catalyzes oxidative dehalogenation reactions, whereas under low oxygen levels, reductive dechlorination takes place. Oxidation of substrate can lead to de-halogenation as a result of the formation of labile products that undergo subsequent chemicaldecomposition(J.M. Bollag, 1998).

(v) Microbial Laccases

Laccases (p-diphenol:dioxygenoxidoreductase) constitute a family of multicopper oxidases produced by certain plants, fungi, insects, and bacteria, that catalyze the oxidation of a wide range of reduced phenolic and aromatic substrates with concomitant reduction of molecular oxygen to water. Laccases are known to occur in multiple isoenzyme forms each of which is encoded by a separate gene, and in, some cases, the genes have been expressed differently depending upon the nature of the inducer.

Many microorganisms produce intra and extracellular laccases capable of catalyzing the oxidation of ortho and paradiphenols, aminophenols, polyphenols, polyamines, lignins, and aryl diamines as well as some inorganic ions. Laccases not only oxidize phenolic and methoxy-phenolic acids, but also decarboxylate them and attack their methoxy groups (demethylation). These enzymes are involved in the depolymerization of lignin, which results in a variety of phenols. In addition, these compounds are utilized as nutrients for microorganisms or repolymerized to humic materials by laccase. Among the biological agents, laccases represent an interesting group of ubiquitous, oxidoreductase enzymes that show promise of offering great potential for biotechnological and bioremediation applications.

The substrate specificity and affinity of laccase can vary with changes in pH.Laccase can be inhibited by various reagents such as halides (excluding iodide),azide, cyanide, and hydroxide. Different laccases appear to have differing tolerance toward inhibition by halides, indicating differential halide accessibility. Laccase production is sensitive to the nitrogen concentration in fungi. High nitrogen levels are usually required to obtain greater amounts of laccase. Recombinant laccase can be produced by either homologous or heterologous means.

(vi) Microbial Peroxidases

Peroxidases (donor: hydrogen peroxide oxidoreductases) are ubiquitous enzymes that catalyze the oxidation of lignin and other phenolic compounds at the expense of hydrogen peroxide (H_2O_2) in the presence of a mediator. These peroxidases can be haem and nonhaem proteins. In mammals, they are involved in biological processes such as immune system or hormone regulation. In plants, they are involved in auxin metabolism, lignin and suberin formation, cross-linking of cell wall components, defense against pathogens, or cell elongation.

The hemeperoxidases have been classified into two distinct groups as found only in animals and found in plants, fungi, and prokaryotes. The second group peroxidases have been subdivided into three classes on the basis of sequence comparison. Class I is intracellular enzymes including yeast cytochrome c peroxidase, ascorbate peroxidase (APX) from plants, and bacterial gene-duplicated catalase peroxidases. Class II consists of the secretory fungal peroxidases such as lignin peroxidase (LiP) and manganese peroxidase (Mnp) from Phanerochaetechrysosporium, and Coprinu-scinereus peroxidase or Arthromycesramosus peroxidase (ARP). The main role of class II peroxidases appears to be the degradation of lignin in wood. Class III contains the secretory plant peroxidases such as those from horseradish (HRP), barley, or soybean. These peroxidases seem to be biosynthetic enzymes involved in processes such as plant cell wall formation and lignifications.

Nonhaem peroxidases are not evolutionarily linked and form five independent families. They are thiol peroxidase, alkylhydroperoxidase, nonhaemhaloperoxidase, manganese catalase and NADH peroxidase. Among all these thiol peroxidase is the largest and having two subfamilies such as glutathione peroxidases and peroxyredoxins(Yoshida, 1998).

CLASSIFICATION OF PEROXIDASE ENZYMES

Peroxidases have been classified into many types based on its source and activity. Among peroxidases, lignin peroxidase (LiP), manganese-dependant peroxidase (MnP), and versatile peroxidase (VP) have been studied the most due to their high potential to degrade toxic substances in nature.

1. Microbial Lignin Peroxidases

Lignin peroxidases are heme proteins secreted mainly by the white rot fungus during secondary metabolism. In the presence of cosubstrate H_2O_2 and mediator like veratryl alcohol LiP degrade lignin and other phenolic compounds. During the reaction, H_2O_2 gets reduced to H_2O with the gaining of electron from LiP, (which itself gets oxidized). The LiP (oxidized) with gaining an electron from veratryl alcohol returns to its native reduced state, and veratryl aldehyde is formed. Veratryl aldehyde then again gets reduced back to veratryl alcohol by gaining an electron from substrate. This result in the oxidation of halogenated phenolic compounds, polycyclic aromatic compounds and other aromatic compounds followed by a series of nonenzymatic reactions. Lignin peroxidase (LiP) plays a central role in the biodegradation of the plant cell wall constituent lignin. LiP is able to oxidize aromatic compounds with redox potentials higher than 1.4 V (NHE) by single-electron abstraction, but the exact redox mechanism is still poorly understood.

2. Microbial Manganese Peroxidases

MnP is an extracellular heme enzyme from the lignin-degrading basidiomycetes fungus, that oxidizes Mn^{2+} to the oxidant Mn^{3+} in a multistep reaction. Mn^{2+} stimulates the MnP production and functions as a substrate for MnP. The Mn^{3+}, generated by MnP, acts as a mediator for the oxidation of various phenolic compounds. The resulting Mn^{3+} chelate oxalate is small enough to diffuse into areas inaccessible even to the enzyme, as in the case of lignin or analogous structures such as xenobiotic pollutants buried deep within the soil, which are not necessarily available to the enzymes (Tsukihara, 2006).

3. Microbial Versatile Peroxidases

VP enzymes are able to directly oxidize Mn^{2+}, methoxybenzenes, phenolic aromatic substrates like that of MnP, LiP, and horseradish peroxidase. VP has extraordinary broad substrate specificity and tendency to oxidize the substrates in the absence of manganese when compared to other peroxidases. It has also been demonstrated that VP is able to oxidize both phenolic and nonphenolic lignin model dimer. Therefore, a highly efficient VP overproduction system is desired for biotechnological applications in industrial processes and bioremediation of recalcitrant pollutants (Vasileva-Tonkova, 2006).

(vii) Microbial hydrolytic enzymes

The pollution of soil and water by industrial chemicals and petroleum hydrocarbons is a serious problem of the modern world. Due to their extensive use, they are found as environmental contaminants in numerous aquatic and terrestrial ecosystems. The use of bioremediation technologies for removing these contaminants provides a safe and economic alternative to commonly used physical-chemical treatment. Bacterial activity is the major process involved in the hydrolysis of organic pollutants. Extracellular enzyme activity is a key step in degradation and utilization of organic polymers, since only compounds with molecular mass lower than 600 daltons can pass through cell pores (Sánchez-Porro *et.al.* 2003).

Hydrolytic enzymes disrupt major chemical bonds in the toxic molecules and results in the reduction of their toxicity. This mechanism is effective for the biodegradation of oil spill and organophosphate and carbamate insecticides. Organochlorine insecticides such as DDT and heptachlor are stable in well-aerated soil but readily degrade in anaerobic environments. Hydrolases also catalyze several related reactions including condensations and alcoholysis. The main advantages of this enzyme class are ready availability, lack of cofactor stereoselectivity, and tolerate the addition of water-miscible solvents. Hydrolases belong to group 3 of enzyme class and may further be classified according to the type of bond hydrolyzed.

Extracellular hydrolytic enzymes such as amylases, proteases, lipases, DNases, pullulanases, and xylanases have quite diverse potential usages in different areas such as food industry, feed additive, biomedical sciences, and chemical industries. The hemicellulase, cellulase, and glycosidase are of much importance due to its application in biomass degradation (Margesin *et.al.*, 1999).

(viii) Microbial Lipases

Lipase degrades lipids derived from a large variety of microorganisms, animals and plants. Recent works have shown that lipase is closely related with the organic pollutants present in the soil. Lipase activity was responsible for the drastic reduction total hydrocarbon from contaminated soil. Research undertaken in this area is likely to progress the knowledge in the bioremediation of oils spill. Lipases have been extracted from bacteria, plant, actinomycetes, and animal cell. Among these microbial lipases are more versatile because of their potent application in industries. These enzymes can catalyze various reactions such as hydrolysis, interesterification, esterification, alcoholysis and aminolysis.

Lipases are ubiquitous enzymes which catalyze the hydrolysis of triacylglycerols to glycerol and free-fatty acids. Lipolytic reactions occur at the lipid-water interface, where lipolytic substrates usually form equilibrium between monomeric, micellar, and emulsified states. Lipases have been classified into two types on the basis of criteria such as (a) enhancement in enzyme activity as soon as the triglycerides form an emulsion and (b) lipases with a loop of protein (lid) covering on the active site.

Triglyceride is the main component of natural oil or fat. This can hydrolyze consecutively to diacylglycerol, monoacylglycerol, glycerol, and fatty acids. Glycerol and fatty acids are widely used as raw materials, for instance, monoacylglycerol is used as an emulsifying agent in the food, cosmetic, and pharmaceutical industries. The study made on triolein hydrolysis from Candida rugosa lipase in the biphasic oil-water system as proven to be effective. The lipase adsorbs on to the oil-water interface in the bulk of the water phase. The lipase then breaks the ester bonds of triolein to produce consecutively diolein, monoolein, and glycerol. During the catalysis oleic acid is formed at each consecutive reaction stage. The glycerol formed is hydrophilic and thus dissolves into the water phase.

Lipase activity was found to be the most useful indicator parameter for testing hydrocarbon degradation in soil (Prasad and Manjunath, 2011). Lipase is of much interest in the production of regiospecific compounds which are employed in pharmaceutical industry. Along with its diagnostic usage in bioremediation, lipase has many potential applications in food, chemical, detergent manufacturing, cosmetic, and paper making industries, but its production cost has restricted its industrial use.

(ix) Microbial Cellulases

Cellulases now promise the potential of converting waste cellulosic material into foods to meet burgeoning population and have been the subject of intense research. Some organisms produce cell bound, cell envelope associated, and some extra cellular cellulases. Extracellular cellulases, hemicellulases, and pectinases have been shown to be constitutively expressed at very low levels by some bacteria and fungi.

Cellulases are usually a mixture of several enzymes. At least: three major groups of cellulases are involved in the hydrolysis process (1) endoglucanase (EG, endo- 1,4-D-glucanohydrolase) which attacks regions of low crystallinity in the cellulose fiber, creating free chain ends; (2) exoglucanase or cellobiohydrolase (CBH, 1,4-b-D-glucan cellobiohydrolase) which degrade the cellulose molecule further by removing cellobiose units from the free chain ends; (3) β-glucosidase which hydrolyzes cellobiose to glucose units. Along with major enzymes, some ancillary enzymes are also present. During the enzymatic hydrolysis, cellulose is degraded by the cellulases to reducing sugars that can be fermented by yeasts or bacteria to ethanol(Beena andGeevarghese, 2010).

Cellulase enzymes are capable of degrading crystalline cellulose to glucose. Cellulases have been used in the manufacture of detergents since early 1990s. Cellulases remove cellulose microfibrils, which are formed during washing and the use of cotton-based cloths. This is also observed as the colour brightening and material softening in the textile industry. Alkaline cellulases are produced by Bacillus strains and neutral and acidic cellulases by Trichoderma and Humicola fungi. In paper and pulp industry, cellulases have been employed for the removal of ink during recycling of paper. The cellulases are added during brewing to increase the juice liberation from fruit pulp and for the production of ethanol from cellulosic biomass(Margesin, 1999).

(x) Microbial Proteases

Proteases hydrolyze the breakdown of proteinaceous substance which enter atmosphere due to shedding and moulting of appendages, death of animals, and also as byproduct of some industries like poultry, fishery, and leather. Proteases belong to group of enzymes that hydrolyze peptide bonds in aqueous environment and synthesize them in nonaqueous environment. Proteases have wide range of applications in food, leather, detergent, and pharmaceutical industry.

Proteases are divided as endopeptidases and exopeptidases based on the catalysis of peptide chain. Endo peptidases further grouped based on the position of active site such as serine endopeptidase, cysteine peptidase, aspartic endopeptidases, and metallopeptidases. The enzymes whose reaction mechanism is completely elucidated are grouped under. The exopeptidases act only near the terminal amino or carboxylic position of chain. The protease that acts on free amino, and carboxyl terminals are called as aminopeptidase and carboxypeptidase, respectively.

The endopeptidase acts on the inner regions of peptide chain. The presence of free amino and carboxyl terminal will have negative impact on enzyme activity. Proteases have been used in the manufacture of cheese and detergent manufacturing industry since many years. The alkaline proteases are used in leather industry for the removal of hairs and parts which are present on the animal skin. Proteases have been employed for the production of dipeptide aspartame, which is a non-calorific artificial sweetener. In the pharmaceutical industry, varying and specific proteases are used in developing effective therapeutic agents. Clostridial collagenase or subtilisin is used in combination with broad-spectrum antibiotics in the treatment of burns and wounds(Prasadand Manjunath, 2011).

REFERENCES

Arora, P.K, Srivastava A, and Singh V P, 2010. "Application of Monooxygenases in Dehalogenation, Desulphurization, Denitrification and Hydroxylation of Aromatic Compounds," Journal of Bioremediation & Biodegradation, 1, 1-8.

Beena A.K and Geevarghese, P.I, 2010. "A Solvent Tolerant Thermostable Protease from a Psychrotrophic Isolate Obtained from Pasteurized Milk, "Developmental Microbiology and Molecular Biology, 1, 113-119.

Bollag J.M, and Dec J, 1998."Use of Plant Material for the Removal of Pollutants by Polymerization and Binding to Humic Substances," Tech. Rep. R-82092, Center for Bioremediation and Detoxification Environmental Resources Research Institute. The Pennsylvania State University, University Park, Pa, USA.

Fetzner S, 2003. "Oxygenases without Requirement for Cofactors or Metal Ions," Applied Microbiology and Biotechnology, 60 (3), 243-257.

Lehninger A.L, Nelson D.L, and Cox M.M, 2004. Lehninger's Principles of Biochemistry, W.H. Freeman, New York, NY, USA, 4th Edition.

Leung M, 2004. "Bioremediation: Techniques for Cleaning up a Mess," Journal of Biotechnology, 2, 18-22.

Margesin R, Zimmerbauer A, and Schinner F, 1999. "Soil Lipase Activity—A Useful Indicator of Oil Biodegradation," Biotechnology Techniques, 13 (12), 859-863.

Prasad M.P. and Manjunath K, 2011. "Comparative Study on Biodegradation of Lipid-rich Wastewater Using Lipase Producing Bacterial Species," Indian Journal of Biotechnology, 10 (1), 121-124.

Que L and Ho R Y N, 1996. "Dioxygen Activation by Enzymes with Mononuclear Non-heme Iron Active Sites," Chemical Reviews, 96 (7), 2607-2624.

Sanchez-Porro C, Martín S, Mellado E, and Ventosa A, 2003. "Diversity of Moderately Halophilic Bacteria Producing Extracellular Hydrolytic Enzymes," Journal of Applied Microbiology, 94 (2), 295-300.

Singh C.J, 2003. "Optimization of an Extracellular Protease of Chrysosporiumkeratinophilum and its Potential in Bioremediation of Keratinic Wastes," Mycopathologia, 156 (3), 151-156.

Tsukihara T, Honda T Y, Sakai R, Watanabe T, 2006. "Exclusive Overproduction of Recombinant Versatile Peroxidase MnP2 by Genetically Modified White Rot Fungus, Pleurotusostreatus," Journal of Biotechnology, 126 (4), 431-439.

Vasileva-Tonkova E and Galabova D, 2006 "Hydrolytic Enzymes and Surfactants of Bacterial Isolates from Lubricant-contaminated Wastewater," Zeitschrift fur Naturforschung, 58 (1-2), 87–92.

Vidali M, 2001. "Bioremediation. An Overview," Pure and Applied Chemistry, 73 (7), 1163-1172.

Yoshida S, 1998. "Reaction of Manganese Peroxidase of *Bjerkanderaadusta* with Synthetic Lignin in Acetone Solution," Journal of Wood Science, 44 (6), 486-490.

Pages: 127-149

BIOTECHNOLOGY AND ENVIRONMENTAL MANAGEMENT

Edited by: **Prof. Arun Arya; Dr. Raaz K Maheswari & Dr. Pawan Kumar 'Bharti'**

ISBN: 978-93-5056-862-0

Edition: **2017**

Published by: **Discovery Publishing House Pvt. Ltd., New Delhi (India)**

6

Macrophomina Management Through Frontier Tools and Techniques
Retrospectives & Perspectives with Special Reference to Jute

Sourav Dutta[1]; Madhumita Roy[1]
Kanti Meena[2]; Rajib K. De[2] and
Asit B. Mandal[2*]

ABSTRACT

Macrophomina phaseolina is a dreadly disease causing soil, seed and stubble borne, necrotrophic fungal pathogen with wide distribution world wide with broad host range, and higher competitive saprophytic ability, rendering it as a serious causal organism in developing diseases in more than 500 plant species, which include economically significant plants like fiber crops, fruits, legumes, vegetables, etc. Subsequent losses incurred due to the varied pathogenicity of *M.phaseolina* cause substantial detriment in annual productivity recurrently over years across locations globally. At the interface of discernible global climate change, enhanced temperature, relative humidity, CO_2 concentration in conjunction with microclimate changes have deemed to increase susceptibility of diverse crops to *M.phaseolina* in natura, under diverse agro ecological conditions to infect plants at almost all growth stages, and thereby could intensify productivity losses. Prophylactic and conventional measures with wide acceptance, used by farmers may not be full proof in halting disease incidence. Also most aggressive third generation fungicides

[1] Techno India University (Biotechnology Department), EM- 4/1, EM Block, Sector V, Salt Lake Kolkata – 700 091, West Bengal (India)

[2] ICAR-Central Research Institute for Jute & Allied Fibres (CRIJAF), Barrackpore, Kolkata – 700 120 West Bengal (India)

and synthetic pyrethroids provedto be not only largely ineffective but also eco offensive by creating environmental pollution owing to their long shelf life and residual effects over years. At this critical juncture, frontier tools and techniques are deemed to be appropriate to avert the loss caused by this deadly pathogen. The application of molecular techniques to identify pathogens correctly, deciphering the molecular mechanism of plant-pathogen interaction, *in silico* techniques to aid in exploration of *M. phaseolina's* genetic and physiological routes of infection, controlling the disease by using synthesized macromolecules and nanoparticles and finally through transgenic development endowed with killer gene/s dove-tailed in productive background efficiently and effectively are expected to be the landmarks. These techniques demonstrate potential to design rational strategies for ensuring economic and environmental friendly crop protection strategies in days to come, which are narrated below briefly.

Keywords: *Macrophomina phaseolina*, Crop plants, Jute, In silico techniques, Bio-molecular technologies, Nanotechnology, Transgenics.

INTRODUCTION

Since the onset of agriculture unconsciously in nature by the prehistoric man, epidemics in plant diseases and sufferings of man have gone hand in hand, depicting the importance of plant diseases and their significance for mankind at large (Anon 2011). Partial starvation, acute hunger and famines are well documented in ancient literatures and treatises. Plants have over centuries developed inbuilt mechanisms through evolution to sustain in environments under varying stress factors (Atkinson & Urwin 2012). The presence of enhanced abiotic and biotic stresses in plants is looming large especially at the interface of discernible global climate change, whose ill effects are emerging very drastically. At the advent of such a juncture that ushers in an age of more aggressive pathogens, which are robust and more adapted to infect a wide variety of species (Saleh *et al.* 2010). Prophylactics, diagnostics and control measures to halt such pathogens have to be revisited with the deployment of most modern tools and techniques. Gaining reputation as one such smart pathogen, *Macrophomina phaseolina* (Tassi.) Goid. has the ability to effectively render useless the immunity of plant, animal and human systems (Arora *et al.* 2012). *Macrophomina phaseolina* is a serious, opportunistic, disease causing soil, seed and stubble borne, necrotrophic fungal pathogen with wide distribution, varied host range, and higher competitive saprophytic ability, rendering it a causative agent of diseases the likes of which include charcoal rot, dry-root rot, wilt, stalk rot, fruit rot, seedling blight, leaf blight, stem blight and damping-off diseases (Omar *et al.* 2007; Babu *et al.* 2010; Vasebi *et al.* 2013). The ranges of its pathogenicity has been recorded in nearly 500 plant species, which include economically significant plants like fiber crops (jute, cotton), fruits (orange), pulses (common bean, green gram), oil crops (soybean, sunflower, sesame), softwood and other forest trees (pine, fir) medicinal plants and weed species etc. (Khan 2007; Sundravadana *et al.* 2011;Gupta *et al.* 2012), which in one or other ways support livelihood. Also an opportunistic pathogen of humans, it is found to have caused fungal keratitis in immuno-compromised humans (Dhingra & Chagas 1981; Premamalini *et al.* 2012) and thus in no way the incidence of this fungus can be ignored. Recent global climatic changeis of serious concern since discernible influx in temperature; relative humidity, CO_2 concentrations and associated microclimate change are evident to exhibit major change in pathogenicity and disease dynamics. Drought, heat, extreme cold, enhanced CO_2, increased salinity,desiccation are the major outcomes, which favour disease spread and aggressiveness. These are expected to enhance susceptibility of *M. phaseolina* in agricultural and natural ecosystems in diverse crops, thus infecting plants almost at all growth stages, and inflicting major crop losses (Ali *et al.* 2014). Losses incurred due to the pathogenic variability of *M. phaseolina* makes heavy dent in annual productivity recurrently over years across locations globally (Gupta *et al.* 2012). Prophylactic and conventional measures with wide acceptance, used by farmers are found to be largely ineffective to halt disease incidence. Also most aggressive third generation fungicides and synthetic pyrethroids proved to be not only largely ineffective but also pose a serious threat to the environment (Panhwar 2005; Gaige, 2010; Anon 2011; Babu *et al.* 2011; Illakkiam *et al.* 2013). At this critical juncture, frontier tools and techniques embodied in the biotechnological approaches are deemed to be appropriate measures to avert the loss caused by this deadly pathogen. The aid of molecular techniques to identify the pathogen, deciphering the molecular mechanism of plant-pathogen interaction at genetic, transcriptomics and proteomics levels, deployment of*in silico* techniques to aid in exploration of *M. phaseolina's* genetic and physiological routes of infection, metabolomics approaches to identify functional component of genes and proteins, use of miRNA, siRNA, antisense RNA technology, directed mutagenesis and *Agrobacterium*mediated gene silencing would be appropriate domains to unzip *Macrophomina*biology and evolving its control measures. To understand differentially expressed genes governing pathogenicity through microarray analysis and qPCR, using different molecular markers - especially most stringent RFLP diagnostics may offer most effective diagnostic tool and of course sero diagnostic and other molecular markers may be used with varied competence. Inhibiting viability using synthesized macromolecules and nanoparticles and finally through transgenics development, wherein plants can be engineered with tolerant genes from alien sources to impart induced resistance to the pathogen (Paulitz 2000; Broughton 2003; Islam *et al.* 2012; Andrea *et al.* 2013; Iqbal & Mukhtar 2014) may be adopted. These techniques demonstrate potential to design rational strategies for ensuring economic and eco-friendly crop protection and seem to help in perpetuation of pathogenic free crops species in days to come (Saleh *et al.* 2010).

Macrophomina phaseolina

Macrophomina phaseolina (Tassi.) Goid (CMI description of pathogenic fungi and bacteria no.275) was first observed by Petrak in 1923, who established the monotypic genus as *M.philippinensis* (Babu *et al*. 2010; Islam *et al*. 2012). Subsequent examination reviewed the taxonomic description of *M. phaseolina*, which was then deduced as follows: Division: *Eumycota*, Sub Division: *Deuteromycotina*, Class: *Coelomycetes*, Order: *Sphaeropsidales*, Family: *Sphaeropsidaceae*, Genus: *Macrophomina*, Species: *phaseolina* (Wheeler 1975; Rayatpanah & Dalili 2012). *M. phaseolina'*sviability in soil and as sclerotia can last for more than 4 years. Although observed both as pycnidal anamorphs and microsclerotia, the latter is found in abundance globally (Aboshosha 2007). The *modus operandi* of the fungus is to initially attack the cortical tissues, which is subsequently followed by oval sclerotia formation. Each microsclerotia is 50-150ìm in size comprising of 50-200 cells, which are united by a septal pore. When in soil, the cells from the microsclerotium germinate producing numerous germ tubes forming appresoria at the tip of the fungal hyphae, which then infects the root of the host plant by penetrating the epidermal cell walls through chemical softening or mechanical/turgor pressure. The secretion of cell wall degrading enzymes aids in the intra- and intercellular growth of the fungi. Thus under favourable conditions i.e., abundance of nutrients in the soil and at optimum temperature of 30° C and also under unfavourable conditions i.e., when the fungus draws nutrition from its microsclerotium due to lack of environmental nutrition, it can infect a plant across all stages in its development and progresses from formation of circular, reddish, necrotic lesions in the emerging hypocotyls, branches or stems, which mature from brown to black to leaf yellowing that leads to finally wilt and thus prematurely killing the plant. Plant death and reduced yield is caused due to the disrupting of the nutrient and water transport as the vascular system of the roots and basal internodes come under attack from this pathogen (Sharmin *et al*. 2012). Aseptate, elliptical, hyaline and thin-walled conidia are produced and dispersed, which aids in fungal survival and infection of new hosts (Islam *et al*. 2012; Gupta *et al*. 2012).

Distribution and Crops Affected

Dubbed as a polyphagous pathogen, *M.phaseolina* affects a wide range of unrelated plant species globally. The geographical distribution of the fungus is found in tropical and subtropical countries. Crops in arid to semi-arid climatic environments of Africa, Asia, Europe and North and South America are largely susceptible to this pathogen. Global climate change elevating the temperature increases the susceptibility of this pathogen in crops (Babu *et al*. 2010; Islam *et al*. 2012). The fungus is most viable at temperature ranges of 30-35 °C and under prolonged drought conditions, wherein the plants do not stand a chance to survive the pathogen attack. Commonly known to cause charcoal rot, the pathogen also causes diseases like ashy stem blight,

sclerotia plug the vessels, affecting the fibrovascular system of the roots and basal internodes by impending the transport of nutrients and water to the upper parts of the plant thus resulting in wilt of the infected plants (Khan 2007). Upon plant death, the dead plant debris becomes the carrier of the fungus thus releasing the sclerotias, which remain in the soil and upon addition of water becomes dislodged and rises to the surface to favour the germination of the fungi under suitable environmental conditions (Khan 2007; Islam *et al.* 2012). The infection of the fungi is associated with several environmental factors like increased heat stress and high salinity. Heat stress is known not only to loosen chitin bonding and degrade lignin in the host plants but also to enhance the metabolic activity of the pathogen. Pathogenicity of the fungi increases upon degrading the lignin present in the host plant. *M.phaseolina* deploys its arsenal of ligninolytic enzymes viz. laccase, galactose oxidase, chloroperoxidase [CPO], lignin peroxidase [Lip], etc. Both CPO and Lip are extracellular enzymes, which interact with the lignin polymer with the aid of cofactors like heme, vanadium or veratryl alcohol. The enzymes affect lignin by the oxidization of the Cl^- to hypochlorous acid [HOCl] or to a similar chlorine electrophile (Islam *et al.* 2012; Ali *et al.* 2014). The pathogen also shows wide adaptability to diverse osmotic and pH ranges. Salt concentrations of 1-8% favour the growth of *M. phaseolina* with optimum levels reaching at about 2-4%. Thus plants growing under saline stress have not only to struggle with salinity (K^+ and Na^+ ion imbalance) but also the salt tolerant pathogen to worry about(Radwan 2014). Presence of a robust pH sensing and neutralizing system, makes the fungi tolerate pH ranges of 3.5 to 10. The fungal genome comprises of pH-regulated proteins (19 acid phosphatases, 2 α-L-arabinofuranosidases, and 7 alkaline phosphatases), which extraordinarily neutralizes both acidic and alkaline environment to favour the growth and make the fungi adaptable to adverse pH ranges (Islam *et al.* 2012).

JUTE AND MACROPHOMINA

Jute, considered to be the 'golden fibre' and heritage of West Bengal state in the Indian Republic is intimately associated with survival of about 4.5 million people alike Bangladesh- another predominant jute growing neighbouring country. This crop is highly vulnerable, especially to biotic stresses like jute apion, Bihar hairy caterpillar, semi looper but maximally to disease causing pathogen *Macrophomina phaseolina*, which are making heavy dent in annual productivity with million-dollar loss recurrently. To save this great loss, leak proof control measures are most wanted (Mahmood *et al.* 2010). *M. phaseolina* causes substantial loss of fiber yield in jute (Sarkar *et al.* 2014). The symptoms of the disease are root-rot, black patches on leaves and stem and signs of defoliation. The disease symptoms were found to be elevated in biotic stress add-on conditions i.e., if the plant pathogenic fungus was present in tandem with nematode interactions (Haque & Mukhopadhyaya 1979; Niblack *et al.* 2011) (Figure 6.2 & Figure 6.3).

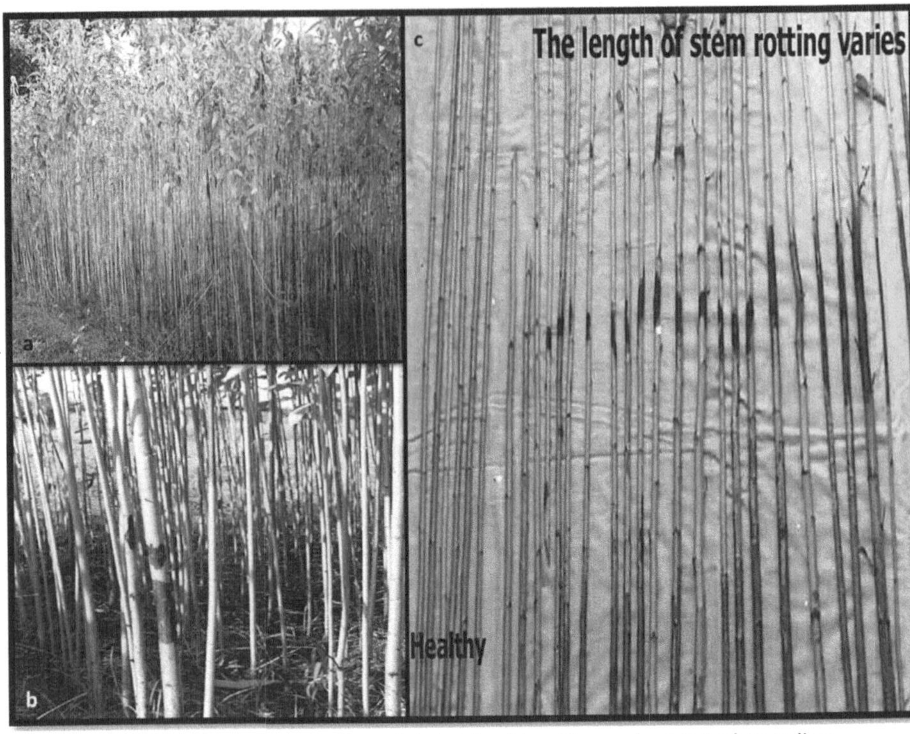

Fig. 6.2: Steps in Infection of Jute Plant by *Macrophomina phaseolina.*

(a) Stem Rot Infected Jute Field.

(b) Advanced Stage of Brown Spot on the Stem: Continuous Rain & High Relative Humidity & Temperature Around 30-35ºC are Congenial for the Infection

(c) The Rotting of Stem may Extend up to 10 - 15 cm or Higher.

Introduction to Jute

Jute is a lingo-cellulosic bast fibre crop belonging to the family *Sparmanniaceae.* The bast fibre is spun into coarse threads, to produce diverse products having demand in domestic and international markets. Among many species only two jute species in the genus *Corchorus,* are cultivated viz *Corchorus olitorius* and *C. capsularis* (Alamri *et al.* 2012). India alone contributes about 80% of global jute requirement of which West Bengal alone provides 80% of the entire produce. Considering its great importance the Colonial Britishers established Jute Technology Research Laboratory (JTRL) as early as in 1938 in Dhaka (presently in Bangladesh) to pursue jute research and development. During the past 74 years of long journey, spectacular achievements have been made in case of variety development in spite of exceedingly narrow genetic base in this self-pollinating crop. More than 35 HYVs have been released from India cultivating on an area of 0.94 million ha with production of 11.27 million bales (1bale=180kg) of which Central Research Institute of Jute & Allied Fibres (CRIJAF) alone has developed and released 15 varieties.

Fig. 6.3

(a) *M. phaseolina* Chokes the Vascular Bundles by the Mycelia it Produces, Causing Drooping of Leaves and Wilting of the Plant, Finally Killing the Plant.
(b) Stem Rot Symptoms show as Reddish Spots in Saplings.
(c) The Coloration Changes from Reddish to Brownish as the Saplings Age.
(d) At the Advanced Stage of Stem Rot, the Rotting may Extend to 10-15cm or Higher.
(e) The Affected Stem can also Break at the Point of Infection.
(f) The Pycnidia Appear Dark Brown with Apical Ostiole for Releasing of Conidia.
(g) Infected Seeds are mostly Produced from Infected Crops.

Estimated quantity of jute produced during 2010-11 deemed to be 1527.7 million tonnes is a landmark achievement. The crop duration has been reduced from 180 to 120 days, productivity increased from 10-12 to 22-24q/ha (potential yield: 40 q/ha) are commendable success in jute research domain. It provides jointly principal inputs to textile, geo-textiles, paper pulp and many other ancillary industries. In total, this cash crop provides livelihood for about 7 million people in entire south Asia. Production of raw jute has inflated from 3.3 million bales (1950-51) to 11.3 million bales during 2006-2007. Although the productivity has been doubled from 10-11 q/ha since independence to 22q/ha during 2006-2007, still there are huge demands for this biodegradable green fibre crop both in domestic and international markets. At the interface of rampant use of synthetic polymers, the area under jute is dwindling about one million hectare over last six decades. Alike other crop husbandry, biotic and abiotic stresses pose serious threats to growing crops and huge loss is being incurred in jute productivity every year globally. Since the productivity of jute is relatively low, grown virtually under near zero management on marginal land in subsistence mode, development and deployment of varieties tolerant to serious insect pests developed either through conventional breeding or through adoption of modern biotechnological approaches is felt urgently essential. Very recently with the aid of plant biotechnological approaches especially through exploitation of somaclonal variation, production of doubled- haploids and transgenic development involving transfer of alien gene/s from heterologous sources to engineer trait of interest especially to inflate tolerance to biotic and abiotic stresses and to produce jute hybrids and premium quality fibres (James 2011).

Macrophomina in Jute/Prophylactic Measures/Control Measures

Corchorus capsularis and *C.olitorius*, the most widely cultivated jute species, suffer severely from stem rot disease caused by *M. phaseolina* (Sharmin *et al.* 2012). Average yield losses incurred due to this pathogen is about 10% but can reach upto 30-40% under severe conditions (Biswas *et al.* 2014). Development of suitable package of practices for successful crop husbandry including agronomic management, plant protection measures and Post-Harvest Technology (PHT) are the successful technologies, which have contributed substantially in the jute R&D. Versatile demand in textile industries, paper pulp and ancillary industries showcased bright prospects for this green fibre crop. Fear of synthetic polymers is looming large owing to its environment offensive to nature; jute owing to its 100% biodegradability offers congenial environmental benefits along with immense capability to improve soil health by adding more organic biomass from the crop to the growing field. Among the conventional measures, treatment with cold and hot water extracts of urine of buffalo and bullock, wherein the uric acid completely inhibited mycelia growth of *M.phaseolina*, farmyard manure, neem and mustard cakes to use of various strategies like hot air treatment, hot water treatment, refrigerated storage, gas storage, copper fungicides, etc. and further treatment with systemic fungicides, the likes of which include borax, aminoathiozol, aminopyridine, benomyl, thiourea, dithiocarbamates, agrimycin, aureofungin, nystain, grisofulvin heated benomyl, triforine, etc. and soil fumigation with sodium methyldithiocarbamate, are the current predominant strategies for treatment of host plants against *M. phaseolina* (Raja *et al.* 1997; Panhwar 2005; Gupta *et al.* 2012). Hydrogen cyanamide (25-100mM) can also be used as it demonstrates moderate antifungal activity by lysis, hyphal distortion, fragmentation, etc. But the problem in using hydrogen cyanamide is that it only shows fungistatic effect and no fungicidal effect (Isaac *et al.* 2008, Kirubakan *et al.* 2008). The use of other bio control agents (BCA) against this phytopathogen is a lucrative idea as these can be an effective alternative to chemical fungicides, which prove hazardous to the environment, but is also an important component for sustainable agricultural practices. Reports have surfaced of a secondary metabolite, 3, 4-dihydroxy-N-methyl-4-(4-oxochroman-2-yl) butanamide, with the empirical chemical formula C14H17NO5 and a molecular mass of 279, obtained from *Pseudomonas aeruginosa* PGPR2 with antifungal activity against *M. phaseolina* (Illakkiam *et al.* 2013; Mahmood *et al.* 2013). Also oil of *Origanum syriacum* showed anti mycoticproperties and is a constituent of essential oiland folk medicines and chitinase biopesticide, both of which inhibits fungus growth (Chowdhury *et al.* 2014; Singh *et al.* 2014). Although BCAs' and fungicides can be used and their synergistic effect studied under diverse rhizosphere and soil environmental conditions, uses and subsequent success of BCAs' are limited with understanding the dynamics between the BCA and the pathogen pool (Paulitz 2000; Alamri 2012). A number of management measures have also been reported and are being applied to reduce the negative effects of *M. phaseolina*. Making rotations of the regular crop with non-host crops for a time period of 2-3 years can effectively reduce loss in crop yield. Wheat and barley are considered poor hosts because they do not bloom and set pods during the normally dry and hot months, and thus, those are more likely to escape infection caused by *M. phaseolina*. Increased seeding rate is also not a good option as high plant populations increases drought stress. Charcoal rot incidence can also be controlled through proper fertilization, application of lime, deep ploughing, irrigation and weed control (Gupta *et al.* 2012). Conventional control measures by using synthetic pyrethroids found to be environment offensive, costly and many a time found to be ineffective, that demands repeated spraying/applications, which is very tedious and cumbersome job at the interface of labour scarcity and environment safety point of view. However, there are severe constraints, as all the current disease management techniques are not always efficient because the dormant microsclerotia of the fungus can infect a plant host again when a favorable opportunity for growth occurs and thus, this demands intervention from cutting edge frontier science. In this critical juncture, application of biotechnological approaches deemed to be most logistic to engineer tolerant characters against various insect pests. Many genes have been reported to be prospective to deploy for development of transgenic plants singly or in combination in controlling constraints. Unfortunately extremely limited work on *in vitro* culture and plantlet regeneration of jute has been done. However, in the recent past a few success reports prospect bright future of development of transgenics in jute (Paulitz 2000), which may revolutionize this novel domain of frontier science.

DIAGNOSTICS

In recent times, there has been a paradigm shift from traditional diagnostic techniques, which require highly skilled diagnosticians, expensive lab equipment, lengthy culturing procedures for correct interpretation and quantifying fungi to using molecular, bio-chemical studies and immunological techniques, which are in vogue in this endeavour including most recent monoclonal antibody technology (Mudalige *et al.* 2011). Great advances have been made in understanding the mechanisms of biological control at the genetic and biochemical levels of the phytopathogens. The role of antibiotics, competition and induced resistance in biological control and their genetic regulation have been understood using the powerful tools of recombinant DNA, gene sequencing, polymerase chain reaction and bioinformatics (Paulitz *et al.* 2000). The various diagnostic and contemporary identification and treatment strategies of *M.phaseolina* can be broadly classified under 'Molecular' and 'Bio-informatics' studies. These branches of science make easier the understanding of the pathogen, the host and the complex reactions occurring within. Fairly a newer field of study, 'Nanotechnology' shows immense promise in understanding matter at the nanoscale i.e., at ~1-100nm (Chowdhury *et al.* 2014). Thus combined, they provided to be the pillars of understanding, with the help of which one can enrich ourpresent state knowledge of the phytopathogen and its interactions with host plant systems. This greater understanding can lead us to efficient diagnosis and further prognosis of the issues at hand.

Molecular Approaches

Traditional techniques used for detection and treatment of plant pathogens are being supplemented/complemented/replaced by molecular, genomics and functional genomic approaches, those that have proved to be more efficient for identification, mapping and cloning of genes that underlie plant stress and defense response by understanding the molecular mechanisms embodied in plant-pathogen interaction. New generation tools and techniques including recombinant DNA, gene sequencing, site-directed mutagenesis, polymerase chain reaction (PCR), antisense RNA technology, miRNA and siRNA technology etc. are worthy of mention in this endeavour (Paulitz 2000; Babu *et al.* 2007; Gurjar *et al.* 2010). The shift from identification and manipulation of individual genes to the global characterization of phenotypes is advanced by the utilization of frontier techniques. Some of these are discussed as follows.DNA hybridization assays, which use complementary DNA sequences (probe sequences – radioactive - ^{32}P or non-radioactive - biotin/digoxygenin) present in the target pathogen can be used to identify the unknown samples using dot blot. PCR methods produce probes inexpensively and at exceedingly faster rate, amplify the specific sequence of interest and moreover also do not depend on the limitations of the amount and quantity of DNA. Chromosome walking, a technique used to identify long stretches of DNA from unsequenced segments bordering a known sequence is used effectively in genome-related research. Thermal asymmetric interlaced (TAIL)-PCR, inverse PCR, Self-formed adaptor PCR (SEFA PCR), SiteFinding-PCR etc. are tools used amply in this endeavour (Liu & Whittier 1995; Paulitz 2000; Tan *et al.* 2005; Wang *et al.* 2007; Wang *et al.* 2011; Babu *et al.* 2011; Biswas *et al.* 2012). Genomic approaches (both structural and functional) are essential to know the genome and attributes functions of different genes, which may be bioprospected and used to understand the molecular grid for unzipping metabolomics and to manipulate pathways. Next generation sequencing is another powerful tool in this context. Molecular marker technologies like amplified fragment length polymorphism (AFLP), random amplified polymorphic DNA (RAPD) etc., have proved promising in identifying the pathogens and can help in deploying right resistant cultivar to combat disease pathogens (Virupakshaprabhu *et al.* 2012). Disease resistance genes can be cloned and characterized to exploit mechanisms for disease management. Pyramiding of resistant genes in commercial cultivar i.e., combining the resistance of many pathogenic lines to obtain resistant varieties which stand the test of time against the appearance of new pathogenic races. Marker assisted selection (MAS) can be used to screen the resistance gene(s) harbouring progeny plants. Functional genomics approaches can be used to generate expression profile to understand the function of the gene(s). But this technique requires high-throughout reverse genetics approaches to test gene function. Real-time PCR, microarray, RNAi, serial analysis of gene expression (SAGE), viral-induced gene silencing (VIGS) or viral over-expression as well as the use of gene knock-out libraries and promoter-trap strategies are some of the techniques used to identify novel defense related genes. DNA microarrays chips are used for expression profiling, genotyping and pathogen identification providing insights into the complex pathways governing defense gene regulation. RNA interference or RNA silencing, crucial for establishing innate immunity against pathogens by suppressing gene expression can be used successfully to discover defense genes in host plants (Yang *et al.* 2010; Kulcheski *et al.* 2011; Ouyang *et al.* 2014; Fossdal *et al.* 2012; Zhao *et al.* 2012; Sharma *et al.* 2014; Kohli *et al.* 2014). Serial Analysis of Gene Expression (SAGE) can provide an accurate picture of gene expression at both qualitative and quantitative levels. Massively Parallel Signature

Sequencing (MPSS) is a highly sensitive technique, which provides an ideal technique for comparing expression profiles from polyadenylated transcripts as well as non-polyadenylated RNAs such as micro- and small interfering RNAs. Promoter trapping enables the analysis of gene function thus expanding our knowledge of the host-plant interactions. Finally understanding post-translational modifications and unraveling the functional components of gene and proteins is also a major component of proteomic studies, which also find massive application in this stead. However use of all such techniques have been found to be extremely limited in *Macrophomina* management and warrants the need of elaborate and extensive experimentation. Strategies have also been devised to destroy wild-type DNA selectively, wherein the change of the nucleotide sequence of a gene or a regulatory element by site-directed mutagenesis based on the resistance of phosphorothioate internucleotide linkages to some restriction enzymes (Olsen & Eckstein 1990). Recombinant Inbred Line (RIL) population of jute developed by crossing resistant and susceptiblevarieties to *M. phaseolina* were used to identify genes involved in response to biotic stimuli. 22% of the genes from this were found to be involved in defense against biotic stresses. Defense related genes identified where related to plant pathway such as phenyl propanoid metabolism, phytohormone signaling, cell wall biosynthesis, and proteolysis among others (Biswas *et al.* 2014). The genetic variability of *M.phaseolina* is deemed to be essential to understand plant resistance management and to enable in designing successful control strategies. This can be obtained by understanding the genomic associations among disease resistance loci with the aid of DNA marker technologies, in construction of genetic linkage maps, characterization of quantitative trait loci (QTL) etc. Molecular linkage maps, used to identify, tag and map disease resistance genes and RAPD, AFLP, ISSR (Inter simple sequence repeats) are the most widely used marker types albeit RFLP is most stringent in pathotype detection (Miklas *et al.* 2000; Miklas *et al.* 2006; H-Delgado *et al.* 2009;Mahdizadeh *et al*, 2011; Mahdizadeh *et al.* 2012; Andrea *et al.* 2013). Microsatellite-based fingerprinting has also been used in *M. phaseolina* to generate complex genomic species-specific fingerprints for various fungal molecular studies especially in identifying genetic diversity (Amal 2012). The presence of double stranded RNA (dsRNA) associated with virus-like particles is found in various fungal species. These dsRNA are resistant to RNase treatment and transmit through cell division followed by spore or conidial production or by cell fusion between genetically compatible strains. Indian isolates of *M. phaseolina* contain the aforementioned dsRNA and determination of the dsRNA in the fungi may serve as a useful character to monitor and manage the spread of the pathogen (Arora *et al.* 2012). Thus all these techniques are expected to enable us to characterize this fungus but also understand ways to check its proliferation (Figure 6.4).

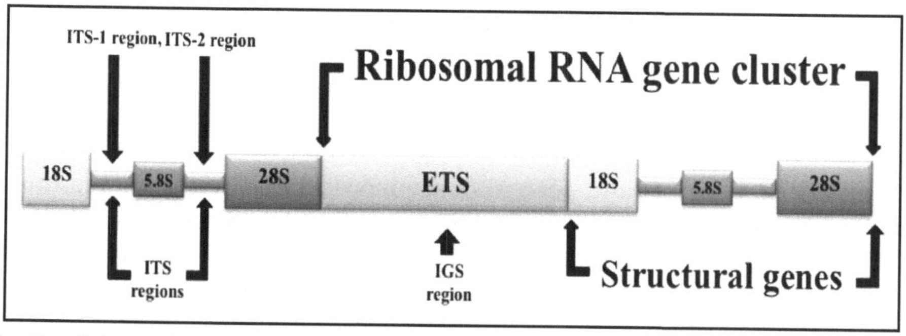

Fig. 6.4: Schematic representation showing general physical map of rDNA gene cluster in fungal genome, which may be used in *Macrophomina* diagnosis

Legends: ITS Internal transcribed spacers; ETS External transcribed spacer/IGS Intergenic spacers.

Bio-informatics

Bio-Informatics began with Alfred Sanger sequencing insulin, ushering in an era of molecular and structural biology, giving a new dimension in understanding of biological queries with the help of computational approaches. It usually deals with large, complex curated data sets, which are often used to reach biological conclusion(Baxevanis & Ouellette 2001; Claverie & Notredame 2007). Present understanding of the pathogen's activity and functions within the hosts' systems is related to the quantum of knowledge regarding genetic make-up, the proteins the pathogens synthesize and what role they play within the hosts (Broughton *et al.* 2003; Illakkiam *et al.* 2014). In this juncture by giving us an understanding of the pathogen by providing clues, bioinformatics can identify and help study the various interactions and processes that occur in and around them.The genome size of *M. phaseolina* is about 49 Mb and about 14,249 protein-coding genes have already been predicted. The pathogen showed to posses' ligninolytic activity as a result of combination of different enzymatic system such as slaccases, lignin peroxidases, galactose oxidases, chloroperoxidases, haloperoxidases, and heme peroxidases (Islam *et al.* 2012). The detection of pathogens from closely related species can be done at ease by the use of ribosomal RNA genes (rDNA) and genus specific internal transcribed spacer (ITS) (P-Quintero *et al.* 2012). These rDNA are highly stable and also exhibit conserved and diverse regions with the genome. Restriction fragment length polymorphism (RFLP), random amplified polymorphic DNA (RAPD), amplified fragment length polymorphism (AFLP), variable number tandem repeats (VNTR) and simple sequence repeats (SSR) can also be used to generate specific primers with the help of which one can identify and differentiate closely related species that can lead to reliable taxonomy, reflective of phylogenetic relationships. Once amplified using techniques like DNA polymerase chain reaction (DAMD-PCR) and SSR –PCR from, products are obtained and subsequently sequenced and aligned against other strain sequences of *M.phaseolina* from NCBI GenBank using BLAST (Basic Local Alignment Search Tool) and phylogenetic analysis. From the sequence alignments obtained, variations may easily be observed between other *M. phaseolina* isolates at species level. Multiple and pair wise sequence alignment can be generated and used to calculate evolutionary distances and percent of sequence similarity values and finally construct phylogenetic tree (Chakraborty *et al.* 2011; Mudalige *et al.* 2011). Differential gene expression between two species one susceptible and one resistant under both infected and uninfected conditions at different time intervals can be studied using a technique called mRNA differential display to identify gene/s that are expressed in the resistant specie and also to study their differences from the susceptible variants (Sharmin *et al.* 2012). The structure of these differentially expressed proteins and enzymes can easily be predicted and modeled after sequence retrieval and physicochemical characterization, finally leading to their use in designing mutagenesis experiments (Pérez *et al.* 2012; Akbar *et al.* 2013).

Nanotechnology

'There's plenty of room at the bottom' was the quintessential lecture delivered by Richard Feynman at Caltech on the 29 December 1959, hinting at the use of nanotechnology for advancements in synthetic chemistry by manipulation of atoms. Decades later in the years 1980-1990s, this sparked the ideational beginnings to the field of nanotechnology. Nanotechnology is the cognizance and the ability to modulate matter at dimension ranges of ~1-100nm. At these dimensions, the chemical reactivity of these materials differs largely from the bulk form, thus enabling novel applications. Vastly increased surface area and unique electronic, mechanical, magnetic and photonic properties empower nanoparticles with the potential to act as entirely new entities compared to their macro or even micro forms (Anon 2007). Research reports in treatment of pathogenic fungi with the use of nanoparticles are well evident in the not so distant past. Silver ions and nanoparticles have exhibited efficient antifungal activity *in vitro* and *in planta* by inhibiting the viability of spores. Silver in microorganisms has shown to alter cell membrane structure and function and interact with phosphorous and sulphur-containing compounds, causing DNA and protein damage especially to proteins associated with ATP production. These multiple modes of action, which target a wide range of biological pathways, provide a safer alternative against pathogens, which develop resistance to synthetic fungicides fast. Although higher doses can prove toxic to humans,ìm concentrations of silver find application in development of various biological and pharmaceutical processes. The use of silver nanoparticles for the treatment of disease on the onset of spores before they penetrate and colonize the host tissue is found to increase the efficacy of disease suppression thus labeling them as efficient fungicide (Jo *et al.* 2009; Krishnaraj *et al.* 2012; Chowdhury *et al.* 2014). Chitosan nanoparticles have

also exhibited promises in effecting inhibition of mycelial growth. The chelating properties of chitosan towards vary many organic and inorganic compounds make it a suitable biopolymer for efficient biocidal activity (Saharan *et al.* 2013; Chatterjee *et al.* 2014). Although such new techniques prove to be a panacea for phytopathogen remediation as they can be synthesized in an environment-friendly and economic way by the application of green synthesis, which can address current issues of chemical management, they are not totally devoid of detriments. The downside of the use of such engineered nanoparticles is the requirement of an efficient environmental tracking system to assess their impact on the environment and human health (Jo *et al.* 2009; Chowdhury *et al.* 2014).

PERSPECTIVES

In the context of future of biotic stress management in jute, the great success of BT cotton is worth mentioning. About 92% of cotton growing area in India is cultivated with BT cotton and production has been tripled within 6 years (James 2011). Thus the possibility of use of transgenics is very tempting and lucrative in redressal of the problems. Genetic transformation is precisely defined as the transfer of foreign gene/s, isolated from diverse sources (homo- and heterologous origin) into a new genetic background of the targeted recipient system. Since its inception in eighties, spectacular achievements have been made to introduce alien gene/s into plant systems for genetic improvisation especially for those characters, which are not amenable through conventional breeding (Qaim 2003). Transfer of gene(s), the likes of which include encode for osmotin protein can induce spore lysis in several fungal species (Abad *et al.* 1996). Since the discovery of restriction enzymes and development of genetically engineered vectors, diverse genes, promoters and with the development of optimized cell technological protocols for *in vitro* cell/tissue culture and regeneration of plantlets, significant strides have been made in crop genetic modulation through genetic transformation by producing desirable transgenic plants. Development of tolerant lines towards biotic threats through genetic management offers a cheap, more permanent and eco-compatible avenue in combating phytopthogen damage for resource-poor jute farmers (Biswas *et al.* 2014). Gene transfer methods like vector less system, which includes direct transfer of naked DNA through particle bombardment or electroporation of genes through membrane permeabilisation using high molecular weight PEG and indirect method by using vectors such as bacteria, viruses, fungi etc are notable. Transgenic plants have been developed in almost all major crops and discovery of novel genes have played major role in this endeavour. In total 29 countries including India produce transgenic plants and 60 countries are having the license to import and cultivate transgenics crops (James 2011). Thus the future for the identification and treatment of *M. phaseolina* in the Indian subcontinent is indeed a bright one. In essence among various tools and techniques,

Agrobacterium mediated genetic transformation has proved to be more reproducible with single locus and single copy insertion, which averts the hassels of multicopy induced gene silencing, frequent in case of microprojectile bombardment. Anyhow since jute is a recalcitrant crop to *in vitro* culture response, fine tuning of the developed protocol is still required, which would have less or zero genotype dependency. Furthermore jute is a fibre crop and hardly consumed as leafy vegetable, majority of which is used in textile and other industrial purposes. Bearing close resemblance with cotton from the viewpoint of use, the scope of direct consumption in human body does not arise. Not much fear is looming large and thus biotechnological approaches especially development of transgenics for *Macrophomina* management seems to be logical and is expected to revolutionize jute husbandry to attain farm prosperity at a sustainable scale in India, in the days to come.

REFERENCES

1. Abad LR, D'Urzo MP, Liua D, Narasimhan ML, Reuveni M, Zhu JK, Niu X, Singh NK, Hasegawa PM, Bressan RA, 1996. Antifungal Activity of Tobacco Osmotin has Specificity and Involves Plasma Membrane Permeabilisation. *Plant Science,* 118: 11-23.
2. Aboshosha SS, Atta Alla SI, El-Korany AE, El-Argawy E, 2007. Characterization of *Macrophomina phaseolina* Isolates Affecting Sunflower Growth in El-Behera Governorate, Egypt. *Int. J. Agri. Biol* 9(6): 807-815.
3. Anon, 2007. Nanotechnology, Commodities & Development, a Background Paper for the International Workshop on Nanotechnology, Commodities & Development, Meridian Institute.
4. Anon, 2011. Climate Change, Precision Agriculture and Innovative Disease Control Strategies. Proceedings of the 24th Training, (Ed. Kumar J.K. and R.P.Singh), G.B. Pant University of Agriculture and Technology, Centre of Advanced Faculty Training in Plant Pathology (Indian Council of Agricultural Research, New Delhi).
5. Alamri S, Hashem M, Mostafa YS, 2012. In vitro and In vivo Biocontrol of Soil-borne Phytopathogenic Fungi by Certain Bioagents and their Possible Mode of Action. *Biocontrol Science* 17(4): 155-167.
6. Amal AA, 2012. Molecular Identification of *Macrophomina phaseolina* by Microsatellite-based Fingerprint. *Plant Pathology & Quarantine* — Doi 10.5943/ppq/2/2/7.
7. Arora P, Dilbaghi N, Chaudhury A, 2012. Opportunistic Invasive Fungal Pathogen *Macrophomina phaseolina* Prognosis from Immuno Compromised Humans to Potential Mitogenic RBL with an Exceptional and Novel Antitumor and Cytotoxic Effect. *Eur J Clin Microbiol Infect* 31(2): 101-107.
8. Arora P, Dilbaghi N, Chaudhury A, 2012. Detection of Double Stranded RNA in Phytopathogenic *Macrophomina phaseolina* Causing Charcoal Rot (in *Cyamopsis tetragonoloba*. *Mol Biol Rep* 39: 3047-3054.
9. Atkinson NJ, Urwin PE, 2012. The Interaction of Plant Biotic and Abiotic Stresses: from Genes to the Field. *Journal of Experimental Botany* 63(10): 3523-3544.
10. Akbar MT, Habib AM, Chowdhury DUS, Bhuiyan MIK, Mostafa KMG, Mondol S, Mosleh IM, 2013. An Insight into the Lignin Peroxidase of *Macrophomina phaseolina*, *Bioinformation* 9(14): 730-735.

11. Andrea M-H, Yuraima M, Dasybel P, Hernán L, 2013. Genetic Variability of *Macrophomina phaseolina* Affecting Sesame: Phenotypic Traits, RAPD Markers and Interaction with the Crop. *Research Journal of Recent Sciences* 2: 110-115.
12. Ali Y, Sikder MOF, Marzan LW, Sharmen F, Khan MM, Hosain MA, 2014. In silico Analysis of Chloroperoxidase and Lignin Peroxidase of Pathogenic Fungus *Macrophomina phaseolina*. *Int J Biol Med Res* 5(3): 4246-4257.
13. Bankole SA, Ikotun B, Ekpo EJA, 1999. Fungal Deterioration of Melon Seeds Stored in Jute Sacks and Polyethylene Bags in Ago-Iwoye, Southwestern Nigeria. *Mycopathologia* 146: 135-146.
14. Baxevanis, A.D. and Ouellette, B.F., 2004. *Bioinformatics: A Practical Guide to the Analysis of Genes and Proteins* (Vol. 43). John Wiley & Sons.
15. Broughton WJ, Herna ìndez G, Blair M, Beebe S, Gepts P, Vanderleyden J, 2003. Beans (*Phaseolus spp.*) – Model Food Legumes. *Plant and Soil* 252: 55-128.
16. Babu BK, Saxena AK, (Srivastava AK, Arora DK, 2007. Identification and Detection of *Macrophomina phaseolina* by using Species - Specific Oligonucleotide Primers and Probe. *Mycologia* 99(6): 797-803.
17. Babu BK, Saikia R, Arora, DK, 2010. (Ed. Gherbawy Y, Voigt K). Molecular Identification of Fungi. Springer Verlag, Berlin, Heidelberg, New York, 1st Edition: 501.
18. Babu BK, Mesapogu S, (Sharma A, Somasani SR, Arora DK, 2011. Quantitative Real-time PCR Assay for Rapid Detection of Plant and Human Pathogenic *Macrophomina phaseolina* from Field and Environmental Samples. *Mycologia* 103(3): 466-473.
19. Biswas C, Dey P, Satpathy S, Sarkar SK, Bera A, Mahapatra BS, 2012. A Simple Method of DNA Isolation from Jute (*Corchorus olitorius*) Seed Suitable for PCR-based Detection of the Pathogen *Macrophomina phaseolina* (Tassi) Goid. *Letters in Applied Microbiology* 56: 105-110.
20. Biswas C, Dey P, Karmakar PG, Satpathy S, 2014. Next-generation Sequencing and Micro RNAs Analysis Reveal SA/MeJA1/ABA Pathway Genes Mediated Systemic Acquired Resistance (SAR) and its Master Regulation via Production of Phased, Trans-acting siRNAs Against Stem rot Pathogen *Macrophomina phaseolina* in a RIL Population of Jute (*Corchorus capsularis*). *Physiological and Molecular Plant Pathology* 87: 76-85.
21. Costanzo S, Ospina-Giraldo MD, Deahl KL, Baker CJand Jones RW, 2006. Gene Duplication Event in Family 12 glycosyl Hydrolase from *Phytophthora spp. Fungal Genetics and Biology* 43: 707-714.
22. Claverie, J.M. and Notredame, C., 2011. *Bioinformatics for Dummies*. John Wiley & Sons.
23. Costanzo S, Ospina-Giraldo MD, Deahl KL, Baker CJ, Jones RW, 2007. Alternate Intron Processing of Family 5 Endoglucanase Transcripts from the Genus *Phytophthora*. *Curr Genet* 52: 115-123.
24. Chakraborty BN, Chakraborty U, Dey PL, Rai K, 2011. rDNA Sequence and Phylogenetic Analysis of *Macrophomina phaseolina*, Root Rot Pathogen of *Citrus reticulata* (Blanco), *Global Journal of Molecular Sciences* 6(2): 26-34.
25. Chatterjee S, Chatterjee BP, Guha AK, 2014. A Study on Antifungal Activity of Water-soluble Chitosan Against *Macrophomina phaseolina*. *International Journal of Biological Macromolecules* 67: 452-457.
26. Chowdhury S, Basu A, Kundu S, 2014. Green Synthesis of Protein Capped Silver Nanoparticles from Phytopathogenic Fungus *Macrophomina phaseolina* (Tassi) Goid with Antimicrobial Properties Against multidrug-resistant Bacteria. *Nanoscale Research Letters* 9: 365.
27. Dhingra OD, Chagas D, 1981. Effect of Soil Temperature, Moisture and Nitrogen on Competitive Saprophytic Ability of Macrophomina phaseolina. *Transactions of British Mycological Society* 77(1): 15-20.

28. Dhingani RM, Tomar RS, Parakhia MV, Patel SV,Golakiya BA, 2012. Analysis of Genetic Diversity Among Different *Ricinus communis* Genotypes for *macrophomina* Root Rot Through RAPD and Microsatellite markers. *International Journal of Plant Protection* 5(1): 1-7.
29. Fossdal CG, Yaqoob N, Krokene P, Kvaalen H, Solheim H,Yakovlev IA, 2012. Local and Systemic Changes in Expression of Resistance Genes, nb-lrr Genes and Their Putative MicroRNAs in Norway Spruce after Wounding and Inoculation with the Pathogen *Ceratocystis polonica*. *BMC Plant Biology* 12: 105.
30. Gaige AR, 2010. Molecular Interactions Between the Pathogenic Fungus Macrophomina phaseolina and its Plant Host Medicago truncatula. M.S. Thesis, Dept. of Biological Sciences and the Faculty of the Graduate School of Wichita State University, Kansas, United States.
31. Gurjar G, Mishra M, Kotkar H, Upasani M, Soni P, Tamhane V, Kadoo N, Giri A, Gupta V, 2010. Major Biotic Stresses of Chickpea and Strategies for Their Control Pests and Pathogens: Management Strategies. BS Publications, ISBN: 978-81-7800-227-9.
32. Gupta GK, Sharma SK, Ramteke R, 2012. Biology, Epidemiology and Management of the Pathogenic Fungus *Macrophomina phaseolina* (Tassi) Goid with Special Reference to Charcoal Rot of Soybean (*Glycine max* (L.) Merrill). *J Phytopathol* 160: 167-180.
33. Haque MS, Mukhopadhyaya MC, 1979. Pathogenicity of *Macrophomina phaseoli* on Jute in the Presence of *Meloidogyne incognita* and *Hoplolaimus Indicus*. *Journal of Nematology* 11: 318-320.
34. H-Delgado S, Reyes-Valdés MH, Rosales-Serna R, Mayek-Pérez N, 2009. Molecular Markers Associated with Resistance (to *Macrophomina phaseolina*(tassi) Goid. in Common Bean. *Journal of Plant Pathology* 91(1): 163-170.
35. Isaac S, Kirubakaran, Sakthivel N, 2008. Site-Directed Mutagenesis, Heterologous Expression of Cyanamide Hydratase Gene and Antimicrobial Activity of Cyanamide. *Curr Microbiol* 56: 42-47.
36. Islam MS, Haque MS, Islam MM, Emdad EM, Halim A, Hossen QMM, Hossain MZ, Ahmed B, Rahim S, Rahman MS, Alam MM, Hou S, Wan X, Saito JA, Alam M, 2012. Tools to Kill: Genome of One of the most Destructive Plant Pathogenic Fungi *Macrophomina phaseolina*. *BMC Genomics* 13: 493.
37. Illakkiam D, Ponraj P, Shankar M, Muthusubramanian S, Rajendhran J, Gunasekaran P, 2013. Identification and Structure Elucidation of a Novel Antifungal Compound Produced by *Pseudomonasaeruginosa* PGPR2 Against *Macrophomina phaseolina*. *Appl Biochem Biotechnol* 171: 2176-2185.
38. Illakkiam D, Shankar M, Ponraj P, Rajendhran J, Gunasekaran P, 2014. Genome Sequencing of a Mung Bean Plant Growth Promoting Strain of *P. aeruginosa*with Biocontrol Ability. *International Journal of Genomics* Article ID 123058, 10 pages.
39. Iqbal U, Mukhtar T, 2014. Morphological and Pathogenic Variability Among *Macrophomina phaseolina* Isolates Associated with Mungbean (*Vigna radiata* L.) Wilczek from Pakistan. *The Scientific World Journal* Article ID 950175: 9 pages.
40. Inventory of Consumer Products, The Project on Emerging Nanotechnologies (2014), http://www.nanotechproject.org/inventories/consumer/.
41. Jo Y-K, Kim BH, Jung G, 2009. Antifungal Activity of Silver Ions and Nanoparticles on Phytopathogenic Fungi. *Plant Dis* 93: 1037-1043.
42. James C, 2011. Global Status of Commercialized Biotec/GM Crops. The International Service for the Acquisation of Agri-biotech Applications (ISAAA).
43. Jiang YN, Haudenshield JS, Hartman GL, 2012. Response of Soybean Fungal and Oomycete Pathogens to Apigenin and Genistein. *Mycology* 3(2): 153-157.

44. Khan SN, 2007. *Macrophomina phaseolina* as Causal Agent for Charcoalrot of Sunflower. Mycopath, 5(2): 111-118.

45. Kirubakaran SI, Sakthivel N, 2008. Site-Directed Mutagenesis, Heterologous Expression of Cyanamide Hydratase Gene and Antimicrobial Activity of Cyanamide. *Curr Microbiol* 56: 42-47.

46. Khan F, Khan MI, 2011. Fungal Lectins: Current Molecular and Biochemical Perspectives. *International Journal of Biological Chemistry* 5(1): 1-20.

47. Kulcheski FR, de Oliveira LFV, Molina LG, Almerão MP, Rodrigues FA, Marcolino J, Barbosa JF, Moreira RS, Nepomuceno AL, (Marcelino-Guimarães FC, Abdelnoor RV, Nascimento LC, Carazzolle MF, Pereira GAG, Margis R, 2011. Identification of Novel Soybean Micro RNAs Involved in Abiotic and Biotic Stresses. *BMC Genomics* 12: 307.

48. Krishnaraj C, Ramachandran R, Mohan K, Kalaichelvan PT, 2012. Optimization for Rapid Synthesis of Silver Nanoparticles and its Effect on Phytopathogenic Fungi. *Spectrochimica Acta* Part A 93: 95-99.

49. Kohli D, Joshi G, Deokar AA, Bhardwaj AR, Agarwal M, 2014. Identification and Characterization of Wilt and Salt Stress-Responsive MicroRNAs in Chickpea Through High-Throughput Sequencing. *PLoS ONE* 9(10): e108851.

50. Liu Y-G, Whittier RF, 1995. Thermal Asymmetric Interlaced PCR: Automatable Amplification and Sequencing of Insert End Fragments from PI and YAC Clones for Chromosome Walking. *GENOMICS* 25: 674-681.

51. Linhai W, Yanxin Z, Donghua L, Junbin H, Wenliang W, Haixia L, Xiurong Z, 2011. Variations in the Isolates of *Macrophomina phaseolina* from Sesame in China based on Amplified Fragment Length Polymorphism (AFLP) and Pathogenicity. *African Journal of Microbiology Research*, 5(31): 5584-5590.

52. Miklas PN, Delorme R, Stone V, Daly MJ, Stavely JR, Steadman JR, Bassett MJ, Beaver JS, 2000. Bacterial, Fungal, and Viral Disease Resistance Loci Mapped in a Recombinant Inbred Common Bean Population ('Dorado'/XAN 176). *J. Amer. Soc. Hort. Sci* 125(2): 476-481.

53. Miklas PN, Hu J, Grünwald NJ, Larsen KM, 2006. Potential Application of TRAP (Targeted Region Amplified Polymorphism) Markers for Mapping and Tagging Disease Resistance Traits in Common Bean. *Crop Sci* 46: 910-916.

54. Mahmood N, Azam MS, Islam MS, Sharmin S, Moosa MM, Hossain MA, Khan H, 2010. Differentially Expressed Transcripts of Wild and Cultivated Jute (*Corchorus spp.*) Varieties Upon Fungal (*Macrophomina phaseolina*) Infection. *Annals of Biological Research* 1(3): 120-127.

55. Mahdizadeh V, Safaie N, Goltapeh EM, 2011. Diversity of *Macrophomina phaseolina* Based on Morphological and Genotypic Characteristics in Iran. *Plant Pathol. J*27(2): 128-137.

56. Mudalige C, Girisha ST, Raghavendra VB, Niranjan MH, Ravikumar K, Sumantha MG, 2011. Molecular Characterization of *Macrophomina Phaseolina*, the Incitant of *Coleus forskohlii* Revealed by Rapd Markers. *International Journal of Life Sciences* 5(1): 44-50.

57. Mahdizadeh V, Safaie N, Goltapeh EM, 2012. Genetic Diversity of Sesame Isolates of *Macrophomina phaseolina*using rapd and issr Markers. *Trakia Journal of Sciences* 10(2): 65-74.

58. Mahmood T, Mahmood I, Mustafa S, Wahab A, 2013. In vitro Nematicidal and Fungicidal Effects on Oil of *Origanum syriacum* from Palestine Against Root-knot Nematode and *Fusarium solani* Plant Pathogens. *European Academic Research* I(6): 1095-1099.

59. Niblack TL, Bond JP, Tylka GL, 2011. Disease Complex Between Nematodes and Other Plant Pathogens. APS-IPPC Joint Meeting Abstracts of Special Session Presentations, Diseases of Plants, *Phytopathology* 101(6) (Supplement).
60. Olsen DB, Eckstein F, 1990. High-efficiency Oligonucleotide-directed Plasmid Mutagenesis. *Proc. Natl.Acad. Sci. USA*, 87: 1451-1455.
61. Omar MR, Abd-Elsalam KA, Aly AA, El-Samawaty AMA,Verreet J-A, 2007. Diversity of *Macrophomina phaseolina*from Cotton in Egypt: Analysis of Pathogenicity, Chlorate Phenotypes, and Molecular Characterization. *Journal of Plant Diseases and Protection* 114 (5): 196-204.
62. Ouyang S, Park G, Atamian HS, Han CS, Stajich JE, 2014. MicroRNAs Suppress NB Domain Genes in Tomato That Confer Resistance to *Fusarium oxysporum*. *PLoS Pathog* 10(10): e1004464. doi:10.1371/journal.ppat.1004464.
63. 'Office of the Jute Commission – Ministry of Textiles', http://www.jutecomm.gov.in.
64. Paulitz TC, 2000. Population Dynamics of Biocontrol Agents and Pathogens in Soils and Rhizospheres. *European Journal of Plant Pathology* 106: 401-413.
65. Panhwar F, 2005. Postharvest Technology of Mango Fruits, its Development, Physiology, Pathology and Marketing in Pakistan. http://www.chemlin.de/publications/documents/postharvest_technology_of_mango_fruits.
66. Prasad RD, Navaneetha T, Rao NN, 2011. Cultural, morphological, pathogenic and Molecular Diversity in *Macrophomina phaseolina* Isolates of Safflower from Southern India. *Indian Phytopath*. 64(3): 247-253.
67. Pérez-Quintero, Á.L., Quintero, A., Urrego, O., Vanegas, P. and López, C., 2012. Bioinformatic Identification of Cassava miRNAs Differentially Expressed in Response to Infection by Xanthomonas Axonopodis pv. manihotis. *BMC Plant Biology* 12(1): 29.
68. Premamalini T, Ambujavalli BT, Vijayakumar R, Rajyoganandh SV, Kalpana S, Kindo AJ, 2012. Fungal Keratitis caused by *Macrophomina phaseolina* – A Case Report. *Medical Mycology Case Reports* 1(1): 123-126.
69. Qaim M, 2003. Bt Cotton in India: Field Trial Results and Economic Projections. *World Development* 31(12): 2115-2127.
70. Roy PK, Roy U, Vora VC, 1993. Hydrolysis of Wheat Bran, Rice Bran and Jute Powder by Immobilized Enzymes from *Macrophomina phaseolina*. *World Journal of Microbiology and Biotechnology* 9: 164-167.
71. Raja V, Kurucheve V, 1997. Antifungal Properties of Some Animal Products Against *Macrophomina phaseolina* Causing Dry Root Rot in Cotton. *Plant Disease Research* 12(1): 11-14.
72. Rayatpanah S, Dalili SA, 2012. Diversity of *Macrophomina phaseolina* (Tassi) Goid Based on Chlorate Phenotypes and Pathogenicity. *International Journal of Biology* 4(2): 54-63.
73. Rayatpanah S, Nanagulyan SG, Alav SV, Razavi M, Ghanbari-Malidarreh A, 2012. Pathogenic and Genetic Diversity Among Iranian Isolates. *Chilean Journal of Agricultural Research* 72(1): 40-44.
74. Radwan O, Rouhana LV, Hartman GL, Korban SS, 2014. Genetic Mechanisms of Host–Pathogen Interactions for Charcoal Rot in Soybean. *Plant Mol Biol Rep* 32: 617-629.
75. Sanyal A, Saha SC, Kundu RK, Sinha SN, Dube DK, 1981. Induction of Carboxymethylcellulase in *Macrophomina phaseolina*. *Folia Microbiol*. 26: 83-88.
76. Saleh AA, Ahmed HU, Todd TC, Travers SE, Zeller KA, Leslie JF, Garrett KA, 2010. Relatedness of *Macrophomina phaseolina*isolates from Tallgrass Prairie, Maize, Soybean, and Sorghum. *Molecular Ecology* 19(1): 79-91.
77. Statistics-World Production of Jute Fibres from 2004/2005 to 2010/2011.' International Jute study group, http://www.jute.org.

78. Sundravadana S, Thirumurugan S, Alice D, 2011. Exploration of Molecular Variability in *Rhizoctonia bataticola*, the Incitant of Root Rot Disease of Pulse Crops. *Journal of Plant Protection Research* 51(2): 184-189.
79. Sharmin S, Azam MS, Islam MS, Sajib AA, Mahmood N, Hasan AMM, Ahmed R, Sultana K, Khan H, 2012. Xyloglucan Endotransglycosylase/Hydrolase Genes from a Susceptible and Resistant Jute Species show Opposite Expression Pattern Following *Macrophomina phaseolina* infection, *Communicative & Integrative Biology* 5(6): 598-606.
80. Saharan V, Mehrotra A, Khatik R, Rawal P, Sharma SS, Pal A, 2013. Synthesis of Chitosan Based Nanoparticles and their *in vitro* Evaluation Against Phytopathogenic Fungi. *International Journal of Biological Macromolecules* 62: 677-683.
81. Sarkar TS, Biswas P, Ghosh SK, Ghosh S, 2014. Nitric Oxide Production by Necrotrophic Pathogen *Macrophomina phaseolina* and the Host Plant in Charcoal Rot Disease of Jute: Complexity of the Interplay Between Necrotroph–Host Plant Interactions. *PLoS ONE* 9(9): e107348.
82. Sharma I, Kumari N, Sharma V, 2014. Defense Gene Expression in *Sorghum bicolor* Against *Macrophomina phaseolina* in Leaves and Roots of Susceptible and Resistant Cultivars. *Journal of Plant Interactions* 9(1): 315-323.
83. Singh G, Bhalla A, Bhatti JS, Chandel S, Rajput A, Abdullah A, Andrabi W, Kaur P, 2014. Potential of Chitinases as a Biopesticide Against Agriculturally Harmful Fungi and Insects. *RRJMB* 3(1): 27-32.
84. Tan G, Gao Y, Shi M, Zhang X, He S, Chen Z, An C, 2005. Site Finding-PCR: A Simple and Efficient PCR Method for Chromosome Walking. *Nucleic Acids Research* 33(13): e122.
85. Virupakshaprabhu H, Adiver SS, Rameshbhat, Narayana YD, Shamaraojahagirdar, Parameshwarappa KG, 2012. Genetic Variability in *Macrophomina phaseolina* (Tassi.) Goid., Causal Agent of Charcoal Rot of Sorghum. *Karnataka J. Agric. Sci* 25 (1): 72-76.
86. Vasebi Y, Safaie N, Alizadeh A, 2013. Biological Control of Soybean Charcoal Root Rot Disease Using Bacterial and Fungal Antagonists *In Vitro* and Greenhouse Condition. *J. Crop Prot* 2 (2): 139-150.
87. Wheeler H, 1975. Plant Pathogenesis. Academic, Press, New York and London 2-3.
88. Wang H, Jones RW, 1995. Cloning, Characterization and Functional Expression of an Endoglucanase - Encoding Gene from the Phytopathogenic Fungus *Macrophomina phaseolina*. *Gene* 158: 125-128.
89. Wang S, He J, Cui Z, Li S, 2007. Self-Formed Adaptor PCR: A Simple and Efficient Method for Chromosome Walking. *Appl. Environ. Microbiol* 73(15): 5048-5051.
90. Wang Z, Ye S, Li J, Zheng B, Bao M, Ning G, 2011. Fusion Primer and Nested Integrated PCR (FPNI-PCR): A New High-efficiency Strategy for Rapid Chromosome Walking or Flanking Sequence Cloning. *BMC Biotechnology* 11: 109.
91. Yang X, Wang L, Yuan D, Lindsey K, Zhang X, 2010. Small RNA and Degradome Sequencing Reveal Complex miRNA Regulation during Cotton Somatic Embryogenesis. *Journal of Experimental Botany* doi:10.1093/jxb/ert013.
92. Zhao J-P, Jiang X-L, Zhang B-Y, Su X-H, 2012. Involvement of MicroRNA-Mediated Gene Expression Regulation in the Pathological Development of Stem Canker Disease in *Populus trichocarpa*. *PLoS ONE*7(9): e44968.

Pages: 150-169

BIOTECHNOLOGY AND ENVIRONMENTAL MANAGEMENT

Edited by: Prof. Arun Arya; Dr. Raaz K Maheswari & Dr. Pawan Kumar 'Bharti'

ISBN: 978-93-5056-862-0

Edition: 2017

Published by: Discovery Publishing House Pvt. Ltd., New Delhi (India)

7

Bioconversion of Organic Waste into Value Added Products using Earthworm and its Impact on Crops

S. Ponmani
C. Udayasoorian
P. Kannan

INTRODUCTION

Agriculture, food processing, pulp and paper, or any cellulose based industry produces massive quantities of solid and liquid waste materials. Disposal and environmental friendly management of these industrial wastes has become a serious global problem. Therefore, much attention has been paid in recent years to develop low-inputted efficient technologies to convert these nutrient-rich organic wastes into value added products for sustainable land practices. Decomposition of complex organic waste resources into odor free humus like substances through the action of worm is termed vermicomposting. However, vermicomposting is stabilization of organic material involving the joint action of earthworms and microorganisms. Although microbes are responsible for biochemical degradation of organic matter, earthworms are the important drivers of the process, conditioning the substrate and altering the biological activity (Dominguez, 2001). Several epigeic earthworms have been identified as detritus feeders which can be reared on large numbers in organic wastes (Taylor *et al.*, 2003). Some of these epigeics, e.g. *Eisenia fetida* (Savigny), *Perionyx excavatus* (Perrier), and *Eudrilus eugeniae* Kinberg, have appeared as the key candidates for organic waste recycling industries (Suthar, 2007).

Dryland Agricultural Research Station, Tamil Nadu Agricultural University, Chettinad – 630 102, Tamil Nadu, (India)

However, agriculture by-products, e.g. animal dung, farmyard manure, and crop residues, are potential sources of plant nutrients. According to a conservative estimation, around 600-700 million tonnes (mt) of agricultural waste (including 272 mt of crop residues) are available in India every year, but most of it remains unutilized. This huge quantity of wastes can be converted into nutrient-rich bio-fertilizer (vermicompost) for sustainable land restoration practices. It is interesting that a great proportion of the crop nutrient input during cultivation returned in the form of the plant residues. Estimation showed that 30–35% of applied N & P and 70-80% for K remained in the crop residues of food crops. Such nutrient rich crop residues must be 'prepared' before they are used as a fertilizer, and earthworms are suitable candidates for the same. According to Lorimor *et al.* (2001), compared to conventional composting system (as commonly used in India to manage crop residues and other related wastes), vermicomposting often results in mass reduction, shorter time for processing, high levels of humus with reduced phytotoxicity. Since organic matter is transferred differently in compost and vermicompost, it can be partly explained by the mutualistic relationship between ingested microorganisms and intestinal mucus (Trigo and Lavelle, 1993).

The composting efficiency and biology of tropical earthworm species, i.e. *E. eugeniae* Kinberg, is well documented in literature. Several workers have reported the vermicomposting potential of *E. eugeniae* by using a variety of waste materials such as animal dung (Dominguez *et al.*, 2001); industrial waste (Senappa *et al.*, 1995), etc. The crop residues, which are produced in a huge quantity, have not been previously tested as feeding substances for *E. eugeniae*. Therefore, there are vast opportunities to explore the composting potential of this species to manage the crop residues and other agriculture by-products.

METHODS OF VERMICOMPOSTING

Pits Below the Ground

Pits made for vermicomposting are 1 m deep and 1.5 m wide. The length varies as required.

Heaping above the Ground

The waste material is spread on a polythene sheet placed on the ground and then covered with cattle dung. Sunitha *et al.* (1997) compared the efficacy of pit and heap methods of preparing vermicompost under field conditions. Considering the biodegradation of wastes as the criterion, the heap method of preparing vermicompost was better than the pit method. Earthworm population was high in the heap method, with a 21-fold increase in *Eudrilus eugenae* as compared to 17-fold increase in the pit method. Biomass production was also higher in the heap method (46-fold increase) than in the pit method (31-fold). Consequent production of vermicompost was also higher in the heap method (51 kg) than in the pit method (40 kg).

Tanks above the Ground

Tanks made up of different materials such as normal bricks, hollow bricks, shabaz stones, asbestos sheets and locally available rocks were evaluated for vermicompost preparation. Tanks can be constructed with the dimensions suitable for operations viz., 1.5 m (5 feet) width, 4.5 m (15 feet) length and 0.9 m (3 feet) height (ICRISAT, 2006) The commercial biodigester contains a partition wall with small holes to facilitate easy movement of earthworms from one tank to the other.

Cement Rings

Vermicompost can also be prepared above the ground by using cement rings (ICRISAT and APRLP 2003). The size of the cement ring should be 90 cm in diameter and 30 cm in height.

MATERIALS REQUIRED FOR VERMICOMPOSTING

A range of agricultural residues, all dry wastes, for example, sorghum straw and rice straw (after feeding cattle), dry leaves of crops and trees, pigeonpea (*Cajanus cajan*) stalks, groundnut (*Arachis hypogaea*) husk, soybean residues, vegetable wastes, weed (*Parthenium*) plants before flowering, fiber from coconut (*Cocos nucifera*) trees and sugarcane (*Saccharum officinarum*) trash can be converted into vermicompost. In addition, animal manures, dairy and poultry wastes, food industry wastes, municipal solid wastes, biogas sludge and bagasse from sugarcane factories also serve as good raw materials for vermicomposting. The quantity of raw materials required using a cement ring of 90 cm in diameter and 30 cm in height or a pit or tank measuring 1.5 m × 1 m × 1 m is given below:

Dry organic wastes (DOW)	50 kg
Dung slurry (DS)	15 kg
Rock phosphate (RP)	2 kg
Earthworms (EW)	500-700
Water (W)	5 L every three days

The various ingredients are used in the ratio of 5:1.5:0.2:50-75:0.5 of DOW:DS:RP:EW:W. In the tank or pit system 100 kg of raw material and 15-20 kg of cow dung are needed for each cubic meter of the bed.

EARTHWORM

Biology of Earthworm

Earthworms are natural invertebrates of agro ecosystem belonging to the family lumbricidae and dominant in the temperate and tropical soils. They are hermaphrodites, both male and female reproductive organs are present in every single earthworm but self-fertilization does not generally occur. At the time of laying eggs, the sexually mature worms have a distinctive epidermal ring shaped area called, the clitellum, which has gland cells that secrete material to form a viscid, girdle like structure known as cocoon. Cocoons are small, with their size varying according to species. The colour of the cocoon changes gradually as it develops from the freshly laid stage to the hatching stage. Though the number of fertilized ova in each cocoon ranges from one to twenty for lumbricid worms, often only one or two survive and hatch.

Cocoon production starts at the age of 6 weeks and continues till the end of 6 months. Under favourable conditions one pair of earthworms can produce 100 cocoons in 6 weeks to 6 months (Ismail, 1997). The incubation period of a cocoon is roughly about 3-5 weeks, in temperate worms it ranges between 3-30 weeks and in tropical worms within 1-8 weeks. Earthworms also have the power to regenerate segments, which are lost. The doubling time i.e. the time taken by a given earthworm population to double its number or biomass, specifically depends upon the earthworm species, type of food, climatic condition etc. For example, the mean doubling time, with reference to density and biomass of *Lampito mauritii* in different organic inputs is 38.05 and 33.77 days respectively while in case of *Perionyx excavatus* it is 11.72 and 16.14 days respectively (Ismail, 1997). The most effective use of earthworms in organic waste management requires a detailed understanding of biology of all potentially useful species (Edward, 1998) population dynamics and productivity in earthworms can not be fully understood unless the life cycle of each earthworm is known. There are studies on life cycle and reproductive strategies of earthworms on temperate species, Indian species (Julka, 2001) and tropical species. Knowledge of reproductive strategies of earthworms comes predominately from studies on temperate species (Jimenez, 1999). Studies on the life cycles i.e. cocoons production, morphology, hatching pattern and fecundity of seven tropical earthworm species have been done by Battacharjee and Chaudhari (2002) for effective vermiculture. Quality of organic waste is one of the factors determining the onset and rate of reproduction (Dominguez, 2000). The quantity of food taken by a worm varies from 100 to 300 mg/g body weight/day. Earthworms derive their nutrition from organic materials, living micro organisms and by decomposing animals. Surface living earthworms feed on food material selectively while deep soil living worms ingest soil as such. The type and amount of material available influence the size of earthworms, population, species diversity, growth rate and cocoons production.

Earthworms voraciously feed on organic wastes and while utilizing only a small portion for their body synthesis they excrete a large part of these consumed waste materials in a half digested form. Since the intestines of earthworms harbour wide ranges of microorganisms, enzymes, hormones, etc., these half digested material decompose rapidly and is transformed into a form of vermicompost within a short time.

Species of Earthworms

There are about 3000 species of earthworms distributed all over world and about 384 species are reported in India. Most earthworms are terrestrial organisms, which live in the soil. But some species like *Pontodrilus burmudensis* lead a comfortable life in estuarine water. Taxonomic studies on the Indian earthworms species have been carried out mainly by Julka (1983). Earthworms vary greatly in size, In India some peregrine species like *Microscotex phosphoreus* (Duges) are even 20 mm long while some endemic geophagous worms such as Drawida *grandus* (Bourus) may reach up to one meter in length. Earthworm occur in diverse habitats, organic materials like manures litter, compost etc are highly attractive for earthworms but they are also found in very hydrophilic environment close to both fresh and brachish water, some species can survive under snow. Most of the earthworms are omnivorous, however Agastrodrilus, a carnivorous genus of earthworms from the Ivory Coast of Africa has been reported to feed upon other earthworms of the family Eudrilidae.

Vermiculturing Process

Earthworms are generally classified as saprophages but based on their feeding habits they are classified into detrivores and geophages. Detrivores feed at or near the soil surface on plant litter or dead roots and other plant debris or on mammalian dung. These worms are called humus formers and comprise the epigeic and anecic forms. *Perionyx excavatus, Eisenia fetida, Eudrilus euginae, Lampito mauritii, Polypheretima elongata, Octochaetona serrata* and *Octochaetona curensis* are few examples of detrivorous earthworms (Ismail, 1997). Geophagous worms, feeding beneath the surface, ingest large quantities of organically rich soil and comprise the endogeic earthworms, *Metaphire posthuma* and *Octochaetona thurstoni* are two common examples of geophages.

Epigeics are surface dwellers and feed on organic matter on soil surface. Endogeic earthworms spend most of their time in the minerals layer of soil and burrow predominantly. Anecic earthworms like *Lumbricus terrestris* predominantly make vertical burrows. Of these three ecological varieties of earthworms, the epigeics and anecics have been harnessed for use in the vermicomposting process. Although a number of earthworm species have been used, one of the most commonly used world wide is *Eisenia fetida*, the tiger or brandling worm. Other suitable species include *Lumbricus rubelus, Eudrilus eugeniae* and *Perionyx excavatus* an Asian species (Edwards, 1995) and Eisenia andrei (Haimi, 1990). As local species of earthworms are excellently adapted to local conditions, Ismail (1995) recommended the 'in-situ' soil community comprising the epigeic and anecic varieties, for the combined process of litter and soil management. He studied the distribution of earthworms in 50 locations. *Lampito mauritii* and *Octochaetona serrata* were found to be the dominating species in the sandy loams and clay loams respectively. The endogeic and anecic earthworms associate with free living soil bacteria to constitute the drilosphere (Ismail, 1995).

The selection of the correct earthworm species for particular vermiculture application is important (Appelhof, 1996). Also the vermicomposts produced -using different species of earthworms show variation in nutrient composition.

A study was conducted on the effect of moisture on the growth, maturation and cocoon production of *Dendrobaena venera,* an earthworm species from Europe. It was considered as less successful species for vermicomposting as it requires relatively high moisture content (Muyima, 1994). Also in a comparative study, Drawida nap1ensis showed relatively slow growth in comparison to other earthworms species although population was not a prerequisite for the production of viable cocoons, indicating that it may be parthenogenetic. Shanthi *et al.* (1993), in India, evaluated the potential of three species of earthworms namely *Metaphire posthuma,* Eisenia species and *Perionyx excavatus* in degradation of vegetable waste. Among all three, P. excavatus was able to withstand greater ranges of moisture and temperature than other species and thus most suited for use in vermicomposting. Contrary to this, *E. fetida* had a wider tolerance for temperature than Eudrilus eugeniae and *P. excavatus.* It tolerates as high as 42° C as well as low soil temperature below 5° C. The quality and amount of food material influences not only the size of earthworm population but also the species present and their rate of growth and fecundity (Chaudhari and Battacharjee 2002). Handricsen (1990) suggested that C:N ratio and particularly polyphenol concentration are the most important factor determining litter palatability in detrivorus earthworms.

Earthworms can be cultured and put to various uses i.e. to improve and maintain soil fertility, to convert organic waste into manure, to produce earthworm based protein food (earthworm meal) for livestock, drug and vitamins source, as natural detoxicant and a bait for fish market (Ghosh, 2004). Culturing of earthworms is done in humid places with proper protection from predators like ants, rats, bandicoots, frogs and toads. Shelter is provided to avoid direct sunlight and water logging conditions due to rain.

The first step in vermiculture is to select suitable feed materials for the earthworms. These can be nitrogen rich material like cattle dung, pig manure, poultry manure etc. or other organic materials like leguminous agro waste. The feed material should not have C:N ratio more than 40. Using carbon material with a very high C: N ratio, like paper and soaked cardboards, may just fatten the worms (Ismail, 1997). A variety of non-standard materials for vermiculturing have been compared. The greatest weight increase of earthworms *Eisenia fetida* was obtained with 50g soil mixed with 150g cellulose waste. Reproduction was most intensive in substrate consisting of 100g cattle manure, 50g soil and 50g cellulose waste. The best results obtained with cotton waste were in combination with cattle manure in the ratio 1:5. Grape cake and tobacco waste gave only marginal increase and the earthworms did not reproduce. An outdoor study conducted using polythene containers to assess the suitability of different organic residues, i.e. soyabean, wheat, maize strover, chickpea straw and city garbage, with *Perionyx excavatus,* showed best growth of earthworms with maize strover (Manna, 1997).

Wooden boxes, cemented tanks, earthen pots, earthen pits lined with either stones or plastics can be used for vermiculturing. Humid and slightly dark places, 40-50% moisture in beds, 20-30° C temperature, pH of 7 and partially decomposed organic matter rich in nitrogen help earthworms to grow faster and produce more cocoons (Kale, 1995). Vermiculturing is also being employed to produce castings for use as agricultural fertilizer. Cuba has developed more than 170 vermiculture centres for the above purpose. Data are also available on the chemical composition of earthworms castings from worms fed with different feed stocks (Werner, 1995). It is widely believed that organic fertilizers, by providing a nutrient rich substrate, support higher earthworm population, whether they feed directly upon the organic matter or upon the microorganisms, which colonize the organic materials. Inorganic fertilizers may also contribute indirectly to an quality of crop residues returned to the soil (Edwards, 1995), although the long term use of inorganic nitrogen fertilizers may some times cause a decrease in earthworm abundance and biomass, particularly if it is ammonia based (Ma, 1990).

VERMICOMPOST PREPARATION

Steps in the Process

Vermicomposting involves the following steps:

- Cover the bottom of the cement ring with a layer of tiles or coconut husk or polythene sheet.
- Spread 15-20 cm layer of organic waste material on the polythene sheet. Sprinkle rock phosphate powder if available (it helps in improving nutritional quality of compost) on the waste material and then sprinkle cow dung slurry. Fill the ring completely in layers as described. Paste the top of the ring with soil or cow dung. Allow the material to decompose for 15 to 20 days.
- When the heat evolved during the decomposition of the materials has subsided (15-20 days after heaping), release selected earthworms (500 to 700) through the cracks developed.
- Cover the ring with wire mesh or gunny bag to prevent birds from picking the earthworms. Sprinkle water every three days to maintain adequate moisture and body temperature of the earthworms.

The vermicompost is ready in about 2 months if agricultural waste is used and about 4 weeks if sericulture waste is used as substrate.

- The processed vermicompost is black, light in weight and free from bad odor.
- When the compost is ready, do not water for 2-3 days to make compost easy for sifting. Pile the compost in small heaps and leave under ambient conditions for a couple of hours when all the worms move down the heap in the bed. Separate upper portion of the manure and sieve the lower portion to separate the earthworms from the manure. The culture

in the bed contains different stages of the earthworm's life cycle, namely, cocoons, juveniles and adults. Transfer this culture to fresh half decomposed feed material. The excess as well as big earthworms can be used for feeding fish or poultry. Pack the compost in bags and store the bags in a cool place.

- Prepare another pile about 20 days before removing the compost and repeat the process by following the same procedure as described above.

Precautions during the Process

The following precautions should be taken during vermicomposting:

- The African species of earthworms, *Eisenia fetida* and *Eudrilus eugenae* are ideal for the preparation of vermicompost. Most Indian species are not suitable for the purpose.
- Only plant-based materials such as grass, leaves or vegetable peelings should be utilized in preparing vermicompost.
- Materials of animal origin such as eggshells, meat, bone, chicken droppings, etc are not suitable for preparing vermicompost.
- *Gliricidia* loppings and tobacco leaves are not suitable for rearing earthworms.
- The earthworms should be protected against birds, termites, ants and rats.
- Adequate moisture should be maintained during the process. Either stagnant water or lack of moisture could kill the earthworms.
- After completion of the process, the vermicompost should be removed from the bed at regular intervals and replaced by fresh waste materials.

Characteristics of Vermicompost

Vermicompost, a product of a non- thermophilic biodegradation of organic material through interactions between earthworms and micro organisms, is a peat like material with high porosity, aeration, drainage, water holding capacity and microbial activity, (Atiyeh, 2000). It contains most nutrients in plant available forms such as nitrates, phosphates, exchangeable calcium, soluble potassium etc (Edward, 1998) and has large particular surface area that provides many microsites for microbial activity and for the strong retention of nutrients. The plant growth regulators and other plant growth influencing materials i.e. auxins, cytokinins, humic substances etc, produced by micro organisms have been reported from vermicompost (Atiyeh, 2000). The humic materials extracted from vermicomposts have been reported to produce auxin- like cell growth and nitrate metabolism of carrots (*Daucus carota*) (Muscolo, 1999). However humic substances can occur naturally in mature animal manure, sewage sludge or paper – mill sludge but their amount and rates of production are increased dramatically by vermicomposting. The nutrient status of vermicompost produced with different organic waste is; organic carbon 9.15 to 17.98%, total nitrogen 0.5 to 1.5%, available phosphorus 0.1 to 0.3%, available potassium 0.15, calcium and magnesium22.70 to 70 mg/100g, copper 2 to 9.3 ppm, Zinc 5.7 to 11.5 ppm and available sulphur, 128 to 548 ppm (Kale, 1995).

How to Use Vermicompost?

- Vermicompost can be used for all crops: agricultural, horticultural, ornamental and vegetables at any stage of the crop.
- For general field crops: Around 2-3 t ha^{-1} vermicompost is used by mixing with seed at the time of sowing or by row application when the seedlings are 12-15 cm in height. Normal irrigation is followed.
- For fruit trees: The amount of vermicompost ranges from 5 to 10 kg per tree depending on the age of the plant. For efficient application, a ring (15-18 cm deep) is made around the plant. A thin layer of dry cow dung and bone meal is spread along with 2-5 kg of vermicompost and water is sprayed on the surface after covering with soil.
- For vegetables: For raising seedlings to be transplanted, vermicompost at 1 t ha^{-1} is applied in the nursery bed. This results in healthy and vigorous seedlings. But for transplants, vermicompost at the rate of 400-500 g per plant is applied initially at the time of planting and 45 days after planting (before irrigation).
- For flowers: Vermicompost is applied at 750-1000 kg ha^{-1}.
- For vegetable and flower crops vermicompost is applied around the base of the plant. It is then covered with soil and watered regularly.

IMPACT OF VERMICOMPOST ON CROPS

Effects of Vermicompost on Plant Growth

Vermicompost significantly stimulates the growth of a wide range of plant species including several horticultural crops such as tomato, pepper, garlic, aubergine, strawberry, sweet corn and green gram. Vermicompost has also been found to have positive effects on some aromatic and medicinal plants, cereals such as sorghum and rice, fruit crops such as banana and papaya and ornamentals such as geranium, marigolds, petunia, chrysanthemum and poinsettia. Positive effects of vermicompost have also been observed in forestry species such as acacia, eucalyptus and pine tree.

Vermicompost has been found to have beneficial effects when used as a total or partial substitute for mineral fertilizer in peat-based artificial greenhouse potting media and as soil amendments in field studies. Likewise, some studies show that vermicomposting leachates or vermicompost water-extracts, used as substrate amendments or foliar sprays, also promote the growth of tomato plants, sorghum and strawberries (Singh *et al.* 2010).

Positive effects of vermicompost include stimulated seed germination in several plant species such as green gram, tomato plants, petunia and pine trees. Vermicompost also has a positive effect on vegetative growth, stimulating shoot and root development (Edwards *et al.*, 2004). The effects include alterations in seedling morphology such as increased leaf area and root branching (Lazcano *et al.*, 2009). Vermicompost has also been shown to stimulate plant flowering, increasing the number and biomass of the flowers produced (Arancon *et al.*, 2008), as well as increasing fruit yield (Singh *et al.*, 2008). In addition to increasing plant growth and productivity, vermicompost may also increase the nutritional quality of some vegetable crops such as tomatoes (Gutiérrez-Miceli *et al.*, 2007), Chinese cabbage (Wang *et al.*, 2010), spinach (Peyvast *et al.*, 2008), strawberries (Singh *et al.*, 2008) and lettuce (Coria- Cayupán *et al.*, 2009).

Nevertheless, despite the large body of scientific evidence showing the positive effects of vermicompost on plant growth and yield, there is also strong evidence that these effects are not general or constant, and that there is great variability in the magnitude of the effects reported in different studies. In fact, some studies report that vermicompost may decrease growth and even cause plant death (Lazcano *et al.*, 2009). The variability in the effects of vermicompost may depend on the cultivation system into which it is incorporated, as well as on the physical, chemical and biological characteristics of vermicompost, which vary widely depending on the original feedstock, the earthworm species used, the production process, and the age of vermicompost (Warman and AngLopez, 2010).

There is also a large variation in the effects of vermicompost depending on the plant species or even the variety considered. This was observed in tomato plants where the replacement of a fertilized commercial potting media with vermicompost had different effects on germination, seedling elongation, biomass allocation, fruit morphology and chemical properties of three tomato varieties (Zaller, 2007). Similar variation was observed in an experiment studying the effects of vermicompost and vermicompost extracts on the germination and early growth of six different progenies of maritime pine Lazcano *et al.* (2009). In this experiment, the speed of maturation increased, relative to the control without vermicompost, in three out of the six pine progenies, decreased in two of the progenies and was unaffected in the other. It may be expected that different hybrids or plant genotypes will respond differently to vermicompost, considering that plant genotype determines important differences in nutrient uptake capacity, nutrient use efficiency and resource allocation within the plant. Different genotypes may therefore enhance root growth or modify root exudation patterns in order to increase nutrient uptake (Cavani and Mimmo 2007), and all of these strategies will determine the establishment of different interactions with the microbial communities at the rhizosphere level. In fact, after the application of vermicompost to sweet corn crops, the different genotypes showed important differences in their rhizosphere microbial community (Aira *et al.* 2010). In light of this evidence, it is clear that vermicompost constitutes a promising alternative to inorganic fertilizers in promoting plant growth.

However, further research into the exact mechanisms and circumstances that stimulate plant growth by this organic substrate is necessary in order to maintain consumer confidence in this type of fertilizer.

Plant Growth Regulating Mechanisms

Vermicompost is a microbiologically-active, nutrient-rich, peat-like material, which when added to plant growing media may influence plant growth directly or indirectly through different chemical, physical and biological mechanisms (Figure 7.1).

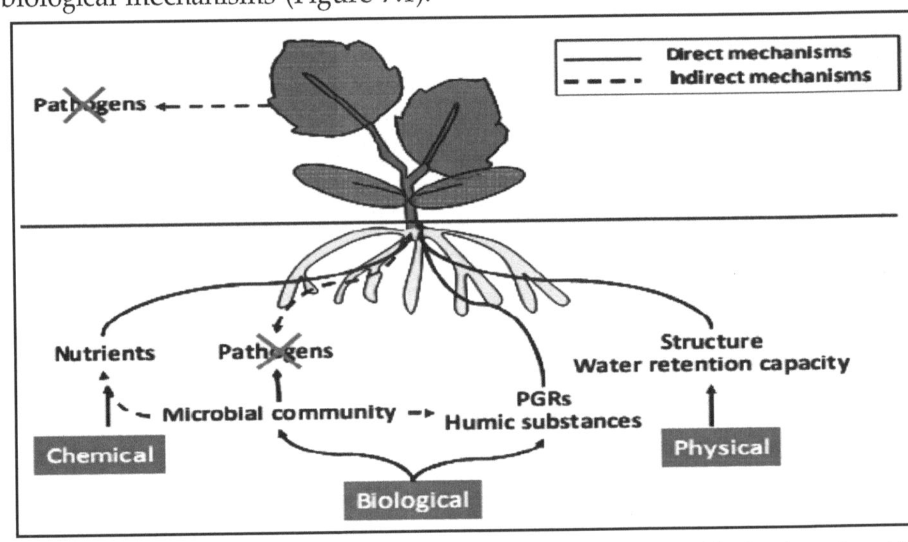

Fig. 7.1: Some of the Proposed Chemical, Biological and Physical Mechanisms by which Vermicompost may Directly or Indirectly Influence Plant Growth and Development

Direct Mechanisms

As regards the direct effects on plant growth, vermicompost constitutes a source of plant macro - and micronutrients. Although some of these nutrients are present in inorganic forms and are readily available to plants, most are released gradually through mineralization of the organic matter, thus constituting a slow-release fertilizer that supplies the plant with a gradual and constant source of nutrients. However, in contrast to chemical fertilizers, the amount of nutrients provided may vary greatly depending on the original feedstock, processing time and maturity of the vermicompost (Campitelli and Ceppi, 2008).

Vermicompost is a finely-divided peat-like material and because of this fine structure, the addition of vermicompost to plant potting media causes significant changes in the physical properties, altering water and air availability in the substrates and conditioning root growth. Nonetheless, the type and magnitude of these effects depends on the physical characteristics of the original growing medium. For example, the bulk density of vermicompost is usually higher and the particle size lower than in some of the most commonly used peat-based substrate; mixing of these two substrates produces a significant increase in the bulk density and water holding capacity, while decreasing particle size and total porosity (Bachmann and Metzger, 2007). Hidalgo *et al.* (2006) reported a significant increase in total porosity and water holding capacity after addition of vermicompost to a greenhouse potting medium comprising a mixture of sand, pine bark and peat. Vermicompost may also have significant effects on soil physical properties. Ferreras *et al.* (2006) observed that addition of 20 t ha^{-1} of vermicompost to an agricultural soil in two consecutive years significantly improved soil porosity and aggregate stability. The number of large, elongated soil macropores increased significantly after a single application of a dose of vermicompost equivalent to 200 kg ha^{-1} of N to a corn field (Marinari *et al.*, 2000). Similarly, Gopinath *et al.* (2008) reported a significant decrease in soil bulk density and a significant increase in soil pH and total organic carbon after application of vermicompost in two consecutive growing seasons, at a rate equivalent to 60 kg ha^{-1} of N. Together these changes in soil properties improve the availability of air and water, thus encouraging seedling emergence and root growth.

Despite the above-mentioned physical and chemical mechanisms, there is much experimental evidence showing that vermicompost enhances plant growth further than expected because of nutrient supply and improvements in the physical condition of substrates. This was first suggested by Scott (1988) and Edwards and Burrows (1988), who observed that small doses of vermicompost added to the potting media of several ornamental species, produced a much larger increase in plant growth than the equivalent dose of nutrients. These effects were maintained even when vermicompost was diluted 1:20 with other potting media, resulting in a dose of vermicompost would be expected to have negligible physical effects. This was also observed more recently in field experiments carried out by Singh *et al.* (2008). Both studies indicated a significant increase in the growth and productivity of strawberries cultivated with 5 and 7.5 t ha^{-1} of vermicompost respectively, in comparison with strawberries cultivated with equivalent doses of mineral fertilizers. Furthermore, many studies have shown that increases in growth and yield often involve changes in plant development and/or plant morphology such as increased leaf area, root volume and root branching (Singh *et al.*, 2008). It has been postulated that such enhancement of plant growth may be attributed to the existence of biologically-mediated plant growth promoting mechanisms.

Vermicompost may influence plant growth directly via the supply of plant growth regulating substances (PGRs). This was first proposed by Tomati and Galli (1995). In these experiments the authors compared the effects of different vermicompost extracts on the growth of Begonia, Petunia and Coleus with the effects produced by auxins, gibberellins and cytokinins, and concluded that there was a strong evidence of hormonal activity caused by the earthworms. Hormonal activity has also been associated with the humic substances present in vermicompost. Zandonadi *et al.* (2006) reported that the humic substances extracted from earthworm compost were capable of inducing lateral root growth in maize plants by stimulation of the plasma membrane H^+-ATPase activity, thus producing similar effects such as the exogenous application of indole-3-acetic acid (IAA). Furthermore, the induction of lateral root initiation by vermicompost-derived humic substances in arabidopsis has been related to the activation of the transcription of some auxin responsive genes (Trevisan *et al.*, 2010). The hypothesis of the auxin activity of vermicompost humic substances is reinforced by the presence of exchangeable auxin groups in their macrostructure.

It has been suggested that earthworms may be important agents capable of influencing the production of PGRs by microorganisms through the stimulation and promotion of microbial activity in organic substrates (Nardi *et al.*, 1988). Nevertheless, some authors suggest that earthworms, and not microorganisms, are responsible for the production of PGRs. Nielson (1965) reported the first evidence of the presence of indole compounds in the tissues of *Aporrectodea caliginosa*, *Lumbricus rubellus*, and *Eisenia fetida*. More recently, El Harti *et al.* (2001) showed that a crude extract of the earthworm *Lumbricus terrestris* was able to stimulate rooting in bean seeds due to the presence of indole compounds of endogenous origin.

Indirect Mechanisms

Vermicompost has also been found to have a wide range of indirect effects on plant growth such as the mitigation or suppression of plant diseases (Figure 7.1). Suppression of plant diseases has been extensively investigated in other organic amendments such as manure and compost (Trillas *et al.*, 2006). Likewise, some studies have shown that vermicompost can suppress a wide range of microbial diseases, insect pests and plant parasitic nematodes.

As regards the suppression of fungal diseases, Orlikowski (1999) observed that the addition of vermicompost extracts to three ornamental plant species significantly reduced sporulation of the pathogen *Phytophthora cryptogea*. Similarly Nakasone *et al.* (1999) observed that aqueous extracts of vermicompost were capable of reducing the growth of pathogenic fungi such as *Botrytis cinerea*, *Sclerotinia sclerotiorum*, *Corticium rolfsii*, *Rhizoctonia solani* and *Fusarium oxysporum*. The addition of solid vermicompost to tomato seeds significantly reduced infection caused by *Fusarium lycopersici* (Szczech, 1999) and *Phytophthora nicotianae* (Szczech and Smolinska, 2001). Nevertheless, Szczech and Smolinska (2001) did not find any significant suppressive effects of a sewage sludge vermicompost on *Phytophthora nicotianae*, in comparison with peat. Edwards *et al* (2006) observed that the suppressive effect exerted by several types of vermicompost on several plant pathogens such as *Pythium*,

Rhizoctonia, Verticillium, and *Plectosporium,* disappeared after sterilization of the vermicompost, and concluded that disease suppression may be related to the presence of biological suppressive agents in vermicompost.

As regards the effects of vermicompost on insect pests and mites, field studies have shown that the addition of vermicompost to soil significantly reduces the incidence of the psyllid *Heteropsylla cubana* (Biradar *et al.*, 1998), the sucking insect *Aproaerema modicella* (Ramesh, 2000), jassids, aphids, beetles, and spider mites (Rao, 2002). Furthermore, some studies show that vermicompost reduces not only the degree of plant infestation, but also the populations of plant parasitic insects in soils. This has been reported by Arancon *et al.*, (2005), who showed that vermicompost produced from food waste significantly reduced the populations of two species of beetles in soil (*Acalymma vittatum, Diabotrica undecimpunctata*), in comparison with inorganic fertilization. Similarly Yardim *et al.*, (2006) observed a significant decrease in the larvae of the worm *Manduca quinquemaculata* after addition of vermicompost to a cucumber crop. Arancon *et al.* (2008) observed a significant reduction in the populations of spider mites (*Tetranychus urticae*), mealy bugs (*Pseudococcus* sp.) and aphids (*Myzus persicae*) after the addition of food waste vermicompost to several vegetable crops (tomatoes, cucumber, cabbage, bush beans and eggplants).

Vermicompost may also have significant effects on both the incidence and abundance of plant-parasitic nematodes in soil. This was first reported by Swathi *et al.* (1998), who found that addition of vermicompost to soil at a rate of 1kg m^{-2} significantly inhibited the incidence of the parasite nematode *Meloidogyne incognita* in tobacco plants. Similar reductions in the degree of plant infestation by *Meloidogyne incognita* were observed by Morra *et al.* (1998), while Ribeiro *et al.* (1998) reported a significant decrease in the egg mass of *Meloidogyne javanica* after the application vermicompost to the growth medium. Arancon *et al.* (2005) indicated significant reductions in the abundance of plant-parasitic nematodes in soil plots amended with different doses of two types of vermicompost, in comparison with the effects of inorganic fertilizers.

According to the mechanisms proposed for compost (Noble and Coventry, 2005), disease suppression by vermicompost may be attributed to either direct suppression of pathogens or to the induction of systemic resistance in the plant (Figure 7.1). Direct suppression of the pathogen by the vermicompost-associated microflora and microfauna may be general or specific, depending on the existence of a single suppressive agent or the joint action of several agents. In both cases, the proposed mechanisms are competition, antibiosis and parasitism. The mechanisms responsible for disease suppression by vermicompost are not yet well known, and the effects of biopesticides are usually attributed to general suppressive effects. Vermicompost increases microbial biomass in soil and changes the diversity and abundance of soil fauna (Arancon *et al.*, 2005), and thus a broader range of organisms may act as biocontrol agents. Furthermore, there is recent evidence showing that the use of vermicompost extracts as foliar sprays in different crop plants effectively reduces the incidence of fungal diseases such as *Phytophthora infestans* (Zaller, 2006), *Erysiphe pisi* and *Erysiphe cichoracearum* (Singh *et al.*, 2003). Reductions in disease incidence are sometimes accompanied by an increase in the production of defence substances by the plant (Singh *et al.* 2003), thus suggesting the induction of plant systemic resistance by vermicompost.

Some of the indirect effects of vermicompost have been related to the change in the microbiological properties of the soil or the potting media. Processing by earthworms during vermicomposting has a strong effect on the microbial community of the initial waste (Dominguez *et al.*, 2010). Vermicompost therefore has a rather different microbial community structure than the parent waste, with lower biomass and activity but enhanced metabolic diversity.

CONCLUSION

The production of degradable organic waste and its safe disposal becomes the current global problem. Meanwhile the rejuvenation of degraded soils by protecting topsoil and sustainability of productive soils is a major concern at the international level. Provision of a sustainable environment in the soil by amending with good quality organic soil additives enhances the water holding capacity and nutrient supplying capacity of soil and also the development of resistance in plants to pests and diseases. By reducing the time of humification process and by evolving the methods to minimize the loss of nutrients during the course of decomposition, the fantasy becomes fact. Earthworms can serve as tools to facilitate these functions. They serve as "nature's plowman" and form nature's gift to produce good humus, which is the most precious material to fulfill the nutritional needs of crops. The utilization of vermicompost results in several benefits to farmers, industries, environment and overall national economy.

***To farmers*:**

- Less reliance on purchased inputs of nutrients leading to lower cost of production.
- Increased soil productivity through improved soil quality.
- Better quantity and quality of crops.
- For landless people provides additional source of income generation

To industries:

- Cost-effective pollution abatement technology.

To environment:

- Wastes create no pollution, as they become valuable raw materials for enhancing soil fertility.

To national economy:

- Boost to rural economy.
- Savings in purchased inputs.
- Less wasteland formation.

REFERENCES

Aira, M. Gómez-Brandón, M. Lazcano, C. Baath, E and Domínguez, J. (2010): Plant Genotype Strongly Modifies the Structure and Growth of Maize Rhizosphere Microbial Communities. *Soil Biology and Biochemistry*, 42 (12): 2276-2281.

Appelhof, M. Webster, K and Buckerfield, J. (1996): Vermicomposting in Australia and New Zealand. *Biocycle*, 37(6): 63-74.

Arancon, N.Q. Galvis, P.A and Edwards, C.A. (2005): Suppression of Insect Pest Populations and Damage to Plants by Vermicompost. *Bioresource Technology*, 96: 1137-1142.

Arancon, N.Q. Edwards, C.A. Babenko, A. Cannon, J, Galvis, P and Metzger, J.D. (2008): Influences of Vermicomposts, Produced by Earthworms and Microorganisms from Cattle Manure, Food Waste and Paper Waste, on the Germination, Growth and Flowering of Petunias in the Greenhouse. *Applied Soil Ecology*, 39: 91-99.

Atiyeh, R.M. Dominguez, J. Subler, S and Edwards, C.A. (2000): Change in Biochemical Properties of Cow Manure Processed by Earthworms (*Eisenia andreii*) and Their Effect on Plant Growth. *Pedobilogia*, 44: 709-24.

Bachman, G.R and Metzger, J.D. (2007): Physical and Chemical Characteristics of a Commercial Potting Substrate Amended with Vermicompost Produced from Two Different Manure sources. *HortTechnology*, 17(3): 336-340.

Bhattacharjee, G and Chaudhuri, P.S. (2002): Cocoon Production, Morphology, Hatching Pattern and Facundity in Seven Tropical Earthworm Species – A Laboratotry - based Investigation. *J. Biosci.*, 27(3): 283-94.

Biradar, A.P. Sunita, N.D. Teggelli, R.G and Devaranavadgi, S.B. (1998): Effect of Vermicomposts on the Incidence of Subabul Psyllid. *Insect Environment*, 4: 55-56.

Campitelli, P and Ceppi, S. (2008): Chemical, Physical and Biological Compost and Vermicompost Characterization: A Chemometric Study. *Chemometrics and Intelligent Laboratory Systems*, 90: 64-71.

Cavani, N and Mimmo, T. (2007): Rhizodeposition of *Zea mays* L. as Affected by Heterosis. *Archives of Agronomy and Soil Science*, 53: 593-604.

Chaudhuri, P.S and Bhattacharjee, G. (2002): Capacity of Various Experimental Diets to Support Biomass and Reproduction of *Perionyx excavatus*. *Bioresource Technology*, 82: 147-50.

Coria-Cayupán, Y.S. De Pinto, M.I.S and Nazareno, M.A. (2009): Variations in Bioactive Substance Contents and Crop Yields of Lettuce (*Lactuca sativa* L.) Cultivated in Soils with Different Fertilization Treatments. *Journal of Agricultural and Food Chemistry*, 57(21): 10122-10129.

Domjnguez, J. Edwards, C.A and Webster, M. (2000): Vermicomposting of Sewage Sludge: Effect of Bulking Materials on the Growth and Reproduction of the Earthworm *Eisenia Andrei*. *Pedobiologia*, 44: 24-32.

Dominguez, J. Edwards, C.A and Ashby, J. (2001): The Biology and Population Dynamics of *Eudrilus eugeniae* (Kinberg) (Oligochaeta) in Cattle Waste solids. *Pedobiologia*, 45: 341-353.

Domínguez, J. Aira, M and Gómez Brandón, M. (2010): Vermicomposting: Earthworms Enhance the Work of Microbes. In: H. Insam, I. Franke-Whittle and M. Goberna, (Eds.), Microbes at Work: From Wastes to Resources. Springer, Berlin Heidelberg. pp. 93-114.

Edwards, C.A and Burrows, I. (1988): The Potential of Earthworm Composts as Plant Growth Media. In: C.A. Edwards and E.F. Neuhauser (Eds). Earthworms in Waste and Environmental Management. SPB Academic Publ. Co. The Hague, Netherlands. pp. 211-219.

Edwards, C.A. (1995): Historical Overview of Vermicomposting. *Biocycle*, 36 (9): 56-8.

Edward, C.A. (1998): The Use of Earthworms in the Break Down and Management of Organic Wastes. In: Earthworm Ecology. CRC Press LLC, Boca Raton, pp. 327-354.

Edwards, C.A. Domínguez, J and Arancon, N.Q. (2004): The Influence of Vermicomposts on Plant Growth and Pest Incidence. In: S.H Shakir and W.Z.A. Mikhaïl, (Eds). Soil Zoology for Sustainable Development in the 21st Century. Cairo. pp. 397-420.

Edwards, C.A. Arancon, N.Q and Greytak, S. (2006): Effects of Vermicompost Teas on Plant Growth and Disease. *BioCycle*, 47: 28-31.

El Harti, A. Saghi, M. Molina, J.A.E and Téller, G. (2001): Production des composes indoliques rhizogénes par le ver de terre *Lumbricus terrestris*. *Canadian Journal of Zoology*, 79: 1921-1932.

Ferreras, L. Gomez, E. Toresani, S. Firpo, I and Rotondo, R. (2006): Effect of Organic Amendments on some Physical, Chemical and Biological Properties in a Horticultural Soil. *Bioresource Technology*, 97: 635-640.

Ghosh, C. (2004): Integrated Vermi-pisciculture - an Alternative Option for Recyclying of Solid Municipal Waste in Rural India. *Bioresource Technology*, 93: 71-75.

Gopinath, K.A. Supradip, S. Mina, B.L. Pande, H. Kundu, S and Gupta, H.S. (2008): Influence of Organic Amendments on Growth, Yield and Quality of Wheat and on Soil Properties during Transition to Organic Production. *Nutrient Cycling in Agroecosystems*, 82 (1): 51-60.

Gutiérrez-Miceli, F.A. Santiago-Borraz, J. Montes Molina, J.A. Nafate, C.C. Abdud-Archila, M. Oliva Llaven, M.A. Rincón-Rosales, R and Deendoven L. (2007): Vermicompost as a Soil Supplement to Improve Growth, Yield and Fruit Quality of Tomato (*Lycopersicum esculentum*). *Bioresource Technology*, 98: 2781-2786.

Haimi, J. (1990): Growth and Reproduction of the Compost Living Earthworms *Eisenia andrei* and *E. foetida*. *Revue d' Ecologie et de Biologie du Sol*, 27(4): 415-21.

Handricsen, N.B. (1990): Leaf Litter Selection by detrivore and geophagous earthworm. *Biology and Fertility of Soil*, 10: 17-21.

Hidalgo, P.R. Matta, F.B and Harkess, R.L. (2006): Physical and Chemical Properties of Substrates Containing Earthworm Castings and Effects on Marigold Growth. *HortScience*, 41: 1474-1476.

ICRISAT and APRLP. (2003). Vermicomposting: Conversion of Organic Wastes into Valuable Manure. Andhra Pradesh, India: APRLP. pp. 4-7.

ICRISAT. (2006): Vermicomposting: Recycling Wastes into Valuable Organic Fertilizer. Andhra Pradesh, India. Global Theme on Agrecosystems Report No. 8. August.

Ismail, S.A. (1995): Earthworms in Soil Fertility Management in Organic Agriculture. In: P.K. Thampan, (Ed.). pp. 77-100.

Ismail, S.A. (1997): Vermicology: The Biology of Earthworms. In Orient Longman Limited, Chennai. p. 92.

Jimenez, J.J. Moreno, A.G and Lavelle, P. (1999): Reproductive Strategies of Three Native Earthworm species from the Savannas of Carimagua (Colombia). *Pedobiologia*, 43: 851-858.

Julka, J.M. (1983): A New Genus and species of Earthworm (Octochaetidae: Oligochaeta) from South India. *Geobios New Reports,* 2: 48-50.

Julka, J.M. (2001): Earthworm Diversity and it's Role in Agroecosystem, VII National Symposium on Soil Biology and Ecology. Abstract Volume, Banglore University of Agricultural Sciences. pp. 13-17.

Kale, R.D. (1995): Vermicomposting has a Bright Scope. *Indian Silk,* 3: 6-9.

Lazcano, C. Arnold, J. Tato, A. Zaller, J.G and Domínguez, J. (2009): Compost and Vermicompost as Nursery Pot Components: Effects on Tomato Plant Growth and Morphology. *Spanish Journal of Agricultural Research,* 7: 944-951.

Lorimor, J. Fulhage, C. Zhang, R. Funk, T. Sheffield, R. Sheppard, C and Newton, G.L. (2001): Manure Management Strategies/technologies. In: White Paper on Animal Agriculture and the Environment for National Center for Manure and Animal Waste Management. MWPS, Ames, IA. p. 52.

Ma, W.C. Brussarrd, L. DeRidder, J.A. (1990): Long Term Effect of Nitrogenious Fertilizers on Grassland Earthworms (Oligochaeta: Lumbricidae): Their Relation to Soil Acidification. *Agric Ecosystem Environ,* 30: 71-80.

Manna, M.C. Singh, M. Kundu, S. Tripathi, A.K and Takkar, P.N. (1997): Growth and Reproduction of Vermicomposting Earthworm Perionyx Excavatus as Influenced by Food Materials. *Biology and Facility of Soils,* 24 (1): 129-32.

Marinari, S.G. Masciandaro, B. Ceccanti and Grego, S. (2000): Influence of Organic and Mineral Fertilizers on Soil Biological and Physical Properties. *Bioresource Technology,* 72: 9-17.

Morra, L. Palumbo, A.D. Bilotto, M. Ovieno, P and Picascia, S. (1998): Soil Solarization: Organic Fertilization and Grafting Contribute to Build an Integrated Production System in a Tomato-zucchini Sequence. *Colture-Protette,* 27: 63-70.

Muscolo, A. Bovolo, F. Gionfriddo, F and Nardi, S. (1999): Earthworm Humic Matter Produces Auxins-like Effect on Daucus Carota Cell Growth and Nitrate metabolism. *Soil Biology and Biochemistry,* 31:1303-11.

Muyima, N.Y.O. Reinecke, A.J and Viljoen Reinecke, S.A. (1994): Moisture Requirements of *Dendrobaena veneta* (Oligichaeta), a Candidate for Vermicomposting. *Soil Biology and Biochemistry,* 26 (8): 973-976.

Nakasone, A.K. Bettiol, W and de Souza, R.M. (1999): The Effect of Water Extracts of Organic Matter on Plant Pathogens. *Summa Phytopathologica,* 25: 330-335.

Nardi, S. Arnoldi, G and Dell'Agnola, G. (1988): Release of Hormone-like Activities from *Alloborophora rosea* and *Alloborophora caliginosa* feces. *Journal of Soil Science,* 68: 563-657.

Nielson, R.L. (1965): Presence of Plant Growth Substances in Earthworms Demonstrated by Paper Chromatography and the Went Pea Test. *Nature,* 208: 1113-1114.

Noble, R and Coventry, E. (2005): Suppression of Soil-borne Plant Diseases with Composts: A Review. *Biocontrol Science and Technology,* 15: 3-20.

Orlikowski, L.B. (1999): Vermicompost Extract in the Control of some Soil Borne Pathogens. *International Symposium on Crop Protection,* 64: 405-410.

Peyvast, G. Olfati, J.A. Madeni, S and Forghani, A. (2008): Effect of Vermicompost on the Growth and Yield of Spinach (*Spinacia oleracea* L.). *Journal of Food Agriculture and Environment,* 6: 110-113.

Ramesh, P. (2000): Effects of Vermicomposts and Vermicomposting on Damage by Sucking Pests to Ground Nut (*Arachis hypogea*). *Indian Journal of Agricultural Sciences,* 70 (5): 334-339.

Rao, K.R. (2002): Induced Host Plant Resistance in the Management of Sucking Insect Pests of Groundnut. *Annals of Plant Protection Science,* 10: 45-50.

Ribeiro, C.F. Mizobusi, E.H. Silva, D.G. Pereira, J.C.R and Zambolim, L. (1998): Control of *Meloidogyne javanica* on Lettuce with Organic Amendments. *Fitopatologia*, 23: 42-44.

Scott, M.A. (1988): The Use of Worm-digested Animal Waste as a Supplement to Peat in Loamless Composts for Hardy Nursery Stock. In: C.A. Edwards and E.F. Neuhauser, (Eds.). Earthworms in Environmental and Waste Management. SPB Acad. Publ. The Netherlands. pp. 231-229.

Senappa, C.O. Rao, C.B.J and Kale, R.D. (1995): Conversion of Distillery Wastes in to Organic Manure using *Eudrilus eugeniae* King. In: Proceeding of 3rd International Conference on Appropriate Waste Management Technology for Developing Countries, NEERI, February 25-28, pp. 1165-1169.

Shanthi, N.R. Bhoyar, R.V and Bhide, A.D. (1993): Vermicomposting of Vegetable Waste. *Compost Science and Utilization*, 1(4): 27-30.

Singh, U.P. Maurya, S and Singh, D.P. (2003): Antifungal Activity and Induced Resistance in pea by Aqueous Extract of Vermicompost and for Control of Powdery Mildew of Pea and Balsam. *Zeitschrift fur Pflanzenkrankheiten und Pflanzenschutz*, 110: 544-553.

Singh, R. Sharma, R.R. Kumar, S. Gupta, R.K and Patil, R.T. (2008): Vermicompost Substitution Influences Growth, Physiological Disorders, Fruit Yield and Quality of Strawberry (*Fragariax ananassa* Duch.). *Bioresource Technology*, 99: 8507-8511.

Singh, R. Gupta, R.K. Patil, R.T. Sharma, R.R. Asrey, R. Kumar, A and Jangra, K.K. (2010): Sequential Foliar Application of Vermicompost Leachates Improves Marketable Fruit Yield and Quality of Strawberry (*Fragaria x ananassa* Duch.). *Scientia Horticulturae*, 124: 34-39.

Sunitha, N.D. Giraddi, R.S. Kulkarni, K.A and Lingappa, S. (1997): Evaluation Methods of Vermicomposting Under Open Field Conditions. *Karnataka Journal of Agricultural Sciences*, 10(4): 987-990.

Suthar, S. (2007): Production of Vermifertilizer from guar gum Industrial Waste by Using Composting Earthworm *Perionyx sansibaricus* (Perrier). *Environmentalist*, 27 (1): 329-335.

Swathi, P. Rao, K.T and Rao, P.A. (1998): Studies on Control of Root-knot Nematode *Meloidogyne incognita* in Tobacco Miniseries. *Tobaco Research*, 1: 26-30.

Szczech, M. (1999): Supressiveness of Vermicompost Against *Fusarium wilt* of Tomato. *Journal of Phytopathology*, 147: 155-161.

Szczech, M and Smolinska, U. (2001): Comparison of Suppressiveness of Vermicompost Produced from Animal Manures and Sewage Sludge Against *Phytophthora nicotianae* Breda de Haar var. *nicotianae*. *Journal of Phytopathology*, 149: 77-82.

Taylor, M. Clarke, W.P and Greenfield, P.F. (2003): The Treatment of Domestic Waste Water Using Small-scale Vermicompost Filter Beds. *Ecol. Eng.*, 21 (2-3): 197-203.

Tomati, U and Galli, E. (1995): Earthworms, Soil Fertility and Plant Productivity. Proceedings of the International Colloquium on Soil Zoology. *Acta Zoologica Fennica*, 196: 11-14.

Trevisan, S. Pizzeghello, D. Ruperti, B. Francioso, O. Sassi, A. Palme, K. Quaggiotti, S and Nardi, S. (2010): Humic Substances Induce Lateral Root Formation and Expression of the Early Auxin-responsive IAA19 Gene and DR5 Synthetic Element in Arabidopsis. *Plant Biology*, 12: 604-614.

Trigo, D and Lavelle, P. (1993): Changes in Respiration Rate and some Physiochemical Properties of Soil during gut transit Through *Allolobophora molleri* (Lumbricidae, Oligochaeta). *Biol. Fertil. Soils*, 15: 185-188.

Trillas M.I. Casanova, E. Cotxarrera, L. Ordovás, J. Borrero, C and Avilés, M. (2006): Composts from Agricultural Waste and the *Trichoderma asperellum* Strain T-34 Suppress *Rhizoctonia solani* in Cucumber Seedlings. *Biological Control*, 39: 32-38.

Wang, D. Shi, Q. Wang, X. Wei, M. Hu, J. Liu, J and Yang, F. (2010): Influence of Cow Manure Vermicompost on the Growth, Metabolite Contents, and Antioxidant Activities of Chinese Cabbage (*Brassica campestris* ssp. chinensis). *Biology and Fertility of Soils,* 46: 689-696.

Warman, P.R and AngLopez, M.J. (2010): Vermicompost Derived from Different Feedstocks as a Plant Growth Medium. *Bioresource Technology,* 101: 4479-4483.

Werner, M and Cuevas, J.R. (1995): Vermiculture in Cuba. *Biocyde,* 37 (6): 57, 61-2.

Yardim, E.N. Arancon, N.A. Edwards, C.A. Oliver, T.J and Byrne, R.J. (2006): Suppression of Tomato Hornworm (*Manduca quinquemaculata*) and Cucumber Beetles (*Acalymma vittatum* and *Diabotrica undecimpunctata*) Populations and Damage by Vermicomposts. *Pedobiologia,* 50: 23-29.

Zaller, J.G. (2006): Foliar Spraying of Vermicompost Extracts: Effects on Fruit Quality and Indications of Late-blight Suppression of Field-grown Tomatoes. *Biological Agriculture and Horticulture,* 24: 165-180.

Zaller, J.G. (2007): Vermicompost as a Substitute for Peat in Potting Media: Effects on Germination, Biomass Allocation, Yields and Fruit Quality of Three Tomato Varieties. *Scientia Horticulturae,* 112: 191-199.

Zandonadi, D.B. Canellas, L.P and Rocha Façanha, A. (2006): Indolacetic and Humic Acids Induce Lateral Root Development Through a Concerted Plasmalemma and Tonoplast H^+ Pumps Activation. *Planta,* 225: 1583-1595.

Pages: 170-186

BIOTECHNOLOGY AND ENVIRONMENTAL MANAGEMENT

Edited by: Prof. Arun Arya; Dr. Raaz K Maheswari & Dr. Pawan Kumar 'Bharti'

ISBN: 978-93-5056-862-0

Edition: 2017

Published by: Discovery Publishing House Pvt. Ltd., New Delhi (India)

8

Yield Maximization of Pigeon Pea Through Promotion of Integrated Disease Management (IDM) Technology

Sanjeev Kumar[1]; S.N.Singh[2]
Rajni Tomar[3]; Archana Rani[4] and
Gyanendra Singh[5]

ABSTRACT

Pigeon pea is an important pulse crop of India and has key role in food and nutritional security as it is a rich source of protein, minerals and vitamins. Of late, the cultivated area and production of pigeon pea have recorded a steady positive growth, but the mean productivity is disappointingly low in comparison to potential yield. To increase its productivity, breeders are trying to develop suitable varieties with subjective spread, growth, duration, and disease resistance under varied agro-climatic growing conditions. Diseases are a continual problem and management practices must be planned for developing sustained production. Each condition that affects plant growth also affects the disease causing organism and the effectiveness of any control measure. In general, conditions that favour rapid, lush plant growth also favor disease development. No single control method is effective in every disease situation. Often a complex of disease interactions defies simple explanations or solutions. Thus to overcome these constraints Integrated disease management (IDM) has been developed for pigeon pea diseases.

INTRODUCTION

Pigeonpea (*Cajanus cajan*), popularly known as tur or arhar is one of the important pulse crop after chickpea in India. Besides being rich source of

1 & 2 Department of Plant Pathology, College of Agriculture, Jawaharlal Nehru Krishi Vishwavidyalaya - Jabalpur - 482 004, (MP) (India)

3, 4, 5 Department of Plant Breeding & Genetics, College of Agriculture, Jawaharlal Nehru Krishi Vishwavidyalaya- Jabalpur - 482 004, (MP) (India)

protein (22.3%), essential amino acids particularly lysine, this crop also help in maintaining the soil fertility through natural biological nitrogen fixation (Rao *et al*, 2002). The ability of pigeonpea to produce economic yields in soils characterized by moisture deficient, makes it an important crop of dry land agriculture. Farmers grow it in various production systems as a mixed crop, intercrop and perennial crop using long established traditional practices. (Chauhan 1990). In India pigeonpea grown in 36.3 lakh ha. and production of pigeonpea is 27.6 lakh tones. The major pigeonpea growing states are Maharashtra, Madhya Pradesh, Gujarat, Karnataka, Andhra Pradesh, Uttar Pradesh, Jharkhand, Orissa, Bihar and Rajasthan contributing 88.2% in total pigeonpea production (Singh and Singh 2014). In Madhya Pradesh, area and production of pigeon pea is 3.50 lakh ha and 2.17 lakh tone (Shrivastava *et al* 2016). However, the average national and state yield of pigeonpea is disappointingly low in comparison to potential yield (Table 8.1).

Table 8.1: Yield Gaps: National vis-à-vis Madhya Pradesh

Crops	Yield (Kg/ha)		Gap	
	FLD	State Average*	Actual (Kg/ha)	Percent
Pigeonpea (Early duration)				
All India	1142	833	309	37.10
M.P	1159	632	527	83.39
Pigeonpea (Medium duration)				
All India	1433	675	758	112.25
M.P	1198	632	566	89.56

* FLD/State Yield-(Avg. 207-08 to 2011-12)

In India, pigeonpea is challenged by a number of constraints which include several abiotic and biotic stresses.

(a) **Abiotic**

1. **Waterlogging and Salinity**: Pigeon pea, a predominantly rainy-season crop experiences waterlogging in high rainfall regions and in soils with low permeability spreading Madhya Pradesh. Water logging and salinity has been recognized as one of the major constraints to pigeonpea cultivation.
2. **Drought**: The inherent deep root-system of pigeon pea imparts high degree of drought tolerance; however, moisture stresses at reproductive phase do severely limit productivity, and sometimes even no yields are realized. This stress also limits symbiotic N fixation.

(b) **Economic:** Lack of stable input and output markets, increased price of cash inputs, no availability of timely credit, labor scarcity, lack of extension support and awareness on improved Varieties and hybrids

(c) **Policies:** Distorted price policies favoring wheat and rice, lack of procurement at Minimum Support Price

(d) **Input supply and mechanization:**

1. Timely availability of quality seeds.
2. Availability of fertilizers and pesticides.
3. Availability of low cost harvesters for reducing the drudgery f. Infrastructure constraints: Improved storage facilities, post-harvest processing, and value addition.

(e) **Biotic**

1. **Insect pests:** Pod fly and Pod borer
2. **Diseases:** Sterility mosaic, *Fusarium* wilt and *Phytophthora* blight

The pest and disease problems are the major bottlenecks in realizing the higher yields (Mayee 2016; Sharma 2016). Through there are several diseases, which attacks pulse crops, the major ones are mentioned in Table 8.2. On a rough estimate in pigeon pea, losses due to pests often exceed 50 percent (Rao *et al* 1990).

Table 8.2: Diseases of national and regional significance

Sl. No.	Name of Disease	Name of Pathogen	Distribution	References
National Significance				
1.	Wilt	*Fusarium udum* E.J. Butler	All over India	Butler,1906; Butler, 1910; Karimi *et al*. 2012.
2.	Stem blight	*Phytophthora draschalari* f.sp. *cajani*	All over India	Kannaiyan *et al*,1981
3.	Sterility mosaic:	*Pigeon pea sterility mosaic virus*	All over India	Khare *et al*, 1975
Regional Significance				
4.	Yellow disease:	*Mungbean yellow mosaic virus*	Tamil Nadu, Uttar Pradesh, Gujarat, Odisha	Kannaiyan *et al*,1984
5.	Dry root rot:	*Macrophomina phaseolina*	Uttar Pradesh, Tamil Nadu, Karnataka, Madhya Pradesh, Maharashtra, Delhi	Kannaiyan *et al*,1984
6.	Cercospora leaf spots	*Cercospora cajani* Hennings	Uttar Pradesh, Bihar	Khan *et al*, 2004 ; Singh and Singh, 2014
7.	Powdery mildew	*Leveillula taurica* (Lév.)	Uttar Pradesh, Maharashtra and Tamil Nadu	Singh and Singh, 2014

Therefore, apart from facing the above mentioned constraints of pigeon pea production, mitigation of disease damage is one of the possible alternatives to boost the production of the country, especially when other than economy; the nutritive value of the crop to the masses is of critical importance. In order to offset the losses caused by disease, farmers often resort to indiscriminate use pesticides leading to pest resurgence, resistance, pesticides residues and associated environmental problems. This has dictated the need to look for other alternatives like use of botanicals pesticides, bioagents, manipulation of cultural practices and lastly the need based use of eco friendly pesticides. Integrated disease management (IDM) combines a wide array of all the above methods and practices for the control of diseases and at the same time protects the environment in the long run as natural enemies are conserved and pesticide use are minimized.

KEY DISEASES AND THEIR DIAGNOSTIC DETAILS

Wilt

It is characterized by slow wilting of plant. The symptoms can be observed after a month of sowing or at the flowering or pod formation stage. The affected plants become yellow in color followed by drooping and finally the whole plant dries up. The symptoms resemble as if the plant is suffering from the drought. The disease can be confirmed whenever the affected stem is cut and opened where the browning of xylem vessels could be clearly seen. It has been recorded that wilting can be partial or total. However, it has been observed that partial wilting is mainly associated with lateral root infection, whereas tap root infection may cause complete wilting.

Phytophthora Blight

The symptoms of the PB on pigeonpea have been described as stem rot, stem blight (and root rot. Generally, pigeonpea seedlings become infected with PB as soon as they emerge. Characteristic foliage blight symptoms are visualized on ≥1 month old seedlings. Blight symptoms first appear as water-soaked lesions on the primary and triplicate leaves which become necrotic within a week when humidity ≥80% and temperature 20-30° C persist. The leaflet lesions are circular to irregular in shape and can be as large as 1 cm in diameter. Stem symptoms appear as brown to dark brown lesions distinctly different from healthy green portions on main stem, branches and petioles. The lesions on stems and branches increases rapidly and extend up to 20 cm, girdle and cracks and dry the stem. It is also common to find stems swollen into cankerous structures. Infected stem and branches break easily in wind. Phloem vessels show smoky gray colored discoloration and xylem vessels remain healthy The PB can be easily mistaken for Fusarium wilt because the general symptoms of these two diseases are similar. An attempt has been made by us to differentiate PB symptoms from Fusarium wilt, based on repeated observations on wilt and PB symptomatology in farmer's field and at research stations on several pigeonpea varieties and hybrids belonging to different genetic make up for the last one decade. Comparative symptomatology distinguishing PB from Fusarium wilt based on visible symptoms at seedling, foliage, stem and roots are given in table 8.3.

Table 8.3: Differentiation of symptomatology of *Phytophthora* blight and *Fusarium* wilt in pigeonpea

Plant Part/Growth Stage	Phytophthora Blight	Fusarium Wilt
Seedling (up to 30 days)	Young seedlings are killed within 3-10 days	Young seedlings gradually wilt and die within 10-30 days retaining dull green color.
Foliage (30-45days)	Water-soaked lesions seen on the leaves and whole foliage gives desiccated appearance	Initial visible symptoms are loss of turgidity, slight chlorosis and drooping of leaves
Stem (45–>75 days)	Brown to dark brown lesions, distinctly different from the healthy green portion. These lesions increase rapidly and usually girdle the stem; infected stems break easily at lesion site.	Dark brown to purple streak band extending upward from soil level and usually seen only on one side of the stem
	Phloem is smoky gray colored and the xylem remains clear.	Characteristic internal symptom of wilt is the browning of the xylem vessels.
	It is also common to find stem and branches swollen at base or else turning into a cankerous hypertropical structures.	In humid weather a pinkish mycelial growth is often observed on the part of the wilted plants.
Root	The roots of the PB infected plants are healthy and can not be uprooted easily.	The roots of the Fusarium infected plants are dried and can be pulled easily.

Sterility Mosaic

It is caused by pigeonpea sterility mosaic virus transmitted through an eriophyid mite, *Aceria cajani.* The affected plant remains stunted with profuse branching bearing large number of small light green leaves due to which the plant appears bushy. The leaves show mosaic with dark and light green to yellowish patches. The branches are without flowers partially or completely. The diseased plant is easily spotted out in the field due to its yellowish and bushy appearance. The disease may cause heavy reduction in yield.

Alternaria Blight

It is considered as a most serious disease of post rainy season crop of pigeonpea in north eastern india and epiphytotics of the disease has been reported in part of Bihar. The severe occurrence of the disease has been reported on july sown crop also. The symptoms of the disease appear as small brownish spots on leaves, which later increase in size and coalesce each other resulting in blighting and defoliation. Spots may appear on pods and the fungus infects seed also.

Mungbean Mosaic

This disease was probably reported first from Sri Lanka. The disease first appears in the form of yellow, diffused spots scattered on the leaf lamina, not limited by veins and veinlets. Such spots slowly expand and in later stages of disease development, affected leaflets show broad, yellow patches alternating with green colour. Sometimes the entire lamina turns yellow. Leaf size is conspicuously reduced in early infections. In peninsular India, disease incidence is relatively higher in late-sown pigeon pea. The vector is whitefly (*Bemisia tabaci)* Typical symptoms include root and basal stem rot with a large number of minute, fungal sclerotia visible under the bark. Plants dry prematurely, particularly when they face drought stress. Disease incidence severe in off -season, irrigated, summer crops in several parts of India, and it is a minor one in the normal-season crop. The pathogen is both soil- and seed borne.

Cercospora Leaf Spots

The first symptoms appear in October on mature leaves, petioles and even on young twigs The spots are triangular in outlinc and are raised above the surface of the leaf. Very rarely, the upper surface is infected. The spots are usually discrete but occasionally several spots may coalesce, forming diseased areas up to 15 × 5 mm in size. In early stage, the spots are dirty brown in colour. Petioles and stems are sometimes attacked. The disease from single spots does not cross midrib or primary vein and confines itself to lamina. Infected leaves start drying and in severe cases defoliation may take place.

Powdery Mildew

The symptoms appear mostly on older leaves, however, in severe cases even young buds and pods also get infected. Symptoms appear as dull red spots, limited by veins, appear on upper surface of leaves and later white powdery patches develop on both the surfaces. Entire lower leaf surface gets covered with powdery growth, leading to defoliation. The disease is also known to cause stunting of young plants and significantly reduces nodulation. In several cases, affected leaves turn yellow with crinkling.

INTEGRATED DISEASE MANAGEMENT (IDM)

Broadly IDM can be defined as "the careful consideration of all available disease control techniques and subsequent integration of appropriate measures that discourage the development of disease index and keep pesticides and other interventions to levels that are economically justified and reduce or minimize risks to human health and the environment. IDM emphasizes the growth of a healthy crop with the least possible disruption to agroecosystems and encourages natural disease control mechanisms".

Goal of IDM

- To increase the productivity with reduced pesticide risk to the producers, consumers and the environment.
- Conserve the biodiversity through augmenting natural enemies of diseases.
- Encourage eco-friendly approach of disease management
- Ensure farm productivity and profitability with reduced inputs on plant protection.
- Empower farmers through periodic training and exposure visits to improve their decision making process.

Why Practice IDM?

1. **Promote a healthy environment**: Persistence of chemicals in the environment, is one of the major problem in the era of modern agriculture. However, more cases of contaminated groundwater appear each year, and disposal of containers and unused pesticides still pose challenges for applicators. Even though long term documentation on the effects of all pesticides is still unavailable, it is generally agreed that fewer pesticides means less risk to surface and groundwater, and less hazard to wildlife and humans.
2. **Keep a balanced ecosystem**: Every ecosystem, made up of living things and their non-living environment, has a balance; the actions of one creature in the ecosystem usually affect other, different organisms. The introduction of chemicals into the ecosystem can change this balance, destroying certain species and allowing other species (sometimes pests themselves) to dominate. Beneficial organisms such as the *Trichoderma* and *Pseudomons,* both of which control diseases, can be killed by pesticides, leaving few natural mechanisms of disease control.
3. **Pesticides can be ineffective**: Chemical pesticides are not always effective. Diseases can become resistant to pesticides when used indiscriminately. In fact, various cases of diseases developing pesticide resistance have been documented to date. Furthermore, diseases may survive in some situations where the chemical does not reach diseases, is washed off, is applied at an improper rate, or is applied at an improper life stage of the diseases.

4. **Save money**: IDM can save money through avoiding crop loss (due to pests), and avoiding unnecessary pesticide expense.
5. **Maintain a good public image**: Recent public outcry about the use of growth regulators and the presence of pesticide residues on produce has heightened pesticide applicator awareness of the level of public concern about chemicals. Consumers are pressuring food stores, which in turn are pressuring producers, for produce that has been grown with as few pesticides as possible. Growing food under integrated disease management can help allay public concerns.

IDM Component

It includes:

1. Sowing a crop variety with resistance to a disease.
2. Modified farm management practices that result in reduction of disease loss.
3. The enhancement of natural control processes.
4. Need based application of pesticides

Based on the above components, a package has been developed for the management of pigeon pea diseases depicted below.

DEVELOPMENT OF IDM PACKAGES

Summer Ploughing

Due to summer ploughing, most of the crop residue which harbor the dormant mycelium/ spores of the pathogen get exposed to the temperature above 40° C for several days. Thus most of the inoculums of soil borne pathogens (*Fusarium spp., Rhizoctonia spp, Phytophthora spp* and nematodes) automatically get killed under hot condition and their number are reduced.

Soil Solarization

In this practice, ploughed fields are covered with a thin polythene sheet for a period of 6-7 weeks during April - May, which results in rising of the soil temperature up to 60° C. The resultant high temperature is lethal to soil inhabiting pathogen, nematode and insects. This practice is very effective in controlling the *Heterodera cajani* and *Fusarium udum* provided the soil is irrigated before polythene covering.

Plant Nutrients

Pigeonpea is a legume crop so it is believed that it requires less amount of nitrogen. Therefore, diammonium phosphate(DAP) @ 100 Kg/ha is applied in the field which provides nitrogen and phosphorus. Application of 20 kg of K/ha reduces the incidence of *Phytophthora* blight. Manures and oil cakes reduces wilt incidence. It increases the population of beneficial microorganism and reduces the population of fungal and bacterial propagules.

Varieties

First major component under IDM is the use resistant or tolerant varieties. Swaminathan, M. S., noted Indian agriculture scientist, stated undoubtedly the most attractive form of defense is provided by disease resistance, for as long as it remains effective it provides protection at no cost to the farmer or the community. Host plant resistance is an imperative tool to manage diseases of major food crops in India, especially pigeonpea. Research efforts so far resulted in development of several high yielding varieties insulated against major diseases. However, most of these lack combined resistant against 2-3 diseases. Therefore, pyramiding of gene(s) conferring resistant to different diseases is required to have multiple disease resistant varieties so that full potential of varieties can be realized at farmers fields. In view of climate change, there is need to screen large number of genetic resources including accessions of related wild species, pre breeding lines and primitive landraces so that donors carrying genes conferring resistance to emerging diseases Alternaria blight, yellow mosaic etc can be identified. Once identified, targeted genes can be pyramided using molecular markers. The improved pigeonpea varieties having good yield potential as well as resistant/tolerant to diseases are mentioned in table 8.4.

Table 8.4: Disease resistant/tolerant varieties of pigeonpea

Disease	Resistant/Tolerant varieties
Fusarium wilt	H 76-65, ICP 8863 (Maruti), ICP 9145, ICPL 267, Mukta, AL 1, BDN 2, Birsa Arhar1, DL 82, H 7 6 - 1 1, H 76-44, H 7 6 - 5 1
Phytophthora blight	ICPL 304, KPBR 80-1-4, KPBR Hy 4, ICPL 150, ICPL 288
Sterility mosaic	ICPL 87051, MA 165, MA166, PDA 2, PDA10, Rampur Rahar Prabhat, Sharda, TT 5, T T 6 Bageshwari, B ahar, DA 1 1, DA-13
Alternaria blight	DA 2, MA 1 2 8 - 1, MA128-2, 20-105
Wilt and Sterility mosaic	Asha, MA3, BSMR 736, Narendra Arhar-1

Seed Treatment

Seed treatment with carbendazim+ thiram(1:2) @ 2.5 g/kg of seed reduces the incidence of wilt and *Alternaria* blight immensely. In *Phytophthora* prone area, metalaxyl should be used for seed treatment @ 2.5 g/Kg of seed (Kannaiyan and Nene,1984). Seed treatment with *Trichoderma* formulations @ 5 g/kg of seed reduces the incidence of wilt considerably (Gouder & Kulkarni, 1999; Kumar *et al*, 2009; Mandhare and Suryawanshi, 2004).

Sowing Time and Season

Date of sowing and season also plays an important role in disease management. *Phytophthora* blight occurs less in pre monsoon sown crops as compared to late sown crops of which early plant stage is caught by cloudy weather and continuous rains. The disease occurs more on plants at the age of 15 to 20 days and the susceptibility decreases with advancing age, being minimum at 120 days. The pre rabi pigeonpea crop escapes the attack of *phytophthora* blight as well as wilt. On the contrary, *Alternaria* blight is serious on pre rabi crops as compared to rainy season crop. Early sowing of pigeonpea reduces the sterility mosaic incidence.

Method of Sowing

Ridge sowing helps in the better crop establishment than the flat bed sowing method. Ridges not only provide proper drainage but also avoid the water to come in contact of plants for the longer duration. Otherwise, water stagnated in the field facilitates caongenial condition for sporangium formation, germination and liberation of zoospores. It also helps in free swimming of zoospore and infection of seedling to cause *Phytophthora* blight disease.

Crop Geometry

The crop geometry influences the crop growth as well as microclimate of the area. The closely spaced plants are more weak and prone to attack of *Phytophthora* blight and stem rot diseases, while widely spaced plant suffer less. The optimum row to row spacing recommended for pigeon pea are 40cm, 50-60cm and 75 cm for early, medium and late maturing varieties.

Inter/Mixed Cropping

Inter/mixed cropping provides diversity in the field and ultimately creates sequential and temporal discontinuity to the pathogen. Crops like sorghum, urdbean, sunhemp, mungbean, and sesame are grown as inter/ mixed crop during cultivation. These crop are of short duration and mature at different intervals and perform better under such conditions. Roots of sorghum exudates hydrogen cyanide (HCN) which inhibit the growth and reproduction of the pathogen.

Crop Rotation

Crop rotation with non host crop helps in reduction of soil borne diseases. Three to four year rotations with tobacco/sorghum and cereal crops reduces intensity of wilt and *Phytophthora* blight diseases.

Sanitation

The pathogens *Phytophthora, Fusarium, Sclerotium* and several others survive in the field on the infected plant debris. Therefore, removal and destruction of the infected plant debris after harvesting or at the time of field preparation, help in reducing the severity of diseases. The mite vector as well as the virus of SDM survives on the perennial plants of pigeon pea growing in the field bund or near the houses. Such plant should be uprooted and destroyed to eliminate the inoculums. In the standing crop also, the diseased plants may be destroyed as soon as they appear in the field.

Chemical Control

In case of severe disease incidence of wilt in the field, drench the soil with carbendazim 50 WP @ 1.0 g/l of water. Control *Alternaria* blight, *Cercospora* blight and powdery mildew by foliar spray at fortnightly interval with carbendazim (0.1%). In sterility mosaic prone areas, soil application of phorate@1kg a.i/ha at the time of sowing can protect the pigeonpea plant from infection of sterility mosaic diseases for the period of 75 days after sowing. Control of vector mites by foliar spray of chemical insecticides e.g., dicofol 18.5 EC (2.5 ml/l) or dimethoate 30 EC (1.7ml/l) reduces the spread of the disease considerably.

Reasons for limited Implementation of IDM at Farmers' Level

- Farmers perceive that the chemical pesticides are easy to apply and act rapidly and their success can be seen by anyone after a brief period only.
- IDM is relatively complex as it requires knowledge of the complex interrelationships within the agroecosytem and demands a farsighted planning.
- The influence of pesticide industry to boost sales of chemical pesticides through their better trained and equipped extension personnel hinders IDM implementation.
- Awareness and participation of the state agriculture departments in IDM implementation and dissemination are inadequate.
- Precise surveillance and monitoring methods are yet to be worked out.
- Shortage of disease resistant as well as multiple disease resistant varieties.
- Preventive measures like summer ploughing, proper showing dates, use of trap crops, crop barriers, collection of damaged parts of plant and their destruction etc. are normally not practiced by farmers.
- ETLs have not been worked out for all diseases for pigeonpea crop region- wise.
- Forecasting and forewarning models are also lacking.
- The techniques of mass production of various potential bio-control agents are still not well developed.
- Non availability of timely inputs like biopesticides.
- Quality control is another problem associated with biocontrol agents, particularly with fungal antagonist and viral preparations.
- Indian farmers are by and large less educated and have a different kind of social and cultural environment, which is also a constraint in introducing modern technology.
- Less efforts for extension and large-scale technology transfer at field level.

- Low status of plant protection workers in the administrative hierarchy.
- Fragmentation between disciplines, between research, extension and implementation and between institutes, all lead to a lack of institutional integration.
- Paucity of fund for research, extension and accelerated training of farmers.
- There is a false notion that IDM means no pesticides, where as just the reverse is true, IDM cannot go without pesticides. Many countries which have already adopted IDM are still using maximum quantity of pesticides.
- Selective pesticides, which are effective against crop disease and safe against natural enemies, are still not very much available.
- Concentrations of pesticide spray material are never proper, being either above the required dose, which becomes phototoxic or leaves great residue, or most of the time it is sub lethal causing development of resistance in pathogens.

Suggestive Measures for Successful Implementation of IDM Strategies

- Periodic disease surveys to update their incidence, distribution, extent of losses, in different situations are obligatory.
- For biologically based IDM approaches involving components like summer ploughing to expose resting stages of pathogens to predatory birds and sun, suitable intercropping system which suppresses diseases and encourage natural enemies, growing resistant cultivars, keeping bird perches to attract predatory birds,, use of biopesticides of microbial and botanical origin to keep disease below ETL.
- Keep pathogen population below ETL by following low cost cultural practices like hand collection and burning of remains of crop,encourage the activity of natural enemies.
- Use organic soil amendments like farm yard manure, neem/karanj/ castor cakes, green manure etc., to improve antagonistic micro flora population in the soil and to reduce disease incidence.
- Avoid indiscriminate use of pesticides to conserve natural enemies and to avoid toxic stress of the environment.
- Strengthen disease monitoring by effective means such as weather based advisory system/ forecasting system.
- Crop varieties with resistance to important diseases need to be developed.
- Knowledge on the economic thresholds of various pathogens in different situations needs to be generated for effective use of plant protection inputs.

- Effective cultural operations, augmentation of natural enemies should be given the due priority.
- Promotion of only those chemical molecules, which are target specific and less hazardous and fit well in IDM.
- Use of biorationals and indigenous technologies should be encouraged as an alternative to over dependence on pesticides and to reduce the environmental hazards due to pesticide usage.
- Periodic pesticides resistance monitoring in key disease like wilt, stem blight, Alternaria blight, sterility mosaic and yellow mosic should be given high priority.
- Periodic monitoring and management of pesticide residues in food chain.
- Encourage the community involvement with effective teams.
- Encourage farmer's participation in identifying the remedies.
- Follow systems based approach rather than disease or crop based approach.
- The strategic research information generated need to be shared with the needy partners through on-farm trials, periodic training and audiovisual aids.
- Participation of ICAR Institutes, SAUs, Non Governmental organizations and industries along with the farming families for effective implementation of IDM.
- Timely supply of critical inputs like seed, quality biocontrol agents, pheromone traps, etc. Both public and private agenicies are expected to ensure that the critical IDM inputs are made available to the farmers on time.

Impact of the IDM Technology

- Reduction in the quantity of pesticides used and improvement in the environmental safety. Reduced cost of cultivation and increase in yield in IDM as compared to the Farmer practices.
- Conservation of natural enemies and enhancement in the activity of the natural enemies.
- Environmental safety.
- Utilization of locally available substrates for creating employment for rural youths.
- Upliftment of socio-economic status of farmers.
- Reduction in the use of chemical pesticides.
- Improves decision making ability of farmers.
- Farmers can adopt only spot application of pesticides.

Do's and Don'ts in IDM

Sl. No.	Do's	Don'ts
1.	Deep ploughing is to be done on bright sunny days during the months of May and June. The field should be kept exposed to sun light at least for 2-3 weeks.	Do not plant or irrigate the fi eld after ploughing, at least for 2-3 weeks, to allow desiccation of weed's bulbs and/or rhizomes of perennial weeds.
2.	Adopt crop rotation.	Avoid mono cropping
3.	Grow only recommended varieties.	Do not grow varieties not suitable for the season or the region.
4.	Sow early in the season	Avoid late sowing as this may lead to reduced yields and incidence of white grubs and diseases.
5.	Always treat the seeds with approved biopesticides/ chemicals for the control of seed borne diseases.	Do not use seeds without seed treatment with biopesticides/chemicals.
6.	Sow in rows at optimum depths under proper moisture conditions for better establishment.	Do not sow seeds beyond 5-7 cm depth.
7.	Use NPK fertilizers as per the soil test recommendation.	Avoid imbalanced use of fertilizers.
8.	Apply short persistent pesticides to avoid pesticide residue in the soil and produce.	Do not apply pesticides during preceding 7 days before harvest.

Wilt

Phytophthora Blight

Sterility Mosaic

Alternaria Blight

Yellow Mosaic

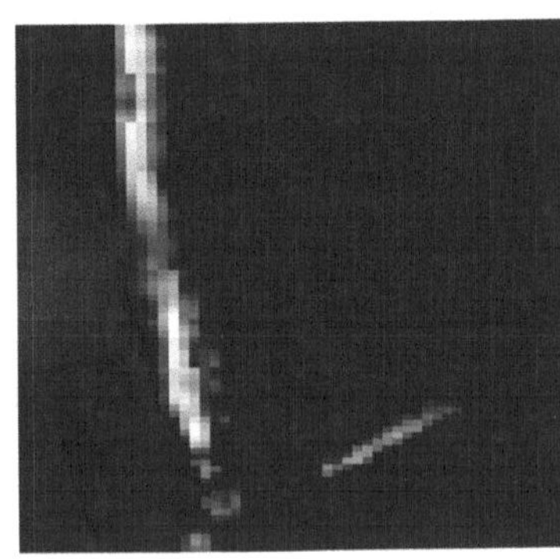

Dry Root Rot

Cercospora Leaf Spot

Powdery Mildew

SUMMARY

Of late, pigeonpea production has shifted from a largely subsistence farming to market oriented commercial production. However, it has not been possible to exploit the full genetic potential of high yielding pigeonpea varieties because of immense losses due to diseases and pests. Management of one single disease in isolation would prove counterproductive; hence it calls for the management of all diseases in integrated manner. An integrated disease management to combat the disease is the right approach.

REFERENCES

Butler, EJ. (1906). The Wilt Disease of Pigeonpea and Pepper. Agricultural Journal of India. 1: 25-36.

Butler, EJ. (1910). The Wilt Disease of Pigeonpea and the Parasitism of *Neocosmospora vasinfecta* Smith. Memoirs of the Department of Agriculture in India, Botanical Series. 2: 1-64.

Chauhan YS. (1990) Pigeonpea: Optimum Agronomic Management. In: The Pigeonpea, pp. 257-278. Nene YL., Hall, SD and Sheila VK (Eds) CAB International Wallingford, U.K.

FAI (1999). Fertilization Statistics 1998-99 pp. III 46-51. The Fertilizer Association of India, New Delhi.

Gouder, SB., Kulkarni, S. 1999. Compatibility Effect of Antagonists and Seed Dressers Against *Fusarium udum*-The Causal Agent of Pigeonpea Wilt. Karnataka Journal of Agricultural Sciences. 12: 1-4, 197-199.

Karimi R, Owuoche JO and Silim SN (2012). Importance and Management of Fusarium Wilt (*Fusarium udum* Butler) of Pigeonpea. International Journal of Agronomy and Agricultural Research. 2(1): 1-14.

Kannaiyan, J, Nene Y L, Raju, TN and Sheila, VK. (1981). Screening for Resistance to Phytophthora Blight of Pigeonpea. Plant Disease. 65: 61-62.

Kannaiyan, J. and Nene, YL. (1984). Efficacy of Metalaxyl for Control of Phytophthora Blight of Pigeonpea. Indian Phytopathology. 37: 506-510.

Kannaiyan J, Nene YL, Reddy MV, Ryan JG, Raju TN. (1984). Prevalence of Pigeonpea Diseases and Associated Crop Losses in Asia, Africa and the Americas. Tropical Pest Management 30, 62-71.

Khare, D., Satpute, RG and Tiwari, AS. (1975). Present State of the Wilt and Sterility Mosaic Disease of Pigeonpea. *Indian Journal of Genetics.* 54: 331-346.

Khan, J., Ooka, JJ., miller, SA, Madden, LV and Hoitink, HAJ. (2004). Systemic Resistance Induced by *Trichoderma hamatum* 382 in Cucumber Against Phytophthora Crown Rot and Leaf Blight. Plant Disease. 88: 280-286.

Kulka, M. and Von Schmeling, B. (1987). In: Modern Selective Fungicides-Properties, Mechanism of Action. Longman Scientific and Technical, pp. 119.

Kumar Sanjeev, Upadhyay JP and Rani Archana (2009). Evaluation of Trichoderma Species Against *Fusarium udum* Butler Causing Wilt of Pigeonpea. Journal of Biological Control, 23 (3): 329-332.

Kumar Sanjeev and Upadhyay JP (2013). Cultural Morphological and Pathogenic Variability in Isolates of *Fusarium udum* Causing Wilt of Pigeonpea. Journal of Mycology and Plant Pathology. Journal of Mycology and Plant Pathology. 43(1): 76-79.

Mandhare, V.K. and A.V. Suryawanshi, 2004. Application of *Trichoderma* Species Against Pigeonpea Wilt. JNKVV Res. J., 38: 99-100.

Mayee CD (2016) Integrated Pest Management for Sustainable Crop Protection from Diseases : What are the Options. 6th International Conference Plant Pathogens and People February 23-27, 2016, New Delhi, India. P. No. 70.

Rao, S.C., Coleman, S.W., Mayeux, H.S., 2002. Forage Production and Nutritive Value of Selected Pigeonpea Ecotypes in the Southern Great Plains. Crop Science, 42: 1259-1263.

Sharma M (2016) Climate Change and Emerging Diseases in Chick Pea and Pigeonpea: Occurrence, Distribution and Epidemiology. 6th International Conference Plant Pathogens and People February 23-27, 2016, New Delhi, India. P. No. 53.

Singh JP and Singh F (2014). Scenario of Pigeonpea Research in India. National Conference of Pulses: Challenges and Opportunities Under Changing Climate Scenariao 29th Sept. 1st Oct. 2014. JNKVV Jabalpur, MP.

Shrivastava V, Khare NK, Kinjulek CS and Naberia S(2016) Symoposium on Physiological Approaches to Enhance Productivity in Pulses Under Changing Climate. 30 April, 2016, JNKVV, Jabalpur, MP.

Pages: 187-203

BIOTECHNOLOGY AND ENVIRONMENTAL MANAGEMENT

Edited by: **Prof. Arun Arya; Dr. Raaz K Maheswari & Dr. Pawan Kumar 'Bharti'**

ISBN: 978-93-5056-862-0

Edition: **2017**

Published by: **Discovery Publishing House Pvt. Ltd., New Delhi (India)**

9

Fungal Pigments and Their Applications

R. Poorniammal; E. Parameswari
T. Anitha and V. Davamani

The population explosion and the environmental pollution in recent years have forced researchers to find new health and hygiene related products for the well being of mankind. Natural dyes/colourants have been used historically throughout the world.

The use of natural dyes/colourants has decreased to larger extent due to the advent of synthetic dyes. Recently, dyes derived from natural sources have emerged as an important alternative to synthetic dyes, which have been reported to have carcinogenic effects. With the worldwide concern over the use of eco-friendly and biodegradable materials, the use of natural dyes/colourants has once again gained interest. The worldwide demand for colourants of natural origin, especially yellow and red pigments, are rapidly increasing in the food, textile, pharmaceuticals, cosmetic, painting and plastics. In the food, textile and pharmaceutical industries, due to the serious environment and safety problems caused by many artificial synthetic pigments, research has focused on processes for the production of safe and natural pigments from natural resources (Cho *et al.*, 2002).

SYNTHETIC PIGMENT

The first synthetic organic dye, a purplish lilac colour, was discovered in 1856 by William Henry Perkin and called "mauve." Over the next 50 years, scores of similar organic aniline dyes, representing every colour and tint of the rainbow, were developed, and many were used to colour food with little thought or testing regarding their safety. Significant toxicity of many

Horticultural College and Research Institute, Tamil Nadu Agricultural University, Periyakulam, Tamilnadu, (India)

early aniline and coal-tar based colours prompted regulators to examine exactly what was being used to colour food (Pratima and Bhat, 2003).

Of the 80 synthetic food colourants sold in 1907, only 16 were deemed to be "more or less" harm-less. By 1907, this list was pared to seven synthetic colourants, which eventually were subjected to "batch certification" to detect and limit toxic impurities. The list of "certified" colours had expanded and contracted over the decades to the current group of nine certi-fied colours chemically classified into four chemical families: azo, xanthenes/fluoroscein, triphenylmethane and sulfonated indigoid (Table 9.1).

Table 9.1: Certified synthetic colour for use in foods

Certified colour name	Common or Industrial Name (hue)	Uses and Restrictions	CFR
FD & C Blue No. 1	Brilliant Blue FCF	Foods generally (Brilliant blue)	74.101
FD & C Blue No. 2	Indigotine (royal blue)	Foods generally	74.102
FD & C Green No. 3	Fast Green FCF (sea green)	Foods generally	74.203
Orange B	–	Casings or surfaces of frankfurters and saus	74.250
Citrus Red No. 2	–	Skins of oranges	74.302
FD & C Red NO.3	Erythrosine(Cherry red)	Foods generally	74.303
FD & C Red No 40	Allura Red (Orange-red)	Foods generally	74.340
FD & C Yellow No 5	Tartrazine (Lemon yellow)	Foods generally	74.705
FD & C Yellow No 6	Sunset yellow (Orange)	Foods generally	74.706

CFR - Code of Federal Regulations

Health Hazards of Synthetic Pigment

The potential for adverse health effects through exposure to synthetic agents in foods is evaluated by risk analysis. Among the synthetic agents, food colours are of major concern in India. In the mid-1980s, there was a growing concern among consumers about the possible adverse effects of additives such as colours, for example, the purported link between tartrazine and hyperactivity in children. A possible link between the ingestion of foods containing synthetic food flavourings and colours and the presence of hyperactive behaviours in children had been suggested.

Permitted colours like ponceau, tartrazine and sunset yellow have provoked allergic reactions in several individuals even at low levels of intake. The allergic responses vary from urticaria to dermatitis, angioedema and exacerbation of asthmatic patients (WHO, 1991). It has also been reported that the consumption of a particular brand of aniseed having very high levels of ponceau 4R, exhibited symptoms of glossitis of tongue in children. Tartrazine was associated with irritability, restlessness and sleep disturbance in atopic or hypertensive children aged between 2 and 14 years. The behavioural changes in relation to irritability, restlessness, and sleep disturbance were associated with the ingestion of tartrazine in some children, and reported that those effects were dose-related (1-50 mg/child).

Abdel Aziz *et al.* (1997) revealed the potential adverse effects of erythrosine (ER, FD & C Red No. 3) on the spermatogenesis in adult mice. The sperm count as well as the percentage of motile sperms were significantly reduced by about 50% and 57% respectively. These findings indicated that ER in the used doses had a potential toxic effect on spermatogenesis in mice and in turn, it might affect its testicular function and reproductive performance. 23 children consumed tartrazine beverage showed increased levels of overactivity, aggressive and/or violent activity, poor speech, poor coordination and the development of asthma and/or eczema.

Many synthetic colours have been widely used as food additives in various processed foods for economic reasons and for their bright colour and stability (Ozaki *et al.*, 1998).

The Prevention of Food Adulteration (PFA) Act in India prescribes a level of 100 ppm of tartrazine, sunset yellow, ponceau 4R, carmoisine, erythrosine, brilliant blue, fast green FCF and indigo carmine to be added to specified food items and a level of 200 ppm in canned foods, jams and jellies.

Tsuda *et al.* (2001) reported the genotoxicity of synthetic red tar dyes (amaranth food red No. 2), allura red (food red No. 40), or acid red (food red No. 106), new coccine (food red No. 18) when orally administered to pregnant and male mice to analyse the DNA damage. The assay was positive in the colon, 3 h after the administration of amaranth and allura red and weakly positive in the lung, 6 h after the administration of amaranth. Acid red did not induce DNA damage in any sample at any sampling time. The three dyes induced DNA damages in the colon starting at 10 mg/kg of new coccine, induced DNA damage in colon, glandular stomach, and bladder. Because the three azo additives examined induced colon DNA damage at a very low dose, more extensive assessment of azo additives was warranted.

Permitted colours usage had also evoked concern because they were being used in excess of the statutory limit (100 ppm) or in foods in which they were not permitted (Padmaja *et al.*, 2004). The safety of repeated exposure to the permitted synthetic colours were questioned.

Status of Permitted Food Colours in India

The type and extent of colours added to ready-to-eat (RTE) foods prepared in the non-industrial sector of India was investigated. Of the 545 RTE foods analysed, 90% contained permitted colours, 2% contained a combination of permitted and non-permitted colours and 8% contained non-permitted colours (Santhanakrishnan, 1981). However in RTE foods with permitted colours, 73% exceeded the 100 ppm, as prescribed by the Prevention of Food Adulteration Act of India, and 27% were within the prescribed levels. Among the permitted colours, tartrazine was the most widely used colour followed by sunset yellow. The maximum concentration of colours was detected in sweet meats (18767 ppm), non-alcoholic beverages (9450 ppm), miscellaneous foods (6106 ppm) and hard-boiled sugar confectioneries (3811 ppm). Among the non-permitted colours found, rhodamine was most commonly used. Some of the foods, such as savouries and miscellaneous foods like sugar coated aniseed and almond milk, are not supposed to contain colours as per the Prevention of Food Adulteration Act, but were found to contain colours (Pratima and Sudershan, 2008). The studies on permitted and non-permitted colours are presented in table 9.2.

TEXTILE DYES

As far as the textile sector is concerned synthetic dyes are exclusively used nowadays which makes almost exclusive use of not only their production techniques but also their uses to manufacture coloured fabrics or yarns having a tremendous environmental impact. To process 1mg of textile, quite large volumes (230-270m^3) of water are needed and this gives rise to enormous volumes of exhausted dye baths containing up to 90% of the chemicals used in the finishing processes, which have to be disposed off. Moreover, a great deal of concern has been raised by the presumed or actual noxious effects of some synthetic dyes on human health which are the sources of skin cancer, disorders and allergic reactions (Francalanci *et al.*, 2001).

Highly coloured substances, known as dyes or colourants, are widely used to impart colour to a boundless variety of materials described technically as substrates. The increased application of these dyes or colourants in dyeing industries and inefficiencies in dyeing resulted in a large amount of dyestuff being directly lost in the wastewater, which ultimately finds a way into the environment. It is estimated that 10-35% of the dye is lost in the effluent during the dyeing process, while in the case of reactive dyes, as much as 50% of the initial dye load is present in the dye bath effluent (Sivakumar *et al.*, 2009). Hence, there is a growing demand for eco-friendly/non-toxic colourants, specifically for health sensitive applications such as colouration of food and dyeing of child textile and leather garments.

Health Hazards of Dyes

Today more than 10,000 dyes are commercially available, most of which are difficult to biodegrade due to their complex aromatic molecular structure and synthetic origin (Nigam *et al.*, 2000). A lot of studies throughout the world, reported about the role of dyes in connection with variety of skin, lung and other respiratory disorders. The extensive use of dyes often poses pollution problems in the form of coloured wastewater discharge into environmental water bodies, which interferes with transmission of sunlight into streams therefore reduces photosynthetic activity (Namasivayam *et al.*, 2001).

Table 9.2: Studies in India on usage of added colours in various foods

Food items	Permitted colours	Non-permitted colours	Reference
(1)	(2)	(3)	(4)
Milk products (ice cream, khoya, chenna), non-milkproducts (sweets, namkins), pulses, miscellaneous(confectionery, soft drinks,spices, condiments and tea)	Tartrazine, sunset yellow, carmoisine, ponceau 4R, amaranth, erythrosine, fast red and indigo carmine	Metanil yellow, auramine, rhodamine B, blue VRS, malachite green, Sudan II, III, congo red	Khanna *et al*. (1986)
Sweets, confectionery, Namkins	Tartrazine, sunset yellow, brilliant blue, carmoisine, indigocarmine, erythrosine, ponceau 4R, amaranth	Metanil yellow, orange II, malachite green, rhodamine B, blue VRS, auramine	Dixit *et al*.(1995)
Pulses (*Cajanus cajan, Cicerarietinum, Phaseolus mungo*), powdered spices (turmeric, chillie powder), non-hydrogenated oils	–	Metanil yellow, orange II, sudan II, III, IV and V, auramine, blue VRS, malachite green, rhodamine B	Khanna *et al*.(1987)
Sweetmeats, turmeric, ice candies	–	Metanil yellow, lead Chromate	Kiple and Ornelas (2000)
Edible oil	–	Butter yellow	Chakravarti (1988)
Sweets, confectionery, softdrinks, ice candies, fruit sweetened juices, edible oils, turmeric, pulses, tea and coffee	Tartrazine, sunset yellow, carmoisine, ponceau 4R, brilliant blue	Rhodamine, auramine, orange II	Babu and Shenolikar (1995)
Jilebi	–	Metanil yellow	Toledo *et al*. (1992)

(Table Contd...)

(1)	(2)	(3)	(4)
Dried ginger, confectionery, pulses, edible oils, potatoes, pickles, prepared foods *viz.*, Biryani	Tartrazine, ponceau 4R, sunset yellow	Rhodamine, orange II, metanil yellow, ultra marine blue	Sudershan (1994)
Confectionery, sweets, biscuits, beverages, jam, jelly, custard powder	Tartrazine, sunset yellow, carmoisine, ponceau 4R, brilliant blue	Amaranth, orange II, metanil yellow, rhodamine B, congored, blue VRS, unidentified chocolate brown	Biswas *et al.* (1994)
Flattened rice, fish, fresh vegetables and cut-fruits		Auramine, congo red, malachite green, rhodamine B	Dixit *et al.* (1995)
Sweets, savoury products, powdered spices (turmeric, red chilli)	Tartrazine, sunset yellow, indigo carmine, amaranth, brilliant blue FCF	Metanil yellow, orange II, sudan I, III, IV, rhodamine B, blue VRS, auramine	Dixit *et al.*(1995)

The presence of these heat and light stable, complex dye molecules in wastewater made the conventional methods of sewage treatment, such as primary and secondary treatment systems, unsuitable. In addition, some dyes or their metabolites are either toxic or mutagenic and carcinogenic.

NATURAL COLOURS

Natural colourants are considered to be safer than synthetic ones, and their applications in foods, cosmetics and pharmaceuticals are growing rapidly. There are a number of natural pigments, but only a few are available in sufficient quantities for industrial production. Production of pigments from microorganisms is advantageous over other sources because microorganisms can grow rapidly which may lead to a high productivity of the product (Kim *et al.*, 1999).

Natural Pigments

The use of food colourants as additives in the food industry is a significant factor for both food manufacturers and consumers in determining the acceptability of processed food (Pattnaik *et al.*, 1997). Currently, the European Union has authorized approximately 43 colourants as food additives, whereas approximately 30 colour additives are approved for use in the United States. These legislations does not distinguish between synthetic and natural colour additives.

The current commercial, naturally derived food colourants have several drawbacks. Anthocyanins are flavonoids and are characterized by their basic flavylium cation structure. The violet, purple colours of anthocyanins are sensitive to oxidation, bleaching by sulfur dioxide and vary with pH, and these factors limit their application to acidic foods and beverages. Also, betanins, carotenoids and chlorophyll pigments contain labile hydrogens and are easily decolourized by oxidation, making them sensitive to light, heat and oxygen. These features limit the robustness of these colour additives during processing, storage and display of the foods to which they have been added. The food colourant curcumin has a different problem, curcumin is the major pigment of turmeric and carries a spicy, curry flavour, which limits its use as a food colourant. Furthermore, the fact that the current, naturally derived colourants are extracted from sources such as fruit skins, seeds or roots means that the colour manufacturers are usually dependent on the availability and external supply of raw materials for the colour extraction Obviously, the pigment profile in the natural sources is prone to variation and the extracted pigment profile is influenced by the extraction procedure employed. Thus, the chemical composition, including the presence of minor components, and the colour and stability properties of the current, commercial and naturally derived colour additives vary significantly among different suppliers and from batch to batch (Downham and Collins, 2000). To say the least, many consumers are likely to be unaware of the exotic sources of some of the currently authorized so-called natural colourants. The red colourant carmine, for instance, is an extract of the female cochineal insect and to produce 100 g carmine colourant approximately 14,000 insects are required. Many of the currently authorized 'natural' food colourants have been accepted by tradition. It has been claimed that if they were to be introduced into industrial food manufacturing today, natural colourants of similar variable quality and exotic origin might not be accepted.

This provides a large incentive to identify alternative ways in which natural colours can be produced in the future.

Microbial Pigments

The pigments from microbial sources are a good alternative that could easily be produced in high yields and capability of producing different coloured pigments. Pigment producing microorganisms and microalgae are quite common in nature. Pigment produced by microorganisms includes carotenoids, melanins, flavins, quinones and more specifically monascins, violacein, phycocyanin or indigo. However, there is a long way from the Petri dish to the market place as only five productions are operated on an industrial scale (Table 9.3).

Table 9.3: Microbial pigments and their properties

Microbial source	Molecule	Colour
(1)	(2)	(3)
Bacteria		
Agrobacterium aurantiacum	Astaxanthin	Pink-red
Paracoccus carotinifaciens	Astaxanthin	Pink-red
Paracoccus zeaxanthinifaciens	Zeaxanthin	yellow
Bradyrhizobium sp	Canthaxanthin	Dark red
Streptomyces echinoruber	Rubrolone	Red
Flavobacterium sp	Zeaxanthin	Yellow
Halobacterium sp	Canthaxanthin	-
Pseudomonas aeruginosa	Phenazine	
Micrococcus sp	Carotenoid	Yellow
Monascus sp	Ankaflavin Monascorubramin	Yellow
Penicillium oxalicum	Anthraquinone	Red
Fusarium sporotrichioides	Lycopene	Red
Cordyceps unilateralis	Naohtoquinone	Deep blood-red
Ashbya gossypi	Riboflavin	Yellow
Blakeslea trispora	ß - carotene	Yellow- orange
Mucor circinelloides	ß - carotene	Yellow- orange
Neurospora crassa *Phycomyces blakesleeanus*	ß - carotene ß - carotene	Yellow - orange Yellow - orange

(Table Contd...)

(1)	(2)	(3)
Penicillium purpurogenum	Unknown	Red
Paecilomyces sinclairii	Unknown	Red
Fusarium graminearum	Aurofusarin	Red
Fusarium culmorum	Rubrofusarin	orange
Xanthophyllomyces dendrorhous	Astaxanthin	Pink-red
Rhodotorula sp	Torularhodin	Orange
Saccharomyces neoformans	Melanin	Black
Dunaliella salina	β-carotene	Green
Haematococcus pluvialis	Astaxanthin	Orange
Spirulina and other blue-green algae	Phycocyanin	Green
Porphyra, Porphyridium and other red algae	Phycoerythrin	Red

The microbial colours have the advantage of being climate independent, do not require large area for their growth and can be produced in any quantity in shorter period. Microorganisms produce a variety of pigments that includes polyketides, carotenoids, phenazines, acylphenols, pyrones, sclertiorins, anthroquinones but most of these pigments are toxic to humans except for carotenoids and polyketides. Further, the carotenoids possess nutraceutical properties which gain more importance in food and textile industries. Among microalgae, two successful stories yield to efficient production of carotenoids such as β-carotene using *Dunaliella* or astaxanthin using *Haematococcus*. The phycobiliproteins or phycocyanin, researchers should first carry out toxicological studies which could allow the use as food colours (Dufosse *et al.*, 2005)

Fungal Pigments

Fungi have a higher advantage among microbial sources of pigments over the other organisms. Fungi can be scaled up in fermentor and because of higher growth rate the yield is also comparatively higher and extraction of pigments from fungi is also easy whether it is extracellular or intracellualr in nature. The fungal pigments are intended to substitute currently used synthetic colourants and/or natural colourants derived from plant materials. In addition, some of the coloured pigments produced by the fungi can expand the current palette of colours used in various industrial applications.

The appropriate use of fermentation physiology together with metabolic engineering could allow the efficient mass production of colourants from fungi. With recent advances in rDNA gene technology, attempts have been made to create cell factories for the production of food colourants through the heterologous expression of biosynthetic pathways from either already known or novel pigment producers (Lakrod *et al.*, 2003).

Biodiversity of Filamentous Fungi: A Promising Source of Colourants

Like plants, filamentous fungi synthesize natural products because they have an ecological function and are of value to the producer (Firn and Jones, 2003). Depending on the type of compound, they serve different functions varying from a protective action against lethal photo-oxidations (carotenoids) to protection against environmental stress (melanins) and acting as cofactors in enzyme catalysis (flavins). Besides providing functional diversity to the host, these pigments exhibit a unique structural and chemical diversity with an extraordinary range of colours.

Several characteristic non-carotenoid pigments are produced by filamentous fungi, including quinones such as anthraquinones and naphthaquinones, dihydroxynaphthalene melanin (a complex aggregate of polyketides, and flavin compounds such as riboflavin. Anthraquinone (octaketide) pigments like catenarin, chrysophanol, cynodontin, helminthosporin, tritisporin and erythroglaucin are produced by *Eurotium* spp., *Fusarium* spp., *Curvularia lunata* and *Drechslera* spp. Yellow pigments epurpurins A to C were isolated from *Emericella purpurea* and azaphilone derivatives (hexaketides), falconensins A–H and falconensones A1 and B2 are produced both by *Emericella falconensis* and *Emericella fructiculosa.*

Monascus spp

Monascus spp. are known to produce well-known azaphilone pigments like monascorubrin, rubropunctatin and more recently, monascusones from a yellow *Monascus* mutant have been identified. Monascorubrin and rubropunctatin have a unique structure responsible for their high-affinity for compounds with primary amino groups (so-called aminophiles). Reactions with amino acids yielded the water-soluble red pigments, monascorubramine and rubropunctamine. In fact, various pigment derivatives with improved functional properties in the colour range of orange-red to violet-red can be produced by *Monascus* fermentations in the presence of different amino acids. However, *Monascus*-fermented rice has been found to contain the mycotoxin citrinin. The production of citrinin together with pigments clearly limits the use of *Monascus* as a producer of natural food colourants. In a recent review article, however, it was suggested that citrinin is only produced by some and not all *Monascus* strains (Carvalho *et al.*, 2003).

Penicillium

Penicillium may be the potential candidate to produce polyketide structure compounds. The new isolate *Penicillium* strain produced violet, red, orange and yellow pigments and these pigments exhibits the monascorubramine components. A new natural food colourant of fungal origin called Arpink RedTM is manufactured by ASCOLOUR BIOTECH in the Czech Republic. The red colourant is an extracellular metabolite of the anthraquinone class and is claimed to be produced by a variety of *Penicillium oxalicum*. It is also said to confer anticancer effects when used in food supplements. *Penicillium* derived pigments have been found to be more stable on exposure to light than other fungal pigments (derived from *Monascus*). Strains of the species belonging to *Penicillium* subgenus *Biverticillium* were known to produce copious amounts of yellow, orange and red pigments on solid media (Mapari *et al.*, 2009).

Aspergillus

Pigments synthesized by micromycetes *Aspergillus* sp are true melanins. Sanjay *et al.* (2007) reported that the pigment obtained from mycelial biomass of *Aspergillus* sp is a safe food colour. The polyketide pigment producing *Aspergillus* species are reported in Table 5.

Fusarium

Fusarium produces naphthoquinone pigments in culture, several of which have phytotoxicity, antimicrobial activity and cytotoxicity. The known pigments, o-methyl-bostrycoidin, o-methyl-fusarubin and bikaverin have been identified as major products in these fungi. Synthesis of naphthoquinones by fungi proceeded *via* the polyketide route by formation of a common precursor, acetyl CoA and malonyl CoA, from primary metabolism. The production of naphthoquinone pigments was mostly studied on nutrient-rich laboratory media for maximal amounts of various pigments and to study their structure.Most investigators have exerted their efforts to cultivate these organisms on submerged condition than solid artificial media.

Thermomyces

Thermomyces pigments exhibits bright pigmentation that varies from yellow to red. the pigmentation varies depending upon the growth, temperature, age and substarte. on the basis of electronic spectra, the intra red spectra and chemical properties, the pigments in thermomyces was found to be similar to aphins, the hydroxylated quinoid pigments (Somasundaram *et al.*, 1986). Toxicological studies were performed on the *Thermomyces* pigment using albino mice. The result showed that due to intake of *Thermomyces* sp pigment for 28 days did not alter the Hb, RBe. WBe. organ weight and histopathology. The *in vivo* antioxidant activity of the pigment was also confirmed. *Thermomyces* sp. can be safely applied to food and the colour remains longer (Poorniammal *et al* 2011).

The stability of the extract was tested in different environmental conditions such as pH,heat, light, antioxidants and chemical preservatives. It has been shown that increasing the pH, temperature or exposure to light does not affect stability of the yellow pigment. The pigment extract was more stable at pH 5.1and 8.0, temperature at 10° C, 20° C and 30° C both in the presence and absence of light, however moderate stability was observed in antioxidants and preservatives. Thus, yellow pigment obtained from*Thermomyces* sp has a high potential to be used as a natural food colorant (Poorniammal *et al.*,, 2015)

ANTIMICROBIAL POTENTIAL OF FUNGAL PIGMENT AGAINST HUMAN PATHOGENS

The antibacterial activity of *Monascus purpureus* was first reported by Wong and Bau. This *Monascus* pigment has antibiotic activities against gram positive bacteria, but nephrotoxic properties have limited its use as an antibiotic. Pigments and citrinin are secondary metabolites derived from the polyketide pathway (condensation of acetyl-CoA and melonyl-CoA). The fungi also produce antibiotic substances against pathogenic bacteria when grown on an appropriate medium.

Secondary metabolites of *M. anka*, ankalactone, which they reported as bacteriostatic. The presence of monascidin A in submerged cultures of *M. purpureus* and *M. atiku*, which they identified as citrinin. They also found that addition of crulenine and ethionine could inhibit citrinin and pigment synthesis. Wild strains and mutants of *M. purpureus* were active against *Bacillus, Streptococcus* and *Pseudomonas*. Solid-state bioprocessing of soybean by *Monascus* is a biotechnological strategy to produce Monascus-fermented soybeans (MFS) with more beneficial components.The antimicrobial activity of total red pigment from *M. purpureus* MTCC 410 recorded more antimicrobial activity, which could yield significant information on the scope for *Monascus* pigments substituted or as an adjunct to chemotherapeutic agents.

TOXICOLOGICAL ASPECTS OF NATURAL PIGMENTS

Consumer awareness towards many natural products leads many of the researchers to explore new and viable alternatives to the synthetics. All natural colours are not suitable for consumption for human beings. Many of them are certified as unsuitable for consumption because they are carcinogenic in nature.

Safety assessment of beta-carotene derived from *B. trispora* has hitherto been limited for genotoxicity and sub acute (4-week) toxicity study (JECFA, 1996). Since it is a potential substitute for synthetic beta-carotene, consumers in general are preferring natural products, the sub chronic (90-day) toxicity study was performed with administration in the diet to both sexes of F344 rats to allow comparison with the results for synthetic beta-carotene. The results showed no adverse effects in the biological system.

The toxicological evaluation of *R. gracilis* CFR-1, in freeze-dried form has been studied to assess its safety as a source of natural colourant and nutritional additive in experimental animals. Acute and subacute studies on freeze-dried *R. gracilis* were conducted on both sexes of albino rats. Acute doses of *R. gracilis* at 0.5-6.0 g/kg of body weight (w/w) did not show any symptoms of toxicity nor mortality of the adult rats. Feeding of low concentrations of *R. gracilis* at 0.1-2.0% level (w/w) for 14 weeks did not induce any significant change in food intake and gain in body weight of the experimental rats compared to control animals. There were no significant differences in the absolute and relative weights of vital organs, hematological parameters, macroscopic and microscopic changes in vital organs and serum enzyme levels between the experimental and control groups. The fecal matter of *R. gracilis*-fed rats did not show any viable cells. The results clearly showed that acute and sub acute oral feeding of freeze-dried whole cells of *R. gracilis* for 14 weeks did not produce any toxic effects on male and female rats (Naidu *et al.*, 1999).

The safety of the natural red colourant extracted from edible algae *Dunaliella* was evaluated in animal model systems. The pigment did not induce any adverse effects in albino rats. The terminal autopsy, vital organs of treated rat groups did not show any biochemical and morphological alteration as compared to untreated animals. On the other hand, *Dunaliella* extract has been shown to have important health benefits as cholesterol, triglycerides and total lipids lowering effect and other additional physiological benefits for human health.

Sanjay *et al.* (2007) evaluated the safety of pigment containing *Aspergillus carbonarious* biomass by conducting acute and subacute toxicity studies in both sexes of albino rats. This study revealed the fact that the feeding of fungal biomass did not show any mortality of rats and there is no significant differences in food intake, body weight, hematological parameters (WBC, RBC, Hb etc.,), organ weight and serum enzymes (LDH, ALP, ASAT, ALAT and cholesterol).

APPLICATION OF FUNGAL PIGMENTS

Pigments produced by fungi are of traditional use in orientalcountries and have been a subject of intense research in the present decades because of its potential for applications. Fungal pigments offer the following benefits and advantages:

- Increasingly attractive to science because of broad ranging activities.
- Easy propagation and wide strain selection.
- High versatile and productive over other sources.
- Fermentation is inherently faster and more productive production compared to any other chemical process.
- Easy to manipulate genes
- Simple and fast culturing techniques allowing continuous bioreactor operation.
- Structural complexity suits for industrial needs.
- Fungal pigments extracted using simple liquid–liquid extraction technique minimizing operation cost.
- Cheap substrates used for bulk production

Food Applications

The best known of the microbial colourants are produced by *Monascus* group, specifically by *Monascus anka* and *M. purpureus*. Traditionally grown on steamed rice, bread, brans and cereal meats, *Monascus purpureus* produces true red mycelium and pigments through solid culture, and has been used in the Orient for many centuries to colour and flavour food and beverages. Fabre *et al.* (1993) reported that the *Monascus* colour incorporated into pork meat products had better colourants and also substitute nitrate salts. Pigments from *M. purpureus* are very stable and suitable for use as a food additive. A noodle making company evaluated the *Monascus* pigment as colourant for flavoring ingredients of instant noodles and found that it was acceptable. Moreover, the *Monascus* fungi contain therapeutic metabolites such as monacolin k (mevinolin), which is regarded as a healthy and nutritious food in Asia.

The *Monascus* pigments were tested for their ability to colour different foods, including meat products. They appeared to be visible substitutes for nitrite salts which are traditionally added to enhance meat colour. Milk and yogurt were coloured with *Monascus* pigment and it resembled like strawberry milk. The products were stable for more than a month. The artificial colouring of sausages is not usually permitted in keeping with the world trend of manufacturing of all natural foods, *i.e.,* with out any synthetic additives in typical to apply red yeast rice to improve the colour and probably their preservatives and flavour too. Baranova *et al.* (2004) reported that the wheat protein – seitan coloured by *M. purpureus* is rich in proteins, did not contain fat and cholesterol and could replace meat products and also improved the consistency of the product.

Textile Application

Pigments from natural sources have been obtained since antiquity and their interest has increased in recent days due to the toxicity problems caused by those of synthetic origin. The synthetic dyes and chemicals used in the dyeing process created several environmental problems. The increasing awareness of health and pollution hazards of chemical dyestuffs has increased the interest in using natural dyes. Among the species examined, common madder (*Rubia tinctorum* L), woad (*Isatis tinctoria* L.) and weld (*Reseda luteola* L.) (Cerrato *et al.,* 2002) proved to be quite interesting sources of red (alizarin), indigo (indigotin) and yellow (luteolin) dyes respectively, either for their agronomic characteristics or for their dyeing properties. In fact, all three dyes were extensively exploited until the commercial success of their synthetic analogues. It has been reported that lowering of the chemical load released with wastewater can be expected by shifting to plant-based dyes and microbial based dyes.

There has been increasing interest in using microorganisms as a source of colour since they require less labour, land, and cost effective solvents for extraction as opposed to higher plant materials. The fungal pigment is one of the best alternate sources to replace synthetic pigments/dyes. Among the pigment producing fungi identified, *Aspergillus ruber*, *Aspergillus glaucus* and *Trichoderma viride* have been reported to produce red, yellow and yellow green pigment, respectively. *Sclerotinia* is a fungus that prefers cool, moist weather, causing diseases of great intensity at temperatures ranging from 15-21° C. De Santis *et al.* (2005) studied that the orange pigment produced by *Monascus purpureus* applied to fabrics, the dyed specimens with different hues depending on the mordant used. Independently of the microbial pigments used, the dyed wool specimens presented a prevailing red or orange shade when alum or stannic chloride was used as mordant respectively. An orange pigment from the fungi *Sclerotina* sp, *Ganoderma lucidum, Coriolus versicolour* and *Amanita muscaria* was extracted from the basidiocarps and applied on silk and cotton fabrics (Perumal *et al.,* 2009).

Pharmaceutical Application

Pharmaceutical industry uses many microbial pigments in their products. Man pigmented secondary metabolites of the microorganism have significant potential clinical applications and many research works are going on for treating many diseases like cancer, leukemia, diabetes mellitus etc. These pigments may act as: antibiotics, anticancer, antiploriferative and immunosuppressive compounds. Some examples of such type of pigments are given below:

Red Yeast Rice (RYR) is a fermented rice product produced traditionally by fermenting cooked rice kernels with yeast Monascusspp (Monascusrubur, Monascuspurpureus, Monascusruberand Monascuspilosus). These Monascus spp. have an important characteristic to produce secondary metabolites of polyketide structure and yellow, orange and red pigments. Monascu-sruberwas used for production of angkak, a fermented rice product with anti cholesterol activity. RYR proved to contain many active constituents such as compounds resembling statins in its structure, unsaturated fatty acid, sterols and B-complex vitamins. Various studies also reported that RYR and statins decreases blood glucoselevels in diabetes.

CONCLUDING REMARKS AND FUTURE DIRECTIONS

The success of any pigment produced by fermentation depends upon its acceptability in the market, regulatory approval, and the size of the capital investment required to bring the product to market. Microbial pigments are not only used as food colorant, flavoring agent and dying agents they are widely applied in medicinal aspects. Apart from food and textile coloring they have been used in clinical therapy to lower the blood cholesterol concentration, Anti-Diabetic Activity, Anti-Inflammation etc.

Further understanding of the biological properties of fungal pigments will not only enrich our instinctual curiosity about colors, but also provide a scientific basis for therapeutic disarming of the pathogens or for borrowing these multifunctional molecules in pharmacologic applications.

REFERENCES

1. Abdel Aziz, A.H., S.A. Shouman, A.S. Attia and S.F. Saad. (1997). A Study on the Reproductive Toxicity of Erythrosine in Male Mice. *Pharmacol Res.*, 35(5): 457-62.
2. Baranova, M., P.Mala, O. Burdova, M. Hadbavny and G. Sabolova. (2004). Effect of Natural Pigment of *Monascus purpureus* on the Organoleptic Characters of Processed Cheeses. *Bull. Vet. Inst. Pulawy*, 48: 59-62.
3. Carvalho, J.C., A. Pandey, S. Babitha and C.R. Soccol. (2003). Production of *Monascus* Biopigments, An Overview. *Agro. Food Ind. Hi tec.*, 14(6): 37-42.
4. Cerrato, A., D. De Santis and M. Moresi. (2002). Production of Luteolin Extracts from *Reseda luteola* and Assessment of their Dyeing Properties. *J. Sci. Food Agric.*, 82: 1189-1199.
5. Cho, Y.J., J.P. Park, H.J. Hwang, S.W. Kim, J.W. Choi and J.W.Yun. (2002). Production of Red Pigment by Submerged Culture of *Paecilomyces sinclairii*. *Lett. Appl. Microbiol.*, 35(3): 195-202.
6. De Santis, M.A., M.A. Gallo and M. Petruccioli. (2005). Assessment of the Dyeing Properties of Pigments from *Monascus purpureus*, *J. Chem. Technol. Biotechnol.*, 80: 1072-1079.
7. Downham, A and P. Collins. (2000). Colouring our Foods in the Last and Next Millennium. *Int. J. Food Sci. Technol.*, 35: 5-22.
8. Dufossé, L., P. Galaup, E. Carlet, C. Flamin and A. Valla. (2005). Spectrocolorimetry in the CIE L*a*b* Color Space as Useful Tool for Monitoring the Ripening Process and the Quality of PDO Red-smear Soft Cheeses. *Food Res. Int.*, 38: 919-924.
9. Fabre, C.E., A.L. Santerre, M.O. Loret, R. Baberian, A. Pareilleux and G. Goma. (1993). Production and Food Application of the Red Pigments of *Monascus ruber*. *J. Food Sci.*, 58: 1099-1102.
10. Firn, R.D and C.G. Jones. (2003). Natural Products - A Simple Model to Explain Chemical Diversity. *Nat. Prod. Rep.*, 20: 382-391.
11. Francalanci, S., S.Giorgini, and A. Brusi. (2001). Sertoli, L'impiego di tessuti ecologici nella prevenzione della dermatite allergica da contatto con coloranti. *Proc. 1st Health and Textile Int. Forum, Biella (Online).*
12. JECFA. (1996). Evaluation of Certain Food Additives and Contaminants. Summary of Evaluations Performed by the Joint FAO/WHO Expert Committee on Food Additive. pp. 1-100.
13. Kim, C.H., S.W. Kim and S.I. Hong, (1999). An Integrated Fermentation Separation Process for the Production of Red Pigments by *Serratia* sp. K.H-95. *Process Biochem.*, 35: 485-490.
14. Lakrod, K., C. Chaisrisook and D.Z. Skinner. (2003). Expression of Pigmentation Genes Following Electroporation of Albino *Monascus purpureus*. *J. Ind. Microbiol. Biotechnol.*, 30: 369–374.
15. Mapari, S.A.S., A.S. Meyer, U. Thrane and J.C. Frisvad. (2009). Identification of Potentially Safe Promising Fungal Cell Factories for the Production of Polyketide Natural Food Colorants Using Chemotaxonomic Rationale. *Microb. Cell Fact.*,8 (24): 1-15.
16. Naidu, K.A., G. Venkateswaran and G. Vijayalakshmi. 1999 b. Toxicological Assessment of the Yeast *Rhodotorula gracilis* in Experimental Animals. *Lebensm Unters Forsch.* 208: 444-448.

17. Naidu, K.A., R. Sarada, G. Manoj, M.Y. Khan, M. Mahadevaswamy, S. Viswanatah, K. Narasimha Murthy, G.A. Ravishankar and S. Leela. (1999). Toxicity Assessment of Phycocyanin – A Blue Colorant from Blue Green Alga *Spirulina platensis*. J. *Food. Biotech.*, 13(1): 51-66.
18. Namasivayam, C., R. Radhika and S. Suba (2001). Uptake of Dyes by a Promising Locally Available Agricultural Solid Waste: Coir Pith. *Waste Manage.*, 21: 381.
19. Nigam, P., G. Armour, I. Banat, M.D. Singh and R. Merchant (2000). Physical Removal of Textile Dyes from Effluents and Solid-state Fermentation of Dye-adsorbed Agriculture Residues. *Bioresour. Technol.*, 72: 219-224.
20. Ozaki, A., M. Kitano, N. Itoh, K. Kuroda, N. Furusawa, T. Masuda and H. Yamaguchi. (1998). Mutagenicity and DNA-damaging Activity of Decomposed Products of Food Colours Under UV Irradiation. *Food Chem. Toxicol.*, 36: 811-817.
21. Padmaja, R., P.R. Jonnalagadda, R.V. Bhat and A.N. Naidu. (2004). Type and Extent of Colors Used in Ready-to-eat (RTE) Foods Prepared in the Non-industrial Sector. *Int. J. Food Sci. Technol.*, 39: 125-131.
22. Pattnaik, P., U. Roy and P. Jain. (1997). Biocolours New Generation Additives for Food. *Indian Food Industry*, 16: 21-27.
23. Perumal, K., V. Stalin, S. Chandrasekarenthiran, E. Sumathi and A. Saravanakumar. (2009). Extraction and Characterization of Pigment from Sclerotinia sp and its Use in Dyeing Cotton. *Text. Res. J.*, 79: 1178-1187.
24. Poorniammal, R, Gunasekaran, Sand Ariharasivakumar, H. (2011). Toxicity Evaluation Offungal Food Colourant from *Thermomyces* sp in Albino mice. *Journal of Sci Ind Rese.*, 70: 773-777.
25. Poorniammal, R. and S. Gunasekaran, (2015). Physical and Chemical Stability Analysis of *Thermomyces* sp yellow Pigment for Food Application. *Int. J.Food. Ferment. Technol*, 5(1): 33-38.
26. Sanjay, K.R., N. Kumaresan, B. Manohar, S. Umesh Kumar and G. Vijayalakshmi. (2007). Optimization of Carotenoid Production by *Aspergillus carbonarius* in Submerged Fermentation Using a Response Surface Methodology. *Int. J. Food Eng.*, 21: 12-18.
27. Sanjay, K.R., N. Kumaresan, K. Akhilender Naidu, S. Vishwanatha, K. Narasimhamurthy, S. Umesh Kumar and G. Vijayalakshmi. (2007). Safety Evaluation of *Monascus purpureus* Red Mould Rice in Albino rats. *Food Chem. Toxicol.*, 45: 431-439.
28. Santhanakrishnan, T.S. (1981). Food Colour and Their Future. *Indian Food Packer*, 35: 104-121.
29. Sivakumar, V., A.J. Lakshmi, J. Vijayeeswaree and G. Swaminathan (2009). Ultrasound Assisted Enhancement in Natural dye Extraction from Beetroot for Industrial Applications and Natural Dyeing of Leather. *Ultrason Sonochem.*, 16: 782-789.
30. Somasundaram, T., S. Sanjay, R. Rao and R. Maheswari. (1986). Pigments in Thermophilic fungi. *Current science*, 55(19): 957-960.
31. Tsuda, S., M. Murakami, N. Matsusaka, K. Kano, K. Taniguchi and Y.F. Sasaki. (2001). DNA Damage Induced by Red Food Dyes Orally Administered to Pregnant and Male mice. *Toxicol. Sci.*, 61(1): 92-9.

Pages: 204-227

BIOTECHNOLOGY AND ENVIRONMENTAL MANAGEMENT

Edited by: **Prof. Arun Arya; Dr. Raaz K Maheswari & Dr. Pawan Kumar 'Bharti'**

ISBN: 978-93-5056-862-0

Edition: **2017**

Published by: **Discovery Publishing House Pvt. Ltd., New Delhi (India)**

10

Integrated Approaches for the Management of Basal Rot Disease in Onion

Srinivasan.V.M;
Krishnamoorthy. A.S.
Daniel Jebaraj. M

ABSTRACT

Basal rot of onion is a serious disease in field as well as in storage. Eight pathogenic isolates of *Fusarium oxysporum* f.sp.*cepae* were collected from different locations of Perambalur District of Tamil Nadu. Among these isolates, *F.o* 6 was found to be virulent. Among the different plant extracts tested bulb extract of garlic showed cent per cent mycelial growth inhibition of *Fusarium oxysporum* f.sp. *cepae* under *in vitro*. Among the fungal and bacterial biocontrol agents tested under *in vitro* against *Fusarium oxysporum* f.sp. *cepae,* the fungal antagonists *Trichoderma viride*-1 (67.77%) and the bacterial antagonist *Pseudomonas fluorescens* -2 (57.89%) were found to be most effective in reducing the mycelial growth. Among the six different fungicides tested against basal rot incidence, Carbendazim 0.1 per cent showed the maximum mycelial growth inhibition and percent disease reduction (11.38%) over control with the highest yield of 9300Kg/ha compared to control 2000Kg/ha.

Key words: Onion, basal rot, Fusarium rot, Plant extract.

INTRODUCTION

Onion (*Allium cepa* var. *aggregatum*) is the second important horticultural crop worldwide, after tomato (Benítez *et al*., 2012). The area under cultivation in India is around 1064 ha with the Production and productivity of 15.118 MT and 14.2 MT/ha respectively. Onion production in India occupies 19.90 % share in world total production. In Perambalur district total cultivated

Department of Plant Pathology, Tamil Nadu Agricultural University, Coimbatore - 641 003, (India)

area is 7.5 ha, production 60.622 tons and productivity 8.04 t/ha. It has great economic importance, because of its medical and nutritional values (Nasri *et al.*, 2012).Onions can be used in almost each type of food either cooked foods or fresh salads. Onions pickled in vinegar are eaten as a snack. The mature bulbs contain starch, sugar, some protein, and vitamins A, B and C (Baloch, 1994). Onion is known for prevention or treatment of many diseases such as coronary heart diseases (Lanzotti, 2006), cancers (Shutenko *et al.*, 1999), cataract (Sanderson *et al.*, 1999) and diabetes (Sheela *et al.*, 1995). The characteristic sulfur containing secondary metabolites alliins (cysteine sulfoxides) cause taste and sharpness, and are criteria for the pharmaceutical quality (Bloem *et al.*, 2005). Another sulfur containing compound thiosulfinates exhibit antimicrobial properties (Peter, 2003). Onion crop is affected many diseases generally caused by fungi and bacteria both in field as well as storage. Pink root (*Pyrenochaeta terrestris*), and *Fusarium* basal rot (*Fusarium oxysporum* f. sp. *cepae*) are the economically important diseases of onion. One of those diseases, Fusarium basal rot is a root and bulb disease of onion grown in temperate and subtropical regions (Brayford, 1996). Basal plate rot is a highly destructive disease of onion found in many countries of the world (Bayraktar, 2010). It induces significant yield losses of the crop worldwide (Ozer and Koycu, 2004). Both infected seeds and soil are the chief source of pathogen inoculum. The fungus causes infection at the basal stem plate of the onion bulb and degrades it, finally destroys the whole plant (Cramer, 2000). Starting from tips of leaves, progressive wilting, yellowing, curving and eventually dying back symptoms appear on infected plants (Sumner, 1995). The disease is prevalent both in the field as well as during storage (Ozer *et al.*, 2003).

Protection of crop plants from disease using fungicides has been the regular practice for many years and it is widely adopted strategy which is yielding a phenomenal result in reducing the disease severity, but this fungus is reported to have developed resistance to some of the fungicides (Anil Kumar, 1979).The spiraling up of the cost of chemical fungicides particularly in under developed countries population to soil, water and air by the accumulation of obnoxious chemical residues due to continuous use of fungicides and development of resistant strains of pathogens to these chemicals are forcing scientists to look for methods which are eco-friendly, safe and more specific to pathogen. Biological control of plant pathogens using antagonists microorganism and plant products is another vital area of plant pathological research in the present day to avoid environmental pollution. Biological approach is eco friendly, does not leave any toxicity, besides being cost effective and can be successfully exploited in the framework of integrated disease management.

One of the main approaches in biological control is the identification and manipulation of the antagonistic microorganisms to suppress the activity of the pathogen. They also stimulate the native antagonistic micro flora. Incorporation of organic amendments in the soil enhance the activity of biological agents and suppress the growth of the plant pathogens besides promoting plant growth (Lucade,1992). Biological control is known to be cheap and effective method for management of soil borne diseases (Sheela,1996). With this background the present study was undertaken to evaluate the efficacy of organic amendments, biocontrol agents, plant extracts and fungicides both individually and in combinations against basal rot incidence in Onion.

MATERIALS AND METHODS

The project work entitled *"Studies on the management of basal rot disease in onion"* in onion was carried out in the pathology laboratory, Department of Plant Protection, Thanthai Roever Institute of Agricultural and Rural Development (Affliated under Tamilnadu Agriculture University), Valikandapuram, Perambalur district, Tamilnadu during 2012-2016. In this study the pathogen causing basal rot in onion. Fungal and bacterial antagonistic have been isolated and tested under *in vitro* and *in vivo* condition. Different extracts of plants, fungicides are also tested under *in vitro* and *in vivo.* The material and methods used in the above experiment finished us follows.

Survey and Collection of Disease Material

We conducted survey in 7 villages of perambalur district and we collected 7 samples of basal rot infected onion plant in infected field and also we collected the rhizoshpere soil for isolation of fungal and bacterial antagonistic in following villages like Thaneerpanthal, Elambalur, Esanai, Ladapuram, Anukur, Valikandpuram and Ammapalayam.

Isolation of the Fungal Pathogen from Basal Rot Sample

The infected plant parts(bulb) showing characteristic symptom of rotten basal part with white mycelial growth were cut in to small pieces (2-3mm).We inoculated the infected plant part into PDA medium under aseptic condition in *in vitro*. The inoculated petriplates were incubated at 28±2° C for 7-10 days.

Isolation of Biocontrol Agent *Trichoderma viride*

Trichoderma viride was isolated from rhizosphere soil of healthy plants in different location of perambalur district,Tamilnadu. Rhizoshpere soil(1g) from different plants were suspended separately in 100ml of sterile distilled water and vertexes for 5 minutes 10^{-1} dilution was transferd to the test tube containing 9 ml of sterile water and 1ml of 10^{-2} dilution was transferred to 10^{-3} dilution and repeated to 10^{-6}.1ml of 10^{-3} dilution was poured on petriplates and add 20 ml of *Trichoderma* selective medium as described by (Elad and Chet, 1983). The inoculated petriplates were incubated at 28±2° C for 7 days.

Isolation of Bacterial Antagonistic (*Pseudomonas fluorescence*)

Pseudomonas fluorescence was isolated from rhizosphere soil of healthy plants in different locations of Perambalur district, Tamilnadu. Rhizosphere soil (1g) from different plants were suspended separately in 100ml sterile distilled water and vertexes for 5 minutes. 10^{-1} dilution was transferred to the test tube containing 9ml of sterile water and 1ml of 10^{-2} dilution was transferred to 10^{-3} dilution and repeat up to 10^{-6} .1ml of 10^{-3} dilution was poured on petriplate and add 20 ml of king's B medium. The inoculated petripltes were incubated at 28±2° C for 7 days.

Testing the Antagonistic Activity of *Trichoderma viride* Against *Fusarium oxysporum* f.sp.*cepae* (Dual Culture Technique)

Trichoderma sp. Isolated from rhizospere w as tested for its antagonistic activity against *Fusarium oxysporum* f.sp.*cepae* by dual culture technique. The different isolate of antagonist and *Fusarium oxysporum* f.sp.*cepae* were grown separately on PDA medium. The virulent strain of *Fusarium oxysporum* f.sp.*cepae* elect for comparison of antagonistic activity. We take the all the isolate of *Trichoderma viride* (*T.v*1 to *T.v*7) A 9mm disc of the test antagonist was cut out using sterile cork borer from the periphery of the 7 days old colony and placed on one end of a sterile petriplate containing 50 ml of sterile PDA medium(Webster,1971 b).Similarly a 9mm disc of pathogen was placed at opposite end and approximately 75mm away from the antagonistic and control (without antagonistic).In each treatment 3 replication were maintained the plates were incubated at room temperature for 3-5 days the radial mycelia growth of the pathogen and test antagonist was measured and the percent inhibition of the pathogen was calculated. Over growth by any test organism was also observed.

Testing the Antagonistic Activity of *Pseudomonas fluorescence* Against *Fusarium oxysporum* f.sp.*cepae* (Dual Culture Technique)

Pseudomonas sp. Isolated from the rhizosphere was tested for this antagonistic activity against *Fusarium oxysporum* f.sp.*cepae* by dual culture technique. The different isolate of bacterial antagonist grown separately on King's B medium (King *et al* 1954). And *Fusarium oxysporum* f.sp.*cepae* were grown separately on PDA medium. The virulent strain of *Fusarium oxysporum* f.sp.*cepae* select for comparison of antagonistic activity and also we take the all the isolate of *Pseudomonas fluorescence*(*P.f* 1 to *P.fi*7).The *Pseudomonas fluorescence* streak on one end of the sterile petriplate containing 50 ml of sterile PDA medium and 9mm disc of pathogen *(F.o6)* was placed at the opposite end and approximately 75 mm away from the antagonistic. In each treatment three replication were maintained. The plates were incubated at room temperature for 3-5 days. The radial mycelia growth of the pathogen and test antagonists was measured and the percent inhibition of the pathogen was calculated. Over growth by any test organisms was also observed.

Percent Inhibition (PI)

Percent inhibition of the test pathogen by the antagonistic strain was evaluated by dual culture technique (Dennis and Webster, 1971). The radial growth of mycelium in mm of antagonistic and pathogen were measured and percent inhibition(PI) was calculated.

$$PI = \frac{C-T}{C} \times 100$$

Where

PI-percent inhibition in growth of test pathogen.

C- Radial growth (mm) in control.

T- Radial growth (mm) in treatment.

Evaluation of Botanicals Against *Fusarium oxysporum* f.sp.*cepae* (Poison Foot Technique)

The inhibitory effects of botanical like bulb extract of garlic and leaf extracts of neem, karunotchi, notchi, pungam, thulasi, bougainvilla, kodukkapuli, prosophis, chenapodium against *Fusarium oxysporum* f.sp.*cepae* isolates was determined using an *in vitro* test on amended agar plates. The 2ml of botanical poured into a sterile petridish then added 50 ml of PDA medium there were three replicate plate for each of the test plates. A 9 mm mycelia plate cut using sterile cork borer from margin of the colonies of *Fusarium oxysporum* f.sp.*cepae* and transfer of middle of 9 cm petrilplates containing amended agar. After three days inhibition at 28±2° C, the colony diameters in the plates were measured on all plates when the mycelia growth of the control reached the edge of plates. A difference in colony diameter between the poisoned medium and the control was calculating the percent inhibition as follows:

$$Mi = \frac{Mc-Mt}{Mc} \times 100$$

Where

Mi- Inhibition of mycelia growth.

Mc- Colony diameter of the control set.

Mt- Colony diameter on the poisoned medium.

Evaluation of Different Fungicides Against *Fusarium oxysporum* f.sp.*cepae*

The inhibitory effects of different fungicides like Propiconazole 25%EC, Tricyclazole 75%WP, Hexaconazole 4% + Zineb 68%, COC 50% WDP, Carbendazim + Mancozeb 63% WP, Mancozeb 75% WP against *Fusarium oxysporum* f.sp.*cepae* isolates was determined using an *in vitro* test on amended agar plates. The 1ml/1g of Fungicide poured into a molten PDA medium. Mix thoroughly and poured into the sterile petriplates (Poison foot technique) (Alice.D *et al.*, 2012). The control plates maintain only PDA. There were three replicate plate for each of the test plates. A 9 mm mycelia plate cut using sterile cork borer from margin of the colonies of *Fusarium oxysporum* f.sp.*cepae* and transfer of middle of 9 cm petrilplates containing amended agar. After three days inhibition at 28±2° C, the colony diameters in the plates were measured on all plates when the mycelia growth of the control reached the edge of plates. A difference in colony diameter between the poisoned medium and the control was calculating the percent inhibition as follows:

$$Mi = \frac{Mc\text{-}Mt}{Mc} \times 100$$

Where

Mi- Inhibition of mycelia growth.

Mc- Colony diameter of the control set.

Mt-Colony diameter on the poisoned medium.

Mass Multiplication or Preparation of Talc based Formulation of *Trichoderma viride*

Grow the antagonistic fungus *Trichoderma* in PDA medium. Transfer mycelia discs grown in PA media to 250 ml conical flasks each containing 100 ml of sterilized molasses yeast medium (molasses-30gm, baker yeast granules-5g, distilled water 1000ml sterilized at 15lbs psi for 1 hour) and incubate for 10 days. The medium can also be prepared in polypropylene bags instead of conical flasks homogenize the mycelia mat along with the broth, mix with talc powder (500 meshes) at 1:2 V/W and shade dry until it attains 20% moisture level. Before mixing with talc powder, assess the spore load of the broth culture using the haemocytometer and it should be between 10^8 and 10^9 spores per ml. After mixing, break the clods and homogenize uniformly. To this mixture add the stickers, carboxy methyl cellulose (CMC)at 5g/kg and pack in polythene bags of 100g capacity. Talc powder is differently named as French chalk powder or soap stone powder (magnesium tri silicate). The shelf life of the product is 120 days.

The required population level at the time of packing is 20×10^7 cfu/g of the product and it should not go below 20×10^6 cfu/g during storage the population (colony forming units) in the product is assessed by serial dilution method.

Mass Multiplication or Preparation of Talc based Formulation of *Pseudomonas fluorescensce*

Transfer a loopful *Pseudomonas fluorescence* culture to 100 ml of sterilized king's B broth (King *at al* 1954). In a 250 ml conical flask under aseptic condition and incubate on a rotary shaker (150 rpm) at room temperature (28±2° C) for 48 hour. Assess the population of *pseudomonas fluorescence* after the incubation period is over (a minimum of 9×10^9/cfu ml is necessary). Adjust pH of the substrate (talc powder) to seven by addition of 150g $CaCO_3$ per Kg of talc powder and sterilize with in an autoclave at 15 psi for 30 minutes on two successive days. Transfer 100g of sterilized substrate (Talc powder) and 10.0g of sticker, carboxy methyl cellulose in to a polythene bag or any sterile container under aseptic condition and add 400 ml of *Pseudomonas fluorescence* suspension. Mix thoroughly and shade dry until it reach moisture content of<20%. The formation can be scored in milky white polythene bags for 3-4 months. The bioformulation should contain a minimum of 2.5×10^{8} cfu/g.

In *vitro* Evaluation of Biocontol Agents, Fungicides, Plant Extracts

The evaluation of biocontol agents, fungicide, plant extracts for the control of basal rot pathogen using efficient strain of pathogen isolated from the farmer's field. The isolated strains of bacterial and fungal antagonist from the soil of farmers field is dual cultured with efficient strain of basal rot pathogen. Also poison foot technique is done for plant extracts and fungicides against virulent basal rot pathogen.

Field Evaluation of Biocontrol Agents, Fungicides, Plant Extracts and Neem Cake followed by the Treatments

The field evaluation of antagonistics, fungicides, plant extract and neem cake against basal rot pathogen *Fusarium oxysporum* f.sp.*cepae* is carried in central farm of TRIARD campus. The experiment was laid out following Randomized Block design (RBD) to compare the 13 treatment (including control) and 3 replications the field ploughed in 2-3 times using cultivator. The biocontrol agents, fungicide, plant extracts and neem cake was applied in soil based on our treatments. The size of treatment plot is 5×3m with 4 rows. We sow the small onion in treated plots in 45×10 cm spacing. Then the irrigated the field in weekly once.

Percent Disease Incidence

The incidence of disease plants (total no of dead plants/ total no of plants at plots) was calculated by one month after planting. Disease severity sample of plants of the plant (20 plants) it asses the following formula:

$$PDI = \frac{\text{Number of diseased plants}}{\text{Total number of plant}} \times 100$$

Treatments:

T1 Soil application of *Tricoderma Viride* @ 2.5 Kg/ha

T2 Soil application of *Pseudomonas fluorescens* @ 2.5 Kg/ha

T3 Soil application of effective oil cakes 150 Kg/ha

T4 Soil application of effective fungicides @ 0.1%

T5 Soil application of *Tricoderma Viride* @ 2.5 Kg/ha + *Pseudomonas fluorescens* @ 2.5 Kg/ha

T6 Soil application of *Tricoderma Viride* @ 2.5 Kg/ha and oil cakes 150 Kg/ha

T7 Soil application of *Pseudomonas fluorescens* @ 2.5 Kg/ha and oil cakes 150

T8 Soil application of *Tricoderma Viride* @ 2.5 Kg/ha + *Pseudomonas fluorescens* @ 2.5 Kg/ha +oil cake 150 Kg/ha

T9 Soil application of *Pseudomonas fluorescens* @ 2.5 Kg/ha +oil cake 150Kg/ha+fungicide @ 0.1%

T10 Soil application of *Pseudomonas fluorescens* @ 2.5 Kg/ha +fungicide 0.1%

T11 Soil application of oil cake 150 Kg/ha +fungicide 0.1%

T12 Effective Plant extract(Garlic) 0.1%

T13 Control

RESULTS

The experiments were carried out on the basal rot disease of Onion comprised, performance evaluation of fungicides, plant extracts, organic amendments and biocontrol agents against the causative agent *Fusarium oxysporum* f.sp. *cepae* of Onion. The results of the above experiments are furnished here under.

Isolation of *F. oxysporum* f.sp. *cepae*

The fungus *F. oxysporum* f.sp. *cepae* was isolated from the infected bulb sample. The isolated culture characters include protrusion of white mycelial growth from the tissue. After five days mycelial mat turned to pink colour. The fungus was purified by single hyphal tip isolation technique on PDA medium. After seven days, a mycelial disc of 10 mm was transferred to PDA slant and incubated at 28±2° C for further study.

Pathogenicity of *F. oxysporum* f.sp. *cepae* on Onion

The pathogenicity test was conducted in pot culture condition. The onion crops were inoculated with isolated pathogen and observed for the symptom development up to 15 d. The inoculated onion plants showed brownish sunken spot at the base of the bulbs. After ten days, the crops were started to dry and shrivel. Whitish mycelial growth were observed in the inoculated onion plants. The upper portion of the inoculated plants were turned to straw colour. These symptoms were similar to the original symptoms observed in the plants.

Morphological and Cultural Characters of *F. oxysporum* f.sp. *cepae*

The mycelial grown on PDA medium was white in the colour up to five days after inoculation. Then the mycelial colour turned to pink in at the center. The reverse side of the colony was also pink in colour. The macro conidia were clavate in shape and the micro conidia are globose in shape. The mycelium covered a 9 cm plate within seven days.

Sensitivity of *F. oxysporum* f.sp. *cepae* Against Different Fungicides under *in vitro*

The interpretations of table 10.7 indicated that the fungicide Carbendazim was found to be more effective in arresting the mycelial growth of *F. oxysporum* f.sp. *cepae*. 100 per cent inhibition of mycelia growth recorded in 0.10 per cent concentration. The minimum inhibitory effect was noticed in fungicide copperoxy chloride. (Table 10.7)

Sensitivity of *F. oxysporum* f.sp. *cepae* Against Different Plant Extracts under *in vitro*

Among the ten plant extracts tested, the bulb extract of garlic was found to be more effective in arresting the mycelial growth of *F. oxysporum* f.sp. *cepae.* 100 percent inhibition of mycelia growth recorded in 0.10 per cent concentration. The minimum inhibitory effect was noticed in the plant extract obtained from neem leaves. (Table 10.8)

Morphological Identification of *Trichoderma viride* Isolates

All the six *T. viride* isolates showed dark green colour growth and produced globose conidia on conidiophore. The mycelial growth were initially white in colour and alter it turned to dark green in colour.

In vitro Efficacy of *Trichoderma viride* Isolates Against *F. oxysporum* f.sp. *cepae*

Among the six *T.viride* isolates, Tv-1 was effective against *F. oxysporum* f.sp. *cepae*. It showed 67.77 per cent mycelial growth inhibition respectively over control. Next to Tv-1, the isolate Tv-4 was found to be effective against *F. oxysporum* f.sp. *cepae*. It showed 65.50 per cent mycelial growth inhibition over control. (Table 10.5)

Morphological Identification of *P. fluorescens* Isolates

All the six *P. fluorescens* isolates showed raised slimy fluorescent green colour colony on the Kings B agar medium. The isolated culture was pure cultured and stored for further study.

In vitro Efficacy of *P. fluorescens* Isolate Against *F. oxysporum* f.sp. *cepae*

Among the six *P. fluorescens* isolates, *P.f*-2 was effective against *F. oxysporum* f.sp. *cepae* causing basal rot in Onion. It showed 57.89 percent per cent mycelial growth inhibition respectively over control. Next to *P. f*-2, the isolates *P.f* 3 and *P.f* 1 were effective against *F. oxysporum* f.sp. *cepae* respectively. It showed 54.38 and 47.54 per cent mycelial growth inhibition over control. (Table 10.6)

Performance Evaluation of Integrated Treatments on the Incidence of Basal Rot in Onion Under Field Condition

Carbendazim 0.1 per cent showed the maximum disease reduction over control which was recorded 11.38 per cent disease reduction. Followed by the treatments with bulb extract of garlic and a combination of *Trichoderma viride, Pseudomonas fluorescence,* neem cake showed the disease reduction over control *viz.,* 12.39, 13.07 per cent respectively. In the control plot 29.86 per cent disease incidence was recorded in the 90th day.

The maximum yield 9300 Kg/ ha was recorded in the plot treated with Carbendazim 0.1 per cent followed by bulb extract of garlic 0.1 per cent and 9260 Kg/ha of yield have been recorded in the plot treated with *Trichoderma viride,Pseudomonas fluorescence,*neem cake and 8980 Kg/ha respectively.

Table 10.1: Field survey on basal rot incidence in different villages of Perambalur district

Name of isolates	Location	Disease incidence (in %)
F.o1	Thaneer pandal	43.33 (30.08)[c]
F.o2	Elambalur	36.66 (38.34)[ef]
F.o3	Ladapuram	23.33 (23.18)[h]
F.o4	Sengunam	30.00 (26.78)[g]
F.o5	Esanai	46.66 (33.76)[b]
F.o6	Anukur	36.66 (38.34)[e]
F.o7	Ammapalayam	40.00 (42.56)[d]
F.o8	Kurumbalur	50.00 (53.21)[a]

* Mean of three replication, In a column means followed by a common letter are not significantly different at the 5 % level by the DMRT, Values in the parentheses are arcsine transformed values

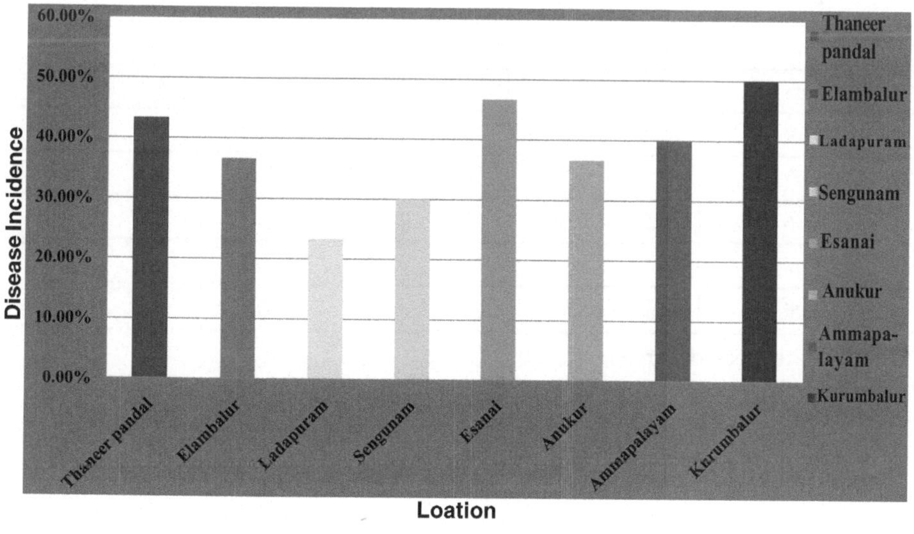

Fig. 10.1: Isolation of *Fusarium oxysporum* f.sp.*cepae* Collected from Different Locations

Table 10.2: Isolation of *Tricoderma viride* from different villages of Perambalur district

Name of isolates	Village
T.v1	Thaneer pandal
T.v2	Elambalur
T.v3	Ladapuram
T.v4	Sengunam
T.v5	Esanai
T.v6	Anukur

Table 10.3: Isolation of *Pseudomonas fluorescens* from different villages of Perambalur district

Name of isolates	Village
P.f1	Elambalur
P.f2	Ladapuram
P.f3	Esanai
P.f4	Sengunam
P.f5	Anukur
P.f6	Ammapalayam

Table 10.4: Isolation and identification of virulent strain of *Fusarium oxysporum* f.sp. *cepae*

Name of isolates	Mycelial growth in different days (cm)						
	Day 1	Day 2	Day 3	Day 4	Day 5	Day 6	Day 7
F.o1	1.0^{b}	2.0^{d}	2.6^{d}	3.2^{d}	3.4	4.2^{c}	4.6^{c}
F.o2	0.4^{d}	1.0^{g}	1.6^{g}	2.2^{f}	2.8^{f}	3.4^{f}	4.0^{e}
F.o3	1.2^{a}	2.4^{c}	3.0^{b}	3.6^{b}	4.0^{b}	4.4^{b}	5.0^{b}
F.o4	0.6^{c}	1.4^{f}	2.0^{f}	2.2^{f}	3.6^{d}	4.0^{d}	4.6^{c}
F.o5	0.2^{e}	0.8^{h}	1.4^{h}	2.2^{f}	2.6^{g}	3.0^{g}	3.6^{f}
F.o6	1.2^{a}	3.0^{a}	3.6^{a}	4.2^{a}	5.0^{a}	5.4^{a}	6.4^{a}
F.o7	0.6^{c}	1.6^{e}	2.2^{e}	2.6^{e}	3.2^{e}	3.6^{e}	4.2^{d}
F.o8	1.0^{b}	2.6^{b}	2.8^{c}	3.4^{c}	3.8^{c}	4.2^{c}	5.0^{b}

* The data are mean of three replications

In the column, means followed by a common letter are not significantly different at 5% level by DMRT

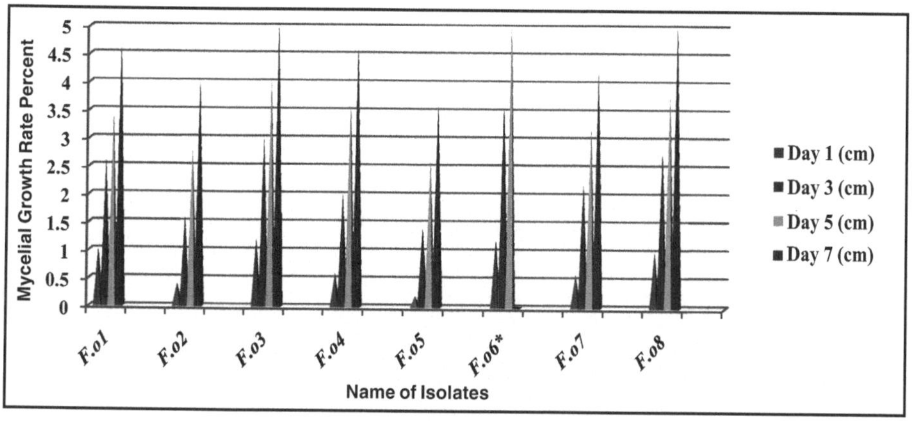

Fig. 10.2: Growth Rate of Different Isolates of *Fusarium oxysporum* f.sp.*cep*

Table 10.5: Antagonistic activity of *Tricoderma viride* against *Fusarium oxysporum* f. sp. *cepae*

T. viride isolates	Mycelial growth at 4 DAI (cm)	Percent reduction over control
T.v 1*	2.9	67.77 (54.89)[f]
T.v 2	3.6	60.00 (50.08)[b]
T.v 3	3.2	64.40 (61.54)[d]
T.v 4	3.1	65.50 (62.32)[e]
T.v 5	4.5	50.00 (52.40)[a]
T.v 6	3.3	63.30 (59.62)[c]
Control	9.0	–

* The data are mean of three replications.

In the column, means followed by a common letter are not significantly different at 5% level by DMRT

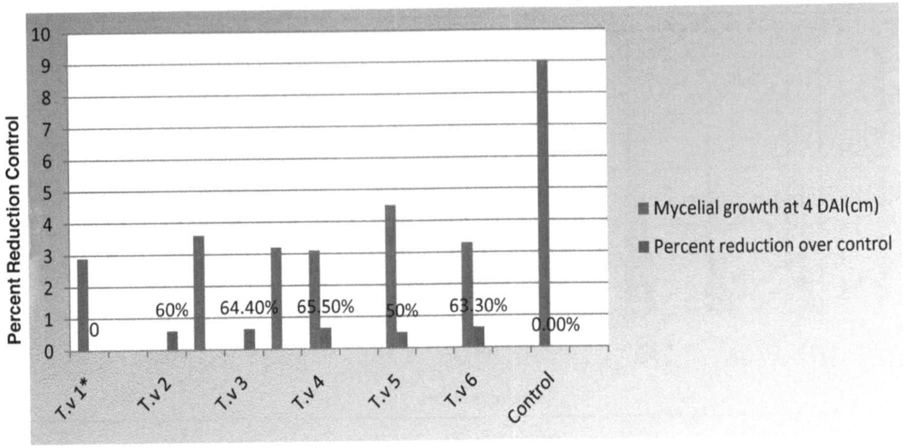

Fig. 10.3: Antagonistic Activity of *T. viride* Against *Fusarium oxysporum* f.sp.*cepae* (*in vitro*)

Table 10.6: Antagonistic activity of *Pseudomonas fluorescens* against *Fusarium oxysporum* f.sp. *cepae*

Name of isolates (Antagonist)	Mycelial growth at 4 DAI (cm)	Percent reduction over control
*P.f*1	6.12	47.54 (43.56)[d]
*P.f*2*	5.74	57.89 (49.83)[f]
*P.f*3	5.91	54.38 (44.64)[e]
*P.f*4	6.53	43.85 (41.45)[b]
*P.f*5	6.20	45.16 (42.76)[c]
*P.f*6	6.36	42.85 (40.76)[a]
Control	9.00	–

* The data are mean of three replications

In the column, means followed by a common letter are not significantly different at 5% level by DMRT

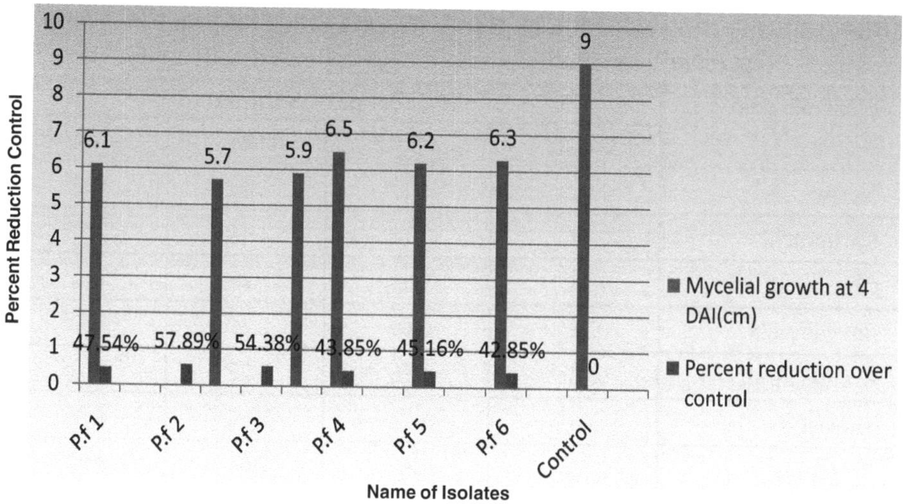

Fig. 10.4: Antagonistic Activity of *P. fluorescence* Against *Fusarium oxysporum* f.sp. *cepae*

Table 10.7: ***In vitro*** **evaluation of fungicides against *Fusarium oxysporum* f. sp. *cepae***

Fungicides	Mycelial growth (in cm)			
	Day 3	Day 5	Day 7	Day 9
Tricyclazole 0.1%	0.00[a]	0.62[b]	0.82[b]	1.24[d]
Propiconazole 0.1%	0.00[a]	0.54[b]	0.75[b]	0.85[c]
Hexaconazole 0.1%	0.00[a]	0.49[b]	0.89[b]	1.63[d]
Copperoxychloride 0.1%	0.10[b]	1.00[c]	2.21[c]	2.13[e]
*Carbandazim 0.1%	0.00[a]	0.00[a]	0.00[a]	0.00[a]
Mancozeb 0.1%	0.00[a]	0.47[a]	0.93[b]	1.00[b]
Control	3.00[c]	6.52[d]	8.46[d]	9.00[f]

* The data are mean of three replications

In the column, means followed by a common letter are not significantly different at 5% level by DMRT

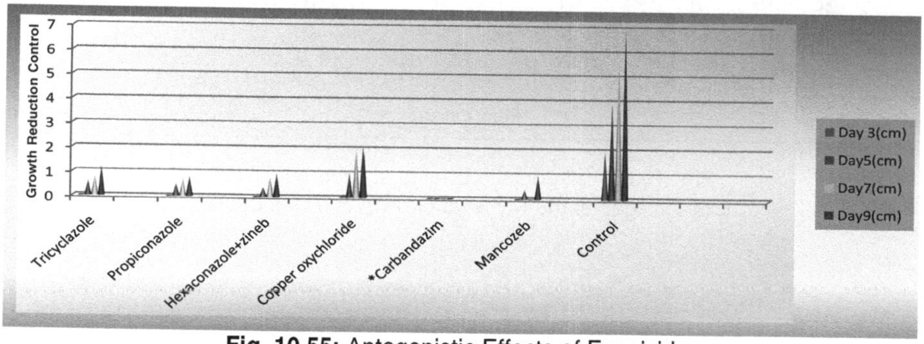

Fig. 10.55: Antagonistic Effects of Fungicides Against the Mycelial Growth of *F.o*f.sp.*cepae (in vitro)*

Table 10.8: *In vitro* **evaluation of plant extracts against** ***Fusarium oxysporum*** **f. sp.** ***cepae***

Plant extracts	Mycelial growth (in cm)			
	Day 3	Day 5	Day 7	Day 9
Neem	1.00[c]	1.49[c]	2.56[d]	3.33[d]
Karunotchi	0.84[b]	1.18[c]	1.34[c]	2.59[c]
Chenapodium	1.23[d]	2.04[d]	3.28[e]	3.87[d]
Bougainvilla	0.78[b]	0.86[c]	2.24[d]	3.52[d]
Kodukkapuli	0.66[b]	1.98[c]	3.25[e]	3.61[d]
Thulasi	1.29[d]	1.74[c]	3.56[e]	3.78[d]
Prosophis	0.38[b]	1.48[b]	2.63[d]	4.92[e]
Notchi	0.00[a]	0.00[a]	0.19[b]	1.34[b]
*Garlic	0.00[a]	0.00[a]	0.00[a]	0.00[a]
Pungam	0.89[b]	1.26[c]	2.48[d]	3.72[d]
Control	3.02[e]	6.35[e]	8.12[f]	9.00[f]

* The data are mean of three replications

In the column, means followed by a common letter are not significantly different at 5% level by DMRT

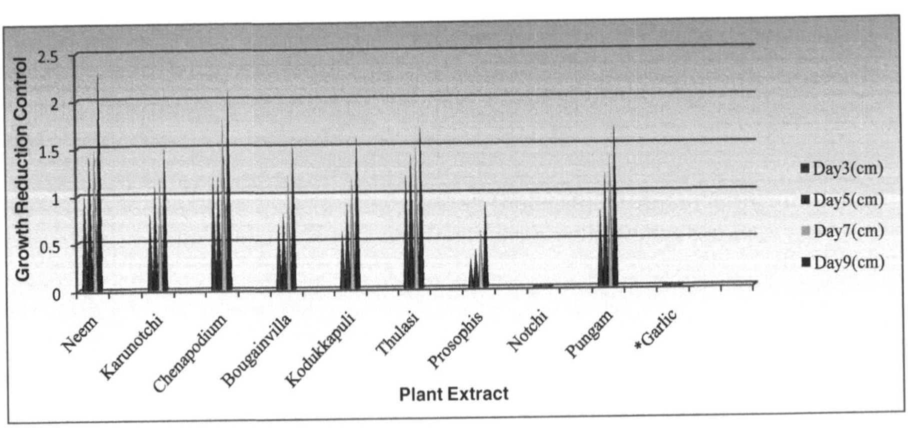

Fig. 10.6: Antagonistic Effects of Different Plant Extract Against the Mycelial Growth *F.* o.f.sp. *cepae*

Table 10.9: Field evaluation of biocontrol agents, organic amendments and fungicides against *Fusarium oxysporum* f. sp. *cepae*

Treatments	Per cent Disease Incidence (PDI)						Yield (kg) Kg/15m^2
	Day-15	Day-30	Day-45	Day-60	Day-75	Day-90	
T1- *Tricoderma Viride*	5.00 (13.73)^{i}	6.65 (18.24)^{efgh}	9.12 (18.02)^{j}	10.55 (18.76)^{g}	12.37 (21.10)^{b}	14.33 (23.78)^{d}	12.21
T2- *Pseudomonas fluorescens*	4.10 (11.79)^{e}	5.98 (13.65)^{bcd}	7.34 (15.81)^{e}	7.36 (15.43)^{a}	13.66 (21.32)^{d}	15.25 (23.36)^{e}	13.23
T3- Effective Neem cakes	2.00 (8.96)^{a}	6.76 (18.43)^{efghi}	8.64 (16.56)^{fg}	9.99 (18.31)^{def}	14.54 (22.63)^{ef}	15.89 (23.96)^{e}	12.65
*T4- Carbendazim 0.1%	3.70 (11.12)^{bcde}	4.24 (11.66)^{a}	6.75 (18.34)^{abc}	8.76 (16.52)^{b}	9.95 (17.82)^{a}	11.38 (19.36)^{a}	13.95
T5- *Tricoderma Viride* + *Pseudomonas fluorescens*	4.00 (11.23)^{f}	6.25 (18.12)^{e}	8.98 (16.98)^{hi}	9.38 (18.01)^{cde}	13.16 (21.32)^{c}	16.64 (23.73)^{f}	13.27
T6- *Tricoderma Viride* + Neem cakes	3.72 (11.11)^{bcd}	5.98 (17.29)^{bcd}	6.71 (18.21)^{ab}	7.24 (15.68)^{a}	9.98 (17.98)^{a}	13.47 (21.58)^{c}	11.24
T7- *Pseudomonas fluorescens* + Neem cakes	4.63 (11.72)^{h}	6.56 (18.21)^{efg}	8.81 (16.31)^{fgh}	9.25 (18.24)^{cd}	12.34 (20.66)^{b}	15.74 (23.21)^{e}	11.71
T8- *Tricoderma Viride* + *Pseudomonas fluorescens* +Neem cake	3.34 (10.53)^{bc}	5.27 (17.76)^{bc}	6.53 (18.12)^{a}	7.26 (15.72)^{a}	12.56 (20.98)^{b}	13.07 (20.97)^{c}	13.47
T9- *Pseudomonas fluorescens* +Neem cake +carbendazim 0.1%	2.95 (9.91)^{a}	4.89 (14.88)^{a}	8.04 (18.01)^{f}	11.39 (19.92)^{hij}	13.81 (21.84)^{d}	15.71 (23.68)^{e}	11.14
T10- *Pseudomonas fluorescens* +fungicide	3.46 (10.84)^{b}	6.81 (18.94)^{ef}	9.12 (18.02)^{j}	11.37 (19.82)^{hi}	14.23 (22.36)^{e}	16.82 (24.23)^{f}	12.21
T11- Neem cake + carbendazim 0.1%	4.29 (11.79)^{g}	5.00 (16.87)^{b}	6.85 (17.43)^{abcd}	9.18 (17.86)^{c}	12.38 (20.21)^{b}	15.71 (23.86)^{e}	11.64
*T12- Garlic 0.1%	3.24 (10.35)^{b}	6.26 (18.22)^{e}	9.78 (18.89)^{jk}	11.00 (19.48)^{h}	12.00 (19.88)^{b}	12.39 (20.44)^{b}	13.89
T13- Control	6.56 (18.12)^{j}	9.78 (18.62)^{j}	13.69 (21.33)^{l}	19.98 (26.58)^{k}	24.67 (29.78)^{g}	29.86 (32.89)^{g}	3.21

* The data are mean of three replications

In the column, means followed by a common letter are not significantly different at 5% level by DMR

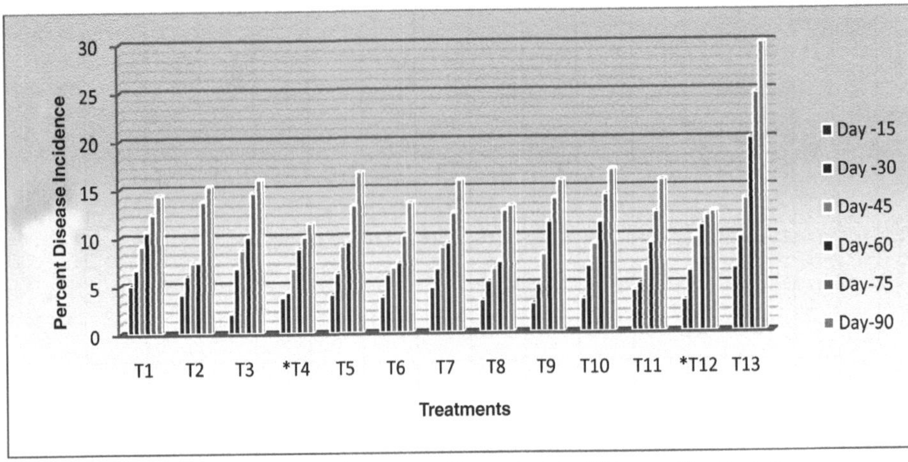

Fig. 10.7: Disease Incidence Recorded in Different Treatments

DISCUSSION

Onion (*Allium cepa* var. *aggregatum*) is an important commercial vegetable crop all over the world. In India, onion occupies an area 10.064 Mha with the yield of 14.2 MT/ha (Indian horticultural database, 2012-2013). Onion is affected by many fungal, bacterial and viral diseases. Among them, basal rot is the major disease accounting for heavy yield losses ranging from 15 to 30 per cent. The basal rot of onion caused by *Fusarium oxysporum* f.sp. *cepae* is a wide spread problem limiting the profitable cultivation and seed production throughout the major Onion growing regions of India. Onion crop is affected many diseases generally caused by fungi and bacteria both in field as well as storage. Pink root [*Pyrenochaeta terrestris* (Hans.) Gorenz, Walker, and Larson], and *Fusarium* basal rot (*Fusarium oxysporum* f. sp. *cepae*) are the economically important diseases of onion. One of those diseases, Fusarium basal rot [*Fusarium oxysporum* f. sp. *cepae,* is a root and bulb disease of onion grown in temperate and subtropical regions (Brayford, 1996). The losses due to basal rot of Onion varied between 16-30 per cent. Yield loss up to 50 per cent has been recorded in susceptible cultivars (Everts *et al.,* 1985) with 90 percent losses during the seedling stage (Davis and Reddy, 1932).Which cause severe defoliation, rotting and degradation of bulbs (Ranjale *et al.,* 2012).

Using single compound may give less effect on target organism and will lead to resistance development in pathogens. The excessive use of chemicals may cause adverse effects on environment. To overcome these limitations and considering the epidemiological synergism, scientists are focusing on the integration of effective and ecologically safer modules for the management of epidemic diseases (Lu *et al.,* 2000). In that way, the present investigation was hypothetically formulated to explore the integrated approaches for the management of basal rot, disease on Onion. The results obtained from the various experiments carried out in this research are discussed as follow.

Isolation and Pathogenicity

The fungi *Fusarium oxysporum* f.sp. *cepae* from onion isolated and subjected to pathogenicity test. The pathogen isolated showed the typical symptoms as in naturally infected plants.

In the present experiment, the artificially inoculated bulbs with *F. oxysporum* f.sp. *cepae* showed the symptoms as formation of sunken water soaked spots covered with white mass of fungal mycelium. The infected bulbs turned to brown coloured and started to rot. In later the mycelial growth was turned to pink colour. The same kind of symptoms was previously reported by various scientists. Differences in Pathogenicity and virulence of different isolates of *Fusarium* have been observed using a set of cultivars of onion, Garlic Seed and Cloves (Cramer, 2002; Jessica *et al.*, 2006; Galván, 2009) and the differences were attributed to vertical resistances of individual cultivar lines. The disease can be very damaging to susceptible cultivars in fields with a history of *Fusarium* basal rot (Howard *et al.*, 2007).

Characterization of Pathogens

Morphological characters of *F. oxysporum* f.sp. *cepae* include white mycelial growth in the initial stage later, turned to pink. The reverse side of the colony was also pink in colour. The macro conidia observed were clavate in shape and the micro conidia were oval in shape. This fungus produces hyaline nonseptate mycelium as well as three types of asexual spores namely microconidia, macroconidia and chlamydospores (Cramer, 2000; Howard *et al.*, 2007).

In vitro Efficacy of Fungicides

In the *in vitro* efficacy test, Carbendazim was found to be effective at 0.1 per cent concentrations against *F. oxysporum* f.sp. *cepae* when compared to other fungicides used in this experiment. It was showed cent per cent inhibition of mycelial growth. Inhibition of fungal growth, spore germination with increased mortality, disruption of fungal developmental stages by carbendazim has been earlier reported by Dugan *et al.* 2007.

Among the systemic fungicides, Carbendazim was highly effective in inhibiting the growth of *Fusarium oxysporium* f. sp. *cepae* in all the three concentrations (0.025%, 0.05% and 0.1%) tested (Dugan *et al.* 2007). Carbendazim 50% WP applied at the rate of 1.4g/L, helped reduced field rotting losses as well as storage losses of onion bulbs by 35 and 40 percent respectively (Dugan *et al.* 2007). Carbendazim at 0.2 per cent was the best treatment amongst the fungicides tested against *Fusarium oxysporium* sp when combined with *T. harzianum* (Rajendran and Ranganathan, 1996).

In vitro Efficacy of Plant Products

Plants are like natural laboratories where a great number of antimicrobial compounds are bio synthesized and in fact they may be considered the most important source of anti microbial compounds. There is growing evidence that these compounds when applied on the other plants, they have the ability to defend the plant from the pathogens (Mohan and Rajinimala, 2006.)

In the current research the experiment was carried out with the ten plant extracts. Among the ten, bulb extract of garlic at 0.1 per cent concentration recorded cent percent growth inhibition against *F. oxysporum* f.sp. *cepae* over control followed by leaf extract of Notchi recorded a considerable per cent growth inhibition (96.67%) against above pathogen.

Use of natural plants products is considered as an alternative to chemical fungicides for the control of phytopathogens (Parka *et al.*, 2002; Kanwal *et al.*, 2010; Riaz *et al.*, 2010a; Jabeen *et al.*, 2011)

In vitro Efficacy of Fungal and Bacterial Antagonist

Although fungicides are primary means of controlling basal rot disease, they have recently come under special scrutiny as they pose potential oncogenic risks when applied to food materials. So biocontrol is the effective alternative method in controlling fruit rot diseases and there was no health hazard in using them. In this phase different isolates of *Trichoderma viride* and *Pseudomonas fluorescens* were tested under *in vitro* and the preeminent one was used for further study.

The fungal and bacterial antagonists were isolated from the rhizosphere soil of onion plants in different area of Perambalur district. *viz.*, Thaneerpandal, Elambalur, Ladapuram, Sengunam, Esanai, Anukur, which are named as *T.v (1-6)* and *P.f (1-6).*

In vitro Efficacy of *Trichoderma viride*

The efficacy of six *Trichoderma viride* isolates, which were isolated from the rhizosphere soil, was carried out by dual culture technique (Dennis and Webster, 1971). Among the six isolates of *Trichoderma viride* tested by the above technique *T.v* 1 isolated from Thaneerpanthal was found to have maximum percent growth inhibition (67.77%) against onion basal rot pathogen followed by *T. v* 4 isolated from Sengunam, recorded maximum per cent growth inhibition (65.50%) over control.

Hydrolytic enzymes produced by *Trichoderma* spp. play an important role in destruction of plant pathogens (Chet *et al.*, 1981). In studying *Trichoderma* isolates and Fusarium proliferatum in dual culture technique, all *Trichoderma* isolates grew faster than the pathogenic fungus (Zeinab, 2014).

Biological control using fungal and bacterial antagonists has been suggested as a potential method to control Fusarium basal rot disease of onion (Cosskuntuna and Ozer, 2008). A combination of Trichoderma sp and pseudomonas fluorescens were most effective for reducing incidence of Fusarium basal rot under pot culture and field conditions (Rajendran and Ranganathan, 1996). Hydrolytic enzymes produced by Trichoderma sp play an important role in reduction of plant pathogens (Chet *et al.*, 1981)

In vitro Efficacy of Bacterial Antagonist

Total six bacterial antagonists were isolated from the rhizosphere soil of onion plants collected from different areas of Perambalur district. Among the six isolates *P. f* 2 isolated from Ladapuram area was found to be efficient and also recorded maximum per cent inhibition against basal rot pathogen (57.89%) over control. Followed by *P.f* 3 isolated from Esanai area showed maximum per cent growth inhibition (54.38%) over control.

Misaghi *et al.*, (1982) reported that the *P.fluorescens* showing maximum antagonism against *Fusarium oxysporum* under *in vitro* condition. Geels and Schippers., (1983) reported that *P.fluorescens* recorded high degree of growth inhibition against *Alternaria solani* and *Rhizoctonia solani* of tomato.

Field Evaluation of Integrated Modules Against Onion Basal Rot

To expose the efficacy of fungicides, plant extracts, biocontrol agents and organic amendments against the Onion basal rot pathogen, an experiment was carried out in RBD at TRIARD farm. The study revealed that soil drenching with Carbendazim 0.1 per cent shown the maximum disease inhibition followed by the bulb extract of Garlic 0.1 per cent recorded the minimum per cent disease incidence. This is on par with the soil drenching with Carbendazim 0.1 per cent. The maximum yield (9300 Kg/ha) was recorded in the plot treated with Carbendazim 0.1 per cent and the lowest yield (2140 Kg/ha) was recorded in the control plot where there were no treatments applied. Carbendazim applied at the rate of 1.4 g/l reduced the field rot and storage rot incidence in Onion (Dugan *et al.*, 2007). Allicin is one of the active principles of freshly crushed garlic homogenates, has a variety of antimicrobial activities (Aankri, 1999).

REFERENCES

Abawi, G.S. and Lorbeer, J.W. (1971). Pathological Histology of Four Onion Cultivars Infected by *Fusarium oxysporium f.sp. cepae. Phytopathology* 61: 1164-1169.

Abawi, G.S. and Lorbeer, J.W. (1972). Several Aspects of the Pathology of *Fusarium oxysporium f.sp. cepae. Phytopathology* 62: 763-772.

Adam Iddrisu Alidu, (2013) Etiology and Control of Bulb Rot Disease of Onion (*Allium cepae.*) in the Eastern Region of Ghana 1-104.

Anonymous (2005). National Onion Association. http://www.onionsusa.org/about/production.asp. (Accessed 27/2/2012).

Apaza, W.E. and Mattos, L. (2000). Reaction of Onion Cultivars to Basal Plate Rot Disease Caused by *Fusarium oxysporum* f. sp. *cepae. Fitopatologia*. 35(4): 231-36.

APS (2008). Compendium of Onion and Garlic Diseases. APS Press, Minnesota, USA. 70pp.

August E. Kehr, Muriel J. O'Brien, Elmo W. Davis, (1962) Pathogenicity of *Fusarium oxysporum* f. sp. *Cepae* and its Interaction with *Pyrenochaeta terrestris* on Onion Euphytica11(2) pp. 197-208.

Awuah, R.T., Kwoseh, C., Kuranteng, S.L., Okpala, R.O.C. and Amoako-Attah, I. (2009) Appearance of *Fusarium* Basal Rot Disease of Onion in the Kwahu Sought District of Ghana. *Ghana Journal of Horticulture* 7: 84-88.

Badino, M., Schiavi M., Falavigna, A. and Fantino, M.G. (1980). A New Technique of Infection by *Fusarium oxysporum* f. sp. *cepae* of Onion Seedlings Grown *In - vitro*. INRA *Versailles* p 111-20.

Barnett, H.L. and Hunter, B.B. (2006). Illustrated Genera of Imperfect Fungi. The American Phytopathological Society. APS press. St. Paul, Minnesota. USA. 218pp.

Bayraktar, H. and Dolar, F.S. (2011). Molecular Identification and Genetic Diversity of *Fusarium* Species Associated with Onion Fields in Turkey. *Journal of Phytopathology* 159: 28-34.

Booth, C. (1971). The Genus of *Fusarium*. Commonwealth Mycological Institute. Kew, England. 237 pp.

Brayford, D. (1996). IMI Description of Fungi and Bacteria Set 127, No. 1263 *Fusarium oxysporium f.sp. cepae*. *Mycopathologia* 133: 39-40.

Barnett, H.L. and Hunter, B.B. (2006). Illustrated Genera of Imperfect fungi. The American Phytopathological Society. APS press. St. Paul, Minnesota. USA. 218pp.

Bayraktar, H. and Dolar, F.S. (2011). Molecular Identification and Genetic Diversity of *Fusarium* species Associated with Onion Fields in Turkey. *Journal of Phytopathology* 159: 28-34.

Booth, C. (1971). The Genus of *Fusarium*. Commonwealth Mycological Institute. Kew, England. 237 pp.

Christopher S. Cramer. (2000) Breeding and Genetics of Fusarium Basal Rot Resistance in Onion. Euphytica 115(3): 159-166.

Corgan, J. (2002). Contributions of the NMSU Breeding Program to the New Mexico Onion Industry. In: Onion Production and Marketing in New Mexico. *New Mexico Cooperative Extension Service Circular* 577.

Coskuntuna, A. and Ozer, N. (2008). Biological Control of Onion Basal Rot Disease Using *Trichoderma harzianum* and Induction of Antifungal Compounds in Onion Set Following Seed Treatment. *Crop Prot.*, 27 (3-5): 330-336.

Craig, W. (2010). Vegetarianism and Vegetarian Nutrition, Andrews University, MI, USA. http//www. Vegetarian-nutrition. Info/updates/onions. (Accessed 03/12/11).

Cramer, C.S. (2002). Current and Future Objectives of NMSU's Onion Breeding Program. In: Onion Production and Marketing in New Mexico. *New Mexico Cooperative Extension Service Circular* 577.

Cramer, C.S., Larsen, T.A., and Muhyi, R. (2003). 2001-2002 Onion Variety Trials at NMSU. *New Mexico Agric Extension* Stn. Res. Rpt. p 22-39.

Cramer, C.S. (2000). Breeding and Genetics of *Fusarium* Basal Rot Resistance in Onion *Euphytica* 115: 159-166.

Dobbs C.G., Hinson W.H., (1953). A Widespread Fungistasis in Soil. *Nature* 172: 197-199.

Dugan, F.M., Hellier, B.C. and Lupien, S.L. (2007). Pathogenic Fungi in Garlic Seed Cloves from the United States and China, and Efficacy of Fungicides Against Pathogens in Garlic Germplasm in Washington State. *American Plant Pathology* 52: 426.

Entwistle, A R. (1990). Root Diseases in Onion and Allied Crops. Boca Raton, Fla. *CRC Press* 2: 103-154.

FAO (2005). UN Food and Agriculture Organization, 2005 (Onions). http//www.answers.com/topic/onion._note 25 (Accessed 1/11/10).

Feng, J., Hwang, R., Chang, K.F., Hwang, S.F., Strelkov, S.E., Gossen, B.D., Conner, R.L. and Turnbull, G.D. (2010). Genetic Variation in *Fusarium avenaceum* Causing Root Rot on Field Pea. *Plant Pathology* 59: 845-852.

Fulton, T.M., Chunwongse, J. and Tanksley, S.D. (1995). Microprep Protocol for Extraction of DNA from Tomato and Other Herbaceous Plants. *Plant Molecular Biology Reporter* 13(3): 207-209.

Galván, G.A., Koning-Boucoiran, C.F.S., Koopman, W.J.M., Burger-Meijer, K., González, P.H., Waalwijk, C., Kik, C., and Scholten, O.E. (2008). Genetic Variation Among *Fusarium* Isolates from Onion, and Resistance to *Fusarium* Basal Rot in Related *Allium* species. *European Journal of Plant Pathology,* 121: 499-512.

Gordon, T.R. and Martyn, R.D. (1997). The Evolutionary Biology of *Fusarium oxysporum.* Annu. Rev. *Phytopathol.* 35: 111-28.

Gutierrez, J.A. and Cramer, C.S. (2005). Screening Short-day Onion Cultivars for Resistancen to *Fusarium* Basal Rot. *HortScience.* 40(1): 157-60.

Harun Bayraktar (2010). Genetic Diversity and Population Structure of *Fusarium oxysporum* f. sp. *cepae,* the Causal Agent of Fusarium Basal Plate Rot on Onion, using RAPD Markers. *Journal of Agricultural Sciences* 16 (2010) 139-149.

Havey, M.J. (1995). *Fusarium* Basal Plate Rot. In: H.F. Schwartz & S.K. Mohan (Eds.), Compendium of Onion and Garlic Diseases. *APS Press, St. Paul, Minn* 10-11 p.

Hicks, N. (2004). Review of Pest and Disease Management in Onions and its Impact on Market Acceptance. Sustainable Farming Fund Final Report 31304. MoFA, New Zealand. 47pp.

Higashida, S., Oshaki, I. and Narita, Y. (1982). Effects of Crop Rotation on Onion Yields and its Microbial Factors. *Journal of Bull Hokkaido Agricultural Experimental Station* 48: 1-9.

Howard, F. Schwartz, David, H. Gent and Michael, E. Bartolo. (2007). Onion Fusarium Basal Plate Rot Identification and Life Cycle. 15pp.

Imtiaj, A., & Tae, L. (2008). Antagonistic Effect of Three *Trichoderma* species on the *Alternaria porri* Pathogen of Onion Blotch. *World Journal of Agricultural Science,* 4, 13-17.

ISTA (2012). International Rules for Seed Testing, Adopted at the Ordinary Meeting 2011, Venlo, The Netherlands. *Journal of ISTA Zurichst* 50: 138-256.

Jenkins, S.F. and Wehner, T.C. (1983). Occurrence of *Fusarium oxysporium f.sp. cucumerinum* on Greenhouse-grown Cucumis Sativus Seed Stocks in North Carolina. *Plant Disease* 67: 1024-1025.

Jessica, A., Gutierrez, R.M. and Christopher, C.S. (2006). Screening Winter Sown, Intermediate-day Onion Cultivars for Resistance to *Fusarium* Basal Rot, *Holtechnology* 177-181p.

Joon, T.L., Dong, W.B., Seun, H.P., Chang, K.S., Youn, S.K. and Hee, K.K. (2000).

Occurrence and Biological Control of Postharvest Decay in Onion Caused by Fungi, Korean Society of Plant Pathology, *Plant Pathology Journal* 17(3): 141-148.

Karthikeyan, M.R., Bhaskaran, K., Radhika, S., Mathiyazhagan, D., Alice, R., Sandosskumar, & Velazhahan, R. (2006). Biological Control of Leaf Blight of Onion by Use of Oil Formulations. *Indian Journal of Plant Protection,* 34(1), 89-93.

Kao C.W., Ko W.H., (1983). Natural Suppression of *Pythium splendes* in a Pasture Soil in South Kohala, Hawaii. *Phytopathology* 73: 1284-1289.

Khatun, H. and Ashrafuzzaman, M. (2008). Fungi Causing Rots in Onions at Storage and Market. *Journal of Bangladesh Agricultural. University.* 6(2): 245-251.

Kishore, C. (2007). Studies on Diagnosis and Management of Fungal Wilt Diseases of Carnation and Gerbera Under Protected Cultivation Thesis Master of Science (Agriculture), *Plant Pathology* 33pp.

Koike, S.T. Gladders, P. and Paullus, A.O. (2007). Vegetable Disease a Color Handbook. Academic Press, San-Diego,USA. 448pp.

Koycu, N.D. and Ozer, N. (1997). Determination of Seed-borne Fungi in Onion and Their Transmission to Onion Seeds. *Phytoparasitica* 25: 25-31.

Kulkarni, Sumitra P. (2006). Studies on *Fusarium oxysporum* Schlecht Fr f. sp. *Gladioli* (Massey) Snyd. & Hans. Causing Wilt of *Gladiolus.* M.Sc.(Agri). Thesis, University of Agricultural Sciences Dharwad (India) 42-76p.

Kyofa-Boamah, M., Blay E., Braum, M. and Kuehn A. (2000) Good Agricultural Practices and Crop Protection Recommendations for Selected Vegetables. *Handbook of Crop Protection in Ghana* 5: 95-108.

Lacy, M.L. and Roberts, D.L. (1982). Yield of Onion Cultivars in Midwestern Organic Soils Infested With *Fusarium oxysporium f. sp. cepae* and *Pyrenochaeta terrestris*. *Plant Disease* 66:1003-1006.

Lopez J. A. and Cramer C. S. (2004). Screening Short-day Onion Cultivars for Resistance to Fusarium Basal Rot. *Holtechnology* 637: 169-173.

Lopez, J.A. (2003). Screening of Onion Cultivars for Resistance to *Fusarium* Basal Rot. MS Thesis. NMSU 19-25.

Lori, G.A., Wolcan, S.M. and Larran, S. (2008). *Fusarium* Yellows of Celery Caused by *Fusarium oxysporium f.sp. apii* in Argentina. *Journal of Plant Pathology* 90: 173-178.

Malathi, S. (2015). Biological Control of Onion Basal Rot Caused by *Fusarium oxysporum*f. sp. *cepae*. *Asian J. Bio. Sci.*,10 (1): 21-26.

Ministry of food and Agriculture (MoFA). (2012). Plant Protection and Regulatory Services Directorate, Ghana, Annual report 2011.

Monte, E. (2001). Understanding *Trichoderma*: Between Biotechnology and Microbial Ecology, *International Microbiology* 4: 1-4.

Necola, S. (2007). *Allium cepa* Variety Evaluation for Organic Farming in the 5th International Symposium on Edible Allianceae. Dronten The Netherlands. ISHS. 45pp.

Norman, J.C. (1992). Tropical Vegetable Crops Arthur H. Stockwell Ltd. Devon, UK. 234pp.

Oduro, K.A. (2000) Checklist of Plant Pests in Ghana. Plant Protection and Regulatory Services Directorate. MoFA, Ghana. 105pp.

Offei, S.K., Cornelius, E.W. and Sekyi-Dawson, O. (2008). Diseases of Crops in Ghana and their Management. Smartline Publishing Ltd., Accra, Ghana. 104pp.

Özer.N, M. Koç and B. Der (2009) the Sensitivity of *Aspergillus niger* and *Fusarium oxysporum* f. Sp. *cepae* to Fungistasis in Onion-growing Soils. Journal of Plant Pathology, 91 (2), 401-410.

Ozer, N. and N.D. Koycu, (1998). Evaluation of Seed Treatments for Controlling *Aspergillus niger* and *Fusarium oxysporum* on Onion Seed. *Phytopath Medit* 37: 33-40.

PANS (1996). Pest Control in Tropical Onions. Tropical Development and Research Institute, London. 109pp.

Pathak, V.N. (1984). Laboratory Manual of Plant Pathology. Second Edition. Oxford and IBH Publishing Co. Pvt. Ltd. New Delhi. 11-12p.

Prakasam.V, Pratibha Sharma. (2012). *Trichoderma harzianum* (Th-3) a Potential Strain to Manage the Purple Blotch of Onion (*Allium cepa* L.) Caused by *Alternaria porri* under North Indian Plains,Journal of Agricultural Science: 4(10)

Rajapakse, R.G.A.S. and Edirimanna, E.R.S.P. (2002). Management of Bulb Rot of Big Onion During Storage Using Fungicides Annals of Sri Lanka Department of Agriculture. 4: 319-326.

Rajendran, K. and Ranganathan K. (1996). Biological Control of Onion Basal Rot (*Fusarium oxysporum* f. sp. *cepae*,) by Combined Application of Fungal and Bacterial Antagonists. *Journal of Biological Control* 10: 97-102.

Retig, N., Kust, A.F. and Gabelman W.H. (1970). Greenhouse and Field Tests for Determining the Resistance of Onion Lines to Fusarium Basal Rot. *Journal of American Society of Horticultural Science* 95: 422-424.

Sara Lager, (2010) Survey of *Fusarium* Species on Yellow Onion (*Allium cepa*) on Öland Master Thesis, Biology and Agronomy Program, Swedish University of Agricultural Science, SLU. 23pp.

Saremi, H. and Bugress, L.W. (2000). Effect of Soil Temperature on Distribution and Population Dynamics of *Fusarium* species. *Journal of Agricultural Science and Technology* 2: 119-25.

Saxena, A. and Cramer, C.S. (2009). Screening of Onion Seedlings for Resistance Against New Mexico Isolates of *Fusarium oxysporium* f. sp. *cepae*. *Journal of Plant Pathology* 199-202p.

Schwartz H.F. (2010). Soil-Borne Diseases of Onion, Fact Sheet No. 2.940 Updated Monday, August 29, 2011 Colorado State University 1-5p.

Schwartz, H.F. and Mohan, S.K. (1995). Compendium of Onion and Garlic Diseases. The American Phytopathological Society. APS Press. Minnesota. USA. 54pp.

Shaner, H. and Finney, R.E. (1977). The Effect of Nitrogen Fertilization on The Expression of Slow Mildewing Resistance in Knox Wheat. *Phytopathology* 67: 1051-1056.

Sinnadurai, S. (1970) A Note on the Bulbing and Flowering of the 'Bawku' onion. Tropical Agriculture Trinidad 47: 77-79.

Sokhi, S.S., Singh, D.P. and Joshi, M.C. (1974). Sources of Resistance to Basal Rot of Onions Caused by *Fusarium oxysporum* f. sp. *cepae*. *Indian Journal of Mycology and Plant Pathology* 4: 214-215.

Somkuwar, R.G., Veere Gowda, R., Singh, T.H. and Pathak, C.S. (1996). Screening of Onion for Resistance to Onion Basal Rot. *Madras Agricultural Journal* 83: 273-275.

Srivastava, K.J. and Qadri, S.M.H. (1984). Some Studies of Damping off Disease of Onion (*Allium cepa* L.). *Indian Journal of Mycology and Plant Pathology* 3: 147-148.

Stadnik, M.J. and Dhingra, O.D. (1995). Reaction of Onion Seeds to *Fusarium oxysporum* f. sp. *cepae* and its Relation to Bulb Basal Rot. Brazil. *Phytopathology* 20(3): 429-33.

Stadnik, M.J. and Dhjngra, O.D. (1996). Response of Onion Genptypes to *Fusarium oxysporum* f.sp. *cepae* During the Growth Phase and in Storage. Brazil. *Phytopathology* 21: 431-35.

Sumner D R. (1995). *Fusarium* Basal Rot. American Phytopathological Society p10-11.

Sunita, S. Chandel and Katoch R. (2001). Chemical Control of *Fusarium oxysporum* f. sp. *dianthi*, an Incitant of Carnation Wilt. *Indian Journal of Microbiology* 41: 135-137.

Swift, C.E, Wickliffe, E.R. and Schwartz, H.F. (2002). Vegetative Compatibility Groups of *Fusarium oxysporum* f. sp. *cepae* from Onion in Colorado. *Plant disease* 86 (6): 606-617.

Tahvonen, R. (1981). Storage of Onion and Their Control. *Journal of the Scientific Agricultural Society of Finland* 52: 27-41.

Trias NGO. (2010). Onions are a Source of Income in Ghana, News letter. *www.Triasngo.org/onions* (Accessed 27/03/2012).

Vigitha Naguleswaran, Kandiah Pakeerathan and Gunasingam Mikunthan, (2014) Biological Control: A Promising Tool for Bulb-Rot and Leaf Twisting Fungal Diseases in Red Onion (*Allium Cepa* L.) World Applied Sciences Journal 31 (6): 1090-1095.

Vijai, K.G., Ashok, K.M., Arti, G., Brajesh, K.P. and Rajarshi, K. (2010). RAPD-PCR of *Trichoderma* Isolates and *In Vitro* Antagonism Against *Fusarium* Wilt Pathogens of *Psidium Guajava*. *Journal of Plant Protection Research* 50(3): 13-22.

Vincent, J.M. (1947). Distortion of Fungal Hyphae in the Presence of Certain Inhibitors, *Nature*.150: 850.

Walker, S., Natalie, G., Christopher, C. (2009). Onion Diseases in New Mexico, Department of Plant and Environmental Science New Mexico State University. Circular 538.

Wheeler, B.E.J. (1969). An Introduction to Plant Disease. John Wiley and Sons Ltd., London, UK. 301pp.

Whipps J.M., (2001). Microbial Interactions and Biocontrol in the Rhizosphere. *Journal of Experimental Botany* 52: 487-511.

Zlata, D., Klokoåar., Jelena, T., Leviã S.N., Maireviã, J.M., Grozdanoviã, V., Mirjana A. and Vasiã, S.R. (2008). *Fusarium* Rot of Onion and Possible Use of Bioproduct. *Natural Science,* 114: 135-148.

Index

B

C

❖❖❖❖❖❖